Voice of Truth

Voice of Truth

The Challenges and Struggles
of a Nepalese Woman

Shanti Mishra

Book Faith India
Delhi

Published by
BOOK FAITH INDIA
414-416 Express Tower
Azadpur Commercial Complex
Delhi, India 110 033
Fax (91-11) 724-9674

Distributed by
PILGRIMS BOOK HOUSE
PO Box 3872
Kathmandu, Nepal
Fax (977-1) 229983

Computer typesetting and layout by
John Snyder Jr.

Cover illustration by Bijay Raj Shakya

ISBN 81-7303-022-7

1st edition

Copyright © 1994
All rights reserved

The contents of this book may not be reproduced, stored or copied in any form-- printed, electronic, photocopied or otherwise --except for excerpts used in reviews, without the written permission of the publisher.

Printed in India by Surya Print Process
New Delhi

DEDICATION

This book is dedicated to my husband Narayan who, not in name only, resembles Lord Vishnu, the redeemer and preserver of all that exists. Him I love most truly, whose wisdom has kept me on course towards my life's goal and safe from the dangers and perils of this world...

... and to Nancy and Douglas Hatch, unique and exemplary in their friendship — friends indeed.

INVOCATION

To the Lord God of heaven and earth be all praise, whose indwelling spirit speaks to our hearts, that truth may spread abroad, that good overcome all wrong, and that the beauty of the Lord shine forth forever.

SALUTE

I am not a writer by profession and so would never have thought to write this book had it not been for a divine urge to record and share with others my experiences, challenges, and unending struggle to serve. I wish to salute she who has been in the front ranks of service to humanity, Mother Teresa, God's gift to the poorest.

GRATITUDE

I express sincere gratitude to my friend Philip Pierce for having read through the manuscript and helping to put it into shape for publication.

FOREWORD

Shanti Mishra is a remarkable person by any standards. Having been associated with her professionally while I was Australia's Ambassador in Nepal, and regarding her as a close friend, I was delighted to have been invited to write a foreword to her book.

Shanti Mishra is remarkable in a number of ways. In the first place, and virtually single-handed, she turned a collection of books into a library of real national standing. Under her leadership the Tribhuvan University Library has become the most important institution in Nepal for academic research. Its resources are available not just in Kathmandu, but to the students at the many far-flung campuses of the University. However Tribhuvan University Library is also a truly national institution, available to and serving the interests of all the Nepali nation.

To have built the Library into what it is today required a person with extraordinary qualities and commitment. Starting with almost no resources, but a great deal of courage and determination, Shanti Mishra took every opportunity to seek out the support which was desperately needed to expand and improve the Library. With resources virtually unavailable in Nepal, a country beset with so many basic needs, she consistently appealed to potential international donors. There are many diplomats who served in Nepal who will remember with admiration Shanti Mishra's unrelenting efforts to obtain financing, training or books for the Library.

I am pleased and proud to say that Australia was one of those countries which assisted the Library. We did so in the knowledge that, with Shanti Mishra at the helm, the assistance would be well used.

Shanti Mishra is well known and highly regarded on the international library scene for her involvement and contributions especially in relation to the problems facing libraries in developing countries, and her achievement in providing to Nepal a library of a standard which attracted international support.

Shanti Mishra is also remarkable in another respect. In a country which, at least as I knew it, allowed very little opportunity for women, Shanti Mishra stands out. Despite all the barriers she managed to rise to the top of her profession and to a position of real importance and influence. In this she earned the respect of all who knew her. She is and will continue to be an inspiration to other women.

I am sure that the readers of this book will be impressed by Shanti's achievements and her very real concern for the well-being of her countrymen and women. I wish her every success.

Di Johnstone
Canberra 26 March 1992

CONTENTS

Chapter **Pages**

Dedication v
Invocation, Salute, Gratitude vi
Foreword vii

1.	Early Divine Urges	1
2.	Breaking Through	19
3.	Embracing an Unrecognized Profession	38
4.	A Golden Age	48
5.	Love and Intercaste Marriage	73
6.	Challenges and Unending Struggles	113
7.	Service to Nepalese Women	184
8.	Planning Social Service -- A Dream	196
9.	Crusade against Corruption	202
10.	The UN General Assembly Thirty-second Session	258
11.	Mission to Bhutan	283
12.	Honour from Without	296
13.	Librarianship on the Global Scene	339
14.	Nepalese Writers and the P.E.N. Club	375
15.	The People's Movement and the Library Episode	398

CONTENTS

Appendix   **Pages**

I.   "Debt to Mt. Everest"; "Shanti"; "How We Felt on Receiving Your Letter, Shanti"   417

II.   IWYCN 1975 Programme   420

III. IWYCN 1975 Report   426

IV. Elimination of All Forms of Racial Discrimination   440

V.   United Nations Decade for Women: Equality, Development and Peace   444

VI. Questions of the Elderly and Aged   453

VII. Policies and Programmes relating to Youth   456

VIII. Elimination of all Forms of Religious Intolerance   460

IX. Notes on Some Unspoken Problems of the Librarians of the Developing World   463

X.   P.E.N. Charter   467

      Index   469

Chapter 1

Early Divine Urges

I was not born with a silver spoon in my mouth. Life was quite hard. I do not remember that I ever had a new dress like other relatives who had a happy childhood full of excitement. Whenever I had to attend wedding parties my mother used to borrow a dress for me. I would refuse to wear the dress at first, as I preferred to go in my own simple outfit. Even in my childhood I must have thought people should be beautiful more in their minds and thoughts than in their outward appearance. My mother always had to explain why I should wear the borrowed dress. At last, to please her, I put it on. She always wished that I, her first child, should look prettier than other girls.

Our family was a joint family where we lived together with our uncles, aunts, and grandparents. It included countless people. In a joint family the seniors look after all the others. Property belongs to the whole family. There was no feeling of yours and mine; everything was ours. Respect for seniors and discipline always prevailed. But education was not regarded as important in those days.

My grandfather was a well-known businessman who used to export *muga* (coral) to India, having imported it from Lhasa. He and his wife died when my father, Jyanki Lall Shrestha and his brothers, Kushav Lall Shrestha and Subarna Lall Shrestha, and his sisters, Amala Devi and Bhawani Devi, had not yet grown up. All the property was taken by elder cousins whose intentions were not good. Thus my father and his brothers and sisters had to undergo many difficulties after their marriages. Even after I was born my father had to live away from home.

1

Early Divine Urges

My mother used to have a terrible time working for the whole family and looking after me too.

I was not a healthy child, maybe because my mother did not have the right food to eat during her pregnancy. I remember once having pneumonia when I was very young. My mother thought that it was just an ordinary cold, but my condition deteriorated so quickly that she started crying, thinking that I was going to die. My father being away from home, his elder brother was the only person left to rely upon. It was not the custom to consult doctors in those days. A *vaidya* (Ayurvedic physician) was summoned. He knew enough, luckily, to give me some medicine, and my life was saved, but for a long time I remained weak after that terrible sickness.

Then I got eye problems and couldn't open my eyes for months. I have a vivid memory of visiting a *gubhaju* (tantric healer) who owned a dog. I opened my eyes, which had been closed for five months, when I heard the *gubhaju* saying, "Look at the beautiful dog barking at you." The dog really was beautiful. My mother was so happy to see that I could see. Though white patches were observed on my pupils for years, no problem arose as far as vision was concerned. It was a great relief for my mother, as she used to hear horrible stories from her in-laws that if a child did not open its eyes for such a long period the pupils would turn towards the inside. God was kind enough to reopen my eyes. And even now I love dogs.

After some years I got the mumps. My mother had some black paste made from some local herbs to apply on the swellings. She thought they would subside after a few days and told me to tolerate the procedure even if it was troublesome. I obediently did my best, but things were out my control. I could not sleep due to the unbearable pain, and the swelling on the right increased to the size of a red bulb. I did not cry because I hated to make my mother worried about me. She herself

Early Divine Urges

noticed this and with the help of my uncles got a compounder (health assistant), a new phenomenon in Nepal, to examine me. When he saw me he showed great surprise and wondered at how I had the spirit to put up with the pain. The next day he came early in the morning to operate. Lots of pus and blood came out. Although it was extremely agonizing and I almost lost my senses, the operation brought great relief. It took quite a long time for the wound to heal. I still have a scar underneath my chin from it. In those days it was a luxury to have a compounder at home. Everyone was a fatalist then and believed that what is lotted cannot be blotted. Since that time I have never been seriously ill.

After the birth of my brother Rajendra and sister Jayanti, my father began to stay with us. It was a great joy for me to have him at home. We did not have a house of our own. We were living in the house of my father's aunt. His earnings were very meagre as a teacher at Juddhodaya Secondary School in Kathmandu. My mother had to work hard to please our aunts and grandaunts so that they would not complain about our staying in their house. After the birth of my brother and sister, she used to get sick from the strain of work.

Being the eldest daughter, I had to start doing the cooking upon reaching the age of nine or ten. I remember I used to play with rag and straw dolls outside the kitchen while cooking with wood, which sometimes did not burn, so that I had to blow again and again over it with a bamboo pipe. Smoke made me cry and got my hands dirty.

One incident is fixed in my memory. I was alone cooking in the kitchen when a burst of bright lightning came into the kitchen through the window. I thought I saw it strike the curry pot and dashed from the scene, crying wildly. My sick mother came upstairs to see what had happened. I could not stop shivering and sobbing for some while and almost lost my

Early Divine Urges

senses. I don't know how, but finally I came back to myself. Even now thunder and lightning scare me.

After the time spent cooking and playing with dolls, I used to read and write with the help of my father and others. I did not have a copybook, pencil, or text. The only thing I had was a slate and a piece of white stone to write with, but I loved my slate very dearly, and whenever I had free time I wrote and read. Though everyone admired me for my urge to learn, they did not particularly encourage it, as female education at that time was hardly given a second thought.

My father was a born artist. He was a good painter and violinist, yet his talents had never been appreciated. I remember when I was a small girl I requested him to teach me how to play the violin. He was not forthcoming and intimated that I should not be aspiring to learn such things. I did not understand why he did not show any interest to pass on his talent to me. I was very unhappy. I loved to hear him play violin and see him painting.

Gradually things got better for my family. My father obtained a tutoring post and taught Ranas to play violin. Many Ranas became his students. Nepal was under the Rana regime at that time. My father went from one Rana mansion to another. His income increased. He even got a request to teach the then Rana Prime Minister Juddha Shumshere's sons Rabi Shumshere and Surendra Shumshere, who were his favourite students. Rabi Shumshere Rana gave him money to buy a house at Durbar Square in Kathmandu for Rs. 3,000 in the late 1940's. I remember very vaguely that the money (all in coins) was brought in *kharpans* (carriers made out of bamboo), as notes were not yet in use. During the counting two or three rooms were filled with coins. I thought as a girl that the Ranas were good, as they respected an artist and gave him due recognition.

Early Divine Urges

It was a happy day for us, especially for my mother, when we moved to our own house. In her in-laws' house, my mother had had to undergo unbearable challenges and work very hard so that we would not be asked not to stay. My mother was a very sociable lady. She tried extremely hard to please the house owners, but I remember that she used to cry to herself when we were small, because she could not share her sufferings with us, nor could she share them with my father, who was usually away from home.

After moving to our new house, I began to concentrate on learning, requesting our neighbours who were teaching children in their house, mainly boys, to include me in the group. They did include me, and without any charge. Sometimes, with my mother's permission, I requested our neighbour to come to our house to teach me. Seeing my keen interest in learning and writing from my childhood, my parents boldly decided to send me to Kathmandu's Shanti Nikunja Secondary School, established in 1945. I was extremely happy that they decided to do this. It was, in fact, one of the happiest days in my life. I was happy but nervous the first day I attended. The school admitted me to class four.

Although it was coeducational, very few girls were in evidence; the majority were boys. All the teachers were men, of whom Messrs. Nanda Lall Joshi and Chitaranjan Nepali were the most active. Some were short-tempered. I still remember how they used to beat boys with sticks and dusters. How lucky I was not to be beaten by the teachers there! I was one of the best students in the class. In the final exam I stood first and was promoted to class five. As a prize, I got a bundle of books, which I still treasure. I was greatly encouraged. Since my childhood I have been a great believer in the Divinity, so whenever good things came my way I always remembered His love and care for me. When I was promoted

Early Divine Urges

to class five, I tried hard to find suitable words to express my gratitude to Him.

I became more serious in my studies, but I never neglected my duty to help my mother and to try to keep our new house very neat and decorated. The ground floor contained storage space, a chicken coop, and a toilet. The first floor was used for receiving visitors. The bedrooms were on the second floor. Cooking and dining was done on the third floor, and the fourth floor was reserved for worship and had a prayer room and an open terrace. After I helped my mother with her domestic chores, I loved to play and dance with my brother and sister.

Some years before the 1950 revolution my father got a message from the palace through an envoy of King Tribhuvan Bir Bikram Shah Dev to appear in audience before him. The day my father was to go to the palace my mother seemed very worried, as no one knew why he had been summoned. Some of my father's friends were already in jail for hatching a plot to do away with the Ranas autocratic regime. Politics was in the air. On one occasion, before we moved to our new house, the police entered into the old one in search of a radio, as at that time people were not supposed to have either radios or foreign newspapers; people were even punished for opening libraries. My mother, with great presence of mind, quickly took our tiny radio and passed it over from one roof to the other to our aunt living next door. The police left disappointed. I do not remember from where the radio was brought. The only thing I remember was that my mother used to hide it covered with rice inside a big *ghyampo* (clay pot). We children loved to tune it and listen to songs.

My father came back late at night from the palace. I did not even hear him coming. The next morning I got up quite early, very curious to know why he had been asked to have an audience with the king. My parents looked very cheerful and

Early Divine Urges

happy. I asked my father what the good news was from his meeting. He told me in brief that the king wanted to learn violin from him. I thought it a great opportunity to be asked to tutor the king.

The first thing the king asked my father to do was to stop tutoring the Ranas. My father did as commanded, but his life style changed completely. He started coming home very late almost every day. He used to bring gold coins and some cash from the king as presents for Dasain and Tihar, the great Nepalese festivals. Still, his salary was not enough to raise our living standard and provide us with luxuries. I remember that the first thing my father brought from the palace was materials needed to build a bathroom inside the house on the second floor. In those days no Nepalese house had a toilet upstairs. Our bathroom with a toilet was the first ever built on the second floor in our community. Our relatives and my father's friends were very critical in the beginning but later on enjoyed taking baths in the white bathtub. The bathroom looked beautiful with all its fittings that were sent from the palace.

A big console with radio and record player was also presented by the king to my father. A movie was shown for the first time in our house when there were no cinema halls in all of Nepal. Once again, the film along with all the necessary equipment was brought from the palace. In one instance, I remember King Tribhuvan himself coming to our house to deliver a film to show to our neighbours, friends, and relatives. Though I wished to see him close up, I was not allowed to do so. I used to think what a wonderful king he was — a king who did not mind coming to deliver a film to an artist's home. My father always talked very highly of him. He used to express the conviction that King Tribhuvan was really the incarnation of the god Vishnu, and his dealings were like those of the kings described in the Vedas. Our relatives and neighbours were very curious about his visit; so many were the unusual things that happened in our home!

Actually I never bothered about all these material gains and just wished I could get an education. No one, though, seemed concerned about my need for one. My happy school life had already come to an end after two years, in each of which I stood first. Unfortunately a rumour that one of the girls had eloped with one of the teachers set my family to worrying, and I was ordered to stop attending. Not that they did not trust me; it was the teachers they could not trust. In those days it was a great disgrace for any family to be associated with a love marriage. I too got a bit scared, being unaccustomed to thinking about such sublime things. In my innocence, I thought that if any teacher eloped with me it would indeed be a great disgrace to my parents, who had already faced enough of a challenge in sending me to the school in the first place.

My dream of getting a good schooling was shattered. My teachers Nanda Lall Joshi and Chitaranjan Nepali came to request my father to send me back to school. They tried their best to convince him of my keen interest to learn and the excellent results in my exam. Success or no success, they seemed very much determined to contribute to the development of female education in Nepal. My father politely refused their request. I spent sleepless nights worrying about how to continue my education.

For their part, my parents and aunts got busy looking for a match for me. These efforts soon paid off, and they were about to settle the date of my marriage. I prayed fervently that something might put a stop to things, being determined to continue my studies by any means. Nothing, not even their decision, could disturb my peace of mind, as I found the presence of God in everything I did, saw, and thought. God inspired and encouraged me to revolt against the decision of

Early Divine Urges

my family to give me in marriage when I was not yet of marriageable age. I did not eat for some days to protest against their decision, and in the end God came to rescue me from the clutches of wedlock. The betrothal of the elder sister of the boy whom I was to marry was cancelled due to social reasons, so the fixed date of my marriage was put back a year, as in Nepalese society younger siblings do not get married before older ones.

During the year the Divine Spirit worked in such a way that my parents changed their attitude and agreed to engage private tutors to teach me at our home. My mother, Krishna Devi, who got married when she was just 14 years old, supported wholeheartedly my yearning for an education. Maybe God changed her outlook; in any case, she now supported my idea of contributing to the development of society, community, and nation. Even at that time I had the strong conviction that society could not change, the nation could not develop, and people's attitudes could not change unless girls and women were given an equal opportunity to be educated. Only quality education could change people's attitudes and impel them to work honestly and sincerely for the development of the nation.

My private tutors were the late Gopal Pandey Ashim, a great promoter of Nepali language and grammar, a writer, and the founder of the Nepali Shiksha Parishad (Nepali Education Council), Bhuwan Lal Joshi, the coauthor of the book *Democratic Innovations in Nepal: A Case Study of Political Acculturation* (Berkeley, University of California Press, 1966), a very widely read publication, and Lava Bahadur Pradhan, a writer and former additional secretary in the Ministry of Education.

My father's income did not permit him to engage private tutors for all the subjects, so I used to tutor myself in some. On the advice of my private tutors, my parents decided to send

Early Divine Urges

me to a girls' school in Kathmandu, Kanya Mandir High School, for about a year so that I could take the S.L.C. (School Leaving Certificate) examination there. This school was established in 1946 to make some headway in the development of girl's education in Nepal. All well-known educationalists helped the school. In those days, especially after the Glorious Revolution of 1950, people from all walks of life gave of themselves. Their interest was not to make money; some even worked voluntarily for institutions and for the country. People were not so self-centred the way they are today.

Having prepared myself with the help of my private teachers, I took the S.L.C. examination. God helped me to get through it. For higher education I was sent to Calcutta University with the financial support of Prince Himalaya Bir Bikram Shah, for whom my father was working as a private secretary after the Glorious Revolution led by King Tribhuvan to put to an end to oligarchic Rana rule in Nepal. The Ranas had ruled for 105 years, during which period the people had had no freedom of speech and education and the king had had no power. He was king in name only.

My father was never interested in politics. He was a man of genuine artistic talent, the most interesting and most handsome man in Nepal, I thought. He never understood the politics the king was playing while engaging him as violin tutor for him and his two sons, Prince Himalaya and Prince Basundhara. The story of the violin and the king's politics was nicely described in Erika Leuchtag's novel *With a King in the Clouds* (London, Hutchinson, 1958).

My father later on realized his own shortsightedness in not having noticed the king's involvement in politics. He was also deceived by one of the king's secretaries, who kept his attention focused elsewhere. Later my father came to know that just before the Revolution of 1950, the king had asked his

Early Divine Urges

secretary to take my father along with him to go to Delhi to deliver his letter to the prime minister of India, Jawaharlal Nehru, the "gem of India" and a heroic freedom fighter. The king took my father's not going to India amiss. My father was all the while blissfully unaware of the dirty trick played by the secretary to alienate the palace towards him.

After that my father was never called back and was asked instead to work for Prince Himalaya. The salary my father got was Rs. 75 per month. He was never happy as secretary, having already been spoilt by the respect shown to him by the king and princes as a violin tutor. He wanted to remain a violinist, not become an administrator, but he had no alternative but to accept the job offered, as he had already left the Ranas who had patronized him. Sometimes he used to tell us that he was happy with Rana students but could not go back to them, as he knew what the royal reaction to that would be. On the other hand, the Ranas would not have accepted him back in the first place, as they would have been troubled by the thought that he had played a role in overthrowing them. Thus whether he liked his secretarial job or not, he had to make do with it.

Whenever I came back from Calcutta during summer vacation, he used to reveal his feelings to me. I understood but could not help him. Sometimes the pain he expressed made me think I should stop accepting the financial assistance I was getting from the prince, but saying or thinking is easier than doing. Even if my father left his job, where would he go? No one could escape the royal presence. I always told him not to worry and to accept whatever came; God was always near to help us. However, I was ever grateful to Prince Himalaya and Princess Princep for the financial support they provided for my education up to the bachelor level at Calcutta University.

Early Divine Urges

After my graduation, Princess Princep Shah, the wife of Prince Himalaya, asked my father to send me to work for her. A bachelor of arts (graduation) was more than enough qualification. It was one of the saddest days for me when my father conveyed to me the message. My heart ached; I had not the least desire to start work just after graduation. My dream was to get a postgraduate degree. I was very firm in my determination to do an M.A. at any cost. Much discussion went on at home about how to get around the royal wish — a very risky business. My parents worried terribly because of my determination bordering on rebellion.

As soon as I got the chance, in 1959, I joined the newly established Tribhuvan University as a postgraduate student in history while I was waiting for a reply from Calcutta University for my admission. Tribhuvan University was started in that same year in the Tripureshwor section of Kathmandu and housed in small buildings with small rooms lacking any facilities; I thought the conditions unfit for a good school or a college. Most of the instructors, though, were good, experienced teachers from India brought in under the Colombo Plan, and a few well-known Nepalese teachers also had posts. I was much used to Calcutta's academic atmosphere, so that it bored me to have to sit in a small, cold room with so few students. My teachers told me that I could get first division marks if I continued my studies at T.U., but day and night I prayed for admission to Calcutta University, then already one hundred years old. God answered my prayer: I got a telegram from my local guardian that I had been selected, one of the 250 successful candidates out of 2,000 applicants. It was a great gift of God for me to be included among them.

Now the question of money arose. There would be no more support from the royal family. My father's salary was Rs. 75, which had to be stretched to cover the whole family, including

Early Divine Urges

my brother's and sister's higher education. I did not want to press my parents too much, as I knew that with so little income they could not support me. I was floating in a dream. Actually I could do nothing but pray. I spent a few sleepless nights crying to myself with a sincere prayer in my heart for help. Then came the Divine Light to guide my mother. I always thought she was the most wonderful woman in the world. She understood my inner feelings. She held me tight and consoled me, and told me with a bright smile that she would support me. I was amazed at her offer. Controlling my continuous sobbing, I asked her how she could do so. She said with great affection, "Dear daughter, don't cry. I had an ornament made with the extra money given by the king; it can be sold and used for your studies in Calcutta." I clasped my mother with great respect, bowing at her feet, and requested her to seek my father's opinion. My father accepted my mother's generous proposal. I could not find suitable words to express my admiration for my mother's wisdom and thoughtfulness, traits unacquired through any formal education. She had been married to my father when she was fourteen.

My father now faced the great problem of how to report to Princess Princep Shah my determination to go back to Calcutta University to obtain an M.A. in modern history. I prayed that my father be given courage. He informed my benefactors with all due politeness that I was not prepared to take any kind of job till I had got a postgraduate degree and that I was determined to go back to Calcutta University for the degree course. Their reaction did not contain anything to cause my father concern. They merely emphasized that they could no longer support me.

I left Kathmandu for Calcutta in 1959 with my father, going by truck along the Tribhuvan Raj Path highway in order to save money. Travel by plane or bus was much higher

Early Divine Urges

compared to truck. This was my first journey by this means of transport. It was interesting but fearful: the road went up and up into the mountains before descending to the Terai region. Though I felt dizzy quite often, I enjoyed the unique scenic views of mountains and green fields, a Shangri-la paradise.

It took 48 hours to reach our destination. I got admitted immediately after we arrived. I felt so happy to be back to my beloved Calcutta University. I studied very hard and scrimped good food, as I wanted to minimize my expenditures and stretch out the money I got from the sale of my mother's ornament as much as possible.

I stayed in an inexpensive girl's hostel. The Calcutta heat, way over 100 degrees Fahrenheit sometimes, made me sick. No fan was available in the hostel. I had two sisterly friends, Subrata Ghose and Sujata Ghose, wonderful girls from a well-known zamindari family from Calcutta who also broke with tradition to get an education, such families being at the time very conservative and attaching very little importance to women and women's education.

These two friends had lost their parents when they were young, and they were left with their brothers to look after. I was much impressed by the love and affection they gave to them. They were very simple, soft-spoken, and kind-hearted women, and also very intelligent. Both dressed simply but neatly. They loved me just like a sister. I too loved them and always loved to be with them in their mansion-like house. I loved to hear them tell the story of their big zamindari joint family, which had already broken apart by then.

They helped me in my studies. I had to study very hard to get through the M.A. examination - a tough competition, given the presence of Bengali and Ceylonese students. The Divine Spirit always guided me in the exercise of courage and hard work to achieve my goals. Nepalese teachers were always

Early Divine Urges

saying that it was very difficult to get an M.A. from Calcutta University, and this fear haunted me like anything. If I did not get through, where could I get more money to continue my studies. By all means I had to pass the examination.

I came back home after two years, in 1961. Having appeared for the examination, I now had to wait about three months to get the result. Those three months were an eternity for me — a nightmare of an eternity, though I was dead sure I would get through. The waiting made me literally sick. My mind and thoughts travelled from Kathmandu back to the examination hall in Calcutta, engaged in the attempt to remember what my answers had been to the questions. When I was able to convince myself that I had done well, then I returned to my reality with great relief. Many were the moments of prayer for me — prayer for good results. I tried to talk to God and tried to be with Him to receive His solace for my unnecessary but unavoidable thoughts, worries, and anxieties. My parents seemed restless, too, though I had remained cheerful in front of them, not wanting to disclose my inner agitation.

Finally a telegram came from Subrata. Before even opening it, I was already trembling like a leaf in a storm. I was sure I had got through, but what would the marks really be? There it stood: Second Division. I jumped for joy and thanked God — a very good pass for getting a job. It was a great and meritorious achievement to have got a second-division M.A. from the hundred-year-old Calcutta University, one of the oldest and best universities of India. Calcutta, the capital of West Bengal state, where still the spirit of its many freedom fighters lives on — B. G. Tilak, G. K. Gokhale, Subhas Chandra Bose; poets, the greatest being Rabindranath Tagore, the winner of the Nobel Prize for literature in 1913 and the first recipient of it in Asia; and the religious saints Ramkrishna

Early Divine Urges

Paramhansa and Swami Vivekananda, great propagators of Vedantic philosophy whose teachings continue to stir people to work for peace in their minds and in the world.

I have always regarded myself as lucky to have obtained my higher education at Calcutta University. My teachers were well-known historians, such as Prof. S. N. Sen, Prof. Tripathy, Prof. K. K. Sarkar, Prof. K. C. Chaudhari and Prof. Majumdar.

My parents, brother, and sister all seemed very happy at my success. It was a great relief for me. I thought that I should immediately start to teach at the University, earn some money and buy enough gold to make an ornament for my mother, in return for the ornament she gave me to support my postgraduate study.

Fortunately there was an opening for the post of instructor in the history department at Tribhuvan University. Having enquired about it, I was told to visit the registrar, Dr. P. N. Suwal, to find out the procedure for applying for the post. I went to see him. He was kind enough to introduce me on the same day to the then vice-chancellor, Mr. Ranadhir Subba, who seemed to enjoy every chance he had to talk in English. I too felt easier talking with him in English rather than in Nepali. I wished I could have talked with him more in Bengali, which had become my second language after my mother tongue, Newari. Though I loved Nepali, I had had little practice in speaking it up till then. Bengalis love their own language so much that they seldom talk in English, so that's why I became proficient in it and grew to love its very sweet and wonderful tones. Vice-Chancellor Subba also knew Bengali. We did in fact exchange a few words in it. He seemed quite impressed with me.

When I came back home the Divine Spirit was whispering to me that I should not worry about finding a job. The next day

Early Divine Urges

I got a call from the University that I had been given the temporary post of instructor to teach history. It was in May 1962 that I joined T.U. Here I was, the first full-time lady teacher on the faculty. How nice it felt! I at once went to the University to collect the appointment letter from the registrar, Dr. Suwal, to whom I expressed my profound gratitude, even as I did to the vice-chancellor. I read and reread the letter. My joy knew no bounds. I was so happy I cried. My salary was set at Rs. 350. I wondered why it was so much when my father's salary as the private secretary to a prince was Rs. 75, living on which had not been easy. Yet we were a happy family. I had never felt poor.

I rushed home, very nearly running, with my appointment letter in hand, and there I bowed at my mother's feet, in the Nepalese gesture of respect and gratitude, and read out the letter. My mother cried for joy and embraced me affectionately. My father was not yet back from his office. I was impatient for him to return; there was no way to inform him, as we did not have a phone. He did eventually come home, though, and I read the letter to him and to my brother and sister, who had also in the meantime come back from college. Happiness reigned. With a big smile my father put his hand on my head and blessed me.

News about my appointment spread very fast, as I was the first woman to have such a position at the University. Women in our community had previously never worked either in offices or in academic institutions. My aunts from my father's and mother's side came to congratulate me by bringing things that are auspicious according to Newar custom: eggs, curds, fish, and fruits. My case was even more unique, as no one in my community, not even a man, had obtained such a position at the University.

Early Divine Urges

My mother was perhaps the happiest one of us all, as she had had to hear much criticism from relatives for sending me to Calcutta. They thought I would turn out to be a loose woman after getting an education abroad and would marry an Indian. But they found me to be the same simple Shanti for all my education, so they too came to congratulate me. They openly regretted what they had said before and took a vow to send their own daughters and granddaughters to school. What could be more heartening to my mother and me than their eager commitment to give an education to their girls. I felt that what I had attained was a great achievement; now the door was open to all girls in our community to study.

My mother and father were very proud of me and my earning ability. My only brother Rajendra and only sister Jayanti also started to enjoy having some pocket money when they went to college. My own happiness depended entirely on theirs. I cared nothing for myself.

My philosophy was somewhat different from that of the rest of the family. I wanted to be very independent and at the same time dedicated to the welfare of the society and the nation — a not very appealing notion to the rest. Sometimes we used to have heated discussions. But my love for my family was deep. My philosophy did not stand in the way of a happy life together. I adored my parents and loved my brother and sister. I all along thought I could never live without them, so I never gave a thought to married life. Many marriage proposals came my way after I joined the University. Maybe I earned a lot, but I knew my father's salary was meagre, and I always wondered who would support the family if I was not around. For the time being I remained single.

Chapter 2

Breaking Through

My experience as a history instructor at Tribhuvan University was highly stimulating. I enjoyed teaching. One of my students was my own former history teacher Mr. Guna Dev Bhattarai. At first I felt uneasy but later on I got over this. During classes I paid him the respect due a teacher; otherwise he was treated like the others. My colleagues were all elderly and mostly from India, having come to Nepal under the Colombo Plan. I was perhaps the youngest instructor and the only full-time lady on the faculty. Everyone showed their high regards for me, which made me feel happy and more emboldened. The instructors from India at that time were highly qualified and dedicated. Nepalese instructors were also well known, not only as subject specialists but also as educationalists committed to develop higher studies in Nepal.

Tribhuvan University was established in 1959 with a few part-time Nepalese instructors and a great number of full-time Indian instructors hired under the Colombo Plan. Its first location was in the Tripureshwor section of Kathmandu. During the first year 80 students were admitted. It was named after the late King Tribhuvan, the leader of the Glorious Revolution of 1950 and the founder of the modern democratic state of Nepal. The first chancellor of the University was the senior queen mother, Kanti Rajya Laxmi Devi Shah, and the first provice-chancellor the junior queen mother, Ishwari Rajya Laxmi Devi Shah. King Mahendra Bir Bikram Shah Dev was the first royal visitor to T.U. and was to become the chancellor later on. The first vice-chancellor was the late Subarna

Breaking Through

Shumshere J. B. Rana, the deputy prime minister of the first elected Congress government headed by the late B. P. Koirala.

I sensed that the queen mothers, both grand in bearing, were very keen to see the University developed properly, in such a way as would provide the quality education so necessary for the development of Nepal. Whenever they came to attend the annual University Day, they called me into their presence and enquired about how things were proceeding, and then went on to tell about the university commission of which they were the chairwoman and vice-chairwoman. Their sweet, soft-spoken voices conveyed the deep interest that they took in having Nepal establish a university of its own. They contributed all the initial funds for the University from their own personal expenses. For instance, they early on donated Rs. 484,000 (an amount sufficient at that time) for the construction of the administration building, though it was finished only in 1984, past their lifetime, which was indeed a shame.

Tribhuvan University is the premier university of Nepal. Courses were first taught in the social sciences and humanities (economics, history, Nepali, and English literature) in small rooms at Tripureshwor, without the facilities normally associated with running postgraduate classes. This is the great irony of every developing county: plans come after the execution phase. Facilities were thought about only after the institution had been running awhile. I could never understand this culture of mine. I always wondered why it seemed impossible to plan things out and to fulfill all the preconditions for running an academic institution before actually trying to run it. Nepalese who accepted the Nepalese way of doing things told me that nothing could start if we waited for all the necessary facilities. I did not agree with them, but I thought it was probably useless to argue.

Breaking Through

I was determined to be a good, dedicated instructor, so I naturally wanted to have good books to consult and refer the students to, but at the time the university collection had only a few volumes on any given subject. Even these few books were kept under lock and key in a few bookcases in a small room. Mr. Purna Prasad Amatya, the assistant librarian, was in charge of this so-called university library. He was the first Nepalese to get a diploma in library science, having graduated from Delhi in 1955. Before joining the T.U. library, he worked in the Trichandra College library and then in the College of Education library, which even now is hardly more than a glorified storehouse.

I used to wonder how teaching could get anywhere without good books and periodicals. I was used to being able to use libraries on the campus of Calcutta University. Calcutta University Library at least looked like a library, though it was not particularly well managed, but the T.U. library did not even look like one. It looked like a randomly filled storeroom of books and lacked good furniture and lighting. I was very disappointed with the condition of it. None of the instructors was happy with it either. At that time, though, I had no idea that the library is the heart of any academic institution, having been educated in India, where the importance of library reading materials was not particularly felt. We were not encouraged to use the reading materials at hand. Instructors always gave notes. We read the notes and left it at that.

It was out of my own love for books that I used to go to borrow regularly from the library. Sometimes I had to spend hours standing in a queue to get a reserved book, as the number of students was large in each class. In the history department, there were 250 students studying for their M.A. Students did not get the chance to question instructors, or instructors the chance to get to know students. However, I

Breaking Through

enjoyed the advantage of being a foreign student: I could go to the instructors during lunchtime if I had some questions to ask. They were happy to help me. Still, I never felt very comfortable about disturbing them too often. Thus I did not take full advantage of the opportunity to be close to them, close enough to engage them in prolonged conversations about things I did not understand.

That was Indian culture. I was really very critical of such teaching by just giving notes. When I joined T.U. as an instructor, I wanted to do away with the distant relationship between instructor and student. Happily, it was not difficult to establish close relations, as there were only a few students in my class. I really wanted to approach teaching and learning as a joint effort, as against the old tradition of the guru imparting knowledge and wisdom to students who had only to imbibe, respect, and obey, not to question. Since T.U. was modelled on the pattern on Indian universities with affiliated colleges, our students were so used to depending on given notes that I did not find them very supportive of my plan to teach them to learn and search for themselves. Whether I liked it or not, I had to prepare notes for the students if I wanted to be a popular instructor.

For all that, I enjoyed my teaching. I loved teaching history. While I was teaching in the University I took so much interest in the subject that I started wanting to go abroad to do Ph.D. work in history, specializing in Nepalese history. Though I obtained an M.A. in modern history from Calcutta University, I knew very little about the history of Nepal, as Nepal was not included in the syllabuses. I had to study British history and Indian history in great detail, and also about the Far East, international law, the Middle East, and so on.

My dream to get a doctoral degree did not materialize because the vice-chancellor, Mr. Ranadhir Subba, and the registrar, Dr. P. N. Suwal, persuaded me, much against my will, to leave the teaching profession so close to my heart and to study library science in the United States, the authorities having begun to realize that quality teaching could not be imparted without a good library. I was requested again and again to go abroad to get training in librarianship, as other senior instructors did not show any willingness to study this unrecognized and unknown subject. I found myself in a great dilemma whether to accept or not to accept the offer, as I too was not aware of the importance of library science and librarianship. As I appeared very hesitant and reluctant to accept, Vice-Chancellor Subba introduced me to the education adviser (for library science) to USAID, John L. Hafenrichter, who was to play a great role in my decision-making process. He too happened to be a historian cum librarian. Having persuaded me, he went to see my father to convince him that I should go to the States for training. Before leaving for abroad, I had a very memorable meeting with the USAID director, John Roach, at which Mr. Hafenrichter was also present.

I left Nepal at the end of 1962. I was somewhat nervous to be going abroad by myself. Luckily I found two Nepalese gentlemen, Devendra Raj Pandey and the late Janak Pyakurel, who were also going to the States by the same flight. We were together up to Washington.

Every moment in the U.S.A. was a new experience for me. I enjoyed every bit of my stay. I found Americans so helpful, so sociable, and so knowledgeable that I thought they were the finest creatures on this earth, I found Washington like heaven — so clean and so beautiful compared to India and my own country. Before going to the States, I never thought that any country could be so beautiful and at the same time so vast and so developed. Even the dogs and cats were well fed. I came from such a tiny, undeveloped country, where 99% of the population still lived under poor conditions, in villages with no good roads, no education, no health service, and few basic amenities. All these thoughts overwhelmed me for a period and set me hoping and praying for the development and prosperity of Nepal.

After an orientation programme in Washington my programme officer, Doris R. Fessler, gave me all the required documents for flying to Nashville, Tennessee, to start training in library science at the Peabody Library School of the George Peabody College for Teachers, one of the best in the States. I was received by one of the staff of the library school.

Nashville is the capital of Tennessee, a state situated in the southern part of the U.S. It is a very beautiful city, surrounded by small hills. I felt at home, as I was very used to mountains, and even small hills made me feel good. I liked the beautiful environment, which was truly scenic. The Peabody campus was also no less beautiful. And I thought that the library school was situated in the best part of the campus.

The library school had quite a number of foreign students: ones from Africa, Burma, China (Taiwan), India, Nepal, and the Philippines. When we all got together, it looked like an international convention.

Nashville is well known, like other southern towns, for its southern hospitality. We foreign students were quite often invited into the homes of American families. People had never heard of Nepal before two Nepalese gentlemen and myself went there to study. I became something of a celebrity, instantly recognizable in and around campus by my Nepalese dress.

Charles U. Coggin, Jr. and his ever-smiling, loving wife Edith were always delighted to have me with them. Their beautiful home became my second home in Nashville. I too loved to be with the Coggins. Theirs was a happy family with two lovely adopted children, Mary and Randy; I felt very fortunate to be a part of it. I called Mr. and Mrs. Coggin my American parents. They always showed great love and affection to me and made me feel thoroughly at home. Mr. Coggin was a prolific writer and a poet. He wrote a very nice article about me, published in the *Tennessee Progress 1963*, and some beautiful poems, three of which I have included in Appendix I.

Before I went to Nashville I was told of the racial problem there. Though I myself did not encounter any problems personally, racial incidents did occur from time to time. Very few black students were seen on campus. I was first put together with a white American in the dormitory. At my request I was given an opportunity to room with a black American, as I wanted to get some insight into why such discrimination was being practised in a developed democratic nation. I got along very well with my black roommate.

When I went to visit American families, I found blacks working for whites. During my visits I asked my hosts why blacks could not eat in the same restaurant as whites when they could cook in their homes. I used to feel very disturbed and sad wherever I saw the sign "Whites Only" posted.

Nashville is full of churches of different denominations. I loved to go to different churches on Sunday. The whites in the South seemed quite religious, yet they could not do away with their racial problem. Whenever I participated in the Sunday classes, I again raised questions about the discrimination, as I always felt there is no discrimination in the eyes of God. Everyone is born equal. I used to tell people how we Nepalese tried to do away with the man-made caste system, though we were not materially as developed as America. They usually did not have good or satisfactory answers to my queries, yet they enjoyed my curiosity. They told me that it would take time to do away with such problems.

Our semester started in September 1962. Most of the students in my class were working library staff from different colleges, universities, and public libraries. They already had working experience in the library profession, whereas I knew nothing about such work. I felt lost in the beginning. Actually I started disliking library science itself. I found the classes very boring, especially subjects like bibliography, classification, and cataloguing, about which I had never heard before. It wasn't the fault of our instructors, though, who were hard-working, helpful, friendly, and devoted.

After a week I went to my adviser, Frances Neel Cheney, the acting director of the school, to try to persuade her to drop me from library science and get me admitted to history courses, so that I could fulfil my longstanding dream of getting a Ph.D. Mrs. Cheney was one of the best known librarians in the States — very knowledgeable, soft-spoken, well-dressed, and beautiful, and the guiding spirit in the library school. She knew all the techniques to appease dissatisfied students. She told me, putting her hands around my neck, not to be unhappy and disturbed. She did not reject my plan to change from library science to history but told me she would have to get permission from my programme officer in Washington.

After this talk I wrote a letter to Ms. Fessler to request the transfer. Mrs. Cheney knew very well that I would not be permitted to change my subject, yet she did not seek to disappoint me. When I got the negative reply, I went to see her again. She again tried with sweet words to convince me of the importance of library science and the library profession, especially in developing countries like Nepal, where I could contribute a lot as a member of this very little-known, rather unrespected calling. I should lay my thoughts of changing my subject to rest.

I was still unhappy. I spent a few sleepless nights before deciding to continue to study librarianship. The Divine Spirit had whispered to me that there were so many who could teach history in Nepal but no one to work for the library profession and library development with dedication and devotion — the most needed academic instrument for ensuring quality education in Nepal. With head and heart I accepted the divine call and went to see Mrs. Cheney to inform her of my decision, to which I attached one condition, that I be enrolled as a postgraduate student, though I had been sent not to get a degree but just for training or auditing. She gave a big questioning smile that read, Why this condition? I explained to her why I should be entitled to get an M.A. degree in library science: In any developing country, and thus in South Asian countries like Nepal, the importance of degrees is great in terms of the respect and recognition they command from society. Postgraduate and Ph.D. degrees were in especially great demand.

Mrs. Cheney understood what I was getting at. She took me to the dean, William C. Jones, to talk about this genuine request of mine to be enrolled as a postgraduate student in the library school. The three of us discussed things awhile. I did most of the talking. The dean took great interest in what I told him about the importance of getting a degree before I returned to Nepal so that I could play a significant role in the development of higher education in Nepal, as chief librarian. One problem discussed was how to get a degree in library science, for which two years of study were required. I told them that since I already had an M.A. in history, I could, if permitted to do so, take more courses than usual in order to complete my studies within one year. The dean and Mrs.

Breaking Through

Cheney agreed to enroll me as a postgraduate student under one condition: They would see my grades for the first semester and then would decide. I thanked God for their encouragement and prayed to Him to help me to be serious in my studies.

I gave all my time to studies. My instructors Mr. A. S. Rescoe and Mr. H. L. Connell, to mention only two, were very helpful. They encouraged me very much. When I thought back on Nepal and India, the U.S. education system seemed superb. The use of the library by students was frequent. The relationship between students and instructors was very good. Class assignments — preparing reading cards from books recommended for reading by instructors, reports on different subjects, and the like — had to be completed on our own, so no student could fool about. Our whole time was devoted to learning in the class and library. It was really a great form of yoga the students practised in the classroom. I don't remember having ever used libraries like that before in my life.

The first paper I presented to the class was on S. R. Ranganathan, the father of the library movement in India. My presentation was warmly applauded. I too learned a lot from this and got some idea of the great challenge I would have to face when I went back to Nepal to work for my unrecognized profession. This strengthened my determination to learn as much as I could during the one year so that I could face the challenge more confidently.

My instructors were always ready to discuss with me how to work and how to manage library services in Nepal. They appreciated and encouraged my enthusiasm to start up a new profession in Nepal. I made plans for school, college, and university libraries with the help of these wonderful instructors.

John L. Hafenrichter was of particularly great help. He wrote almost every week informing me about the library situation in Nepal, especially with reference to the Central

Library management and staff. His letters, which I still treasure reading, were real eye-openers, painting a true picture of Nepalese educationalists and their negligence of library development. Whenever I got his letters, I felt renewed stimulus to press ahead with my studies and to query my instructors about such problems.

I met Mr. Hafenrichter only once while I was studying in the States. We discussed in detail my plans on how to go about my work at T.U. until he returned. Alas, he never did. His term as library adviser terminated without prior notice at the time he was packing to ship out to Nepal. This was shocking news to me. After that I never heard from him again, try though I did to contact him. Once I read in a USAID report that he was working in Vietnam. I sent a letter to him but never got a reply. He loved Nepal greatly and wanted to help me to develop librarianship there. I thought it highly unfortunate to have to do without his services.

After I decided to continue my studies in library science, my head knew only libraries and library services. I was very well aware of the condition laid down by the dean that I do well in the first semester. Accordingly I worked very hard to learn unwanted subjects. But once I was determined, I started to love the whole field, I began to think of it as the great science of collecting and storing knowledge, so essential if any human being is to perfect himself in his own chosen field. It is the science which helps people to become wise, informed, and scholarly. Without it information and knowledge cannot be managed for use. Without well-managed information, development is not possible. The U.S.A., Russia, Germany, France, and other industrialized countries know how to respect the contribution made by librarians to their national life.

My mind changed totally, and I became a staunch advocate of the library profession within a short time. This transformation drew me deeper and deeper into the subject, enabling me to get top marks in almost all subjects in the first semester. Mrs. Cheney and the dean were very pleased with my grades and gave me permission to enroll as a postgraduate student — one of the happiest moments in my life.

The second semester was not that hard because I had finally accepted my major. During it I got a letter from my programme officer informing me of a visiting programme to university libraries in different parts of the U.S. It was a great temptation, no doubt, to have such an opportunity to visit a host of places from the east to the west of the great nation, but I did not want to miss classes, and I had already signed up for too many to finish the course within one year. I wrote back to this effect. Ms. Fessler was quite surprised at my reply and wrote me a very nice letter appreciating my deep interest in the studies and assured me of her help if I had a particular place I wanted to visit the coming semester. My foreign friends were also puzzled at my peculiar ways. I had become quite well known among them and the instructors. It was not me, it was God who showed the way every moment.

The second semester also went quite well. My spirits went on rising. After the second semester I requested Mrs. Cheney to allow me to take a practical course on small college libraries, school libraries, and university libraries in Michigan. I selected Michigan University Library because the head librarian was Dr. E. W. Erickson, who had been in Nepal to start the Central Library under a USOM project, as reported by Mr. Hafenrichter in a letter to me. I wanted to know from him personally about his experience in Nepal.

My request was accepted enthusiastically. I had a full month to be with Dr. Erickson in his well-managed library, receiving training from the staff in different sections of the library under his direct supervision. I thought it was a great piece of luck to

Breaking Through

have this opportunity. Every moment was one of learning and sharing, especially with Dr. Erickson, a wonderful librarian who made service to those thirsting after knowledge the motto of his library. I loved hearing him speak about his work in Nepal of establishing the Central Library. I got many tips and much encouragement and inspiration from him. He and his staff gave me an unforgettable and touching send-off at the end of my in-service training course. Later he kept up correspondence with me in spite of his busy job. I am ever grateful to him.

Among the letters he wrote that I have treasured was one to the vice-chancellor of T.U. congratulating him for having selected me for the course. Another one worth mentioning is dated many years later, August 13, 1970. In it he expressed the following thoughts:

> ... I was pleased, but not surprised, to hear the many nice things Mr. James Green had to say about you and your work in Nepal. It is gratifying to know that my "baby" has been so well taken care of. History will be able to say that Erickson was the midwife to the Tribhuvan [University Central] Library but its growth and development was due to the devoted and expert care of Shanti Shrestha (Mishra).

After Michigan I went to Middle Tennessee State College Library in Murfreesboro, Tennessee, to gain more practical knowledge. I was given a warm welcome there. Everyone on the library staff helped me in whatever way they could. I liked the library, even though it was very small in comparison to Dr. Erickson's. I loved small things because I was from a small country and I had to start in a small way. I learned from the library and made plans on the basis of what I learned. Its director, Catherine Clark, gave me a very nice recommendation letter, having received remarkably good reports from her staff, who were surprised by my work in the library. For years I carried on correspondence with both her and her staff. It had truly been a wonderful experience.

During the short vacations too, at my request, Mrs. Cheney used to organize visits or training in different libraries. Before I went to the U.S. to study library science, I knew nothing about public libraries, so after I took a course on the subject I felt the need to visit a good example of one. I was sent to Atlanta to be shown the main branch of their public system. Its director, John Hale Jacobs, received me. The library was superb, a model anyone could profitably follow. I saw much being done in every section and was greatly impressed. I wished for Nepal a library like it.

After a tour of the whole grand facility I had an opportunity to spend some hours with its dynamic director. Mr. Jacobs took keen interest in my story of the situation of libraries in Nepal. He did not begrudge his time and answered my queries regarding my plan to start my professional career in Nepal when I went back after study. He was so pleased with my idea and enthusiasm that he wrote letters about me to the chancellor of T.U., the late King Mahendra and to the vice-chancellor, congratulating them for sending me abroad to study library science. He sent copies of these letters to me — a joy and inspiration.

Some other unforgettable training I got was at Columbia University School of Library Service in New York. This course on comparative librarianship was organized especially for foreign students, and it fell during the break at Peabody. I enjoyed the workshop very much because I could deal with possible problems I would face when I took up my duties as a

Breaking Through

librarian. The coordinator was an energetic black lady, Dr. Dorothy Collings. Whenever I met strong, active ladies I always felt uplifted, as I wanted to be a strong working career woman myself. We became good friends. She sent a wonderful report to my school about my accomplishments in the workshop. This workshop was designed to bring together students from other countries who were completing periods of study at library schools in the United States or Canada and to give them an opportunity to exchange ideas about their training and experience and to apply them to situations in the countries to which they would return.

During the training period we took a tour of the Dag Hammarskjöld Library at the U.N. and were exposed to a wonderful talk programme on the U.N. depository library system. We got a list of depository libraries in the world. I went hurriedly through the list to check whether Nepal was represented and was very much disappointed not to find it included.

The next day I talked with Dorothy about how I could go about getting a depository library established in Nepal. She was so kind as to arrange an appointment with Harry Winton, chief of the U.N. Depository. My meeting with him was very fruitful. He looked very favourably on my request to establish a U.N. depository in Nepal and asked me to make a preliminary request to get approval from our government and the resident representative at the UNDP Nepal when I returned to Nepal. He gave me every assurance of success, which made me very, very happy.

After returning from the States I did approach our government officials and the resident representative of UNDP, Herbert H. Grantham, for their approval to make T.U.C.L. one of the U.N. depositories. The education secretary, Mr. Pradhumna Lall Rajbhandari, and Mr. Grantham showed great interest and very quickly gave their approval to write to Mr. Winton for the required recognition. When I received the letter of recognition in 1965, it was a moment of great personal triumph.

After my visit to the Atlanta library, my interest in children's libraries grew. I was highly impressed by the services provided to children in the library, so I took a course in school library management and enjoyed it thoroughly. After the course I wanted to have some practical training; I requested Mrs. Cheney to arrange for me to work in a good school library for some days during my break from classes. She was always kind to me, and for three weeks this is what I did. I enjoyed every moment of serving the children. American children — so different from our children — are always coming to you with queries: one small girl from kindergarten, for instance, asked me about the red spot (tika) on my forehead. They loved reading stories in illustrated books. They read fast and with great interest. From this I realized that good libraries with good books can create good reading habits among children.

In America good schools do have good libraries. Whatever I learned and saw I did with Nepal in mind, and I wondered if the schools there would ever have libraries of their own. I have never been pessimistic, so I see everything as being possible. If all educationalists work sincerely, Nepalese schools also will someday have good libraries. My optimism keeps me going.

I finished the formal courses prescribed in the course-book and the non-formal practical training planned by my adviser at my special request within one year. By September 1963 I was packing my things. Some of my foreign friends wanted to see what I was taking back. I had nothing to show them but books, catalogues of library furniture, tools, and magazines, one tape recorder, one pair of binoculars, some shirts for my brother, and some dresses for my sister. They seemed surprised not to see any luxury items. I did not buy things because I wanted to save scholarship money to be able to give something to my parents, who had always supported me in my pursuit of knowledge.

These friends wondered how I managed to save the money, and I told them that I didn't spend money on American clothes; I didn't go to movies; I always wore my national dress (sari and blouse), even in cold weather, and used only one warm coat. My determination to save money made me warm even without enough warm clothes in winter. Further, I didn't eat out; I shared an apartment with a friend and cooked myself; I ate the cheapest foods, but these were my favourites: chicken, milk, and fruits (nothing beats southern fried chicken washed down with milk). I avoided expensive ice cream, cakes, and juices and was quite happy to do so.

It was wonderful to be back to home sweet home. My father, mother, brother, and sister were waiting at the airport to welcome me back. What a thrill it was to touch down in my own small but beautiful country. Snowy mountains and the temples around the valley welcomed me back. I gave a big namaste to all of them, seeing in them the presence of God. Tears of joy streamed forth when I saw my dear parents and dear brother and sister waiting for me.

I had heavy bags on my left shoulder and a big tape recorder in my right hand, not at all well balanced, and I could feel myself trembling a little while walking. Foreign friends were always quick to offer to carry my tape recorder for me throughout my journey from the U.S.A. to Great Britain, Rome, and Switzerland, but at the end of my trip in Kathmandu this custom was unpractised. It was a bit difficult for me. No wheeled carriers were yet available as in other airports. Still, I was very proud to be carrying the tape recorder, as I knew that no one in our community would have anything like it, and looked forward to playing it in front of my relatives and friends.

It took quite a while to go through customs. At first I was very impatient, as during my one year in America I had got used to having things done on time, but at last I disposed of all formalities and went out of the office to meet my family. Our way of expressing our love and affection is very different from that of Americans. My mother seemed very happy and was full of tears of joy. I bowed down to my mother and father and then gave a big loving smile to my brother and sister. My sister tried to carry the tape recorder but failed. I gave my shoulder bag to my sister and the tape recorder to my brother. It was very heavy, he said. We had to wait for a taxi for some time. Taxis were not seen in those days in the numbers they are now. I sat between my parents and together we reached our home at Jhochhe Tole, Durbar Square in downtown Kathmandu. This house had always been close to my heart.

I went to the fifth floor, where our prayer room was situated, to thank God for my arrival after getting a good education in librarianship from the U.S. I prayed to Him to give me the spirit needed to work for the development of libraries and the library profession in Nepal, where none of the importance was attached to it I had seen in America. After this brief prayer I opened my handbag and took out some dollars I had saved for my mother. The tape recorder was for my father so that he could record his violin playing. I gave the camera and binoculars to my brother. For my sister I had a dress with the initials of her name on it. Some handsome kitchen items were displayed. Everyone in my family seemed happy. My mother was happy because I had not changed into an American girl with cropped hair, polished nails, red lips, and a dress instead of a sari.

Breaking Through

I had brought a Better Home Catalogue in which I saw a plan of a house that was much to my liking. I showed it to my father and told him that we should buy a plot of land and build a house like the one in the catalogue. My father took great interest in designing and constructing houses. He was pleased to discuss the house in the catalogue. Nevertheless, I was in a bit of a fix — whether to spend money I had saved in the U.S. to buy ornaments for my mother or to buy a plot of land and build the house in good surroundings — with lawn, garden, flowers, and trees far away from the crowded downtown. I left the choice to my mother. My mother was very thoughtful and very different from other women. She supported my idea to get away from the city to some quiet place and give the city house on rent.

It was great fun to be discussing all about our future. After one full year I was again enjoying a meal prepared by my mother with all our family members, but after the long journey from the U.S. I was indeed tired, so I went to bed promptly, full of thanksgiving to God.

It was a beautiful morning. My mother came to my room, sat close to me and said, "Dear daughter, I really am very proud of you. You look beautiful and bright, but if you can rest for some days before you go to the University you should, as I know once you start working you won't stop. But if you think you should go I have no objection." I enjoyed her feeling and concern for me. I remained the whole day with her, telling her of all the beautiful things about America, American people, my library education, and my determination to serve T.U. and the nation.

Chapter 3

Embracing an Unrecognized Profession

It was in February 1964 that I joined Tribhuvan University as chief of Tribhuvan University Library. The post of librarian had been advertised in the newspaper *Gorkhapatra*. I applied for the post. When I went for the interview I found myself to be the only candidate. I was not happy about the fact, as I wanted to compete with others.

It was a very interesting interview, held in the office of the vice-chancellor. The representative of the British Council, Mr. W. L. Clough, had also been invited to be a member of the interview board. I enjoyed every question from all its members. I was quite sure I had not disappointed them.

The administration of the University under the vice-chancellorship of Mr. Ranadhir Subba was not slow to get things done. The registrar, Dr. P. N. Suwal, was also very cooperative and full of spirit and vitality. After just one day I received a letter of permanent appointment as the chief of the library. My pay was Rs. 350 per month.

When I entered the grounds of Tribhuvan University as its librarian, a new registrar, Prof. J. B. Budhathoki, took me to the library to introduce me to the staff — Assistant Librarian Purna Prasad Amatya and two other employees, who were working in a not altogether pleasing environment. Only two small rooms were allocated to the library, one for the staff and another as a reading room for the teachers and the students. I was given a table.

I immediately called a meeting of my staff to tell them that I wanted to bring about radical change in the library with their

Embracing an Unrecognized Profession

help. I told them what a library should be like and briefly described library services in the U.S.A. While I was sitting there in my office, all the various libraries I visit in the U.S.A. came back one by one in front of my eyes, like a documentary film on American libraries.

For a while I was blue in the face, looking at the university library of which I was in charge. It did not look like a library at all; it looked like a old store in need of cleaning. Some of its 1,200 books were kept on so-called racks made of wooden planks supported by bricks; some were piled on the table of the assistant librarian. Registrar Budhathoki, who was in favour of open access, told me that he had ordered Mr. Amatya to put the books on such wooden planks instead of keeping them under lock and key. Mr. Amatya was aware of the fact that if books were lost he might have to pay for the loss.

I heartily supported the idea of open access — the most important factor in attracting readers and creating good reading habits. Given the registrar's position, I was hopeful I could change the situation, but things didn't happen that way. The registrar seemed to be swayed by Mr. Amatya, who was more solicitous of staff opinion than a professional assistant librarian need have been. I wanted radical change quickly.

Fortunately it was mentioned in T.U. regulations that the library was directly responsible to the vice-chancellor, so I sought a direct approach to the latter, having always respected rules and regulations as conducive to development and smooth operations. As soon as I became the librarian I tried to go through the existing T.U. rules and regulations thoroughly and to proceed accordingly. Thus I thought I should get approval of my plan to improve the condition of our less than ideal library from the VC in order to avoid the bureaucratic stop and go. He immediately gave his approval in writing, and I plunged into work.

Embracing an Unrecognized Profession

Now the problem was the registrar, who was used to giving his approval to Mr. Amatya for everything, be it to buy a pencil. I later became familiar with the latter's hesitation to make decisions on his own. The registrar for his part may have thought I was trying to deprive him of his authority to control the administration of the library. Indeed some people tried to create misunderstandings between him and me from the very beginning of my work. He was told that I was a supporter of the former registrar Dr. Suwal and was naive enough to believe things without testing their veracity. He was well known, too, for his hot temper. He had fired some appointees of the former registrar. I never thought he was a crooked man, but he did listen to false reports and took unreasonable decisions harmful to the institution. Though good at heart, he could be easily moved by unscrupulous people.

Full of enthusiasm, I started to work. One fine morning I was called by the registrar to his office. My first thought was that he had called me to assent to my plan to develop the existing library, as the plan had been already approved by the VC. I was in a cheerful mood. As soon as I entered his office I greeted him. To my great surprise he didn't return my gesture, pretending as if he was immersed in some files.

I said to him, "Registrar sahib, are you busy? Should I come back later? Didn't you send a message that you wanted to see me?"

He was of dark complexion. He looked even darker with the anger now in his face. I did not expect to find him in that mood. What could I do but stand and wonder? He looked at me with red eyes and told me rudely to sit down. I occupied a seat in front of his big desk. I remained as cheerful as I had been when I entered his office. His angry face didn't disturb me a bit.

I asked him, "Are you all right, Registrar saheb?"

Embracing an Unrecognized Profession

He immediately came back in a harsh voice, "You are not supposed to go to the VC to get his approval for any plan for the library. These things go through my office."

This was a great shock to me, as I didn't expect such low forms of expression from high officials like him. I asked what was wrong with getting the VC's approval directly. I was, I told him, directly responsible to the VC. My straightforward manner only served to irritate him further. The truth didn't appeal to him or reason soothe his temper.

I wanted to retaliate, but I controlled myself and came back from his office without having reached any compromise. I was, however, determined to get things going for the library. I could sense he would be a stumbling block, but I knew God would be with me. After such an unexpected turn of events I went to the VC to report about the registrar's negative attitude. Mr. Subba was a different breed of character: gentle, soft-spoken, with very vivid, slow, and halting expressions. Meeting him and discussing with him the University and the library was always a source of inspiration and encouragement to me. He assured me of his continued support and told me not to pay any heed to the registrar but to develop the library as I had planned. It meant much to me to receive his praise and support. I thought that the University was lucky to have him as its vice-chancellor.

Following my plan, I managed to get steel book racks, reading tables, and magazine tables made by local producers according to specifications in the furniture catalogue I had brought from the States. It was a pleasure to be able to supervise the carpenters in making the first library furniture under my tenure. At my request one more room was also added to the existing library. I decorated three rooms with new library furniture and got good lights fixed on the ceiling. All the planks supported by the bricks were replaced by the racks.

Embracing an Unrecognized Profession

Flower pots were set up to make the library attractive and the environment one in which readers would come to add new things to their knowledge. Beautiful sayings and captions brought from the U.S. relating to libraries and education were posted on the walls.

Nothing made me happier than to see the rooms allocated to the library start to took like a library. Within six months of my taking charge, people could see a radical change. It was not as easy a task as I thought to bring such change about, as I had to fight and throw my weight around to get a proper budget for the library.

I had another unpleasant run-in with the registrar in the office of the rector, Mr. Sharada Prasad Upadhyaya. It had been a very pleasant afternoon. I had told the rector in his office about my future plans for the library and found him also taking interest in the library's development. Suddenly Registrar Budhathoki entered the office and, seeing me, made a long face. I greeted him. His response was very cool. I picked up where I had left off. I could notice him becoming very restless. He began to argue with me about the budget.

"Where can you get that money?"

I told him that since he was the registrar it was his responsibility to get it.

He started up and said, "Who are you to assign me my responsibility? Don't show your damned spirit with me. We've already done you a great favour by sending you to the U.S. Now you do what we say, not what you want to do."

I couldn't control myself. I banged on the rector's desk and told the registrar, "Don't dare to say that the University has done a favour to me. I have done a great favour to the University by sacrificing my deep desire to do a Ph.D. in history to study librarianship, which has no recognition and scope in Nepal." I realized I was almost shivering with rage

Embracing an Unrecognized Profession

and would have said many more things, had not the rector, gentleman that he was, soothed me and requested me and the registrar not to get carried away. His room had become a battleground of words between the two of us. People close to the room started peering in, wondering what it was all about. I have a bad habit of not being able to control my anger. Usually I don't get angry in the first place, but I just can't tolerate people speaking or arguing without any basis in fact. I was thankful to the rector for having made the registrar tone down and for having put a stop to his unreasonableness. It may have finally dawned on the registrar that I was no pushover. He seemed used to putting everyone down with his high voice — the voice of an army officer. There was no arguing with him. When he said yes it was yes, and when no it was no. I felt later that God taught him a lesson for arguing with me for nothing. He later on realized I was not a yes lady. I promised myself never to go to him again, hating to invite any more arguments.

The next day rumours about the argument between me and the registrar spread throughout the University. The staff and teachers were eager to know more about it from me. I didn't say a word, knowing the nature and ways of Nepalese, who just add oil to the fire, thus creating even more misunderstanding. Actually I wanted to forget the quarrel and to get on with the task of serving the teachers, students, and staff.

Some experienced staff, such as Hakimbaje, tried to explain to me the Nepalese way of working: not to work too hard or too honestly and sincerely, as sincere, honest, hard workers are not appreciated in a country under a curse.

The common Nepali expression is *satile sarapeko desh* (the country cursed by the woman who committed suttee), the reference begin to the wife of the former prime minister

43

Embracing an Unrecognized Profession

Bhimsen Thapa (term of office 1804-1837), who after glorious service to the country ended up in prison and suffered an ignominious death.

Hakimbaje (Mr. Chhatra Prasad Mainali, an accountant), who was efficient, active, and bright, though he lacked any higher education, used to offer his help and cooperation. Though I appreciated his concern, I told him I didn't like to work slowly and wanted to break with tradition by working hard and honestly; otherwise we would always lag behind. I tried to explain how America had developed. He just smiled at my explanation and insisted that I would realize one day the truth of what he said.

It took some months to make the three rooms look like a library. After changing the appearance of the library, I wanted to organize the collection by classifying and cataloguing it according to the Dewey decimal classification system, a universally accepted system developed in America. But when I was studying library science in the U.S., Mr. Amatya got approval from the T.U. Syndicate to use the Indian Colon classification system, having himself been educated in India. This was the brainchild of S. R. Ranganathan, the father of the Indian library movement. The system has its advantages but is difficult for library users. I had done, it may be recalled, a paper on the contribution of Dr. Ranganathan to library science during my study in Peabody. I was very much impressed by his writings and speeches. He was a man worthy of praise. I always felt that the libraries in South Asia could take pride in his service to the library world. Thus I was never against the Colon system, but on the basis of my one year of education in the Dewey decimal system I became convinced of its ease of use for Nepalese.

I told Mr. Amatya that he would have done better not to have reclassified the books according to the Colon system. He was not a man to argue with, being capable of playing politics. In this case, he went to the registrar to complain about my intention to change Colon to Dewey. I was asked by some members of the Syndicate to write a paper on why I wanted the latter. I immediately wrote up these reasons and gave the paper to the vice-chancellor to submit to the Syndicate. All the members were convinced. Mr. Amatya seemed very unhappy, though he didn't say anything. Within a month each book of the collection had a Dewey number on its spine. Card catalogues were provided for easy reference. Both teachers and students were pleased to be able to use them. I was very happy at the way things were going.

After completing the furnishing and organization of the library, I wanted to show it to others, especially people who could help to develop the library and librarianship in Nepal. I thought the best way to bring people to the library was to organize displays on the occasion of national and international events. The first big display I organized was to mark the celebration of International Red Cross Day.

T.U. authorities seemed very appreciative of what I had done for the library and library service at Tripureshwor. Next I wanted to turn my attention to the Central Library (situated at Lal Durbar, now the site of the Yak and Yeti Hotel). Originally established as a USAID project in 1958 to provide library services throughout the country, it unfortunately had to be dropped, and the collection of 9,000 items, classified according to the Dewey decimal system, was handed over to T.U. along with a green jeep bearing the tag number 1375. The University at that time had only that one jeep, which was used by the VC, the rector, the registrar, and the librarian. I made a routine of stopping in only shortly at the library at Tripureshwor and spending more time at Lal Durbar.

Embracing an Unrecognized Profession

The Central Library was handed over not only with its collection but also 14 of its staff, about whom I had a very accurate report from Mr. Hafenrichter. Some of the Central Library staff were hard workers. As soon as the American supervisor left the library, Mr. N. B. Manandhar, a professional librarian, was put in charge. Most of the people under him behaved not like his staff but like his friends. All of them loved to have a good tiffin of *chiura* (pounded rice) and chicken prepared by the library peons. After the meal they enjoyed visiting their friends in the nearby National Trading Corporation on office time.

I was quite surprised to find this lax atmosphere at the Lal Durbar library. At the beginning I was not sure how to establish some semblance of discipline in the place. Gradually I worked on the staff to convince them of the need to change, and they in fact tried to be cooperative and helpful in the effort to reorganize library services according to my plan. Though they seemed to have some reservations about my disciplined office work, they didn't say so openly; I only heard rumours to this effect. It was reported to me that as soon as I left the library they stopped working. It was hard for me to believe this, and for some time I let things drift, wanting to see for myself what was up. I knew that one aspect of Nepalese life was to try to please the boss by giving false reports. They secretly called me, by the way, "the boss without a cap" (Newari: *topali maruma hakim*), as in Nepal women do not wear anything on their heads. It seemed that it was hard for them to accept a strong, disciplined lady at the top. In any case, they showed very disciplined work in my presence.

At first I used to tell them the exact time I would be coming to the Lal Durbar library, but later on I stopped this practice. I wanted to do some checking up. I was very disappointed to find much truth to the report of their not working in my

Embracing an Unrecognized Profession

absence. Therefore I decided to stay in Lal Durbar almost the whole of my time and to spend very little of it in the Tripureshwor library. I got things done without any trouble for some time. But it didn't last: some of the staff were so spoilt that they couldn't maintain the pace I wanted. Soon they were back to their old ways without my knowledge.

It was in the best interest of the university library, then, that Prof. Budhathoki was replaced by Dr. Trailokya Nath Uprety. A pair of well-known educationalists, Sardar Rudra Raj Pandey as the new vice-chancellor and Dr. Trailokya Nath Uprety as registrar, were appointed to run the University. I was of course sorry to see Mr. Subba, a great supporter of library services, have to leave.

Chapter 4

A Golden Age

The new vice-chancellor, Sardar Rudra Raj Pandey, and the new registrar, Dr. Trailokya Nath Uprety, were great friends of the library and the library profession. They spoke up for the development of T.U. Central Library and its services and were always active in this regard. They came to the library very often to check up on its use by teachers and students. These frequent visits were a great source of inspiration to me and my staff. It was indeed great good fortune to have them in the University. They always regarded me as one of the key persons on their team to run the University. They never made any decision impacting on the library without my advice. This made me feel so happy that my heart and mind were filled to work with team spirit to achieve the goal of making T.U. Central Library a model of its kind in the country. My seniors gave me what amounted to a free hand and lent their never-failing support to me to develop the library in the way I planned.

I was short of staff to run the library at Tripureshwor from 8 a.m. to 7 p.m., the idea being to stay open as long as possible so that the teachers, students, and university staff could enrich their knowledge even with the limited resources made available to them. My request to increase the number of staff for Tripureshwor library services was immediately approved by the T.U. Syndicate. The posts were advertised shortly thereafter in the *Gorkhapatra*. An interview board was formed, and I was included as one of the members to select the candidates, as at that time the authorities always gave all department heads a say in selecting their staff.

I found some of the candidates to be very good. My requests were honoured. Among them was Mr. Narayan Prasad Mishra, in whom I saw a light of devotion and sincerity. I requested him to look after library services in the library at Tripureshwor along with some of the old staff. Though he had no experience in library work, he managed to handle the library services very well, even better than the others. I was very happy with him and his creative drive, a quality that is essential to providing services to readers. His way of talking to the readers was very appealing, and his writing in Nepali was perfect. Teachers, students, and library staff at Tripureshwor were glad he was there. Eventually I requested him to take full responsibility for running the library at Tripureshwor. The old staff members were not happy, but that was to be expected, because their tendency was to grumble only and not to work in the way I wanted them to.

Since Mr. Mishra took full responsibility of the Tripureshwor library, I could give my full time to the library at Lal Durbar. Thousands upon thousands of books had to be processed. The library was heavily used by everyone. It served as a university, national, and public library all in one. I applied the knowledge I gained from my one-year postgraduate course to improve the existing library services. I received encouragement from every corner. Even people in charge of government offices, such as Education Minister P. N. Uprety, Chief Justice Bhagawati Prasad Singh, Attorney General Shambhu Prasad Gyawali, Finance Secretary Dr. Bhekh Bahadur Thapa, Education Secretaries Pradhumna Lall Rajbhandari and Dirgha Raj Koirala, and Senior Advocate Ramananda Prasad Singh, became sources of support.

Having brought about radical change in the role of the library and its services for the academicians to see, I moved to raise the status of librarians by seeking some definite participatory role in one or another of the higher bodies of the University, such as the Senate and Academic Council, this in

A Golden Age

line with practices followed by the universities of both developed and developing countries. I compiled information on the composition of such bodies from the United States, Great Britain, India, Pakistan, and other countries to convince the authorities on the basis of example. I made a special request to Attorney General Shambhu Prasad Gyawali to include the librarian as ex-officio member in the list of members of the Senate and Academic Council, which list he was compiling for an amendment to the T.U. Act. He hesitated to make this change just because I visited him and requested him to do so; he wanted all the information before saying yes. I admired his way of going about things: he didn't come to conclusions without first getting the facts, but once he was convinced of something he supported it fully, confident that it would be good for the institution, not just one or two individuals. I thanked God for giving me the wherewithal to convince Mr. Gyawali, who was so kind as to propose the change to the Senate meeting, being seconded by Chief Justice Bhagawati Prasad Singh.

I was delighted at this important step taken in 1965 to raise the status of librarians and the library profession. Now I could play a well-defined role in the development of the University by participating in decisions taken by the Senate. This encouraged me to go ahead and work harder for the development of the library.

Almost all the members of the Senate were very supportive of quality education. Every member of the Senate and Academic Council had a definite role to play. They never came to attend meetings without first going through the agenda sent to them. They always had questions and always made suggestions on how to approach higher education in a way that served the country's interests. Everyone's contributions were

A Golden Age

worth recording, and they were recorded. All the speeches were worth listening to and noting down.

My role in the Senate and the Academic Council as the chief of Tribhuvan University Library was much appreciated by members desirous of providing quality education, as they realized that such education isn't born in a vacuum; it needs a number of academic tools, with the library heading the list. Their appreciation increasingly inspired me to plan the library services to support the academic objectives of the University.

As planned, I spent more time at Lal Durbar. The library still shared jeep number 1375, donated to the library by USAID. I never faced any problem in using the vehicle to commute from Tripureshwor to Lal Durbar and to bring processed books back from there. The authorities were very understanding and never pulled rank. They cared for their subordinates, and the latter respected them. They never succumbed to *chakadi* (sycophancy), a practice described in Prof. Dor Bahadur Bista's book *Fatalism and Development: Nepal's Struggle for Modernization* (Hyderabad, Orient Longman, 1991). I didn't have to visit their houses to fawn on them and so was able to devote more time to my work (these days 75% goes for *chakadi*, 20% for tea, and 5% for work).

Although I spent most of my time engaged in technical and administrative management at Lal Durbar, I came to Tripureshwor every day for a short time, as this was the place where I could meet teachers, students, and university staff and authorities. I felt strongly that contact with them was very vital to running the library efficiently. Another tack I took at Tripureshwor, as mentioned previously, was to plan displays on events of national and international importance as a means of drawing public attention to them. I believed that well-organized displays based on informative materials could educate people within the space of a few glances. I called on the services of Mr. Mishra, who was a gifted writer, to make appropriate captions and texts for the displays.

The first display was in 1963, on the occasion of International Red Cross Day (May 8). The contributions made by Henri Dunant, the founder of the Red Cross, to the alleviation of human suffering were beautifully spelled out in big letters, the importance of blood donations being captioned in the never-to-be-forgotten slogan *ragat dan jiban dan* (a gift of blood is a gift of life), which is still used in posters published by the Nepal Red Cross and publicized widely by the important newspapers. Some editors, such as the late Ram Raj Poudyal, Gopal Prasad Bhattarai, Ram Chandra Neupane, and Iswar Man Singh of RSS, even carried library news whenever I requested them to.

It was then, all in all, a great public hit and grand success. I even had the opportunity to welcome Princess Princep Shah (the founding president of the Nepal Red Cross Society), Princess Helen Shah, and other members of the royal family to the library and to show them the display. They all seemed very cheerful and impressed while looking around, and appreciative of our efforts to provide information on the Red Cross to the public.

My staff and I were very satisfied with our first attempt to display an exhibit. I thanked Narayan Prasad Mishra for his wonderfully evocative captions. The Tripureshwor library was doing fine under his supervision. How I wished that all my staff were like him in assuming responsibility on their own instead of having to be goaded into action.

At the Lal Durbar library I was not getting very far with my staff. They were so different from what I wanted them to be, which was more service- and work-oriented, more friendly towards me, and more supportive of my plans and programmes. Instead I found them lacking in devotion. Perhaps

A Golden Age

they were merely reacting to the administrative changes. The American spirit was still alive in me, so I couldn't bear to see people not working. Still, I didn't want to hurt their feelings by uttering unseemly words or scolding them for not being sincere in their work. They did work if I stood right in front of them, and then it was as if they were the most disciplined staff in the world, but the tragedy was that as soon as I left, they enjoyed getting together to gossip. Our culture, I thought, encouraged them to (I didn't want to blame them directly).

I was at a loss how to help them to change their ways so that they would take responsibility for the work I assigned. I used to discuss this with my superiors. They offered words of support for my plan to improve the climate of the work place: If staff members made trouble, they should be removed. Such firm assurances from the registrar gave me the strength to go ahead with my plan — to try to reform idlers and, failing that, discharge them. I really hated the prospect of removing any of my staff, as they had my affection, if not my respect, so the first thing I did was to bring Mr. Mishra to the Lal Durbar library, hoping to turn into an example his way of working, his devotion to the library, and his willingness to take responsibility for things I assigned — an ideal worker.

Before I requested him to come to Lal Durbar I used to share with him my problems with the staff there. Even if I complained about their negative approach, he tried to defend them by saying that persons could not be bad themselves. A bad situation and system could make them bad, so that if I, as the boss, could create a good atmosphere by loving them and showing them the way, they would easily reform. It was then that I requested him to help me in my move to get good work out of them in order that library services might reach all those who needed them. He immediately accepted my request to go to Lal Durbar.

A Golden Age

I called a meeting in Lal Durbar to inform my staff of my decision to bring Mr. Mishra to help me to provide better management of library services, as had been done in the Tripureshwor library. Though they admired my decision they didn't look comfortable. Almost 99% of my staff at Lal Durbar were Newars. They loved to chat in the Newari language and felt a little uneasy to have a Brahmin among them. They thought that Mr. Mishra did not know Newari, so when he came to work for the first time they were grumbling in Newari, "*Bahuncha ola, khub jyahimhaha, chalakthe cho*" (a Brahmin has come, very hard-working, and seems very clever). As it happened, he knew Newari quite well. He told me that he might have problems with the staff, but I knew he could tackle them.

In the beginning he was very popular. Everyone loved to hear him talk. The problem started when he took to defending me whenever they criticized me as a boss (they were still calling me "the boss without a cap"). In Nepal it was still not easy for men to accept women as their superiors. I could well imagine how they might have felt.

I was very particular about time. I wanted my staff to come punctually. Thus when they came to office late they usually asked at the counter, "*Topali maruma hakim ola*?" (Has the boss without a cap come?) If the answer was yes, they got worried and said "*Ka syata!*" (Now we're done for!) If the answer was no, a big smile came on the latecomers' faces as they went to sit in the sun or in the corner. Then the same routine of gossiping started, and the main topic was the boss's effort, strongly criticized, to bring change to library management.

They wanted Mr. Mishra to join them against the hatless boss, but he patiently tried to explain that the hatless boss did everything for the greater good of the library and library services, so that people would come to appreciate the role of libraries in nation building. The staff, in other words, should try to see things differently. It was not what they expected to hear, so gradually they stopped criticizing me in front of him. Instead they conspired how to create problems for the both of us and for my plan of implementing rules.

When I took charge of the library at Lal Durbar, it was not being used as much as before, during the time of Dr. E. W. Erickson. The users generally were people who were well known to the staff, so no rules and regulations were strictly enforced. Our staff and their friends could check out as many books as they wanted. Due dates had no meaning. The library had become like a club and now looked like a mismanaged storehouse. The library staff usually spent more time with their friends in the National Trading Office adjacent to the library than in the library itself. When they were in the library they loved to gossip and then go eat a good tiffin with different kabobs prepared by the lower ranking staff of the library. Thus it was but natural for them to criticize me when I laid down the rules: Everyone had to come on time and stay in the library during office hours; library hours should be increased; books should be returned on the due date; the number of books one could borrow should be fixed etc.

I gave Mr. Mishra responsibility for the circulation section. In spite of his colleagues' protest, he was determined to help me to implement regulations. I strongly believed that without the rule of law and strict discipline nothing could be achieved. Though they grumbled behind my back, I never found them saying anything openly against what I was doing. Instead they showed their anger to Mr. Mishra. Poor Mr. Mishra! He didn't disclose all this to me for months. He came on his bicycle but could never go back on it, as some staff member almost every

A Golden Age

day did some such mischief as putting pins in the tyres of it to make the air leak out.

When things finally became too much he told me the story. I got very mad at him, too, for hiding everything from me. I discussed the situation with the vice-chancellor and registrar. They advised me to transfer a new man, Mr. Pant, to Lal Durbar to help Mr. Mishra. Poor fellow, he didn't last long, though he tried to become one of them, even going so far as to eat buffalo meat, which he as a Brahmin was not supposed to do, and to use Newari slang while talking. This, Mr. Pant disclosed to Mr. Mishra when he submitted his resignation. By this time his own brother was mad at him for using the slang at home. Likewise some other staff also left Lal Durbar instead of opposing the others' ways. Thus only Mr. Mishra was left to fight the battle as a lone crusader. He was not shaken, as God was guiding him to help me. There were many instances and incidents I could mention here, but then the chapter would grow beyond sound limits.

As planned, I extended the library hours so that government officials and others could use its services as before. To this end I made a duty chart outlining the shift programme for my staff. They immediately refused to come other than between 10 a.m. and 5 p.m. The man who staffed the counter threatened not to come, and the person who kept the library key refused, being under pressure, to keep it. It was indeed a critical time for me, and I was greatly worried. Mr. Mishra told me not to be; he would take the key and open the library according to my schedule. I could hear a divine whisper in his assurance. Thus I was determined to face the challenge.

I went to the vice-chancellor and the registrar and reported the insubordination. Without hesitating, they dismissed all the troublemakers at my request. Some were transferred to other offices. Having witnessed the dismissal and transfer of some of

A Golden Age

their numbers, the remaining staff decided to mend their ways and help me. I thanked God for His continuous guidance.

I was of course grateful to the vice-chancellor and registrar for their quick action and support. They did not act rashly, however. They watched my work and activities very closely. If these were self-serving and not geared to the betterment of the library, I don't think they would have acted as they did. The most important qualities of any good administrator, I believe, are the power (1) to make prompt decisions based on the facts, (2) to reward the best and punish the worst, and (3) to forget one own's self-interest and not to fall prey to sycophants but to devote oneself to promoting the institution.

This whole episode merely strengthened my resolve to offer better library services in order to achieve the academic goals set by the University.

Though I was the chief librarian, Vice-Chancellor Pandey used to involve me in other activities too. He always gave me opportunities to be present whenever foreign visitors, including scholars and ambassadors, came to visit him. I was also included on a team which got together to think of how best to develop the University. The vice-chancellor had the remarkable quality of appreciating and knowing how to use people's talents and skills for the good of the University. He didn't stay the whole day in his office, meeting whoever came and drinking tea. He very often went to the various departments and to the library to observe activities and keep an eye open for such talent. He used to tell me that you should use skilful people, even if they're the kind that sound off, for the benefit of the institution.

Once he asked me to become the registrar of the University, as he was apparently impressed by my management of the library, but I politely refused, wanting to make the library a model. He then requested me to work as the member secretary

A Golden Age

of a committee on Nepalology, of which he was himself chairman. A well-known historian, he wanted to preserve and disseminate the large fund of knowledge available on the country's history and culture. This committee was the nucleus of the present-day Centre for Nepal and Asian Studies (CENAS), which developed in its present form because of the direction he provided.

The registrar, Dr. Trailokya Nath Uprety, also gave me unfailing support in my efforts to develop the library. Without it I wouldn't have had the ten happy years in the history of the library I did have. He was very hard-working, supervising the activities of all administrative and academic staff from *chaukidars* (gatemen) to professors. Even at midnight he might be seen making the rounds of the campus to check up on the *chaukidars* on duty. No one complained about his supervision and checking; rather, his efforts were appreciated, and everyone demonstrated some pride in their work. I felt that if the boss was hard-working a good staff would show support.

Dr. Uprety was one of the first American returnees and he had many plans to bring change to the University. He was anxious to introduce a self-service cafeteria on campus to provide good food to academicians, administrators, and students. A cafeteria committee was formed under his chairmanship. I was requested to become the member secretary. I happily accepted, as I too wanted such service for my readers so that they could use the library longer.

The self-service cafeteria was a new phenomenon in Nepal. Dr. Uprety got a Swiss volunteer, Irma Ruegg, to do the managing. She was good at her job. The teachers, students, and staff had to get over feeling uneasy about taking the food themselves and returning the cups and plates for washing. I vividly remember how I used to carry trays and plates for others back in order to show them how we should get used to

A Golden Age

self-service. I loved the system when I was a student in the U.S.; it was great fun then and now. I enjoyed helping to manage the cafeteria in Nepal. Everyone eventually got used to self-service and appreciated such dining facilities. The cafeteria itself looked very neat and clean and displayed the menu nicely written on a board with the prices. Other government offices and corporations followed later on in our footsteps. We used to have people coming to see our service. Dr. Uprety was quite happy with my work. Team spirit was inspiringly high in those days. Anything worth doing was done with heart and soul.

With the opening of the cafeteria, the library began to be used more. I was extremely happy to see more readers in the library in Kirtipur.

The library building was inaugurated in 1967 during the visit of the Indian deputy prime minister, Morarji Desai, the building having been constructed with Indian aid money. As the time of the inauguration drew near, the library still didn't have enough furniture and books to fill the different rooms. One day Vice-Chancellor Pandey called me to his office and asked me to move both the libraries to the Kirtipur campus before all classes started being held there. If the move could be done on time, he would ask the prime minister to inaugurate the building during the visit of Morarji Desai. I too thought this a good idea. I told the vice-chancellor I would try my best.

The transfer of thousands and thousands of books from two libraries was not going to be an easy task. A thought came in my mind: if I could use Peace Corps volunteers working in different parts of Nepal, it would facilitate things, as they all knew Dewey numbers and could arrange books numberwise while packing and reshelving. I immediately went to see the Peace Corps director, George Zeidenstein, to see what he would say. Like his predecessor, Willi Unsoeld, he had always been helpful to me. I still remember how he assisted me in

A Golden Age

obtaining the library's first Peace Corps volunteer in the early 1960's — Dorothy Miller, a retired professional librarian. She was a great help to me in cataloguing and classifying. I remain ever grateful to Willi and Jolene Unsoeld, George and Sondra Zeidenstein, and James H. and Jane E. Martin.

With the help of more than a dozen Peace Corps volunteers and the Nepalese staff, all the items from the two libraries were moved to the Kirtipur library building much faster than I thought possible. Afterwards I made a small speech expressing my appreciation and admiration for the Peace Corps spirit. The vice-chancellor and the registrar were surprised to see the library in Kirtipur so well arranged and decorated within such a short time. Everyone thought the move would take at least a month. Instead it took just ten days. I felt that the move had a divine touch. The few words of appreciation and admiration from persons like the vice-chancellor and the registrar mattered a great deal to me. With the outside help I had been able to keep my word.

A most expressive building with beautiful Nepalese wood carving on its facade was inaugurated on October 23, 1967 by Prime Minister Surya Bahadur Thapa in the presence of Deputy Prime Minister Morarji Desai amid a colourful function. A host of dignitaries from Nepal and members of the diplomatic corps were present. Eloquent speeches were made by Morarji Desai, Vice-Chancellor Pandey, and Ambassador Shriman Narayan of India on the importance of libraries in higher education. I, too, made a short speech to draw the attention of all present to the need for moral and financial support for the development of T.U. Central Library so that my mission to make it a model of its kind in Nepal, where the importance of the role of libraries and library services had yet to be recognized, would be a success. It was one of the happiest moments in my life. The speakers' wonderful words ring in my ears even now. We were off to a good start.

After the inaugural function, Ambassador Narayan and the Indian Cooperation Mission director, Mr. M. Ramunny, expressed interest in providing some funds for furniture and books, as I had made the point of telling them that a library was not only a building but a collection of good books with reading facilities for teachers and students (the Indian aid had been given just to construct the library building). It was the first library building ever erected in Nepal. It was designed by the Swiss architect Robert Weise, who also drew up the master plan for the Kirtipur campus by doing field work day and night, and in the absence of any approach road to the campus. His wonderful master plan remained only a plan — a sad story indeed. If it had been realized our Kirtipur campus would have been turned into one of the most beautiful campuses in the world, as we have a wonderful and unique landscape with mountains viewable round about. The defect of our system is that when authorities change, policies also change without so much as a second thought being given to the existing ones. This is what happened to Robert Weise's master plan.

A few weeks after the inauguration, I discussed with the vice-chancellor and registrar the interest shown by the ambassador and the Cooperation Mission director in providing funds to furnish the library with reference books and furniture. They encouraged me to explore the matter, which I proceeded to do. I was impressed by the willingness on the part of the Indians to support the library; they requested me to give them a list of needed material. Their assurances spurred me on.

I immediately arranged a meeting with Mr. Weise and a British furniture designer, Mr. R. Qualtrough. Mr. Qualtrough and I set about designing the furniture for, among other places, the circulation counter, the periodical room, the reference

A Golden Age

room, the browsing area, the seminar hall, and the newspaper room. We made a list to submit to the Indian Cooperation Mission director. I called another meeting of senior professors to ask them to select the reference books they needed for their teaching and research. Among them were the late Prof. B. D. Pandey, Prof. Shiva Shankar Singh, Prof. Shamba Dev Pandey, and Prof. Dhruba Man Singh Amatya. They all contributed to the effort of making the list. It was a wonderful joint undertaking of the sort that seemed endemic to that time.

I submitted the list to the director of the Indian Cooperation Mission, and prompt action was taken to get all the books and furniture requested. Within a few months all the Godrej racks had arrived, along with the wooden furniture designed by me and Mr. Qualtrough and made in Balaju under the latter's supervision. It was a joy to behold: every room fitted out with new racks and furniture. In Nepal it was unheard of to have different types of furniture for the different rooms housing the different service points. The library looked no less organized and beautiful than any library in a developed country. My office with well-designed furniture looked so grand that some teachers went to complain to the vice-chancellor and the registrar about it: "Why should the librarian have such an office?" They were given a good reply; it was the meeting place of scholars, foreign visitors, and dignitaries, so it was the pride of the University to have such a model office.

I came to know about this whole affair later on and wondered why people could not appreciate good things and why they let unnecessary jealousy get the better of them. I was not put out, though; rather, our authorities' reply made me extremely happy. I always loved to do things in some better way if I could. I wanted to make every room of the library, including my office, a model, so that if others wanted to copy them they could easily do so. Every distinguished visitor from

A Golden Age

within and abroad praised my office and the library as a whole. Quite a number of high officials from different government corporations and bank offices sent their carpenters to take the measure of the furniture in my office and seminar room. It was indeed a great source of satisfaction to me. Those were the golden days. One and all felt proud of the library, and this was the reason why a visit to it was so often part of the schedule of such distinguished visitors as princes and princesses, presidents, ministerial delegations, eminent scholars, and writers from different nations.

The ambassadors posted in Nepal used to bring their friends who visited the country to the library. These visits were a source of encouragement. I would like to mention some of the ambassadors and other diplomats and foreign friends who gave me continuous moral support in my endeavour to make the library a model in Nepal: the American ambassador Henry Stebbins and his wife Barbara, the British ambassador A. R. H. Kellas and Mrs. Kellas, the French ambassador Jean Français, the Indian ambassadorial couples Mr. and Mrs. Shriman Narayan and Mr. and Mrs. Raj Bahadur, the Israeli ambassador Mordechai Avgar and his wife Shoshana, the Canadian ambassador James George, the Japanese ambassador Hedimichi Kira and Mrs. Kira, the Australian ambassador Patrick Shaw and Lady Shaw, the Pakistani ambassador Mr. Inayatullah, the first secretary of the French embassy Henri Charut, the chargé d'affaires of the Burmese embassy U Maung Maung Gyee, and the deputy chief of mission of the U.S. embassy Peter Burleigh.

Further, Marjorie Lindsey (the president of American Women of Nepal), Dr. Quint Lindsey (Ford Foundation adviser to His Majesty's Government), and Father Casper J. Miller were all great friends of T.U. Central Library. They always gave me opportunities to be present at important

63

A Golden Age

receptions, dinners, and gatherings. USIS directors and their wives — Mr. and Mrs. Sentress Gardner, Mr. and Mrs. G. Richard Hopwood, and Mr. and Mrs. Thomas C. Dove — were also faithful supporters, bringing visitors to the library on their own initiative and thereby giving me the chance to meet still other dignitaries, educationalists, planners, and policy-makers. They also presented many good books to the library.

Our library had a wonderful link with the USIS and the British Council. I believed that cultural relations between Nepal and other countries could be greatly strengthened through books and the written word. British Council representative Mr. Robert Arbuthnott and his beautiful and graceful wife Robina gave me strong backing. He helped me to get not only large donations of new books but also to buy badly needed British books and periodicals with Nepalese currency. He, too, used to bring eminent visitors to the library.

I got regular invitations to parties where I met all kinds of people to whom I could talk about the library and its role. I felt it very necessary to go to such parties, where people enjoyed foreign drinks and I enjoyed talking about the library. I was very conservative about drinking liquor, so much so that I never indulged, having had the idea that the people of my country should not drink, as we could not afford to. It was always awful to see people drunk at parties. I used to feel very ashamed. Some people cried and some laughed after consuming excessively. But it was also fun to watch them. I used to wonder why they lost control of themselves. Maybe it was because they did not have access to such foreign drinks at home.

Mr. Arbuthnott's five years of never-failing help for the development of T.U. Central Library was praiseworthy indeed. He was one of the most friendly representatives the British

A Golden Age

Council ever had, and he kept busy by thinking up new ways of helping to develop every aspect of education and culture in Nepal. Even now he is remembered by Nepalese who knew him as one of the most wonderful and extraordinary diplomats Nepal ever encountered. He remained a great friend of the library till he left Nepal in 1972. To show my deep appreciation for his support, I organized a farewell party at my small T.U. staff quarters, inviting the VC, registrar, and some educationalists. When the time came, it was very hard to say good-bye.

The support of Mr. Ramunny, the Indian Cooperation Mission director, is also worth mentioning. Having seen to the furnishing of the library, he one day came to visit it. I took him around and then led him outside in order to tell of my desire to have a planned garden around the library building. He immediately understood my intention of asking his help in making the outside mud-filled plots into nice flowerbeds. It seemed that he too was a great lover of gardens. With a smile appreciative of my aim, he said he would see if he could help. I was overwhelmed with joy at his offer. God, I thought, was helping me everywhere. I love gardens, I love flowers, I love trees — all the soul of real development, where you can always feel the presence of God. It is said that one hundred years ago the Himalayan countries had the richest environment, not only in Asia but also in the world, but today we have more butchers than protectors of nature. Our so-called development is pushing us to destruction. But if we love God we must protect our environment.

Within a short time I was informed by the director that his staff would help to plan the garden and estimate the cost. Everything went along smoothly and quickly, and within a short span of time a garden had been created to welcome readers and visitors to the library. The garden greatly enhanced

A Golden Age

the library building. Natural beauty conduced to a pleasant atmosphere I saw readers enjoying the blooming flowers and the large carpet-like lawn. Sometimes I used to get very mad at people for plucking the flowers. They showed great surprise when I told them not to, as the reason they did so was to offer them to gods and goddesses. My straight answer — all the flowers in the garden were already offered to God (I saw Him accepting this offering) — produced astonishment. Some used to give me a smile; others showed anger. I had to engage someone to watch the garden. Even the watchmen seemed unhappy at not being allowed to let people pick the flowers, but he knew I meant business, so he did his duty. The library garden remained as beautiful as I hoped it would.

Of all flowers I love roses most, but the library didn't have enough space to have a separate plot to plant roses. Still, when someone really wishes for something sincerely, it will come. In 1968 the president of India and former professor Zakir Husain came to the library during his state visit. His visit to the library was arranged by the government. I was really thrilled, as I knew he was one of the greatest educationalists in India and a man who loved books. When I was informed I arranged a small but attractive display on him and his many provoking thoughts. He, it turned out, was also a great lover of roses. After his visit to the library I received the happy news from the Indian embassy that a rose garden would be created in his name across from the library building. Within a year a beautiful rose garden with about 125 kinds of roses came into being. It was superb. One can easily forget everything when in the presence of the beautiful roses — pink, red, purple, and even black (rare) —, which bloom at different times of the year, though especially in April. All book lovers and rose lovers came to visit the library and the rose garden. The library was blooming as a flower of wisdom, and the roses were

A Golden Age

blooming as the gift of nature to humankind. I took great pride in both.

Carl M. White, the renowned educationalist, said that the true university is its collection of books. The library is the soul of a university — a growing organization. It can never be stopped from growing. Thus I always looked for more books to be added to the library collection. During the visit of the Indian planning minister D. P. Dhar to the library on April 30, 1973, I discussed the need for new reference books and back volumes of Indian professional periodicals. Mr. Dhar seemed to me as much an intellectual as a politician and showed a keen desire to provide such items to the library. His remarks — "This library has grown with a sense of dedication and service exhibited by the very talented librarian. This visit has been a source of inspiration for me" — overwhelmed me. I broke this happy news in writing to all the department heads and requested them to help me in making a list of needed books and periodicals. This they did enthusiastically. I was very grateful to them for their cooperation and help. Hardly anyone was remiss. It was a great thing for me to have their support and cooperation whenever needed. Only some few teachers grumbled and complained, being leery for some reason — perhaps jealousy of the growing collection —, but I felt that it was a weakness of their own not to be able to appreciate others' work. The planning minister's visit had unquestionably enriched the library.

Another visit worth mentioning was that in 1969 of Mr. V. K. R. V. Rao, the union minister for education and youth services of India. He was one of the country's most well-known economists and a great lover of books. He spent more time in the library than any other distinguished visitor. He had lots of interesting and searching questions for me. I was impressed by his interest in book selection and collection

A Golden Age

techniques and wished that all our teachers and readers had been as interested. He checked the books on his subject, economics, and remarked that the librarian seemed to be more energetic than the teachers, as he failed to find newly published books which were so needed for the classroom and wondered how they could satisfy themselves with old ones. His remark in the visitors book was: "Pleasantly impressed by this upcoming library. The progress it has made is rapid but requirements indicate an even faster speed for the future." Some good books on Indian economics were donated after his visit.

Almost all the resident embassies were regular donors of reading material to the library. Once, in 1974, the Russian embassy held a grand display of scientific books in the City Hall. Our science teachers and I were very impressed by all the publications and their low prices. After consulting these teacher, I expressed to the ambassador of the USSR, Boris E. Kirnavotsky, my desire to buy the scientific publications, thinking they would be quite useful for teaching and research purposes but told him that there was not enough money in the library's funds. To my great surprise, he sent me a message that I could purchase them with a 75% discount. I thought it was a wonderful offer. With the permission of the university authorities, I bought all the books on display and enriched our science collection with little expenditure; it was almost like a big donation. Our science teachers were very happy at my success. Our library had at that time very few books on science, as postgraduate science classes were started only in 1965. Scientific books had therefore been on my priority list of acquisitions.

When I was studying in the United States, I came to know a little about the Asia Foundation's Books for Asia Programme, started in 1954. Now that I was faced with a shortage of

A Golden Age

books, especially on science, the memory of the foundation came back to me. I got a booklet about it and took note of some of its objectives: to support Asian initiatives to strengthen institutions and distribute English-language books and journals to Asian schools, universities, libraries, research centres, and other academic institutions that could not otherwise afford or even obtain quality American books. These were mostly donated by U.S. publishers. I strongly agreed with their philosophy that book donation could contribute to national development by providing free access to information and strengthening academic institutions.

I sent my request to the head office for book donations. The Asia Foundation headquarters in San Francisco promptly sent me an encouraging letter requesting me to contact the Asia Foundation branch office in Delhi. The next day I wrote a letter to that office. Their reply made me no less happy: they invited me to come to Delhi to select books from their collection. I broke the news to the vice-chancellor, registrar, and all the faculty members. Before leaving for Delhi, I discussed in detail which books to select with our science and arts faculty. Once there, I was treated to the sight of brand new books lined up on the racks waiting for librarians like me.

I enjoyed spending my time choosing books for our library, more so than sightseeing. From then on, for some years, I made at least one trip annually to the Asia Foundation in Delhi. Whenever books from the Asia Foundation arrived, I displayed them after processing to draw the attention of teachers, students, and other library users to them. I was very shocked when the Asia Foundation office ceased operating in Delhi due to political reasons. Since I was not into politics I could not understand why India felt it had to close such a worthwhile private, non-profit organization. After learning of the closure, I started requesting high officials in the U.S. embassy in Nepal

A Golden Age

to open a branch in our country, but only recently has one materialized.

Having acquired American books, I approached German universities at the suggestion of German scholars who visited the library. Thousands of books on science were given as gifts over a period of years by these institutions. The support and help from German scholars like Prof. András Höfer of the University of Heidelberg's South Asia Institute, Prof. Willibald Haffner of the University of Giessen, Prof. Albrecht Wezler of the University of Hamburg, and Prof. Bernhard Kölver of the University of Kiel is particularly worth mentioning, as is that of Ambassadors Dr. Hans-Ulrich Meyer-Lyndemann and his wife and Eduard Mirow and his wife.

The Japan-Nepal Friendship Society also at my request donated thousands of books on different subjects. They were selected by Japanese professors of different universities for our library. The presidents of the Japan-Nepal Friendship Association Mr. Shinrokuro Hidaka and Mr. Tatsu Kambara and Ambassadors Hidemichi Kira, Hiroshi Nemoto, and Haruhisa Kobayashi also gave never-failing support to enrich our collection. It still gives me great pleasure to think of them and their wives, who always were so affectionate and inspiring to me.

It was surely due to the appreciable good will shown towards T.U. Central Library by the Japanese embassy in Nepal that Crown Prince (now Emperor) Akihito and Princess (now Empress) Michiko visited the library on February 25, 1975. I was extremely happy to welcome them. I found them extraordinarily interested in knowledge and information and equally keen to develop educational and cultural relations between Japan and Nepal. After their visit I thought that the Japanese were truly fortunate to have them as heirs to the

A Golden Age

throne. They seemed to me to be a unique symbol of love and affection — ever concerned for the welfare of Japan.

Also worth mentioning is the story of my efforts to enrich the periodical section of the library. Periodicals, the backbone of research, had no place in the library when I took over — not even *Newsweek* or *Time*. With the help of the British Council I subscribed directly to some important periodicals for different departments, making payment to London in Nepalese currency. Such service was not available either through USAID or the USIS, though I did get some magazines as gifts from the latter.

It was very distressing not to have a good collection of periodicals. I was deep in prayer to find some important ones, such as *Chemical Abstracts* and *Biological Abstracts*, for the science departments — chemistry, physics, botany, and zoology — when Fulbright professors started teaching in these departments under the Fulbright Programme. This programme was started in Nepal in 1961 under the purview of the U.S. Educational Foundation. It was a piece of good fortune for our library to have Fulbright teachers using it. I made known our interest in serving them by contacting the directors of the Educational Foundation. Messrs. Krishna Raj Aryal, Terence R. Beck, and J. Gabriel Campbell were soon close friends of the library and always cooperated with me wholeheartedly.

As soon as the Fulbright teachers arrived in Nepal, the director himself brought them to the library to introduce them to me. I thus became quite close to the teachers from the very beginning. I could share my ideas concerning the development of the library and their role in helping me to encourage the students and teachers to use it. Before leaving Nepal, most all Fulbright teachers donated the books and periodicals they had brought with them from abroad. Some of them were truly ideal teachers, I thought. Dr. Henry D. Weaver, Jr., a chemistry professor, was one of them. It was he who helped me to get

A Golden Age

the back volumes of *Chemical Abstracts* from the beginning to 1971 as a donation from the American Chemical Society. We both together wrote a letter of request and thanks to its president. I came to be very proud of the periodical collection. The subscription cost of *Chemical Abstracts* now is more than Rs. 482,000 per year.

Encouragement, inspiration, support, and cooperation from within and without were bestowed upon me like blessings from heaven, inducing me to work harder and harder to speed the advancement of T.U. Central Library and to help the University to achieve its academic goal of imparting quality education to the country. Everything shone bright in the library, a torch of wisdom and knowledge to light the way for teachers, students, and scholars towards the development of the country. God's grace and peace always prevailed in the library in those days. I used to feel very proud of my profession. It was a golden period in the history of the library indeed!

Chapter 5

Love and Intercaste Marriage

My love story is not like that of Romeo and Juliet. It is not a modern teen romance either. It is quite different — something very unique. It did not start in college. It started at work: I was working and not aware that I was in love. I was and still am very reserved about such matters. I had in fact decided not to marry, as I was very afraid I might lose my chances to continue my work for my country, male domination being what it is in our society. If I didn't find a good husband, I would have to be content with being a housewife, looking after my spouse and the children — an intolerable prospect.

Some divine spirit had already worked in me, leading me to give my life to service to the library. I loved this work; the library had become my soul. I had learnt from God to worship my work. I saw the presence of God in it. Thus it was that I started to love and admire Narayan Prasad Mishra unconsciously, as I found him also worshipping his work in the library. I sensed that we had the same goal: to reach God through our good service to the people.

A library is a temple of learning where you can serve scholars, planners, decision makers, and politicians as a philosopher, guide, and friend. I loved to serve; he too loved to serve. What we both wanted was service that would be an outlet for our divinely guided drive to help others. I told him the story of my changing my mind to become a librarian when I saw the Peabody library staff serving scholars, teachers, and students, thus realizing that here was a profession that would really take me out into the world and satisfy my desire for service. I also told him how people had reacted to my decision

Love and Intercaste Marriage

to become a librarian with a litany of discouraging comments. People thought I was a great fool to choose such an unrecognized profession. He listened to my story with great interest.

When he joined the library he had not had any idea of library science and the library profession. From the beginning, though, he took great interest in the library work. I remember so vividly when he entered my office for the first time with his appointment letter. He was dressed in a beautiful sweater woven by the prisoners of the Central Jail in Kathmandu. His keen dark eyes and beautiful smile tugged at my heartstrings. I felt immediate confidence in this quick-witted, handsome young man who did not treat me like a poor unrecognized librarian in those days when I was still having bitter experiences trying to earn respect. I responded from deep within to his respect and soft-spoken voice. I welcomed him wholeheartedly. Not knowing why, I started to tell him about my disappointments and my unhappiness with my existing library staff; he listened sympathetically and with great attention and offered his sincere service to work for the library. In the days that followed he became not only a member of my staff but also a close friend and counsellor. He made my working life happier.

I found Narayan to be a gifted writer. He and I worked together writing down things for different programmes for the library. I found out that he was a very versatile stylist and could write poems; he also produced captivating captions for displays and news for RSS, the national news agency. His life had been filled with unusual experiences, which deserve a separate volume of their own, a volume perhaps he himself will write one day. It is an exceptional story, just as he is an exceptional, extraordinary Brahmin gentleman with great,

Love and Intercaste Marriage

independent ideas, a keen intelligence and a wonderful sense of service.

He was born and brought up in Bhaktapur, 18 kilometres from Kathmandu. There the family of thirteen, centred around his parents, two sisters, and four brothers, lived in a traditional house with a courtyard for playing. His goal, like mine, had always been to get a good education. In the beginning he used to walk from Bhaktapur to Kathmandu to attend the college for higher education, as in those days there was no college in Bhaktapur. His abiding interest was in the law profession, and he dreamed of becoming a sincere and honest member of a law firm to provide legal counsel to the poor, in a society where the poor have always been the victims of injustice.

When his elder brother left the joint family to provide a more comfortable life for his own family in Kathmandu, Narayan decided to take some job while studying in the college to give solace and support to his parents, whose main interest in life had been to raise money to decorate the Shipadole Mahadev temple with a gold finial and to bring water to pour on the head of Lord Shiva. His parents were unhappy because in those days it was a disgrace to see a son's family moving out of the joint family. Moreover, the eldest son was one of the first persons in all of Bhaktapur to get a higher education.

Jobs were hard to find, and when the opportunity arose to work in the Gorkhapatra Chhapakhana (Gorkhapatra Printing Press) for Rs. 45 a month, Narayan jumped at it. He told me that, what with his 16 years and youthful good looks, he had been an immediate hit at the office among the staff and with the boss. He made his parents and sisters, the latter already married at the age of 10, very happy with his earnings.

Narayan was an exciting contrast to the rest of my staff, who did things in a routine way and only under pressure. From the first I thought Narayan was the right man at the right time

Love and Intercaste Marriage

to show the other staff members what an ideal worker should be like. Some time after joining the library, he told me he would give his best to the library, leaving me more time to do all the planning and meeting with and convincing of people in position necessary for developing the library and its services. He believed I had a real future.

With his advice and help, I gained in self-confidence. He at once became a close friend. We read books and discussed them. We had always something to talk about. He loved our great poet Laxmi Prasad Devkota, Nepal's most versatile literary genius. After office hours he often read from his favourite books by that author, such as *Sulochana* (an epic) and the verses of *Muna Madan*. Devkota was the only poet with multiple talents that Nepal has ever produced. He was a great lover of books and libraries, having once been fined for helping a library during the Rana regime.

I was always at ease with Narayan. He too seemed at ease with me. I never thought, though, that I was in love. I was treating him exactly like a brother and never imagined I would marry him. But one of the first things that happened to him and me when we both were attracted to each other was the extraordinary coincidence that we each found ourselves saying the same things the other had been thinking. How wonderful it was that we liked the same books and the same people. It struck me as unexplainable luck. Narayan began to tell me I was wonderful, absolutely wonderful; not a lady boss in a thousand, he said, would behave like me, nor a male boss for that matter.

As I became better acquainted with the self-confident Narayan, it became easier for me to talk about things we both were interested in — literature, administration, management of the University, the situation in Nepal, and life in developed

Love and Intercaste Marriage

countries. Narayan and I began to see each other regularly before and after office hours. We fell in love.

Actually I do not remember when we first expressed our love. Courtship is quite different in our culture, the more so in our case, as our relation was also one between boss and staff member. He was very clever at hiding his feelings from others. No one suspected for years that we were in love. With God as our director, we were great actors on the stage, behaving like supervisor and assistant one minute and lovers the next. It was a hard act indeed. But we were extremely happy in our love affair and library work. We walked together through villages, along riversides, and past religious monuments and enjoyed a kind of companionship that we had not known before. I used to be charmed and spellbound by his wonderful poetic words about our love and future plans.

Sometime, we felt, we should let the world know about our love. Alas, we could not, as we knew our families would not accept the fact, Narayan being from a very conservative Brahmin, and I from a Newar Shrestha family. Intercaste marriages were not accepted easily in those days, nor are they now, but we were guided by divinity to break through the man-made caste system and the traditional marriages arranged by the elders of the family. Though men and women are born equal in God's eyes, in Nepal they have been divided into four castes: Brahmins (the highest), Kshatriyas (warriors), Vaisyas (businessmen), and Sudras (sweepers, butchers, and the lowest untouchables). We had the Muluki Ain (Law of the Nation), but the laws were laws on paper only. Foreign friends living in Nepal tried to implement that law by giving employment to the lowest — a very praiseworthy act.

We agreed on all subjects except one, namely, the library profession. Narayan was a man of farsightedness and very realistic in outlook. He always found time to expound on the

Love and Intercaste Marriage

low profile of librarians and librarianship in Nepal, where people did not see their necessity for education. Nepalese society itself had to be changed, he said, to get better recognition for the profession. This was the great challenge to be faced if I wanted to be a pioneer of the library profession in the country. I always turned a deaf ear to him whenever he talked about the low image of librarians, as I had the strong conviction that I could face the challenge with him, come what may.

He never said no to any of my requests, and this proved to be a boon. As luck would have it, in 1967 the Indian Aid Mission offered a diploma-level scholarship in library science at Delhi University. When we learned of it, I prayed the whole night to God to whisper to Narayan to accept it. Though I was sure he wouldn't reject my request, I trembled with fear to put the question to him. He knew, though, what my request would be and gave me his usual wonderful accepting smile. I thanked God.

Narayan went off to Delhi for two years of unsought higher study at Delhi University, one of the best universities of India, on the recommendation of Tribhuvan University. I missed him terribly. Life was rather gloomy during his absence. For the first time in my life everything bored me. We wrote to each other regularly, he more so than I. He is a really gifted letter writer. His letters were exactly like his talking, and the next best thing to it. I loved to read and reread them — a source of true joy. I tried to be prompt in replying, but my library work kept me tied down. And letter writing had never been one of my strong points.

I have treasured and saved all his letters. I wish I could one day publish them, the way the love letters of Browning and other writers have been published. But I know it's not possible,

Love and Intercaste Marriage

because our society is not open to the extent that Western society is. My wish will likely remain a wish.

I felt those two year pass like two centuries. It was one of the happiest days of my life when I heard his voice again after such a long absence. He called me at home from the airport as soon as he arrived in Kathmandu and came directly to the library to meet me and to see what changes there were in it, and only then went home with his belongings. I was so thrilled by and appreciative of this gesture, as I was dying to see him. His own feelings were similar. At the end of this short visit, I urged him to go home and pay respect to his parents, who were also eagerly waiting for his return. This he did, but then he again came back to the library with all the materials on library services collected for me during his study period.

I always loved to get information on libraries and the library profession from different countries, especially from South and South-East Asian countries, in order to compare the library services others offered with our own; if I found anything being done better I tried to copy it, as I strongly believed that we should not hesitate to learn from any country if it suited our needs. I found Narayan's knowledge of library science very profound, as he also worked hard to get not only his postgraduate degree in library science but also to enrich his knowledge of different aspects of librarianship so that he and I could work together to develop the library as a model for the country — my longstanding dream. He became a great asset to the library.

Back from India, Narayan seemed more romantic and enjoyed telling me about the love affairs of his Delhi friends and their marriages. He became increasingly keen to get married. We became engaged, though it could not really be called an engagement, only an understanding between us, as we could not make an announcement, nor did we even tell our

Love and Intercaste Marriage

close friends about our commitment to marry. The time was not yet right. We both were trying our best to please our parents in all possible ways by providing all available luxuries — a new bungalow, built according to the design I brought from the U.S.A., and a car, bought with my two years' salary — so that my family would not object to our marriage. Narayan gave all his earnings to his parents. We both had a strong conviction that if we did everything to make them happy they would not do anything that would make both of us unhappy.

It was harder for me to break the news of my love to my family than for Narayan to do so to his, because our society is male-dominated, so it is not regarded as bad for a man to marry a woman from the outside if he loves her. Narayan convinced his parents very easily. I was nevertheless surprised to hear of their acceptance of his proposal to marry me, who was lower in caste. An unseen divine force had worked to change their attitude. Their acceptance was a great gift from God.

Now my turn came. I was nervous and hesitant — ashamed to tell my parents, whose fondest dream for me was an excellent marriage with a rich man's son within the same caste, as in our community wealth played a more important role than education. Wealth was everything; it was worshipped. I was always against such a philosophy. I agreed with the notion that the love of money is the root of all evil.

My family must have somehow sensed our affection, because everyday I told them about Narayan's help in my work, but they could not have imagined that I wanted to marry him. Once I tried to bring up the matter but I found myself dumb, unable to say anything for fear that they might object, given their different attitude towards marriage.

Love and Intercaste Marriage

Before I could tell of my determination to marry Narayan, something unexpected, terrible, and unbearable happened in our family, striking like a thunderbolt — the tragedy of my mother's death in 1968. The doctor told us that it had been due to a brain hemorrhage, but this was too impersonal for us to understand. For weeks and months afterwards there was not a moment that I did not think about her and cry alone, away from the other family members, not wishing to add my sorrow to theirs. My younger sister and brother cried wildly for days. My father was also long unable to keep back tears.

For the first time I learnt what death was like and what it meant. Everyone who knew my mother said she was a remarkable woman — an ideal traditional housewife who gave of her best to educate her children, not shrinking to face the criticism of society. I thought I was the most unfortunate of creatures to have lost her love and to care even before I was settled down in life. Now my responsibility to the family as its eldest child was all the greater — to give love to and care for my younger brother and sister and to care for and respect my father. I thought it was my duty to make them as happy as I could.

After the death of my mother there was a lot of talk among our relatives and my parents' friends on our having not arranged marriages for me and my brother and sister before we reached twenty; they thought that marriage should take place between fifteen and twenty years of age. They even once expressed what an unlucky woman my mother had been not to have witnessed the marriages of any of us. I was very hurt by their unnecessary remarks.

I thought I should talk to my father about arranging marriages for my brother and sister before breaking the news of my marriage with Narayan. I was looking for a woman for my brother, one who could take care of my father and keep our

Love and Intercaste Marriage

household in perfect running order, as my mother had done. In the same way, I looked for a handsome man as a match for my sister. Many proposals were brought by the matchmakers. We selected just such a beautiful woman, Renu, for my brother and a handsome man, Pushpa Lall Shrestha, for my sister with their approval, having arranged for the pairs to see each other. We did not consult their horoscopes. I broke tradition with the help of my father because I was afraid that if their horoscopes did not match we would have to forego such fine in-laws.

Selecting the bride and the bridegroom was thus a felicitous joint effort. According to our custom no one should get married if some elder in the family, such as a grandparent or parent, has died within the past year. My father, having consulted our house priest and astrologer, fixed the date for their marriage just after the death anniversary of my mother.

We threw ourselves into arranging everything for the wedding in the traditional way. I went to Princess Princep Shah to inform her, as she had shown deep concern to me at the untimely death of my mother. I was encouraged to share my sorrow with her whenever I felt the loss of my mother's love. I cried before her without inhibition; she was a great source of solace to me. Having kept abreast of my plans to arrange marriages for my brother and sister, when the time came she gave generous wedding presents, including gold rings and saris, to my sister. She discussed their marriage with me just as my mother would have done if she had been alive. And it was especially during this planning that I missed my mother. I knew it would have been happier had she lived. I was strongly convinced of the truth of the saying "What is lotted cannot be blotted," but I had an equally strong conviction that my loving mother's spirit was everywhere and could never die. I prayed that she might make me always victorious over sadness.

Love and Intercaste Marriage

The traditional wedding ceremonies were held in a very grand manner for both my sister and brother. On the first day of my brother's wedding, we invited all our relatives and friends to our house to bless him before he went in procession to the bride's house. Narayan was busy arranging for a music band and the bus to carry people downtown, from where they would walk to the bride's house.

Marriages in Nepal usually take place during certain seasons, which are fixed by well-known astrologers, so that it was a hard task to get a music band to arrive on time, as they got many calls from different marriage parties. The bandmasters could demand what rates they liked. Narayan did a remarkable job of getting them to come punctually.

In those days only men could go in procession to the bride's house. All of our male relatives and friends, then, left with the bridegroom, my brother, so as to arrive at the time given on the invitation card. The procession, lighting its way with oil lamps, had a stirring traditional look to it. I was indeed proud.

The next morning the procession came back to our house with the bride and bridegroom. I joyfully welcomed my dear brother and my new sister-in-law. But I was not the first to do so, as this honour fell to the seniormost females of our community. They were called *thakali naki* and *thakali naku* and were the only ladies privileged to welcome officially the bride and the bridegroom to all rituals. They would lead them inside the house and give the house key to the bride. Then I jumped forward to welcome them and hold them together. Tears rolled down my cheeks — a sign of happiness mixed in with memories of my mother. My brother also showed the same emotion. He and his wife made a handsome couple and looked like they belonged to one another.

A grand marriage party was organized with a mixture of modern and traditional features. It was a combined party for both my brother and sister together. Almost all of our relatives and friends were invited. They brought different types of wedding gifts for my sister according to our custom. Everyone came up to me to express admiration of such a well-managed party. I was very flattered to hear myself talked of as a wonderful, selfless sister.

On the third day the marriage procession came from my sister's bridegroom. This procession was very traditional in the Newar sort of way, having arrived, namely, without the bridegroom. It was the bridegroom's father, older relatives, and friends who came to our house. We gave them a warm welcome by offering them cigarettes, a variety of dry fruits, and betel leaves and nuts. In accordance with custom, the elders spent the night in our house. We were expected to serve them a good dinner. My two aunts and my father were quite busy looking after them.

As soon as the procession reached our home my sister started to cry. I joined in the lamenting, knowing that we had to part the next day. We spent the night together, sharing all kinds of thoughts up to midnight. We awoke to a beautiful dawn and got busy preparing for all the rites that had to be performed before the bride could be taken to the bridegroom's place. My aunts and my sister's friends helped to dress her. She looked absolutely stunning in her wedding gown: a gold brocade Benares sari, shawl, and gold and diamond ornaments.

It took at least one hour to finish the ceremony, during which my father formally handed over my sister to the eldest male of the groom's family, who had to tie a silver ornament called in Newari *tuti-bagi* on both legs of the bride before she joined the procession. Then my father, with the help of my brother, carried my sister on his back up to the gate and put her into a festooned car, to be conveyed to the bridegroom's house. My sister was weeping loudly, which made me sad and

Love and Intercaste Marriage

nervous. Weeping has always been a part of Newar weddings. It is said that it is inauspicious for the bride not to weep. But in my sister's case weeping was natural because we had all been very close and very loving. It was hard and sad to see her go to someone else's house. I prayed that my sister and I would have the fortitude to accept the separation. My new sister-in-law was nearby to console me.

My father, brother, and aunts kept busy packing all the wedding presents given to my sister, as whatever was given by relatives and friends and the dowry given by the parents had to be sent with the bride on the same day. Her dowry included a range of household goods needed for settling down in a new house, such as a bed, wardrobe, dressing tables, sofa set, cooking utensils, and a collection of silver plates and vessels, along with dozens of saris and matching blouses.

Usually the dowry is given to daughters in compensation for their being deprived of the right to inherit their parents' property. Thus parents try to give as much as they can, not in cash but in kind. Nowadays the dowry includes modern conveniences, such as TV sets, refrigerators, washing machines, and even houses and cars, if the parents can afford them. A kind of competition is observable among the rich.

My father and brother came back with tears in their eyes and told me how difficult it had been to see my sister leave weepingly after a brief ceremony in front of the temple of the god Ganesh (the elephant God), during which the priests of both parties, in the presence of the fathers of the bride and bridegroom and other elders, spoke some edifying words.

The priest of the bride's side said, "Today we have handed over our innocent, loving Laxmi-like daughter to you and request you humbly to look after her as your own daughter and make her happy."

Love and Intercaste Marriage

Then the priest of the groom's side assured my father that everything would be done for the bride's happiness in her new home and promised that they would treat her as their own daughter. These mutual promises were reassuring, as by Nepalese custom daughters lose everything in their own house as soon as they get married — an awful prospect to have to look forward to. Once daughters get married, they cannot count on staying in their parents' house even if they have trouble with their in-laws or husband; to do so is a disgrace to the family. What a tragedy, I have always thought.

Our home without my sister seemed rather gloomy for days, and I missed her very much, but my new sister-in-law soon filled the void left by her absence by showing her own love, care, and respect to my father, brother, and me. She quickly adjusted herself to our family and took her share of responsibility for our domestic affairs. I was extremely happy with her. I thanked God for such ideal mates both for my brother and sister, and I knew they did too. This had been one of the goals in my life: to see my brother and sister happy in their married life. Now my new responsibility was to make my father as happy as I could in spite of his having become a widower in middle age. Fortunately my brother and sister-in-law were ever mindful of the same need and made every effort to give to my father all the love and attention he used to get from my mother, a model traditional wife who did not eat any meal without first drinking water touched by my father's big toe. That was the custom in those days. I wish that my father had been equally as devoted to her. Alas, that could not be the case in our male-dominated society. Whenever I thought of the traditional relations between husband and wife among us, I hated the very idea of marriage, but when I met Narayan I knew he was going to be an ideal husband — a combination of the best qualities of both the traditional and modern

Love and Intercaste Marriage

husband —, and this was my dream, as I wanted to keep our old values too.

After the marriages of my brother and sister days and months passed, yet I could not get up the courage to tell my father about my decision to get married myself. Too many thoughts roamed in my mind, making me restless and nervous. Narayan was insisting constantly that we break the news of our informal engagement to my father. I asked him to have more patience, as this was not a task I could easily do myself.

Then suddenly a divinely inspired thought flashed through my mind that I should first convey this news to Princess Princep, with whom I had shared many things in the past. At the time she was doing her M.A. in Nepali literature at the University, so I received many visits from her in my office whenever she came to use library materials. Narayan helped her in finding needed information. She was quite impressed with his service and admired him for his rich knowledge of literature; she had a wonderful ability to appreciate people's qualities. I remember once her having admired my well-disciplined administration and management of the library, having been stopped by the peon who stayed outside of my office. He had asked her to write her name on a slip of paper, and this she had done. When I got the slip I became so nervous that I almost swooned, wondering what she would think of my office practice, which was rather different from the practice of other offices, where people could enter at any time they wanted. I never wanted to be disturbed by unannounced visitors and tried my best to have appointments made. Moreover, it would have been impossible for me to see everyone even if I had wanted to. I never liked to meet people just for meeting's sake. It was to go against our culture not to keep the door open to everyone at any time of day. Naturally I became the target of criticism, but I hardly cared.

Love and Intercaste Marriage

Happily, Princess Princep did not mind at all but warmly praised my practice when I went to receive her. She told me, "Shanti, I admire your administration, and your peon is just as disciplined as you want him to be. He would not let me enter your office without writing my name on the slip." I was thrilled and encouraged to hear such positive remarks on my administration. I used to hear from some revolutionary-minded teachers that royalty never cared to abide by the rules, but I always found the opposite to be the case. I told the princess that I needed such cooperation from all the readers to keep the library running properly, as I strongly believed that the rule of law and strong discipline was needed to develop any institution in the country and the country as a whole. Princess Princep always listened carefully to what I said.

While we were in conversation Narayan entered my room with some new information for her. She asked him to join us. To my great surprise she constantly glanced back and forth between him and me, seemingly studying us very closely, in the manner of a keen psychologist, to find out how close we really were. I felt a bit uneasy under her penetrating look and gave a signal to Narayan to leave us, which he did. She remarked how helpful he had been. Though I wanted, in response to such pleasing words, to tell her I was in love and already engaged, I hid my feelings on that day. As soon as she left Narayan came hastily to ask whether I had told her about our engagement. I giggled and told him I felt very shy. He was so disappointed that he almost lost his patience. Then I proposed to him that we tell her together when she came the next time. He at once rejected the idea, saying that I was closer to her than he was. I understood his point well and promised to tell her about us.

After a few days she came to my office straight from class during tea time. I offered her a cup. She was in a cheerful

Love and Intercaste Marriage

mood, but I was trembling inside. My heartbeat increased rapidly and my cheeks and ears turned so red that she asked me what was wrong with me and whether I had anything to tell her. I thanked God for her query. I just said nothing but bowed my head. She said not to feel inhibited but to express myself freely. When I told her that Narayan and I were in love and wanted to get married, I could not bring myself to look into her face. For a moment Princess Princep and I were quiet. She gave me time to return to normal. Then I slowly looked up at her to see how she had taken the news. She was beaming; I knew she had accepted us.

She asked me to call Narayan. He entered with his usual quick smile. She put some penetrating questions to him about the marriage and was impressed by his replies. She was delighted and happy for us. I told her, though, that I didn't have the courage to inform my father about our marriage plans. The princess took up my battle to break with tradition. "If you really love one another and have decided to marry, go ahead, and I'll talk with your father about it myself." Narayan and I were sure that my father would never say no to a royal request, as he was always more than ready to heed royalty, whether he liked to or not.

I was not present when Princess Princep told my father about our love and desire to wed. He raised no objections, and together they fixed the date. On May 8, 1970 I married a Brahmin from Bhaktapur who had been my fiancé for seven years. For the wedding I wore a heavy silk Benares sari, gold earrings, and bangles given to me by Princess Princep. Our wedding ceremony took place at the Saraswati Temple at Swayambhu, a scenic place sacred to the goddess of learning. Princess Princep sent everything required for the rites and an old Brahmin to perform the wedding rituals.

Love and Intercaste Marriage

I went with my father, brother, sister, and sister-in-law in a white car to the temple before Narayan's parents arrived in the company of his close friend Sunder Keshar Pundit Chhetri. They did not make us wait long.

Everything was in place, but now we had to wait for Princess Princep Shah. She had many engagements on that day, May 8, International Red Cross Day. As a founder and the current chairwoman of the Nepal Red Cross, she had to hoist the flag and grace the function that morning at Red Cross headquarters. Afterwards she came directly to the temple. As soon as she arrived, the wedding rituals started. Vedic hymns were chanted and we, the bride and bridegroom, were asked to exchange rings. Then we garlanded each other in front of the goddess and made three rounds of the temple, and in the end bowed down to my father, Princess Princep Shah, and Narayan's parents.

To our great surprise and joy, a few *gaines*, traditional low-caste folk singers, unexpectedly appeared with their typical locally made instruments and started spontaneously to play and sing beautiful songs of blessing for a happy married life. It was more touching and fun to have such singers singing pure Nepalese tunes than a modern band playing cinema hits. I gave some money to these unforeseen guests as a token of appreciation for their contribution to our wedding, the first intercaste marriage in our community.

It was a very lovely brief ceremony. My close friends Nancy and Douglas Hatch kept themselves busy taking photographs from the beginning. Afterwards Princess Princep arranged to have her beautiful red car take us to our small rented house in the compound of Akhanda Shumshere J. B. Rana at Lal Durbar.

The renting of those lodgings was an interesting story in itself. Mrs. Rana had requested us to find a single foreigner for

Love and Intercaste Marriage

the house, where once the first Peace Corps library volunteer, Dorothy Miller, who worked for me at the University, had lived at our recommendation. Before we fixed our wedding date, Narayan went to Mrs. Rana to tell her that a friend of his wanted to move into that house on May 7, just a day before our marriage. She was happy to hear of the arrival of another foreign tenant, who was in fact Narayan, he being unsure whether she would rent if he told her the truth. He played this trick on her with the connivance of Princess Princep. When Narayan brought all his luggage, Mrs. Rana was utterly surprised to see him moving into that house. Afterwards the princess phoned her about our marriage.

We went to this house in the princess's car unaccompanied by a wedding procession, a modern music band, or the dowry. We also broke with the traditional procedure of having two days of rituals at home and parading through town behind a band. Neither Narayan nor I approved of displaying pomp and spending money for unnecessary things. People constantly spoke against the evils of social custom but rarely followed through on their convictions. We wanted to be an exception.

My husband decorated the flat so well that I could not believe my eyes. I did not know of his hidden talents. The room looked better than any nuptial chamber I might imagine. We spent a few hours in it together for the first time in our lives. There was no fear of anybody's disturbing our new-found tranquillity.

Then we got ready for the wedding party, to be hosted by Princess Princep in the name of my father, in the Park Restaurant at Ratna Park in Kathmandu. Perhaps our party was the first such ever held in the restaurant, which at the time was run by Hotel Soaltee. Wedding feasts usually occurred in the homes of the bride and bridegroom, hosting many guests for many days — a real social evil. Princess Princep's brother

Love and Intercaste Marriage

Prabhakar Shumshere J. B. Rana, the manager of Hotel Soaltee, overflowed with buoyant energy and saw to it that his staff made everything just right for the occasion.

My father had distributed the invitation cards some days before with only our first names (Shanti and Narayan) written on them. Narayan was more known to all our circle as Mr. Mishra than as Narayan, and we didn't want anyone to know of our relation till they saw us together at the party. As we expected, many friends had asked Narayan whom I was to wed. His simple and quick reply was that he didn't know. They would find out at the party. It was very suspenseful. We thought we were wonderfully successful actors on the world's stage, as none of our friends and not even our staff could guess the truth.

The party started at 7 p.m. It was a well-managed affair. The food was prepared by the gourmet cooks of the Soaltee; the tables were attractively decorated. All of our relatives were in attendance without a grumble in them about our intercaste marriage. It was a great joy for me to see even the conservative elders of our community enjoying the party. I saw them dressed as I had never seen them before. When I told them they looked gorgeous, they told me it was their first time in a restaurant, so they thought they should put on some finery. They did not stop quipping till they left. Some of their remarks were touching: "The groom is very handsome with a smiling face." "Shanti is a wonderful daughter to get married only after arranging marriages for her brother and sister. She is more than a son. Her father should be proud of her" "How do you eat standing? Who does the serving?" Some were whispering questions about how to eat with forks and spoons, having been used to using their fingers. They feared others would laugh at them if they saw them eating with their hands.

Love and Intercaste Marriage

All the ladies drifted towards a corner, too shy to go get food from the table themselves, it being Nepalese custom at wedding feasts for people to sit on the floor and have others serve them. They also confessed to one another that they had not brought any *gagri* or *bata* (big brass pots and pans), the usual wedding gifts given to brides, thinking it would not look nice for them to take such things into the hotel. Most of them gave me money as a wedding gift. Thus I had to do without the beautiful traditional gifts. It was a delight, though, to hear their talk. They said they had never had such a good buffet dinner before, where they could take as much of any item as they wished. Some were filling up on *dudhbadi* and *rasvari*, round sweets made of milk and sugar.

I received less attention than my husband, as everyone knew me already. My friends and Narayan's friends were also invited. They were utterly surprised to find me and Narayan the bride and bridegroom, but after their initial dumbfoundedness they congratulated us wholeheartedly and came up with lots of pleasing jokes.

At about 8 p.m. Their Royal Highnesses Prince Himalaya and Princess Princep came to grace the party. They both looked very graceful and cheerful in their royal party dress. Prince Himalaya met Narayan for the first time. The prince congratulated him and me in his soft, affable voice. He looked quite impressed with my husband and I was happy, as I esteemed the prince very highly, not only as a prince but also a person. I never heard him raise his voice. His behaviour was always very humble. Whenever I talked with him I never felt uneasy. He was always full of praise for me and for my work — a great inspiration indeed.

Then came another royal guest, Princess Sharada Shah, and her husband Kumar Khadga Bikram Shah. Kumar Khadga was a college friend of Narayan's. My husband was indebted to him for his having found him a good job, long before his marriage to the princess. Narayan used to tell me how much he missed Kumar's good friendship.

The whole affair was wonderful and colourful. It looked more like an international gathering than a Nepalese wedding feast, what with all the ambassadors from almost all the embassies in Kathmandu and all the heads of aid missions that had dealings with the library. A host of Nepalese dignitaries were also present. People were surprised to find so many diplomatic cars around the Park Restaurant. The line reached all the way up to the British Council, half a kilometre away. No one had sent regrets; everyone invited was present.

It was not until 10 p.m. that all the guests finally left. My father, Narayan, and I were all tired from standing so long to welcome the guests. Nancy and Doug had kept busy as usual taking snaps of the gathering. Now the food was left to be enjoyed by all of us, including my father's younger brother Subarna and his wife Kedar. The food was so good that we went on eating and talking for hours. Then Narayan and I went back to our rented house, and my father and the other members of the family to Sanepa.

Our house had a small kitchen, a small bedroom, and a tiny bathroom. The drawbacks of the place were naturally not so small, but we were happy there. So it was good-bye to Sanepa and the start of a new life, a married life. I was at first a bit lonely and missed my family and home surroundings, but I realized that this was unavoidable.

Because we were both caught up in the library work, our honeymoon was put off. By the third day of our marriage we were back to working in the same spirit as we always had, and at times, I felt, with an even better spirit, since we were happier and free to work together uninhibitedly.

Love and Intercaste Marriage

After some days, though, I came down with something awful — stomach problems and vomiting. I thought I just had worms, but my husband was more anxious. At my request he fetched some antiworm preparation available in medical shops, but even after I took the medicine, my sickness remained the same. We both were quite ignorant of the signs of pregnancy. Not knowing it could occur so soon, we became very worried about my sickness.

My husband consulted a health assistant, his childhood friend Sahila (Narayan Dass Karmacharya), who asked us to bring urine and stool samples. I continued to worry, but then the report came: the sickness was the first sign that I was going to have a baby. At first I was thrilled, but my joy turned to tears as it slowly dawned on me that I was not psychologically ready for a baby. My idea had been that babies came naturally and automatically only after some years of married life. We could not help being rather unhappy that we did not have any idea of birth control techniques. Later on we became wiser, and better off for it.

The first person I disclosed the news of my pregnancy to was my previously mentioned friend Nancy Hatch, an American Peace Corps volunteer working for me in the library. She was also expecting her first child, in her fourth year of marriage. She gave me many tips regarding pregnancy. When I told her my misguided views on the subject, she had a good laugh and then gave me some books on sex to read. Neither my husband nor I had ever read such books before. Nancy asked me to consult a doctor, but I was too shy to.

My morning sickness never disappeared. It was not only morning sickness, though; I was sick after every meal, and this made my life quite embarrassing. My husband thought of all sorts of things to cheer me up. I remember him bringing many varieties of food and preparing them himself for me. We always had splendid meals but I could never keep them down. I'll never forget the hurt expression on his face whenever I vomited up his gourmet delights. In my ignorance, I thought that so much vomiting would have a bad effect on our coming child. Finally one of the books on pregnancy and birth that Nancy gave me, by Alan F. Guttmacher, eased my worries. My sickness too eased up some.

In spite of my sickness I never stayed home from work. But I starved myself during office hours, as I did not like my staff to hear my regurgitations. Nor did I want my married life to be disturbed by my regular library work. This divine urge kept me strong even during my sickness.

Just after four months of our marriage, to our happy surprise, I received an invitation from the British Council to visit libraries in Great Britain with my husband, and my husband got an invitation from the United States Department of State to visit the U.S.A. to participate in the Multinational Librarian Project under its International Visitor Program. This latter is designed to give foreigners in positions of responsibility an opportunity to meet and exchange ideas with some of their counterparts and to observe the American cultural, economic, and political scene.

When the ambassador of Israel, Mordechai Avgar, and the ambassador of France, Jean Français, both friends of T.U. Central Library, came to know about the British and American invitations, they also extended their own to visit their two countries for a short time. We thanked God for this unexpected opportunity — the honeymoon we had been waiting for.

The vice-chancellor, Sardar Rudra Raj Pandey, and the registrar, Dr. Trailokya Nath Uprety, arranged everything to make the trip enjoyable for us. For the first time ever a clothing allowance was given, in accordance with a new

Love and Intercaste Marriage

regulation applicable to all teachers and members of the T.U. staff going to foreign countries on invitation.

I was worried about my pregnancy and was not sure whether I could travel. I consulted Dr. Bethel Fleming, whom I had always greatly respected for her continual contributions to the development of medical services in Nepal. She was one of the founders of Tansen Mission Hospital, Shanta Bhawan Mission Hospital, and maternity and child welfare centres in villages of the Kathmandu Valley just after the opening of Nepal in 1950's. Her husband Dr. Robert Fleming's contribution not only to the field of ornithology but also to the establishment of United Mission to Nepal, including its medical services, will long be remembered by Nepalese. One of the most remarkable workers of UMN, Jonathan Lindel, has given a wonderful account of the Mission in his book *Nepal and the Gospel of God*, published by UMN in 1979. Before the establishment of Shanta Bhawan Hospital, Dr. Bethel served with head, heart, and soul the people of Bhaktapur, Kirtipur, and other villages — an extraordinary woman about whom one could write volumes. There is in fact a book about the Flemings called *The Fabulous Flemings of Kathmandu* by Grace Niles Fletcher (New York, E. P. Dutton, 1964). Dr. Fleming immediately gave me a green signal along with her blessings to go ahead with the trip to Europe. I was freed from my worries.

Travelling around Great Britain, France, and Israel after just three months of marriage and expecting a baby was one of the most exciting things that ever happened to me. It was so exciting that I could hardly believe it was true. Eventually we made half a world tour, visiting libraries, seeing scenic places, and enjoying ourselves immensely wherever we went. In every country we were invited to, we were given never-to-be-

Love and Intercaste Marriage

forgotten VIP treatment by the government, and this included a car and a guide. We felt very honoured.

Although the trip was supposed to be something of a honeymoon vacation, we kept looking for new knowledge that might help us to solve problems facing our library and to improve its existing services. Wherever we went we met top librarians, scholars, and educationalists: Mr. J. D. Pearson, librarian of the School of Oriental and African Studies, University of London, Mr. P. D. Haslam, secretary of the Library Association, Dr. G. E. Harrison of the Department of Oriental Manuscripts, British Museum, Mr. and Mrs. S. C. Sutton of the India Office Library, Mr. M. H. Lawrence of the House of Commons, Mr. A. J. Wells of the British National Bibliography, Mr. S. P. L. Filon of the National Central Library, Mr. L. J. Anthony of Aslib, (The Association for Information Management), Ms. Parker of the Science Museum Library, Mr. Chapman of the Bodleian Library, Oxford, Mr. Johnson of the Book Centre, Dr. K. W. Humphreys, librarian of the University of Birmingham, and Mr. P. E. Tuker, librarian of the University of Warwick.

One of the highlights of our visit to Great Britain was a dinner hosted by Mr. Rayner Unwin of George Allen Unwin Ltd., London, in our honour at the Garrick Club. Representatives of well-known British publishers and the Book Development Council were present along with fellow librarians.

After such a wonderful trip together, my husband left for the U.S.A. for three months on his own. I wished I had been invited too, but I was also happy in one way that I had not been; my baby was growing big fast and moving inside me. Thus we parted company at Heathrow. I flew for home. The separation was painful for both of us and I cried.

Love and Intercaste Marriage

Back from my tour, I could no longer hide my pregnancy. Everyone noticed. I was still sensitive about it, so I tried to constrict my belly as much as I could and covered it with a dangling shawl so that my staff and library visitors would not find their eyes wandering so easily.

In the library I launched a further expansion of activities in the British and Israeli spirit. Gradually different sections were added. During my visit to Cambridge and Oxford, I had been very impressed by their dissertation collections, so I started to collect dissertations by Nepalese and foreign students submitted to the University. I added this dissertation collection to our growing Nepal Collection, which I established in 1967 under the impulse provided by the Tennessee Collection at Peabody. Having started from scratch, the Nepal Collection has now more than 20,000 items. I felt very proud of this collection whenever I saw foreign and Nepalese scholars using it. My main goal was to create interest among foreign friends who wanted to know more about Nepal and to help our own people to write books and articles on it. The British Council helped me a lot by getting rare books on Nepal to add to the collection, as our library, being new, had lost the opportunity to collect them when they were less rare. The Nepal Collection has been a great attraction not only for Nepalese scholars, but also for scholars from India, the former USSR, the United States, Great Britain, France, Italy, and Germany, to name but a few. It caused me extreme joy whenever I thought about how I had achieved my goal and how my trips had broadened my knowledge.

The three months alone passed quickly almost without notice, as I kept myself busy planning, arranging, and rearranging different sections in the library. Suddenly, just a week before my husband arrived, I started to think of my own

Love and Intercaste Marriage

problem, that of finding a place to live. I was living in my father's house.

During the early years of my married life I had to make many difficult adjustments. Finding a proper house to live in proved to be a problem even at that time in Kathmandu. I was without any money, as my salary was all going to pay back a loan I had taken to buy a white Toyota car for my parents and the rest of the family, and gold bangles and chains for my mother. In those days, having a car was a mark of distinction. My parents were very happy to have it, but I felt very inadequate because I seemed to be of no help to my husband.

I had never thought of opening a separate account in the bank for my earnings, having never cared for private wealth, which tends to make people inhuman and unloving, and having always felt that whatever I earned belonged to the whole family. I never liked the word "mine" but loved the word "ours." If it were not for this feeling and my deep respect for my parents, I could easily have succumbed to the temptation to become a wealthy woman after my marriage. For nine years I gave whatever I earned to my parents. I took great pleasure in breaking our tradition of dowries. I always loved to give and hated to take. Moreover, I wanted to make my father feel that I was more than a son to him and cared for his happiness and comfort and that of the other members of the family. I knew how hard fathers had to work to provide their daughters with a proper education and a good dowry. It was totally different in my case. There was no dowry. I was living just like an ascetic or a sage: no home of my own to stay in, no bed to sleep in, no furniture, and no utensils for cooking except a few stainless steel pots and pans and a small jar for carrying water given to me by Princess Princep.

My husband also had to give a large portion of his salary to his elderly parents, so after the wedding our life was

Love and Intercaste Marriage

challenging. But God created me and my husband to face the challenge resolutely; our life was happy and full of promise.

We found a small house in the university quarter without running water and electricity. We were the first couple to move in and were grateful to Dr. Trailokya Nath Uprety for having provided us with the house at our request. Before my husband's arrival, I threw myself into the business of furnishing and decorating with the help of my close friend Nancy Hatch. I borrowed two small beds with mattresses. Nancy sewed the curtains for all the windows. Doug, her husband, remodelled boxes into racks for the storeroom and kitchen.

Nancy had been my readiest helper ever since she joined the library as an American Peace Corps volunteer and remained so from the very beginning of my marriage. She was an extraordinary lady who loved Nepal and Nepalese who were committed to the development and welfare of their country. She spoke Nepali better than any foreigner I knew. She always wore Nepalese dress: a sari and a blouse. She was very friendly and sociable, an ideal Peace Corps volunteer who could adapt to any situation. She and her wonderful, loving husband Doug worked for more than two years, from 1966 to 1968, in Doti in the far western part of Nepal, a most backward area, where she had had to walk hours to fetch water. Teachers in a local school, they were greatly loved by the villagers. While working in the University from 1968 to 1969 after their return from Doti, they lived on the ground floor of a typical Nepalese house that had no running water and cooked on a kerosene stove. Their place was clean and attractive, with a *radhi* (a rough wool carpet), *sukul* (a Nepalese mat made out of straw), and clay pots. Without her never-failing help and encouragement, my early married life would have been very difficult. I was thankful to God for giving me such a unique friend.

Within a week Nancy had decorated everything in such a miraculous way that the empty and uninviting house turned into a beautiful, sweet home. Using money given as a wedding gift by relatives and friends, I bought a handsome metal-topped oval coffee table made in Kashmir and two round stools. The price of the table was Rs. 250. Our drawing room cum bedroom looked prettier with that table in it. Nancy and I worked quite hard before and after office hours to get things in shape, in spite of my reservations that it might be too much for me, as the expected delivery date was just three weeks away.

On the very day of my husband's arrival I started to feel uneasy while working in the library, so I went to Prasuti Griha (the first maternity hospital in Nepal, established in September 1959) to consult my doctor, Kanti Giri, one of the most dedicated female doctors in Nepal. She immediately admitted me to the hospital and advised me not to go to the airport to receive my sorely missed husband. I almost cried because our separation just after marriage had been very painful, and I wanted to see him as soon as he arrived, knowing that he too would be looking for me in the airport. I waited for him in the hospital.

With a face showing signs of nervousness, he came to see me direct from the airport. Dr. Giri, the hospital's superintendent, gave us the chance to be by ourselves in her office so that we could share our joy and happiness. It was one of the gladdest moments in our lives.

After a while I was transferred to a room for detailed checkups. Unbearable labour pains started. The chief matron of the hospital, Mrs. Manu Bangdel, kept me cheerful with her smiles and talk, and Dr. Bethel Fleming stayed with me throughout. Her presence made me feel secure, and the loving

Love and Intercaste Marriage

care backed by her reassuring smile made my labour pains seem lighter. I felt her presence to be divine.

I was in the labour room for hours, but my baby refused to come through the normal passage, so the doctor decided to deliver it by caesarean section. My dear husband got so nervous that he almost fainted at the news of the operation, before having put his signature on the hospital form. Strangely, though, I was not even a bit nervous, being thoroughly committed to getting my baby born safely by any means. Before being transferred to the operation theatre, I told my husband, who was standing with speechless pain in his heart and tears in his eyes, and the other family members who had come to be with me not to worry but pray for a safe delivery. Within a short time I was in a different, peaceful world. I knew nothing of what happened.

Dr. Giri and her team were successful. My daughter was born on January 18, 1971. Dr. Giri handed over my daughter fresh from the womb to Dr. Bethel, who was as loving as a grandmother. I was told later that she brought my daughter with a beaming smile from the operation theatre to show to my husband and our other family members. I came back to the world after six hours. I was told that I had been calling for Dr. Bethel in a murmuring voice, and I was so happy to find her right by my bedside when my senses returned. I heard Dr. Bethel saying, "Shanti darling, you have a lovely daughter all right." I held her hands very tightly and thanked God and her for blessing me in this way — my joy and my dream.

Many foreign and Nepalese friends visited me to offer congratulations. It was thoughtful of my husband to bring a baby book from America so that I could get visitors' signatures. Dr. Alan F. Guttmacher, the author of the book *Pregnancy and Birth*, and his wife visited me in the hospital and gave me a signed copy of it, being just then in Nepal.

Love and Intercaste Marriage

Twelve days in the hospital was too long for me, as I had had no chance to be alone with my husband since he had come back from the States. Thus I was extremely happy to be discharged. Nancy kept herself busy arranging everything in the house at the Tribhuvan University Professors' Quarter for me and my baby. She had all the necessary things waiting: diapers, baby powder, warm clothes, and the like. Dr. Bethel gave me a book entitled *Baby and Child Care* by Dr. Benjamin Spock, the most widely recommended handbook for parents ever published. Authoritative, illustrated, and indexed, it was a good guide to me. But of course I also had Nancy as a practical guide on how to take care of the baby. I followed her and Dr. Bethel's advice strictly. In doing so, I broke with our social code by giving my baby solid food, including vegetables and bananas, even before the traditional rice-feeding ceremony.

Pragya grew very fast. She was a healthy baby. My father-in-law wanted to have a very quiet rice-feeding ceremony in the fifth month after her birth. Nancy took photos. My father-in-law was dumbfounded to see my daughter relishing so the solid food; we had not told him that she was already used to it. Nancy and I were smiling and casting knowing looks at each other. According to Nepalese custom, the rice-feeding ceremony takes place at different ages for sons and daughters: for sons after six months and for daughters after five.

Annaprasan is the term used for this rite of feeding a child solid food for the first time, on a day chosen by the family astrologer as promising all favourable auguries. Our daughter's rice-feeding ceremony was very simple and short. For the occasion, her maternal grandfather was supposed to bring gold earrings and thick silver anklet rings (*kalli*) for her, an expensive sari for me, and a suit for my husband, his son-in-law. In my case, as I love to break with unnecessary social custom, I requested my father not to bring all these things. I was happy that he listened to me, but nevertheless he came with a small chain for his granddaughter and some fruits for us — just the right gesture. My sisters-in-law were also present on the happy occasion.

In the beginning we had no maid, as money was a problem, but life proved difficult without one to look after my daughter, so to earn a little more money my husband and I looked for some projects to work on before and after office hours. We never gave a second thought to disturbing our library work, even if we had to sacrifice many things. By the grace of God a project was proposed to us and the library staff by the executive director of CEDA (Centre for Economic Development and Administration), Pashupati Shumhere J. B. Rana, whom I always found to be a very dynamic, broadminded, and forward-looking person with a genuine interest in the development of his institution. As far as experience goes, he has been unique among Nepalese administrators in seeking out persons to serve under him not on their ability to bow to his wishes but because of their true competence to do the job required of them.

CEDA had been established in 1969 and was housed on the first floor of the library before it acquired a building of its own. It was an autonomous institution existing under a tripartite agreement between His Majesty's Government of Nepal, Tribhuvan University, and the Ford Foundation and was destined to play a remarkable role in the economic development of Nepal.

I thought it was just fine having Mr. Rana's office in the library building so that the library could advertise its services to all the important Nepalese visitors, such as secretaries of H.M.G. and general managers of corporations, who came to see him when asked to do so, usually by a simple telephone call, as he had such an irresistible Rana personality that no one, not even high officials, could say no to him. Cars with white plates stood in front of the library. So many Nepalese dignitaries who never had time to visit the library, even at my request, couldn't help but do so now. They saw its services and took time to compliment me on them. I used to be so happy, as a few words of appreciation and admiration from one's own people have a way of being much more meaningful and inspiring than lots of appreciation from outsiders. I was determined to help Mr. Rana by every means I could.

One day I heard from him and Ford Foundation adviser Dr. John Dettmann that they wanted to help the library, but under one condition: the library should serve the needs of CEDA too. They had decided not to have their own library, as T.U. Central Library was already in a position to cater to CEDA's needs. I was thrilled to hear such a progressive idea coming from a Nepalese citizen. I wished our faculty members were like this. Every department wanted to have a separate library and bypass the Central Library's facilities — a very narrow outlook. I always felt that a small nation like Nepal should do away with the philosophy of "yours and mine" and adopt a new philosophy of "ours." I never felt that the Central Library was meant only for the University; it should serve all Nepalese who needed services, as then even as now Nepal had no good national library or public libraries worth mentioning.

I immediately took the proposal to Vice-Chancellor Rudra Raj Pandey and the registrar, Dr. Trailokya Nath Uprety, for their approval. The project, to be financed by CEDA, would involve the collection of all scattered government documents - published and unpublished, confidential and non-confidential - as basic tools for in-depth research work. I was extremely happy, as it was a great opportunity at the same time to enrich the Nepal Collection of the library. Moreover, it would help me out financially too.

Love and Intercaste Marriage

I took my new-born baby along with me to the library while working from morning to late at night, about twelve hours a day. My child was a true gift from God. She never gave me any trouble by crying and even seemed to understand the challenges we faced. I used to feed her according to a fixed time schedule and tucked her away in a small carton in a corner of the storeroom of the library while working. My library staff were greatly surprised at her unusually peaceful nature.

Working hard, we were able to make some extra money from the CEDA project. With it we decided to pay for the expenses of having a girl to look after and play with my daughter. A small Magar girl named Maya, aged twelve years old, was found in a nearby village. I was delighted to have her, though she had some drawbacks. She was one of those who liked to follow her own ways, looking herself somewhat like a baby to my urban mind. She used to boast that she had had great experience in looking after her mother's five other children. My husband and I loved to listen to her offering her grandmotherly advice. To my daughter Pragya (meaning "wisdom") she was a goddess.

Maya, who had no idea of city life, nevertheless fitted into our family extremely well. Her mind was always on her job. It was captivating to watch her adapting herself to a situation so different from that of her village, where every aspect of life was backward. In spite of her looks, she had an air of utter maturity about her. Having worked as her mother's helper since she was six years old, she had a natural feeling for her job, being experienced very much in the way that the eldest child of a big family develops talent in dealing with small brothers and sisters.

Thanks to Maya's care and love, Pragya became a strict disciplinarian in her own way. She would not stand for any

Love and Intercaste Marriage

disobedience or rudeness. By the time she was six years old, I was conscious that she was much more efficient than I was. By the time she was a fourteen-year-old student at St. Mary's High School, the first missionary girls' school in Nepal (established in 1955), she was devoted to books of high moral tenor and would read them again and again. She always wanted to prove worthy of the school's name and always had high praise for mothers and sisters like Winfred, Rita, Benigna and Maria — all committed to girls' education.

My most understanding husband and I planned not to try to have a son — a passport to heaven after our death, as in Hindu society funeral ceremonies can be performed only by sons. God made us very bold to ignore this foolish and ridiculous code. We'll wait and see where we go after our death. We are extremely happy with only one daughter.

After marriage and the birth of my child, the divine urge in me to continue my work was of even greater force. It was up to educated folks like us to improve the social status of girls, who would themselves then be able to take on the burden of bringing reform to society. Why attach more importance to sons than to daughters? (This was one of the sentiments I expressed in an interview, conducted by the talented Mrs. Rupa Joshi, that appeared in *The Rising Nepal* on May 2, 1985.)

Over a period of years we had managed to save some money from my pay, my husband's salary, our foreign tours and, in time, project money. We planned to use it to build a house on land close to the University bought by my farsighted husband for Rs. 4,500 before our marriage with savings from his scholarship money. We told about our plan to build a small house to our close friend, the architect Robert Weise, and he took interest in designing it for us. We had in mind a small house, but he surprised us by his plan for two houses: a medium-sized house to rent to foreigners and a small house for

Love and Intercaste Marriage

us to live in. I told him that we did not have enough money to build even a small house, and that a second house was out of the question. He just laughed out loud at our ignorance and explained how to build a two-storeyed house with mud mortar and low-cost Nepalese bricks inside and Chinese bricks outside. He was sure that this house with its Nepalese style roof and Chinese bricks could easily be rented out, as the land around the house was superb. The house would command a view of snow peaks to the north and a river to the east, both attractions for nature-loving foreigners. If he designed a small house as we wished, no foreigner would lay an eye on it. There would not be any chance for us to make the money we needed to lead a comfortable and independent life, he told us. He even predicted that we might be fired from our jobs, as we both, from the beginning of our careers, spoke the truth and criticized corrupt practices wherever they turned up. He was showing remarkable concern for how to make our life secure. We were convinced by his words and in the end decided to build first the two-storeyed house.

My husband and I did not have the slightest idea about construction. The whole task of erecting the house in the most economical way was discharged by Mr. Weise and his contractor. Without him we would never have ended up with such a wonderfully beautiful place to call our own. His service was strictly volunteer. How fortunate we were to have his expertise. He was an extraordinary architect, having designed, among other buildings, the Hotel Annapurna, Hotel Yellow Pagoda, Hotel Malla, and all army headquarters buildings and living quarters. In Sikkim, besides a host of hotels, schools, and residences, he was instrumental in renovating Rumtek and the Royal Palace monasteries and in planning the Palace Secretariat in Gangtok, to name just a few of his accomplishments. During our house construction period we

Love and Intercaste Marriage

became increasingly closer to him and his wife Lotti. She presented us with well-designed curtains, made by her personal tailor under her supervision, for all the rooms. She helped as Nancy had for the house in the University Quarter. I thanked God for providing us always such wonderful friends in times of need.

The house was completed in 1976, a structure without a gate and approach road. No running water or electricity was available. Our house was the first one to be built in that area, Kuleswor-Balkhu, which was then full of trees, with the beautiful Bagmati River flowing gracefully through it. No concrete houses had sprouted up, and it was so peaceful and so close to nature that I always saw the divine presence there.

After completion of the house, tradition dictated that we have a ceremony performed by house priests for its blessing, but we preferred the blessings to come from those admirable persons committed to Nepal's educational development. We decided to invite Father Marshall Moran, the priest of the Himalaya, Mother Rita, the principal of, and Mother Winfred, one of the founders of St. Mary's School, and Dr. Robert Fleming, the coauthor of *Birds of Nepal* (Kathmandu, self-published, 1976), a great artist, and the husband of my surrogate mother, the late Dr. Bethel Fleming. Dr. Fleming presented me with one of his masterpieces of art, a picture portraying a village in Pokhara against the Himalayan background. Their presence was indeed a divine blessing.

Within a short time, we got many enquiries from foreigners about our house, as foreseen by Mr. Weise. One party came to offer advance money for years, so that we could complete the small house attached to the garage. Mr. Weise at once put his energies into building the house, probably the smallest one in Kathmandu but wonderful nevertheless. It was so well designed that it became the focus of attention of all passers-by. We were

Love and Intercaste Marriage

naturally proud to hear favourable comments about it from our friends. It took a shorter time to complete than the previous house, as my husband by now had a general idea of what construction and supervision entailed. Mr. Weise was happy to observe my husband's interest and grasp of technicalities, as this meant that he did not have to devote as much time to oversight as he had to previously.

Within a very short period, with the help of friends, including carpenters and bricklayers from Kirtipur and other labourers from our own neighborhood, the small gem of a house was ready to move into. We were happy to be living in its sunny spaces, so easy to maintain and keep clean. My husband and I loved to do all domestic chores ourselves without outside help. Pragya grew older and Maya went off and got married, even before she had reached the marriageable age. This occurred against our wishes and her own too, and under great pressure from her parents, who threatened to commit suicide if we refused to send Maya back to the village. It was one of the saddest days in our life.

My husband liked to get outdoors and was an enthusiastic gardener who knew how to grow huge cauliflowers and radishes. I used to gather seeds from all around the world. Because I like things that respond to attention I always enjoyed combining homemaking with a career, though most of my friends never felt they could. I loved cooking and home decorating. I liked to experiment with recipes from the cookbook and recipes of dishes encountered on my foreign trips to see what my husband would say; he, too, liked to help me decipher cookbooks. My foreign friends had high praise for my cooking, and my husband even higher.

Thus with the grace of God we happily settled down to life in our cosy small home. The first foreign visitor to visit was from the U.S.A: my husband's teacher and friend Prof. George

Love and Intercaste Marriage

S. Bonn. Prof. Bonn, a reputed library expert, had worked as the Rockefeller Foundation adviser to Delhi University, where my husband had met him during his higher studies. Prof. Bonn, who had visited us even before we had our home, was delighted to see us settled in. During his visit he kindly offered to help us to buy a small car. Oh, what an offer! Within six months a new red Subaru (cost: $3,100) arrived to us as if it was a gift of his to us. Although we started our married life without anything, from the beginning some unseen divine force seemed behind everything to make it brighter. We remain always grateful to God.

Chapter 6

Challenges and Unending Struggles

The National Education System Plan was introduced in 1971 in line with the partyless Panchayat policy calling for planned national reconstruction. All aspects of education were to be unified into one productive system geared to the needs and aspirations of Nepal and the Nepalese; values unproductive to society — that is, ones not oriented to work and development — were no longer to be fostered. Almost all countries in South Asia had already launched reformed education plans with some vigour to eradicate illiteracy. The advent of the Panchayat system had burdened His Majesty's Government with a great responsibility to show the people its deep concern for better education. The rapid expansion of education during the period 1951-70 (321 primary schools with 8,505 students in 1951 as against 7,256 with 449,141 students in 1970, 11 secondary schools with 1,680 students in 1951 as against 1,065 with 102,704 students in 1970, and two higher institutions with 250 students in 1951 as against 250 with 17,200 students in 1970) combined with the lack of well-defined education policies and objectives had produced a number of problems which needed to be tackled by the new plan.

The new plan itself was not bad at all. It adopted many good points from the British as well as American education systems. My husband and I, though, thought that it had practical drawbacks. It did not mesh with our social reality, so that unless teachers and those they taught changed themselves it would definitely fail. We became critical commentators of the plan and tried to point out both its weak points and strong points. This was not appreciated by the architects of the plan; rather, they became hostile to us. My husband not only spoke out but also published articles. For his efforts he was given a very strict warning that if he continued to speak and write he would have to leave his position, but he and I kept our pledge to ourselves to help the New Education System Plan by engaging in constructive criticism, such as our articles published in *Gorkhapatra* on August 26, September 2 and September 9, 1972.

I always wondered why the elite did not speak out. They always complained at not having the freedom to do so, but I never felt any such lack. We are born free and God has bestowed upon us the power of freely expressing our opinions; if we sincerely wish to enjoy that power no one can stand in our way. The sad fact is that when people do not speak out then things are bound to go wrong.

One instance I remember was when the late King Mahendra spoke against the current system of education during his address to a conference of the Professors Association of Tribhuvan University in 1966. Attacks on the existing education system plan immediately began to be heard. Before that conference, no teacher ever thought to attack it. Conversely, when the New Education System Plan came out, praises were heaped on it as if the plan was a magic wand for bringing radical change to education. The expectations of its architects were too high; no thought was given to the possible obstacles to reform, such as the jealously guarded power of the teachers and the high cost of equipping all the academic institutions with better libraries and laboratory facilities. The teachers, good and experienced though they may have been, knew nothing about the semester system being introduced. I myself rather looked forward to adopting it, having liked it when I was studying in the United States. It kept teachers and

Challenges and Unending Struggles

students busy in their pursuit of knowledge, and the use of libraries was superb under it.

Shortly after the implementation of this system in the University, I was happy to find teachers and students using the library in the way I expected. Library attendance increased. More classes and reading tables were added. What a joy it was for me to see all the reading rooms full of students. I made a very impressive chart with the help of my staff to show the use of the library since the introduction of the semester system. I even had an article, "Semester System and Library Use," published in *The Rising Nepal* on June 22, 1973. I was determined to support the system, even though the architects of it paid little attention to the role played by libraries in schools, campuses, and the University.

I wanted the missing chapter on libraries written, so I submitted a plan to the education minister and friend of T.U. Central Library, Gyanendra Bahadur Karki, in October 1971. My move was not welcomed, and I felt compelled to approach the palace, my philosophy being to start at the bottom and only if not successful go to the top. I wrote several letters to the private secretary to the crown prince, Mr. N. P. Shrestha, and to the crown prince himself. This tactic made more enemies than friends. It crippled library activities in fact. Misfortunes come in train, as the old Nepali saying goes, and now it was happening to me.

The vice-chancellor, Dr. Trailokya Nath Uprety, who was very supportive of my move and my plans for the library, did not wish to continue in his office for a second term. He left the University, and this was a great blow to the development plans for the library. As long as Dr. Uprety was in charge of the University, I never had any problem, even after Sardar Rudra Raj Pandey, a great promoter of education and the library, left the University for reasons of health. But with the New

Challenges and Unending Struggles

Education System came a new vice-chancellor and his team, with ideas that ran counter to the development of an ever-growing library. A group of jealous and narrow-minded persons worked actively against my plans. In our culture knocking people down to size has always been a favourite pastime, if the head of an institution is not strong enough to assert his authority.

Tribhuvan University lost its unified character and became a collection of thirteen institutions, which were broken down in turn into different campuses. It was a radical and expensive step to incorporate all these private colleges, which had been running on their own private zeal and low salaries; they were offered salary increases and brought under the University administration. All the colleges thus lost their individual character and were put under one or the other institute of the University and given the status of campuses. The change posed a great problem for a small university — a big white elephant.

I heard many heart-rending stories from the principals of private colleges when such institutions, which they had cared for and nurtured, were taken over by the University. All the people in power and position acted as if they heard and saw nothing, doubtless thinking that they would lose their posts if they pointed out the new plan's shortcomings. Moreover, if anybody wrote critical articles about the NESP, newspaper editors were ordered not to publish them. Having started to publish my husband's series of articles in the *Gorkhapatra*, the editor one day called to inform him that he dared not publish the remaining articles. I was not happy, as I always thought that editors should not have to accept such interference but be able to make decisions for themselves. No man or system is perfect, and anyone with a good brain and some experience might have something to say about a plan that would keep it from failing. My husband and I took exception to the strong tradition of automatically praising anything put forward by His Majesty's Government, which tended to make people with power intolerant of any, even healthy, criticism.

From the very beginning I was sceptical about prospects for the plan's success. Junior teachers were made the deans of institutes and chiefs of campuses — a step utterly contrary to a social setup in which respect for seniors weighs so heavily. Knowledgeable senior staff lost interest in the University, victims to their ingrained nature of not raising a bold voice and of not complaining but saying yes to everything; their back talk and criticism was done within four walls.

When my husband and I came to know about the situation, we decided to bring out another article supplementary to the earlier series of articles on NESP so that the people in power would open their eyes to this problem and appoint experienced senior teachers to important posts. This was indeed a bold step. It made newly appointed deans and chiefs very uncomfortable, and they took it as if it was a personal attack. Actually we were not against them but the system as it stood.

Some of them made unpleasant comments about the article in front of us, though they had no arguments to counter us with. Some respected scholars and teachers, such as Prof. Kamal Prakash Malla, did ring us up, though, to congratulate my husband. I kept up the fight, even though I started to lose support for the library. My real struggle was just beginning — a great challenge I would have to face.

Even after I submitted the neglected library plan to the National Education Committee for introduction into the NESP, no one seemed to take notice of it, though most of its members, such as Dr. Mohammad Mohsin, Dr. Harkha Gurung, and Thakur Man Shakya, were known to me as good friends of the library. I was very curious to know what the people in charge of handling the proposal, who always pretended to be busy, had done. I hated to see my plan lying around forgotten, having worked days and nights with my husband under a divine urge to prepare it. We slept fewer hours those days, and I made at least two calls a day to enquire about things. Though they assured me that they would introduce my plan, I had little hope because most of the senior educationalists of Nepal who thought of libraries as the heart of any academic institution were no longer on the scene.

One day what hopes I had were soundly dashed. There came the very disheartening news of the removal of the chief librarian as an ex-officio member of the T.U. Council (Senate) and Technical Committee (Academic Council), this in spite of my repeated requests not to be removed. I had had a wonderful ten years sitting on these planning and policy-making bodies and felt I had made a great impact. It had been an important podium for keeping everyone informed on what a key role the library could play in the development of quality education.

For some days I could not decide how I would go on now with things and became so restless that sleep evaded me for several nights. I was gripped by the fear that the library profession and T.U. Central Library's development, which I had pushed so radically for over the past decade, would go downhill. I had no one but my husband to share my troubles with. His words and thoughts gave me solace.

I was by all means determined to get ex-officio membership back. I prayed and prayed. Then the idea came that I might appeal as a last resort to Crown Prince Birendra, who was involved in the formulation of NESP — a daring step which might create more misunderstanding and anger among those who had removed the librarian from the list of council members. Given divine guidance, nothing could stop me. With a deep prayer in my heart I wrote my appeal in August 1971. To my great gratification, the crown prince responded positively and gave the order to the Ministry of Education to include the chief librarian on the council.

This welcome news was kept secret for some time. Before it was broken to me I found that some people's attitude changed completely: they told me they were trying to get something done for me. I sensed victory in the air. In January 1972 I got a reply from the ministry that I would be nominated by King Mahendra as a member of the council. I wished I could have obtained an audience with the king and the crown prince to express my gratitude for this forthright decision, but for a lowly librarian to seek an audience might have been ridiculed by the palace secretaries, so I suppressed my wish. I was extremely happy; it was one of the highlights of my professional career. I had won the battle with the help of my husband.

I joyfully waited for the formal letter from the University informing me of my nomination as ex-officio member of the T.U. Council. Two letters, one dated January 11, 1972 from the Ministry of Education and the other dated April 16, 1972 from the University, were delivered to me, though not as an ex-officio but as an individual member. This was a letdown for me, as I preferred to represent not myself but the library profession. Still, by the grace of God and the king, I was able to continue raising my voice for the cause.

Before I attended the first meeting of the T.U. Council I was called by university authorities and told that it would be better if I did not raise the issue of the missing chapter on the library, especially with reference to T.U. Central Library. I was surprised beyond words at their unprofessional behaviour. My natural yearning for the truth suddenly burst out of me: it was God who had given me the freedom of expression and speech, and these could never be compromised; I would never stop crusading for the cause of the library profession and T.U.

Central Library. My words did not please them; they did not prolong their argument with me. I was sad I had to speak that way, but what alternative did I have?

The first meeting of the T.U. Council that I attended as a nominated member was very interesting. I was proud that I was there representing the library. I did not keep quiet. I raised some very pertinent questions regarding, first of all, the role of the Central Library in relation to the institutes, the research centres (such as the Center for Economic Development and Administration (CEDA), the Centre for Nepal and Asian Studies (CENAS), the Research Centre for Applied Science and Technology (RECAST)), and the campus libraries and, secondly, the branch library of T.U. to be opened at Trichandra Campus to serve all valley campus teachers and students, which was planned during the time of Vice-Chancellor Uprety, verbally and in writing.

My queries pleased neither the T.U. authorities, the deans of the institutes, nor the directors of the research centres. They became hostile, not directly but indirectly. I was disappointed not to have the support even of Dr. Trailokya Nath Uprety's successor, Vice-Chancellor Surya Bahadur Shakya, who had backed me for a decade as the chairman of the T.U. Library Committee when he was the principal of T.U. College. I had always regarded him highly and tried to think how he could have changed so. I sought appointments many times to discuss problems faced by T.U.C.L. and campus libraries with him. To my great dismay I was allowed to meet him just two times, for very short periods, during his whole tenure of four years. It was depressing beyond imagination. I resigned myself not to press him.

I learnt something for the first time: how power could change people in our culture, where sycophants abounded. I was advised by some old hands to compromise with power, but

Challenges and Unending Struggles

I was not born for such cravenness. Though determined to face the coming challenges, I started to miss former Vice-Chancellors Sardar Rudra Raj Pandey's and Dr. Trailokya Nath Uprety's support. If they could have continued on in their posts, the library would have become not only unique in South Asia but one of the best in all of Asia, I thought. Now things were topsy turvy. I spent more and more time trying to clear away obstacles than working for the development of T.U. Central Library.

The library became the main target of attack from different quarters. Things were on the verge of collapse. I was stripped of all my administrative, financial, and professional powers. The library was divided like spoils among different institutes, departments, and research centres, losing at last its character as a central library. It was put under the Kirtipur Campus Coordination Committee and called Kirtipur Campus Library instead of T.U. Central Library, which had been directly under the vice-chancellor. I was incensed.

I wrote several letters to the vice-chancellor and the rector complaining about the unwise decision taken by the committee to block T.U.C.L.'s academic activities, which were so essential to helping teachers and students adjust to the new education system. Under the new arrangement the dean of CENAS, Dr. P. R. Sharma, became the first chairman of the Kirtipur Campus Library Committee. This committee functioned not only as an advisory but also as an executive body. This was another challenge to be faced. I no longer felt free to put forward my own professional ideas. Every minute became a struggle.

One day I was shocked to see a job offer for the post of documentation officer in CNAS without any library science degree requirement. Even the government used to consult me before fixing qualifications for professional posts, but my own university had brought out the advertisement without my knowledge. I immediately called the registrar, Mr. Jagat Mohan Adhikari, a friend of T.U.C.L. even before he became the registrar, and the dean of CENAS, Dr. Sharma, to request cancellation of the advertisement, very politely telling them that no university should neglect basic qualifications for any post. The dean reacted negatively for, as I later discovered, he already had a person in mind for the post. No change was made in the advertisement even after several written requests. To my great surprise, though, I got a letter from the registrar appointing me as an expert to interview Dean Sharma's groomed man, S. B. Thakur, who besides lacking a library science degree was at that time not even a Nepalese citizen, having come from Darbhanga in India.

The registrar's letter was the same as an order, coming as it did from the head of university administration. I did not know what I should do. Should I be submissive to his implied request to curry favour with him and Dr. Sharma at the cost of doing harm to the newly budding library profession and the standards set by T.U., or should I continue my crusade? By nature I hated to take my stand against an individual when the system was at fault. In this case the dean could have given his man another equivalent post till he got his degree in library science, but according to our tradition anything that comes down from someone more powerful is regarded as the final word, even if it is contrary to the common good. Just arguments meant little or nothing.

As a strong believer in God, I practised some yoga (which means to be close to God) before making my decision, which was to challenge the wrong decision the university authorities had taken. I wrote back a letter of three pages, explaining why I refused to be the expert needed for the interview. I stated that

Challenges and Unending Struggles

my intention was not to reject the candidate but to protect the university from mismanagement.

The chairman of the T.U. Service Commission at the time was ex-Chief Justice Bhagawati Prasad Singh, a devotee of Lord Krishna. He came to my office to try to convince me to participate in the interview. I was glad he did not insist strongly; he understood my stand. I took the opportunity to draw his attention to the fact that even an experienced professional librarian could not apply for the post, as a 1st class M. A. (Hindi) was made compulsory for the documentation officer (a professional library post). Later I wrote letter after letter to the rector, Dr. Mohan Man Saiju, who used to show appreciable regard for me even before he became rector, and then to Vice-Chancellor Shakya, pleading with them to intervene. Alas, they read my letters but did nothing more. Then it was that I remembered what Lord Jesus said in the Bible, "They hear but don't understand; they look but do not see, for their hearts are fat and heavy, and their ears are dull."

The dean thus got his candidate appointed as documentation officer; he had been interviewed by the dean himself and Mr. Kamal Mani Dixit, a literary man. I lost the battle but was proud to have taken a stand against wrongdoing, something unusual and very hard to do in our culture. I thanked God for giving me courage to revolt in the interests of the profession, the institution, and the country.

The rector and chairman of the T.U. Library Committee, Dr. Mohan Man Saiju, from whom I had expected firm support for the library, left the University to join the Planning Commission. During his tenure of office, about two years, he had failed to address the library's rankling problems. Mr. Jagat Mohan Adhikari was promoted to succeed him from the post of the registrar. Mr. Adhikari was a very soft-spoken gentleman with whom I never had any hot arguments, but he was helpless before Vice-Chancellor Shakya and had no alternative but to carry out orders from the top.

In one instance I remember, he was given instructions to buy the private collection of Nepali literature owned by Bipin Dev Dhungel. This he did without informing the T.U. Central Library Committee and also without my knowledge. Such action was against the standing policy, which had been adopted by the University at my request so that no persons could purchase books or other materials for the library acting on their own.

When I was informed by him after the fact, I wrote him back my objections. He said demurely, "Shanti, I know your nature, for which I have had respect from the time I worked as the principal of the college in Birgunj, but I'm helpless. I got the order from the top, so please do not oppose the purchase." I was sympathetic with him, yet I decided not to compromise; I requested him to submit the list of all books purchased so that I could get it through the Library Committee. He was cooperative, and within a short time I had the list.

The Library Committee constituted a subject committee chaired by the head of the Nepali department, Dr. Basudev Tripathy, to evaluate the collection. I was extremely happy to get their positive report on the collection, which consisted of rare books and periodicals on Nepali literature. I was proud to be able to acquire the collection, as except for Madan Puraskar Pustakalaya, the child of Kamal Mani Dixit and a treasure of Nepali literature and the Nepali language of which every Nepalese should be proud, no other library had such rare materials so useful for any research on the subject. It also helped to enrich our Nepal Collection. All the teachers and researchers were also happy to be able to use it.

Challenges and Unending Struggles

The continuing struggle for T.U. Central Library and the profession never seriously affected my working spirit. I continued to follow my divinely guided urge to keep the library going the way it should go. My visit to Israel in 1970 had strengthened my conviction that if people have a firm determination to contribute to the development of home, society, and nation, nothing can stop them. Israel is ever developing, turning its deserts into beautiful gardens and even contributing to the developing process of the Third World in the midst of continuous attacks from all sides. Many a time while fighting for the library, I used to feel as if I was a Jew at the time of Roman rule.

One of my prime goals at the time was, in spite of my criticisms of it, to support the New Education Plan. In a circular dated August 27, 1973, I reminded the university authorities of the plan I had submitted to open T.U. Central Library extension services at Trichandra Campus to provide library facilities to valley teachers and students. I was given verbal assurances that the matter would be referred to the T.U. Technical Committee for approval. I was thrilled and waited for a quick decision. Alas, the Technical Committee took no decision and unnecessarily returned the proposal to the Library Committee for further discussion. Though downcast, I was determined to convince all the committee members — the rector, the deans of all institutes, and the directors of the research centres — to reissue their approval and put the ball back in the Technical Committee's court.

The Library Committee assembled on September 18, 1973. No discussion and no arguments took place. The committee, under the chairmanship of Rector Saiju, agreed to resubmit the proposal to the Technical Committee for its approval, with a brief note on the willingness of the British Council representative, Robert Arbuthnott, to help provide textbooks for the branch library. He offered his support at the same time I was trying to convince high officials in His Majesty's Government not to issue notices to the British Council to close its libraries in Pokhara and Birgunj, as I knew these libraries provided needed services to our students and teachers. I was even ready to offer my supervision voluntarily if the government would allow them to be under T.U. Central Library and the British Council jointly. But unfortunately at that time there was a wave of opposition to any foreign projects. Even missionary schools like St. Xavier's and St. Mary's were ordered to follow strictly a curriculum based on Nepali textbooks and to make Nepali the medium of teaching — an unfortunate decision indeed.

I waited again to get approval to implement my plan, less expectant than before. To my surprise, decision no. 19 of the T.U. Technical Committee was forwarded to me, giving me the go-ahead to start a library extension programme at the Trichandra Campus but without any definite policy and directives. I was at a loss again, as nothing was clear about how to implement the plan submitted on June 18, 1973 to Prof. Sankar Prasad Pradhan, the principal of Trichandra Campus, four months before the approval from the Technical Committee reached me. Mere approval would not be enough, I knew. I was already deprived of my administrative and financial power. Without staff and the necessary furniture, I wondered how they could expect the branch library to open. My dream to provide library services to valley students and teachers remained a dream — nothing else. My resolution to serve campuses in the Valley did not materialize and my goal to support the NESP vanished into thin air.

I was extremely sad, but this did not keep me from writing another letter to the Technical Committee requesting them to give me back my lost power and citing all possible valid

Challenges and Unending Struggles

reasons for them to do so. The Library Committee had already acceded to this, and as it consisted of the deans of institutes and the directors of the research centers, that is, members of the Technical Committee, I thought things would go smoothly. A rumour reached me, though, that the chief librarian, who had been made directly responsible to the vice-chancellor under the University Ordinance of 1959, then to the registrar under the decision of the National Education Committee, and finally to the rector according to the University Chart, would never have a status equal to that of professor, and other professional librarians, such as reference librarians and chief cataloguers, would never be equal to readers and lecturers. During the tenure of Vice-Chancellor Sardar Rudra Raj Pandey, and supported by the registrar, Dr. Trailokya Nath Uprety, I had managed to raise the status of every professional librarian, but now things were in flux. Again T.U. Central Library was put strictly under the Kirtipur Campus Coordination Committee and deprived of administrative and financial power. In the meantime CEDA was brought under the T.U. administration, and the documentation project, which was handled by T.U. Central Library under my charge, also came to an end. In spite of my request not to, all the equipment and vehicles bought by CEDA to serve the project were taken away by the Coordination Committee.

All of these were discouraging and very deplorable decisions. For days and months I could not decide how to act. Everything seemed very dark. I found no support for such a good cause. Request after request to make T.U. Central Library better able to serve the academic community was turned down. Usually I'm not given to crying, but for once I did. I prayed for the courage to transform every stumbling block into a stepping stone.

Challenges and Unending Struggles

Then another rumour surfaced: a spark of hope that a mid-term evaluation of NESP would be conducted by a team of educationalists appointed by the palace Jaanch Boojh Kendra to assess its impact on the existing educational structure. I waited very eagerly to learn the truth of the rumour.

One fine morning I read the news that a team of scholars was to carry out just such a mid-term evaluation. I debated carefully with myself whether I should approach the team with my huge files full of complaints, plans, and request letters. It would be again a very bold and risky move, as I knew nobody would think about libraries as being indispensable academic instruments — a truth not generally recognized outside the library profession in developing countries like Nepal. I discussed my decision very intensely with my husband for a few days. In the end I wrote a long letter with all supporting documents to Crown Prince Birendra (the present king of Nepal), who was then involved in the formulation of NESP. A similar letter was also sent to the team. The most active members of the team were Thakur Man Shakya and Dr. K. P. Malla, with both of whom I had had several meetings in T.U. Central Library and also in the Jaanch Boojh Kendra opposite the palace. Their manner of dealing with me at that time was cordial. I thought that the crown prince might have given some directive to them to look into my file seriously. In the meantime I got a very encouraging response from the private secretary of palace, N. P. Shrestha, thanking me for the letter I wrote to the crown prince. I fervently expected to see all my recommendations for T.U. Central Library and the campus libraries included in the mid-term evaluation report.

God listened to my prayers. The report came out in 1977. My heart beat fast and my fingers were trembling as I turned to page 25 — "Development of Libraries." What a relief and joy to find a separate section on libraries and the key role to be

Challenges and Unending Struggles

played by T.U. Central Library in particular in providing library services by establishing branch libraries not only in but also outside Kathmandu Valley, and by starting a training program to produce the manpower to run the libraries. I was extremely happy and shouted for joy. I had won the battle alone with the help of God. I thanked God and prayed to Him to give me more energy and a greater spirit to work for the advancement of library services.

The report of the mid-term evaluation team was very critical of Tribhuvan University's fickle management, citing the example of T.U. Central Library, which was put under different officers at different times. The University was severely attacked for its failure to achieve its expected goal of improving the quality of education according to the standards set by NESP. The university authorities were not pleased. I expected as much. Gradually I insisted that they implement the report by giving me back my administrative and financial powers so that I could fulfil my duties smoothly and speedily, but they showed no signs of doing so. No part of the budget was allotted for the library programme. I again raised the question in a meeting of the T.U. Council as a member nominated by the king for a second term. I was surprised to find all the members very non-committal — neither supportive nor opposed.

Within a short period a change in the top officers of the University came about. The rector, Jagat Mohan Adhikari, became the vice-chancellor. Dr. K. P. Malla, one of the mid-term evaluation team members, succeeded him as rector, and Gopal Dhoj Shrestha remained on as registrar. I was happy that Mr. Shrestha did not have to go, as he was the first person appointed registrar from the administrative staff. The posts of vice-chancellor, rector, and registrar had always been monopolized by the teachers. Alas, he too later changed totally.

Challenges and Unending Struggles

His attitude towards my library work become less and less supportive.

One of the more deplorable decisions Registrar Shrestha made against me is deeply engraved in my memory. It hurt me so deeply that even now my blood pressure goes up to think about it. A low-level library staff member from Patan whom I myself had recommended for his job was caught red-handed stealing library material, and I initiated action to have him punished and fired. Mr. Shrestha, though, appointed a one-man commission, Prof. S. Rimal, to conduct an enquiry. A month later I was given a letter of warning by the registrar in which I was told not to harass the staff. My temper knew no bounds, and I felt like hitting back hard. How could I run the library if evils were not punished? I fought him till, unexpectedly, he had to resign before the completion of his term.

I was equally pleased when Dr. Malla, who took great interest in my plans to solve library problems as a member of the mid-term evaluation team, came in as rector. He was a regarded scholar, academician, and author of trenchant articles. I thought we would get along well, but he proved to be no exception to what happens when power and position come into play and make a man unable to distinguish right from wrong.

At the beginning of his term of office, I felt that a renaissance period for T.U. Central Library and other libraries would be ushered in under his rectorship. The first thing I wanted was his support for gaining back the lost distinction between professional and non-professional library staff based on the model created by the father of the Indian library movement, Dr. S. R. Ranganathan, and approved by the Indian government for all Indian universities and colleges. It had been adopted by the T.U. Syndicate in 1970 during the time of Sardar Rudra Raj Pandey and Dr. Trailokya Nath Uprety.

Challenges and Unending Struggles

I went to Dr. Malla to discuss the matter. He seemed somewhat put off by my request and, expressing how busy he was, said he would call me back. Weeks went by without a call, so I phoned his personal assistant (P.A.) to remind him of my request. After a week or so I got a message that I should prepare a chart of all professional and non-professional library staff and send him a copy for study. I was happy to make a copy of a chart I had prepared in 1970 that was adopted by the T.U. Syndicate.

Again there was no response for months. Then to my great surprise I heard from an outside source that he had circulated the chart to the junior campus librarians, that is, those who were new to the profession with just a diploma-level qualification in library science. Most of the university staff had been given scholarships to go to different library schools in India, this according to my own plan and the 20-year plan prepared by my husband at the request of the former vice-chancellor Jagat Mohan Adhikari. By that time my husband had already left the library profession as he thought, rightly, that people tend to look askance at a husband-and-wife team. Though he was now working in the T.U. administration as deputy registrar, from time to time he was requested by Mr. Adhikari to plan changes for the library services. And so it was that he was asked to draw up within seven days a 20-year plan for library development in the University — a herculean task that he somehow managed to complete on time. I did not understand why I was not asked to work on the plan. In any case, I was ever grateful to the vice-chancellor for agreeing to my proposal to send T.U. staff to India for at least five years so that the professional manpower problem would be solved.

I was quite often denied the opportunity to be on the selection board. If I had been given more of a say, I would surely have broken with tradition and sought out creative, sincere, dedicated, and qualified persons for higher study. It wasn't long, though, before I had no voice in the selection, as I was very critical of selection procedures. I wanted the best candidates from the working staff of the T.U. and campus libraries to be sent. When scholarships are granted in universities of developing countries, the people doing the selecting tend to lose their sense of judgement; they pick close relations and *aphno manchhe* (their own people) without giving any thought whether they are fit for such a profession. Tribhuvan University was no exception to this rule: every Tom, Dick, and Harry got a chance to get a library education; my own library staff were not selected, despite my strong recommendations. Against T.U. rules even two outsiders, both related to a T.U. official, were sent in their place. This irked me to no end, but I had no power to undo the wrong.

I always questioned within me why people were the way they were. God is in everyone's heart, yet not everyone hears him. I revolted by writing against such malpractices from time to time, but no one usually listened to reason, which seldom has a place in our culture. I was warned not to write such letters again. I had started my career as a librarian under good educationalists who supported me with praise and appreciation for more than 10 years, during which time T.U. Central Library rose from nothing to achieve recognition as a model for the country. But after that golden period this all disappeared, to be replaced by opposition, envy, and jealousy. It was a struggle for survival.

Suddenly one afternoon I got a letter from Rector Malla informing me of a meeting of the library chiefs of all campuses, both professional and non-professional, in the T.U. meeting hall in Tripureshwor. The purpose was to discuss the chart, especially with reference to the qualifications mentioned on it. I at once suspected something was up, and I could well guess what the outcome of the meeting would be. It was a well-hatched plot to create misunderstanding between me and the other professionals over the issue of qualifications for higher posts like chief librarian, librarian, reference librarian, and chief classifier. I made a master's degree in library science compulsory for those posts which are equivalent to professorships and readerships in order to gain equal status with the teaching staff of the University. When I made the chart in 1970, I held strictly to the T.U. University Teachers' Chart so that no one could raise any voice against it if and when the T.U. Syndicate and the T.U. Senate approved equal status for the professional library staff. If I had put only a diploma-level qualification, my chart would have been immediately rejected. How could I ask professor, reader, or lecturer status for the chief librarian, librarian and other professionals without similar qualifications? But I knew very well that colleagues and other junior professionals who did not have an M.A. in library science would not understand, as the greatest weakness of mankind is to make everything revolve around oneself. If something brings personal gain it is supported, even if it lowers standards, and if there is no such gain it is rejected, even if it raises them.

The meeting was called to order by Rector Malla in the afternoon. Quite a number of professionals and non-professionals turned out for it. I was happy to see all of them together, but they kept long faces and asked lots of unnecessary questions regarding the degrees mentioned in my chart. Their attitude and behaviour did not surprise me a bit; I was expecting it. I knew I was sincere in my move to get due recognition for the professionals so that they could contribute fully to the development of the institution. If my professional friends refused to understand, there was not much I could do. I became the target of attacks at the meeting. The rector was very quiet, not intervening at all. Perhaps he was satisfied that what he had planned so carefully, to create misunderstanding between me and the other professionals, was working. No decision was taken at the meeting.

Gradually I became very alert to the rector's every move. The next thing he did was to take the same person against whose appointment as documentation officer without library qualifications I had protested and transfer him to T.U. Central Library from Nepalgunj, where he had been relegated from CENAS a year before for his misdeeds. This the rector did without consulting me or seeking my approval.

One morning Mr. S. B. Thakur came with his transfer letter. I was not mad at him but mad at the decision of the University, as I knew by his nature that the new appointee would never be an asset, having been seemingly made to create problems for others. This man had a special knack of spreading false stories about anyone who disappointed his expectations. Well, what of it? Welcoming him to my staff, I told him to abide by library rules and regulations strictly and to carry out the functions assigned to him. I would not tolerate otherwise. He vowed to carry out his duties in the directed ways. I reiterated that not he but the University system had been my target when I raised my voice against his appointment as documentation officer. This had been necessary because at that time I was trying my utmost to raise the status of professional librarians. How could I remain silent when a professional post was given to a non-professional? I was deeply concerned that all future professional posts would become the playthings of people in power if this precedent was set.

As it turned out, Mr. Thakur was later sent to India to get a diploma in library science, so when he came to work under me he had his qualification. I thus had no more cause for complaint and expected good things from him. But it was not

Challenges and Unending Struggles

to be. Before long he was again stirring up trouble — not coming on time, not paying any attention to his assigned duties, creating misunderstanding among the library staff, and breaking library rules and regulations. I then remembered what our elders said: black remains black even if you try to mix white in with it, and a born devil's brain always remains the workshop of evil deeds. He delighted in nonsensical arguments just to disturb the smooth management of the library.

Though I was a little surprised at his suddenly extreme behaviour, I sensed that he got some undue encouragement from the rector, because around this time the latter unnecessarily formed a five-member committee under my chairmanship to deal with library affairs; it included the new troublemaker. This was done without my knowledge and in spite of the recently implemented library development plan already approved by the mid-term evaluation team. Rector Malla was keenly intelligent and, like a good chess player, he picked four other members who were also not pleased with my recommendation regarding professional posts in the University. At the same time, he also provided his friend, the professional librarian Madhab Prasad Sharma, with temporary employment and gave him a contract-based salary equal to mine without my knowledge.

I was not against the rector's steps but merely surprised at every one he took. I had always had sympathy for Mr. Sharma because he too had received a library education in the United States, even before I had. He started his professional career at the College of Education library, and from there he moved on to the USIS library and the palace library but always, unfortunately, success had eluded him. Whenever he was out of a job I used to suggest that he join T.U. Central Library, but he never listened to me.

Challenges and Unending Struggles

Naturally I was now happy to see him in the University. The rector's plan to groom him for my job did not succeed, however, as Mr. Sharma was too gentle, not a person to speak out or act. He was included on the library committee formed by the rector. Though I was appointed as the chairwoman of that committee, the rector cavalierly directed all files to Mr. Sharma. How could I carry out my work without all the information I needed? If the rector did not want me to work on the committee, why did he appoint me as its chairwoman? I would not have raised a finger if he had appointed anyone more to his liking. I could no longer tolerate his devious ways and wrote a protest letter requesting him to hand over to me all the files and information he gave to Mr. Sharma if he wished to see me continue working in my present capacity. Soon a call came from his P.A. that I should go to see him. One afternoon shortly thereafter I did.

Dr. Malla greeted me like a war general, his face all aflush. Never had I seen him in such a cock-fighting mood. He put my protest letter in front of him and asked me in a totteringly angry voice why I should have written such a thing. I too immediately lost control of my temper and a war of words was carried on for some time. At last, in desperation, he said that since no one was indispensable I could leave my job if I was so inclined. My fiery answer came back: "You should leave your own job, not ask me to leave mine. You've lost your sense of duty and responsibility as the rector to encourage dedicated and sincere people like me. And you, rector, you are not worthy of your post if you behave this way. Before you came here I had great respect for you and your intelligence and literary skills. Now you've gone out of your way to misunderstand me, and one day your conscience will prick you."

Challenges and Unending Struggles

When I had finished my tirade he told me he had to see some other persons, so I left him alone. This incident reminded me of a similar one, in which I told him I could not break library rules by entertaining his request as the head of the English department to buy several copies of the same title; he had banged the door of my office closed and stomped off. My relationship with him did not improve until he resigned from his post.

The other members of the five-member committee obviously felt encouraged to oppose me. Unnecessary discussions were held during every meeting. They even went to the extreme of making a separate report without my knowledge and submitting it to the rector. I did not care a bit, having become stronger after that afternoon with the rector in my divinely guided determination never to compromise with those whose thoughts had gone astray. As chairwoman, I submitted my own report on library development without the signatures of the other members, who refused to give theirs. I finished my job, in any event, on time. I never enquired about the whereabouts of those reports.

Another vague and unverified rumour that Rector Malla was negotiating with a non-professional, Mr. Krishna Man Manandhar, for a book on library science was already circulating through the office of the Curriculum Development Centre (CDC) and all over the campuses. This naturally outraged not only me but other professional colleagues, who dared not protest. How were such things possible in the University? At first I did not believe it. How could he stoop so low? But whether I believed it or not it was fact. Once again I put my pen to paper to protest to Rector Malla and to Dr. Rajendra Kumar Rongong, the director of CDC, against such an unwise step and demanded that he advertise and invite quotations for writing a book on library science, as provided for in the T.U. regulations. If no professional came forward, the rector could go ahead with his plan to negotiate with Mr. Manandhar, whom I regarded as a good library worker but not the right person to be asked by T.U. to write a book on the subject. It was an absolute disgrace to the library profession, I thought.

Thus my struggles continued during the tenure of Rector Malla till he resigned from his post. His was the shortest term as rector, as far as I know.

My never-ending struggle was not, I thought, self-centred; it was all for the library profession and for building T.U. Central Library.into a model for the country. I failed to understand why no support came from concerned authorities the way it had before. Opposition was everywhere. I began to think and analyse like a philosopher: Was I too aggressive? Was I too ahead of the times? Why else should people at the top avoid a harmless person like me. My great "weakness" was to attend to my job and keep strict discipline in my office — against the cultural trend.

I always tried to be close to God, with all sorts of questions for Him alone by myself, whenever I was troubled. I read Ramakrishna Paramhansa, Vivekananda, the Gita, the Bible and, among the English authors, Russell, Butler, and Swift to seek the answers to my queries. When I read these I found great solace and learned patience for all the human foibles so damaging to the development process of this earth. Shakespeare's *Macbeth, Julius Caesar,* and *Hamlet,* written so long ago, are still so true of any society.

Now my problem was how to deal with T.U. authorities like the rector and the registrar, who seemed so determined not to support my mission in any way. Emotionally I was exhausted. Then unexpectedly the news of the change of personnel was announced over Radio Nepal. Vice-Chancellor

Challenges and Unending Struggles

Adhikari, Rector Malla and Registrar Shrestha resigned due to student unrest.

Soon everyone in the University, especially the staff of the General Administration Section, were busy getting things ready to welcome the new group: Vice-Chancellor Mahendra Prasad (a medical doctor), Rector Ram Chandra Bahadur Singh (a professor of history), and Registrar Yubaraj Singh Pradhan (a professor of English). A big clay pot with *dahi* (curds) was put on top of a *gagri* (water pot) and placed in front of the university entrance. We senior staff were given flower bouquets to welcome them with. I knew the rector and the registrar but not the vice-chancellor, who was not from the teaching staff but from the medical profession. I was very eager to welcome them. The new vice-chancellor, projecting a pleasant personality, gave a very interesting and thought-provoking speech in reply to the warm welcome accorded by us to him and his colleagues.

I was so impressed that I could hardly wait to request him to visit the library to talk about its problems and immediately asked him for an appointment during his inaugural tour. His response was very encouraging. Within a week he was back and made very inspiring comments about my work. "A wonderful library of which the University can be proud" were his words. He told me about his own interests in library development and what he had done, for example, for the Bir Hospital library development programme, for which he had sent a lady to get library training in the United States when he was working as the superintendent of the hospital.

He assured me of his support in solving the existing library problems. I was happy and encouraged indeed. Firstly I wanted to recover the lost equal status of professional librarians, including the chief of T.U. Central Library, to that of professors, readers, and lecturers. I discussed this with the

Challenges and Unending Struggles

vice-chancellor and with the rector and registrar. All of them were very agreeable to my demand. With rising spirits I began the formal paperwork containing the request. The rector was quick to forward the proposal with his recommendations to the vice-chancellor, who immediately gave his approval to upgrade the status and pay scale of the chief librarian and other professionals who had been effectively demoted in 1972. I felt a surge of happiness and relief and started to sing a verse from the *Gita* proclaiming that truth cannot be defeated.

I was also reminded of a sentiment expressed in the famous best-selling book *Ring of Truth* by J. B. Philip given to me by Eileen Lodge (who is the founder of the Nepal Leprosy Trust, having dedicated herself in the 1950's to the welfare of lepers in Nepal): to walk by faith and truth, which is what we have to do in this life, is never easy. This had always encouraged me tremendously, as it taught me that the challenges I ran up against were the very signs that I was walking by truth and according to conscience (the voice of God). If we wish to see peace on earth, we must work for it in this life. I again remembered the role of the prime minister Bidur of the *Mahabharata*, who always spoke the truth without fear, even in front of the king and his counsellors.

I was for some time in a very jubilant mood, organizing various academic programmes (on national and international occasions), seminars, and training sessions and inviting ministers and other high officials to inaugurations as chief guests of the library. The main objective in having them present was to highlight the importance of the library and its services in every walk of life, as the media usually attach importance to such functions.

One of the interesting functions we had in the library was the ceremony involving the late veteran politician Surya Prasad Upadhyaya, the home minister of the first elected Congress

Challenges and Unending Struggles

government in 1960. He came to the library to hand over his private library formally to Vice-Chancellor Prasad. In doing so he made a very impressive, if brief, speech, on his decision to house his collection in T.U. Central Library after having heard so much about its being the pride of the nation and about its services to all who needed information. He wished that everyone would have easy access to his collection, which covered a variety of subjects, including some rare books on Nepal and newspaper cuttings from 1954 onwards. It was a useful tool for researchers on Nepal. I expressed deep gratitude to him and also regret at the unintentional delay in arranging the take-over, the university authorities having been somewhat reluctant to accept his collection at the time, as he was a Congress Party member. I was in favour of doing so, having a philosophy of my own that knowledge should not have any boundaries. His collection contained a vast store of knowledge, so why not accept it? Unfortunately blame was placed on me for the delay in accepting his collection in the month Mr. Upadhyaya had wanted to hand it over. Once, at the request of the VC, I visited him with my husband to talk about his decision. He talked fretfully, and it seemed that some misunderstanding had already been created. I too did not mince my words — a policy I have adopted regardless of person. He at once understood and regretted his tone of voice. At my request he also donated a few almirahs to keep his books in.

After the function I took him to the area where I planned to house his collection and took some photos for the record. He looked very happy to see his collection better managed and more accessible to users than it would have been in his own house, and I too was happy that the donor was happy.

My cheerful outlook and energetic activities nevertheless seemed disturbing to some people in the T.U. Personnel Administration Section. At least I came to suspect this when I

Challenges and Unending Struggles

did not receive the promised letter upgrading my post, as recommended by the rector and registrar and approved by the vice-chancellor. The Personnel Administration Section raised many unnecessary questions, kept my file pending, and tried in many ways to create misunderstanding between me and the authorities.

For the first time, too, I had an unexpectedly unpleasant discussion with the vice-chancellor about a letter I had written to the foreign secretary, Mr. Jagadish S. Rana, requesting him to include in their upcoming programme a visit to T.U. Central Library by UN Secretary-General Kurt Waldheim whom, during my meeting with him in the UN in 1977, I had personally asked to visit when he came to Nepal. His warm response to my request so thrilled me that when I heard about his planned arrival I at once wrote the above-mentioned letter. I could not imagine anything wrong in making such a request. The vice-chancellor told me not to write letters directly to anyone anywhere without his permission in the future.

For a while I was dumbfounded and could not understand why the same vice-chancellor who encouraged me to go ahead on my own at the beginning of his term should change his attitude so. I stared at him expressionless for a minute and then came back to my senses and asked him why he insisted on censoring my correspondence. I did not get any sensible reply, so I told him I would continue exercising the same freedom of expression I had been doing ever since I joined the University — a temple of learning where the freedom of speech was supposed to mean something. My blood boiled within me but I controlled myself. No further unpleasant comments were exchanged.

The vice-chancellor looked quite disturbed by this turn of events. Things were exacerbated by the fact that the foreign secretary, Mr. Rana, was from his village. In the end I told

Challenges and Unending Struggles

him that if he would send a circular to all sections stating that all letters should go through his office, I would gladly abide by the rule. The simple fact was that I had got recognition for T.U. Central Library from the UN as its depository for Nepal in 1964, and I wanted to have the secretary-general visit what was, so to speak, his own library while he was in Nepal, in the hope of gaining some additional support to make the depository more serviceable throughout the kingdom. My great hope again remained a hope.

I continued my struggle and at the same time became more and more known among the foreigners living in Nepal through my library services and my other academic activities. I was interested in strengthening relations between Nepal and other countries and believed very strongly that such could be accomplished through the spread of information and intellectual endeavours. Almost all the embassies and cultural centres, such as the USIS and the British Council, regularly invited me and my husband to their different functions.

Once I had the opportunity to inaugurate the newly renovated USIS library together with the American ambassador Douglas Heck. This was during the tenure of a most active USIS director and a wonderful friend of libraries Diane Stanley, who contributed much to deepen cultural relations between Nepal and the United States. This rare honour accorded to a librarian was a boost to the not yet well-recognized profession. Now I miss her presence and support — a lady to be remembered forever. Such USIS staff members as Mr. Nanda Ram Bhakta Mathema, Mr. Aditya Prasad Puri, Mr. Bishnu Raj Jha, Mr. N. P. Shrestha, and Mr. Ram Pradhan were also very supportive of T.U. Central Library.

Our library had also had a close relationship with the Israeli embassy since the time of Ambassador Avgar, a great friend of

Challenges and Unending Struggles

Nepal and T.U. Central Library. Another equally active Israeli ambassador, Mr. S. Z. Laor, requested me to participate in the Third International Conference of Friendship Associations to be held in Israel so that I could visit some libraries and information centres with which to establish partner relations for the exchange of materials. I was extremely happy to accept the invitation.

It was to be my second visit to Israel, a unique country indeed. After nine years I noticed much change everywhere. Rays of development shone wherever I went. I wished that Nepal could also develop in such a way. During the conference, attended by more than thirty-eight participants from nineteen countries, I was encouraged to participate actively in the deliberations. I even had an opportunity to make a brief speech in the presidential house in the presence of President Yitzchak Navon of Israel. The hospitality we received from him was warm and abundant. I found him open to and concerned about the needs of developing countries like Nepal. Left and right I encountered people with an exceptional hunger for knowledge and information, enthusiastic in their love for Israel.

Then another invitation came from the USSR to participate in a programme to visit the libraries there. It was going to be my first visit to any communist country. Naturally I was happy. It was initiated by the ambassador, Dr. Kamo B. Udumyan, a good friend of T.U.C.L. He was very active and outspoken, and I used to discuss with him the achievements of the great leader V. I. Lenin, who wrote more articles on libraries and their importance for educational, cultural, and political development than any other world leader in history. I remain grateful to the Russian ambassadors B. E. Krinavotsky, Dr. Kamo B. Udumyan, and A. K. Vezirov, each of whom took admirable interest in the development of T.U.C.L.

Challenges and Unending Struggles

All the necessary arrangements, including passport, were made. Two days prior to the day I was to leave Nepal, two messengers from the vice- chancellor came to my house in the evening to tell me that I would not be allowed to go to the USSR. I was shocked and could make no sense of it. I was already packing, so I told them to convey to the vice-chancellor my resolve to go ahead with the trip unless he sent me his order in writing, as I had already been given permission by the University itself. The next day the messengers were back to inform me that I should visit the vice-chancellor without fail at his residence, it being Saturday. After much hesitation I decided to do so with my husband. We took our small motorbike. I did not enjoy the ride at all; too many unpleasant things were going through my head. I always hated unnecessary hot arguments with anyone, even though they are sometimes necessary for resolving issues.

We reached our destination more quickly than anticipated. The vice-chancellor surprised us with a big smile and showed us into his large living room, which was furnished with an attractive sofa set and many souvenirs from the different countries he had visited. Offering us tea in beautiful cups, he told me that he had summoned me to his house just to wish me a happy journey; he had never intended to stop me from visiting the USSR. He had sent his messengers, he said, because he had not received clearance from the top — a blatant lie, I knew. Expressing appreciation for his good wishes, we returned home to pack my things to fly to Moscow. It is still a source of wonder how and what changed his mind that way.

I left Kathmandu the next morning for Moscow via Delhi. The six-hour trip to Moscow by Aeroflot was quite pleasant. The beautiful airplane hostesses' hospitality was wonderful. Some of them may have been stout but they were all warm-hearted. On arrival I was received by Russian friends with their normal reserved smiles. They drove me to a hotel of traditional architectural design which I liked very much.

My visit had begun. I was deeply impressed by my trips to different cities and libraries, especially the Lenin Library and the Library of Foreign Languages. With the director and chief librarian of the former I had a very useful meeting that centred on the exchange of scientific publications. In Moscow I went out by myself without any guide early in the morning in the hope of talking with Russians in the streets close to the hotel. They seemed, however, to be very cautious. Moreover, language was a great problem. Everything seemed so different. I saw men and women who were well dressed according to our standards sweeping extraordinarily broad streets with long brooms. Russian women were digging ditches, wielding picks and shovels as road maintenance workers, and painting the huge buildings.

In Leningrad I saw many beautiful and scenic things well preserved since the time of Peter the Great, and I enjoyed my visit to Riga, a beautiful city where I felt very much at home.

I returned to Moscow from Riga on a very cosy Latvian train, and more interesting and memorable programmes were planned, including visits to the Patrice Lumumba University (and meeting with its vice-rector, Leonid N. Khariakov), the exhibition of Peoples' Economy Achievements, the Presidium of the Supreme Soviet, the All-Union State Library of Foreign Literature (and meeting with Elizabeth A. Lomakina, its deputy director), and the State Lenin Library (and meeting with its director, Dr. Nikolai Semionovich Kartashov).

I had many queries for all the high officials with whom meetings were arranged, but everything was very fixed and very formal. I began to feel like a bird in a golden cage. They did not seem to like my going out by myself. I was given a big black car with an interpreter to travel around in. This was so different from my experience of moving about freely in my own and other countries that it made me restless. Nevertheless, my trip to the USSR was very successful. I was very grateful to all my Russian friends, especially to Ambassador Dr. Kamo B. Udumyan and the late Mr. I. B. Redco. The latter (a particularly great friend of Nepal) and his wife received me amiably in his very tiny apartment. While I sat eating Russian dishes prepared in my honour, Mrs. Redco asked many questions about my trip. Mr. Redco showed all his work on Nepal written in Russian. I requested him to translate them into English so that they could be read by Nepalese and other scholars. Mr. Redco was a great admirer and user of T.U. Central Library. Once he expressed his opinion that his publications would not have been so well written if he had not had easy access to its Nepal Collection — a repository of information and resources on the country. Because of him, T.U. Central Library had the opportunity of serving a good number of Russian scholars doing research on Nepal. I have always had high regards, no matter where they come from, for scholars who love Nepal and Nepalese. I want my country to be known all over the world; it has a rich culture and tradition different from other South Asian countries.

It was always wonderful to come back from any trip to be with my family again and to start my usual challenging work in the library. Once I was back in the office, my senior staff immediately reported to me that some of the outside junior librarians had been given appointment letters under the unusual condition that they first work in the Central Library for three months of training (they had already received one year of diploma-level training in India).

I had raised my voice against this during a meeting of the interview board, which consisted of the vice-chancellor, the registrar, and Mildred Nance (a professional librarian, the wife of William Nance, the educational programme officer of USAID). I was told that the discontented junior librarians had gone to the VC's house to complain. During that meeting the vice-chancellor, Dr. Mahendra Prasad, had shifted all the blame on me for engineering such conditions and then slipping away from the library to Russia. This was just another misunderstanding between me and my professional colleagues artificially created during one of my absences.

One afternoon the new appointees came to me with the vice-chancellor's story. Up till then I had not believed it, but when the group of librarians themselves came, I had to. For a while I hesitated whether I should expose the truth to them. It was really beyond my imagination that such a false charge could have been made. All along my policy had consistently been to raise the status of these very librarians, not to lower it. In the end I decided to expose the truth and told I was never in favour of the mentioned condition but totally against it, because in any interview people are either accepted or rejected, so there was really no sense in giving an appointment letter with such a condition. Moreover, these librarians had already been working as junior librarians in the different campuses for a long time after receiving their diplomas.

I showed them the draft version made by the university authorities against my will. They listened to me very carefully, yet I could easily notice in their faces the human weakness to believe more readily people in power than people of lower status. Truth has no place in such a culture. Still, they left with a contented smile after I showed them another letter I had written to the registrar requesting him not to mention the condition on the appointment letter. After this incident I totally changed my strategy for dealing with the authorities. I could easily sense that this period was not going to be a bed of roses.

Challenges and Unending Struggles

The new registrar, Prof. Yubaraj Singh Pradhan, had a quite sympathetic attitude towards existing library problems. He never tried to avoid me but always welcomed me into his office to discuss such problems — a good sign indeed. He himself, being a writer and a professor of English, understood quite well the importance libraries have, in any kind of education system, in uplifting standards. I did not know him well until he was appointed the registrar of the University, so it was a happy surprise for me to hear his voice being raised for the cause of T.U. Central Library. However, I hesitated to trust people instantly, having been deceived many a time by people whom I greatly trusted. Thus, though the registrar showed his keen interest to help, I reacted less enthusiastically than I should have. In any case, I requested him to advance the pending file on the upgrading of the librarian's post and to get approval for a vehicle, which was important for expanding planned library programmes and services to other campus libraries. I told him that Tribhuvan University Central Library was the first institution to have a jeep (no. 1375, donated by USOM). It was also used by the vice-chancellor and the rector because at that time it was the only vehicle the University had, but now, even though there were more than a dozen vehicles in the Central Office alone, the library was not given one.

The registrar immediately asked me to include the cost of a vehicle in the new budget, even though a circular from the government was cautioning against buying vehicles due to a financial pinch it was facing. The University, though autonomous, had to depend fully on government funds, as it made no money educating students. Higher education in Nepal must be one of the cheapest in the world. The annual fee is $10.34 for undergraduates, $12.41 for graduate students, and $15.31 for postgraduates.

Challenges and Unending Struggles

The registrar's suggestion cheered me. I at once broke the news to my staff. My lower staff greeted it heartily, as they would no longer be burdened with bundles of books and periodicals to carry on their shoulders from the post office and bookshops in Kathmandu — a distance of five kilometres. It had been always painful for me to see them doing this.

As soon as I got this green light, I went to the Finance Ministry to convince the concerned officials of the urgent need for the vehicle in spite of their objections. Having obtained their consent, I started to hunt around for a good light Japanese vehicle which would consume a minimum of petrol and provide a maximum of service at a reasonable price. I sent my staff to collect catalogues from the different Japanese motor agencies. After going through these, I consulted some of my Japanese and Nepalese friends and in the end decided to purchase a new Toyota Starlet for Rs. 125,000.

The agency was quick to procure the vehicle, and one morning there it was, in front of the library ready for inspection. I was not happy with its yellow colour, but the agency promised to change it. Thus I told the agency to hand it over to the General Administration Section to be entered into the T.U. property register. My staff was already taking to the vehicle, no. 6664, which was to be ours for good the next morning. Or would have been, had not foul play occurred overnight, and a decision been made not to let the library have it.

That fateful day the whole staff eagerly awaited the arrival of the vehicle. They became so impatient that they went to Tripureshwor, where all the T.U. authorities carried out their official duties, to enquire why the vehicle had not been sent; they fully expected to come back to the library in it after picking up some book parcels from the Foreign Post Office. To their shock and amazement they learned that the new vehicle

Challenges and Unending Struggles

had been given to the dean of the Institute of Management and that a run-down Landrover long ago donated to the University by UNICEF would be given to the library after it was first repaired.

It was already four o'clock when my staff came back. They reported everything in detail, down to the instigators and collaborators. This was too much to swallow. That a university, a temple of learning, should be the scene for such conniving was a disgrace. Where to go and complain? It had been the decision of university authorities like the vice-chancellor and the rector not to provide T.U. Central Library with that new vehicle.

T.U. Central Library was directly under the rector, Ram Chandra Bahadur Singh. As a person, I had always found him gracious. Even before he became the rector, he used to greet me with a smile whenever he saw me on the street or in a crowd. His behaviour was never that of a pompous, rich bureaucrat. He was tall and looked like a general, even though generals don't normally smoke cigars. He loved to talk about birds, dogs, and other animals. Struck by his simplicity and gentility, I never imagined him to be a scion of the Thakuris, the highest Kshatriya class. But slowly I realized that he had become a different man now that he occupied the chair of the rector.

I began to dig into his genealogy. Some thought that I was naive not to have known that he was from the family where everyone was addressed as *babusaheb* or raja, which is what his sycophants called him in the office. I never addressed him that way, though I was advised by some to do so and talk about how much trouble buying the vehicle had been so that he might change his mind or at least know how he had been misled by his sycophants, who always surrounded him in such a way that he could never use his own intelligence. During his tenure

Challenges and Unending Struggles

these sycophants were busier looking after their own interests than those of the University. I used to challenge them very openly, not to denigrate them but to reform them so that they would take the right path. One good quality I found in them was that they never got angry with me; they kept their anger hidden. I realized this when they played dirty regarding the newly purchased vehicle. I never blamed the rector for that act, as I knew he was not mean-spirited, but blamed all his sycophants. Knowing full well that the whole foul business was hatched overnight, I decided not to let the matter become a bone of contention with the rector. I was tired of fighting and I told my staff not to worry about the vehicle.

After some time the old Landrover was sent to the library. I knew it was going to be a white elephant that guzzled petrol, yet I had to use it. Giving thought to the well-being of the University had no place under the present circumstances, I gradually realized, though my mind refused to accept the fact. By the grace of God every incident would make me stronger still.

One outcome of all this was that I became a bit more careful to transact business confidentially. Since Registrar Pradhan had always been supportive of the library profession, I wanted the pending file on upgrading the status and pay scale of librarians to be advanced as quickly as possible during his tenure of office. It had been kept pending from 1972 to 1979.

One morning I went to see him with my request. He took great interest and assured me of his help. Though reserved by nature, he loved to crack jokes. He sweetly told me not to worry, since he had great regards for my library work. If I were in politics, he said, I would have been another Indira Gandhi. I felt flattered and was happy he had mentioned Indira Gandhi, whom I had great respect for. She was really a wonderful and extraordinary prime minister, better than any

Challenges and Unending Struggles

other prime minister India had produced after Nehru. As a woman, I used to take great pride in her and loved to read anything on her or by her. I always thought we needed more women like her and Prime Minister Golda Meir of Israel to run the countries of this earth so that male domination would fade away and the world would be a better place to live in, having a mother's care and love.

After a brief conversation with the registrar I came back greatly confident that he would push the matter. My confidence was justified: he got the recommendation from Rector Singh, approval from Vice-Chancellor Prasad and the okay from the T.U. Council in such a way that no sycophant could mess things up. It was one of the happiest days of my life to get due recognition for my profession after such a long, long, struggle (10 years). I received an official letter upgrading my post to the same level as a professor (equivalent to the post of secretary in H.M.G.). What a joy! I was ever after grateful to the vice-chancellor, the rector and especially to the registrar, Yubaraj Singh Pradhan, for the part they played in this.

This news spread all over very swiftly. Some people seemed envious and critical. Again some unrelated, baseless questions were raised before I was given the new salary. I knew it would be like a water bubble. In the meantime another rumour surfaced that the vice-chancellor had been asked to resign before the expiry of his term of office due to recurring student unrest. Within a week the rumour was no more rumour but a fact. The vice-chancellor was succeeded by the rector, Ram Chandra Bahadur Singh, and Registrar Yubaraj Singh Pradhan by Mr. Netra Bahadur Basnet, former dean of the Institute of Agriculture and Husbandry. The post of rector remained vacant for some time — a very unusual situation for the University. Many names were in the air as to who would be the new one.

Challenges and Unending Struggles

I was a bit hesitant whether I should press the pending matter or wait for a rector to be appointed.

I went to see the new registrar several times. He, too, took great interest in library matters and acknowledged the importance of libraries and information retrieval for higher education; there was much praise for my contribution to T.U.C.L. Naturally I was happy. I told him the sad story of the pending file and of my not receiving the salary I was entitled to. He assured me that immediate action would be taken so that I would get just compensation. Soon he had the okay from the new vice-chancellor, who had already cleared the matter when he was rector. The active sycophants could not follow along at all because the move was too fast. I went to express my gratitude to the VC and the registrar for such promptness. From then on the salary came.

The vacancy of the post of the rector was eventually filled; Dr. Chandra Prasad Gorkhali, professor of zoology and an ex-president of the University Teachers Association was appointed by the king, the chancellor of Tribhuvan University, on the recommendation of the vice-chancellor. I greeted his appointment, as he was an assiduous user of T.U. Central Library, and there was thus reason to expect his support for my plans for the development of T.U.C.L. and the library profession. During his tenure I never had any disturbing arguments regarding library matters. He never raised any objection to the agenda set for Library Committee meetings.

It was during this time that I put the crucial matter of loss of library books on the agenda to be dealt with exclusively in the upcoming meeting. It was discussed also in several later meetings. The issue was crucial because I had a file of baseless decisions on the loss of books at the various campuses made by the former registrar Gopal Dhoj Shrestha and sent to me by the vice-chancellor, Jagat Mohan Adhikari, for my opinion. These decisions involved penalizing the library staff by forcing them to pay 50% of the loss. During their tenure I had intentionally delayed voicing my opinion and taking the matter to the Library Committee, being too tired to fight at the time. The members, moreover, were all busy dealing with student unrest.

Now, during the several Library Committee meetings, I really had to work hard to convince all the members — the deans and heads of departments — that the library staff should not be held responsible for the loss of books and other library materials. I distributed a good number of articles on loss of books written by professional librarians from different parts of the world. I was happy to find later that every member had read these documents well. They formulated many questions, which I was pleased to answer. Some of the members were narrow-minded and could see no reason not to hold the library staff fully responsible for the losses. However, after long discussions over several meetings, the rule I drafted not making library staff responsible was approved by the Library Committee, though they deleted a clause I included to punish like a thief any library staff, including the chief, if he or she was found guilty of stealing any reading materials from the library; I had thought this clause very important in any developing country. I was nevertheless extremely happy at the rational approach taken by Library Committee members. If the rule had not got through, no one would have continued to work in the library. Every library, of course, must have an honest, dedicated staff, but such dedication should not involve having to pay for others' dishonesty.

During the Library Committee meetings I found the rector, Dr. Gorkhali, to be very unassertive, though I expected a firm yes or no from him. He was a man whose philosophy was typically Nepalese: never argue if it's going to cause you trouble. He was always slow to make decisions but very fond

Challenges and Unending Struggles

of telling interesting, exemplary stories from different literary sources he had dipped into. It was always a pleasure to listen to him. I used to express my wish very frankly to him that he make such good stories the basis of action. He had no answer other than a smile.

The library saw little development during his tenure. Vice-Chancellor Singh told me openly that the library was not on his list of priorities. It was a period of four years' lull. Tribhuvan University also began to lose its academic character. It became more a platform for politics than the temple of learning it was conceived to be. Authorities were busy pacifying students and teachers by providing facilities unrelated to academic needs. Student unrest was the main cause of the quick rotations among T.U. administrators. The government was on the lookout for any person who might have a knack for appeasing the students, if only on the surface, to fill the post of vice-chancellor.

Vice-Chancellor Singh was unusually successful as a vice-chancellor, managing to serve his full term of four years. When his term was coming to an end, many teachers and other interested candidates entered the race to succeed him. They performed their kowtowing to ministers, palace secretaries, and other high officials. It was not a terribly dignified selection process for such a respectable post. With this in mind, I requested my husband to write an article on the procedures followed by other universities that might be worth copying. He did so and published it in some Nepali newspapers under a pseudonym. He hid his identity because he had once been deprived of a due promotion for speaking the truth and writing openly about the problems of Tribhuvan University. We both had become more cautious, yet we kept up our mission to work for library, university, and country even though we lacked power and position.

Challenges and Unending Struggles

It had become almost a convention to have the rector promoted to the post of vice-chancellor. Thus Dr. Gorkhali expected to occupy the chair of the vice-chancellor after his predecessor left. He had, in fact, not a few connections with those in high circles, so everyone expected him to move up the ladder. But he lost out to Mr. Mahesh Kumar Upadhyaya, the dean of the Institute of Humanities and Social Sciences, his junior, who was appointed to the post by the king at the recommendation of the selection committee, which was headed by the education minister. Mr. Upadhyaya's former bosses, Rector Gorkhali and Registrar Basnet, were taken aback, and many critical comments were heard about his appointment.

Mr. Upadhyaya was very sociable and had a pleasing personality. I knew him from the time he first became dean. He never missed the Library Committee meetings I called. His comments and remarks were always very supportive of library development and the library profession, so his promotion from dean to vice-chancellor, jumping the two posts of rector and registrar, did not bother me as it did most other senior university officials.

A week after his appointment I went to see him in his office. He was in a very jubilant mood. I conveyed my congratulations once again and then expressed my hope of obtaining his support for developing T.U.C.L. in the way I had planned. Words I had not heard in a long time rang forth: library services would be his priority, as he wanted to raise the quality of education. In the beginning, whenever he introduced me to foreign friends at receptions and parties, he would say, "Meet our chief librarian at the University — a legendary lady whose contribution to the birth of T.U.C.L. and the library profession in Nepal has been unique." He was always full of pleasing words and could make good speeches on any topic, which even his critics praised.

Challenges and Unending Struggles

But gradually he turned into a man more of words than deeds. He began to depend more on his advisers than on his own good sense and preferred outward, showy activity to thinking deeply within himself. Soon his own few selected but wrong-headed and narrow-minded advisers were running the University. It was all politics among themselves, the authorities. I was told by reliable teachers that, on the advice of these right-hand men, he had tried to remove Rector Gorkhali and Registrar Basnet from their posts so that he could have his own team of people. I was sad to hear the story because I never believed in such cronyism, which was practised to the detriment of those willing to serve honourably. The intrigues to compel the rector and the registrar to resign went on for some time, but both were strong enough to thwart them.

The term of Mr. Basnet came to an end, and he left of his own accord, not caring to stand for a second term. He was succeeded by Dr. Parthibeshwar Prasad Timilsina, an economics professor who was appointed on the strong recommendation of the vice-chancellor and his advisers. Dr. Timilsina had qualities similar to those of Vice-Chancellor Upadhyaya, with one exception: he loved to read and think. Having been educated in the USSR, he knew the importance of information and library services. At the University he had worked in different high posts, so I knew him quite well. He was tactful and shrewd and knew how to feel others' pulses. I had never seen him gloomy; always he was smiling. Thus I felt quite uninhibited in discussing library problems and development programmes with him. At my first meeting with him as registrar, I received assurances of his support. He told me that he was aware of the existing problems and had suggestions for quick solutions. I trusted him because he had helped to enrich the collection of economics texts when he was

Challenges and Unending Struggles

head of the department. He had spent considerable time in the library.

The stance taken by the new vice-chancellor and registrar encouraged me to push library interests once again. When I heard that a task force had been working to bring out a new University Act, I thought I should not miss the opportunity to renew my standing request to include the chief librarian as an ex-officio member of the University Council. I called on the vice-chancellor, the rector, and the registrar towards this end, noting the fact that the chief librarian had been included in 1963 in the list of members of the T.U. Senate at my request but was dropped in 1970, after which year I was twice nominated in my own person by the king to the T.U. Council. I was sure that the chief librarian would be extended this privilege, as the new vice-chancellor and registrar were the chief architects of the new act.

According to convention the University Act had to be passed by the National Panchayat (unicameral partyless legislature) before it could come into effect. I was a little worried that the Education Ministry might create problems. My worries faded, though, when an active young politician, Mr. Keshar Bahadur Bista, who was once a student at T.U. and an active user of the library, was appointed the education minister. I had full confidence and every hope that he would support my request to include the chief librarian in the T.U. Council. Alas, it all came to naught.

When I came to know about the dropping of the chief librarian from the list of members by the vice-chancellor's advisory team, my mind began to reel. How could the vice-chancellor, the rector, and the registrar deceive me so? I couldn't believe it at first, so I went to see the vice-chancellor to find out the truth. As soon as he saw me he flushed all over and tried to explain it away by shifting responsibility to others.

Challenges and Unending Struggles

I decided not to argue with him but to go to the education minister to inform him how I had been deceived, thinking that he, as a young minister, would definitely understand my rational request and support me.

I was in for a shock, though. The minister took a long time to deign to meet me. Finally he came down and asked me to get into his car. He told me he could do nothing, as the Act had been already reported to the king and sent to the Social Committee of the National Panchayat to be brought up for debate in the National Panchayat session. He dropped me at Pulchok, five minutes from his place. His cool response had a sickening effect on me for some days. After he was appointed minister, I had admired the undulant tones of his speeches, but now I had to agree that "you can't judge a book by its cover."

Learning that the T.U. Act had been reported to the king, I made an effort to see two of the king's influential secretaries, Mr. Narayan Prasad Shrestha and Mr. Chiran Shumshere Thapa, who looked after higher education. I never felt at ease in dealing with Mr. Shrestha, a fidgety man who wanted everything explained to him in one minute. I had known him quite well since 1961, when he was teaching English literature at the University before he joined the palace staff. He was no exception to the baneful effects of power and politics. I was mentally prepared to put my problem to him within the twinkle of an eye. He advised me to see the education minister and added his recommendation for the inclusion, but no assurances were given.

I then went to see Secretary Chiran Shumshere Thapa. I had known him a long time also, since 1963, before he joined the ranks of palace officialdom. I met him for the first time at a dinner party given by the then United States ambassador, Henry Stebbins. He was quite different from Mr. Shrestha: consummately diplomatic as against the latter's unbridled military nature. Still, I never felt uneasy in his presence. He always received me with a smile and at times he impressed me so much that I was buoyed by a conviction that he was the right man to solve the problems. Alas, his actions never matched his words. Ideally, palace secretaries should be messengers of God or like the prime minister Bidur of the *Mahabharata*, speaking always the truth for the good of the people.

The secretary listened very attentively to my statement of the problem, that of getting ex-office membership in the T.U. Council, and assured me that he would look into the matter carefully. He advised me to go to the chairman of the Social Committee of the National Panchayat, Mr. Rabindra Nath Sharma, a seasoned politician. The latter gave me a very encouraging welcome when I went to see him. He suggested that I bring him background information dealing with my request. I respected his methods and immediately provided all the documents and books I had on librarian membership in university and academic councils in different countries of the world.

During my second meeting with him, I found him quite supportive of my request. He told me he would do all he could to get the librarian included as an ex-officio member in both councils but added that without Education Minister Bista's approval, his efforts might be to no avail. I understood him fully and so decided to go to the latter's father, Prof. Dor Bahadur Bista, to raise the question with him, in the expectation that he would understand me better than his son. I had always esteemed him very highly as a scholar and writer, and he had always displayed the utmost respect towards me whenever we met. Usually I hated to disturb people in their homes, yet I made an exception in this case because the time

Challenges and Unending Struggles

was too short. Moreover, the effort was not for my sake but for that of the library profession.

Prof. Bista led me into his drawing room by way of a beautiful garden. His wonderfully demure wife came to greet me, attended by a servant with tea. The air of warm hospitality made me hopeful that I would receive the help I was looking for. After the tea and friendly exchanges I brought up the matter at hand, showing my host all the documents I had assembled and narrating my visit to his minister son. I asked Prof. Bista to convey my request once again and to set matters straight if anybody created any misunderstanding, as I had nothing against his son and high regards for his speeches and the tactful replies to queries put to him by Nepal Television and others.

I told Prof. Bista that after hearing such speeches I had decided to invite his son to the library as chief guest to address and distribute certificates to the participants of a month-long library science course held in T.U. Central Library, knowing he would give an impressive speech, one supportive of the development of library services and the library profession in Nepal. I had invited all the senior teachers and heads of departments and many foreign friends and government and corporation officers to that function so that everyone could see and hear firsthand the new education minister.

Any kind of function organized by the library on occasions of national or international importance never took more than one hour. That was an established convention. But the new education minister made everyone wait more than two hours for his arrival. Most of the senior professors and foreign friends left for other engagements before Minister Bista arrived. I got terribly worried and prayed nothing unfortunate had happened to him. Making calls here and there, I finally received information from his P.A. that he was meeting with

Challenges and Unending Struggles

our vice-chancellor, Mr. Upadhyaya, who was also to attend the function. I again called his P.A. to ask whether it was an emergency meeting; it was not. This made me mad because I had fixed the time in consultation with his P.A. on several occasions.

I always cherished European and American punctuality — a necessary criterion for development. Thus when the honourable minister came to the function with the vice-chancellor, I could not keep myself from expressing my displeasure at his unexpected unmannerliness. I told him while welcoming him that he had broken library tradition by coming so late. He looked quite taken aback and spoke critically. Some people told me later on that I should not have spoken that way to the minister, as in our culture we are supposed to perform *chakadi* (be openly submissive) to people who are in power and position. I told them that it was a fact that he had come so late. Moreover, by divine prompting, I was so used to speaking frankly that I could never think that it was wrong of me to do so.

I'll always remember one incident well: The late King Mahendra came to the library for tea during an annual function at the University in his honour, no other suitable venue being available at the time. The king saw "No Smoking" signs everywhere in the library and surprised me by his unexpected question, "Shanti, can I smoke?" I at once replied, "No, Your Majesty, because smoking is prohibited in the library." He gave me an appreciative smile in recognition of my strict management and graciously told me he would go outside the library to the garden to light up. I was so thrilled by his support for library rules that I requested him very humbly to go to my office, where smoking was not prohibited. This he did, accompanied by the graceful and beautiful Queen Ratna.

Challenges and Unending Struggles

It was a great moment of encouragement and inspiration for me.

After the departure of the royal couple, some people told me that I should not have said no to the king. My reply to them was very simple: I found the king more understanding of library rules than ordinary people. A foreign friend, the journalist Keith de Folo, asked me why I did not bend my head and body with folded hands, like most of the high officials do in front of royalty. Mere gestures do not represent loyalty; it is only dedicated work based on truth that shows real loyalty to the king and nation. I never feared the king, because he was the father of the nation and I was his daughter. Daughters speak freely with fathers. This was the case with me when I talked to the king. My friend Keith de Folo, an American free lance, was impressed with my reply.

Prof. Bista was listening to all of my story very carefully. When I was through I expected him to make some remarks, but he kept quiet. His silence surprised me. Then I thought I should again request him directly to talk to his son about my plea for the cause of librarianship. I did. His response was cool beyond belief. He told me that his son was busy, so he might not have time to talk with him about my request. That was not what I had expected from him. Hopes shattered, I left his residence.

After this disappointing visit I became strengthened in the conviction that I was in no one's service but God's. I thought and rethought the question whether I should continue my struggle for membership or not. I prayed for the courage to take a bolder step, but my conscience, the divine urge, whispered to me to go no further, as dirty politics had already polluted the situation, not only in education but in every field. People had become more self-centred. Love for country and its development was fading. A World Bank report had already

Challenges and Unending Struggles

classified Nepal among the least developed countries. The poor were getting poorer, the rich richer. Having heard the divine whisper, I became more a thinker and philosopher and less a librarian. From then on I began to sing the Serenity Prayer very often:
God grant me the courage to change the things I can change, the serenity to accept those I cannot change, and the wisdom to know the difference. But God, grant me the courage not to give up on what I think is right, even though I think it is hopeless.

In any case, my spirit and urge to work for the development of T.U. Central Library and the library profession grew day by day. No one could stop its speedy growth. The library increasingly became known for its strict management and reliable information services within and without. Book donations from different foreign countries — including Britain, the United States, Japan, Germany, the Netherlands, India, and the USSR — were made to the library, a sign of their good will towards it. At my request, the Asia Foundation provided a good number of books both for the university library and for campus libraries scattered in different parts of the country. My mission, after making T.U.C.L. a model in the country, was to help all the campus libraries to develop in such a way that they could cater not only to the teachers and students on campus but to the local community as well, especially to school children, so that their reading habits would be well engrained when they went to college. Nick Langton, the assistant representative at the Asia Foundation, was a great friend of T.U. Central Library. It was always a joy for me to have him visit and discuss book donations and other projects to boost my development plan.

Challenges and Unending Struggles

Once I had a very long discussion about my problems, especially about the complaints made by my senior library staff at not getting as many opportunities to go abroad as staff members from other libraries, who didn't have to work as hard as they did. Due to lack of control by the central office, there was no proper policy at that time to regulate who would be sent for such training, seminars, and conferences. All the institutes and research centres were free to send people at will without informing T.U. Central Library (central in name only) when some chance came to send teaching, library, or administrative staff abroad. Usually everything was done in a hush-hush manner as if to hide the fact that some crony was being sent; this was very wrong. After hearing me out, Mr. Langton assured me that he would discuss with Jon L. Summers, the Asia Foundation representative in Bangladesh, my request for financial support to send two of my senior staff to Singapore for a short observation tour of the libraries there. I was quite hopeful, as Mr. Summers was also a great friend of T.U.C.L and usually visited me whenever he made trips to Kathmandu from Bangladesh. Whenever I met either him or Nick, I urged them to establish an Asia Foundation office in Kathmandu. My reason for doing so was because it would make it easier to select books for the University and other campuses and to get quick responses to other calls for help for possible new library projects.

Within a short time I received a letter from Nick approving my request for the Singapore training. I was extremely happy to send members of my staff abroad to broaden their knowledge.

In the meantime I was planning a project to provide T.U. Central library service to the members of the National Panchayat, to be started as a part of the Nepal Collection with the help of the Asia Foundation. My deep urge was to provide

Challenges and Unending Struggles

information services like those of the Library of Congress in the U.S. so that the nation's leaders could perform their job better, having at their disposal the work and procedures of other parliaments of the world. My interest to provide such services only increased when members of the National Panchayat came to use the library to solve procedural problems. I took tremendous pleasure in providing all the available materials in the library. If they asked for a particular title, I provided several related documents as well. They often expressed great praise for my library services, saying, "Shanti herself has become an institution." I also wanted their support for getting T.U.C.L. recognized as the national library, just as the Jewish National and University Library is both the national library of the Jewish people and the library of Hebrew University.

I always thought T.U. Central Library should provide its services to the population as a whole and contribute to the building of the nation. In a small, poor nation like ours, we could not be empire builders, but on the other hand could not afford to create too many isolated pockets either; we should have a feeling of oneness — not yours or mine but ours. I always felt that T.U. Central Library should be not only the pride of T.U. but also of Nepal as a whole.

I once submitted my proposal to have T.U. Central Library recognized as the national library to the palace for its approval. Unfortunately my proposal was forwarded to the National Education Committee for discussion. I knew nothing would come of this. In the meantime the member secretary, Dr. Mohammad Mohsin, shifted responsibility from himself by forming a committee of six members under the chairmanship of Dr. Harkha Gurung, then a member of the National Planning Commission, to discuss my proposal. A few meetings were held. My proposal faced opposition from some members, such as Ramesh Jung Thapa (the director of the Department of Archaeology) and Kamal Mani Dixit (the secretary of the Madan Award Trust), who did not care to understand my position. I repeatedly told them that I was not an empire builder. My main urge was to make the existing T.U. Central Library services accessible to all.

I knew quite well that the government had too many other priorities to be bothered with libraries, including the national library. In 1968 a library committee under my convenorship had been formed by H.M.G. to draw up a plan for the development of libraries in the country. I submitted a brief action-oriented plan that laid strong emphasis on improving the existing National Library, but the plan remained on paper for years. This was the reason why I submitted the above proposal. Unfortunately it, too, remained only on paper. I was again misunderstood.

Another donation came from Dr. Hugh B. Wood, the executive director of the American Nepal Education Foundation, who had been making extraordinary contributions to the educational development of Nepal since 1955. He has written countless articles on education in Nepal and compiled the first bibliography ever produced on Nepal, when I was studying at Peabody. I wrote to him for a copy of it — my first correspondence with him. I was extremely happy to get the bibliography along with a friendly reply, which I still have in my files, as I have great respect for any foreigner who loves and contributes to the development of my country.

It had been my long-cherished desire to meet Dr. Wood, and one afternoon I did, when Dr. T. N. Uprety brought him to the library to introduce him to me and to discuss his Books for Nepal project. Dr. Wood's keen interest in library services greatly impressed me; if all the educationalists of Nepal had been like him, library development would surely have received top priority. Under his Books for Nepal, T.U. Central Library agreed to distribute books collected by him from different sources in the United States to different campuses in Nepal, having first selected the volumes needed for the University. The university teachers did a good job of identifying, at my request, books needed for their subjects. All the campus chiefs were also happy to be receiving useful reading material.

Dr. Wood visited Nepal almost every alternate year, during which time he gave receptions to educationalists and distinguished persons. I always enjoyed his receptions, usually held in the hotel where he stayed. Dr. Uprety also used to hold receptions in his honour. My husband and I have always been included on his guest list. At one of the receptions, Dr. Wood whispered in my ear his wish to donate his own Nepal collection to T.U. Central Library, part of it during his lifetime and the remainder after his death. This made me happy as well as sad: happy because T.U. Central Library would acquire the unique collection on Nepal he started even before the library was established — a grand addition to the Nepal Collection of the library; sad because I always liked to see good people live on and on. My fear was that some disease might have forced him to express such a wish. Later on I found that this was not so. He is still young at 86 and is still collecting and sending books. He has already sent quite a number of them from his own collection on Nepal, which is kept separately under his name in the Nepal Collection. When he saw this he asked why I did not amalgamate it with the existing Nepal Collection. What an admirable question, I thought. Most people prefer to be given prominence, but not Dr. Wood. I told him I could have done so but wanted to draw the attention of distinguished visitors to his collection, thinking that they might be inspired to donate their own collections. He smiled appreciatively and refrained from further comment. I always attach importance to such collections — a real academic resource for scholars pursuing knowledge.

During the coronation of King Birendra, T.U. Central Library had the opportunity to welcome many distinguished visitors from different countries. Their visits resulted in many donations of books and other materials to the library. Under the Netherlands Literature Programme, the government of the Netherlands provided gifts of very expensive professional periodicals and books dealing with topics in the natural and social sciences. At my request, they continued their gift programme for more than five years (1976-1981).

I highly appreciate this way of giving donations: selection was never dictated; with the help of department heads and subject specialists, I was allowed to select any periodical or book published in any country (they did not have to be publications of the Netherlands). It was of great help to me when I was struggling to get more funds to purchase necessary periodicals for the library, in a year when the library budget was heavily cut. Thus I was extremely happy with the Netherlands' gift.

The visit of Japan's Crown Prince Akihito (the present emperor) with his beautiful wife Princess Michiko (the present empress) to the library was a very memorable one. I expressed my deep gratitude for their interest in T.U. Central Library. A video was made by a Japanese cameraman during their visit. Afterwards the library again received quite a number of books from the Japan-Nepal Friendship Association and, pursuant to the order of the crown prince, the government of Japan sent regularly two important Japanese quarterlies, *Monumenta Nipponica* and *Japanese Quarterly*. They are still coming.

It was not only from foreign friends; donations began to pour into the library from library-minded Nepalese too. I felt inspired by the trust Nepalese friends bestowed upon me by

Challenges and Unending Struggles

deciding to house their collections in T.U. Central Library. To harbour such trust was not easy in our culture, where suspicion and scepticism are the order of the day.

The first big donation of Sanskrit books was the collection of Pandit Harsha Nath Khanal, the father of the poet Guna Raj Khanal, better known these days as the poet Ramdas, a great disciple of Rama (the great ideal king of the *Ramayana*, the Hindu epic written ten thousand years ago). I always found him deeply devoted to the teachings of Rama. He wrote many books. I even now remember very well his visits to the library in Kirtipur and his recitations in my office from his books on Rama with tears in his pious eyes. He was like a great actor of religious drama taking me close to God. Even then people were finding less time for such things as provided a moral boost to oppose materialistic urges. He always had much praise for the library and for me. I never could forget his beautifully inspiring and loving words when I was busy in his house supervising the packing of those valuable books in Sanskrit, to be loaded in a jeep and taken to the library: "Shanti nani (a loving address for a girl), today, I feel, you are my daughter and I am giving these books as a dowry. And I am happy to give away these books to you, who can better care for the stored knowledge in them for all the Sanskrit scholars and others who aspire to knowledge." I was very touched.

The second big, and welcomed, donation came from General Shingha Shumshere J. B. Rana. Before learning of his collection, I had tried my utmost to acquire Kaiser Library — a unique private collection and one of the biggest in this part of the world, but had failed due to the sudden death of Field Marshal Kaiser Shumshere J. B. Rana. Just after taking charge of T.U. Central Library, I came to know from my foreign friends that Field Marshal Kaiser Shumshere had a good library. I requested him by phone to allow me to visit him. He

Challenges and Unending Struggles

was so kind as to invite me for lunch. After a quiet meal he gave me a tour of his library, telling me all the details of it. I was utterly surprised at his memory, an index to his whole collection, which he started in 1909 and which became one of the great personal libraries of Asia. I was so impressed by the collection that my whole thinking turned towards acquiring it for the University. His collection is very rich in works on history, culture, literature, religion, art, and above all on Nepal — all so needed for research purposes by the University. He showed great interest in getting my help to organize his collection in a scientific way. But alas, he suddenly passed away. The news of his death made me very sad, and my dream to organize the collection and to bring it under T.U. Central Library administration remained a dream.

I did not know that Field Marshal Kaiser's brother Shingha Shumshere had a collection of his own. I was introduced to him by General Samrajya Shumshere J. B. Rana at a grand dinner party hosted by him and his wife, Rani Saraswoti Kumari, at his Shah Mahal (a Rana palace). The party was graced by the crown prince, Birendra (the present king), and attended by diplomats and distinguished persons from different walks of life in Nepal. It was my first dinner party at a Rana palace. The environment was not particularly appealing to me, yet I enjoyed watching all the beautifully dressed Rana women and men. Everyone seemed to have an air of sophistication.

General Samrajya was kind enough to introduce me to the crown prince as his daughter Netra Rajya Laxmi Shah's private tutor. Netra was preparing to take an M.A. examination in history as a private candidate. I had been requested to tutor her. Even in those days high-class Ranas did not like to allow many freedoms to their women. Netra was not permitted to go to the University for her postgraduate studies. She was an extraordinarily well-disciplined student, ever ready to learn.

Challenges and Unending Struggles

Her thoughts on the Rana family system tended to be openly critical — something uncommon among Rana women. She herself was very simple; unlike others, she abjured fashion but was nevertheless beautiful, with winsome, lotus-like eyes. My relationship with her became very close. We shared our thoughts on development, education, women, and social service. I became not only her tutor but also a friend. It was a great joy for me to see her pass with good results. Afterwards she wrote a book entitled *The Anglo-Gorkha War 1814-1816* (Kathmandu, self-published, 1970), which has been widely read.

One day Netra informed me of a luncheon invitation from General Shingha at his residence, Mana Mandir, in the Thapathali section of Kathmandu. It was a surprise for me, and I accepted without any hesitation. I reached his place at exactly 12 noon. He and Princess Rama, the sister of the late King Tribhuvan, welcomed me at the door and took me to his small but well-decorated drawing room. After a while he led me to another small building in the same compound. He himself opened the room and gave me a happy surprise by showing me his library and his beautiful Victorian bookracks and table. He expressed in diplomatic tones — not in the overbearing way of some Ranas — his wish that I help him to organize his library in a scientific way. I at once accepted, as I found his collection to be a treasure trove. I thanked God for leading me to another library which one day might be donated.

I did not express my thoughts to the general that day. How could I? I was quite determined, though, to try to convince him to donate his collection to T.U. Central Library so that it could be well preserved for future generations. I had already heard many depressing stories of many rare books, especially on Nepal, disappearing from Kaiser Library, and it would have been sad if the same thing happened to the Shingha collection.

Challenges and Unending Struggles

After my visit to his library I told him I would be only too happy to start work on his collection before or after my library hours and praised his interest in knowledge and in the library profession. I had enjoyed the lunch with him and Princess Rama, a real princess, so soft-spoken and full of kindness, love, and concern.

I did not wait for summer to start my work in his library. I started in the winter. The library was on the ground floor — almost too cold to endure, even with a tiny heater —, yet I enjoyed working there in the hope of obtaining the collection for T.U. Central Library. My hope kept me quite warm even in those severely cold surroundings. General Shingha was visibly impressed by my enthusiasm and spirit. At some point I requested him and the princess to visit T.U. Central Library at Kirtipur to give them a better idea of what scientific management was. They immediately accepted my invitation and visited the library on April 18, 1972, writing in the visitors book, "Much impressed by the care taken about the books. I have decided to give the collection of my books numbering more than five thousand books to the Tribhuvan University Library." His words overwhelmed me; I was seized with joy and gave thanks to God, while expressing deep gratitude to them for their divinely guided decision.

After the couple's visit, I had a long talk with the general about the procedure for handing over property to the University and about his wish to finance a separate building for his collection adjacent to T.U. Central Library in the future. At that time it would have cost several lakhs of rupees. I supported his plan and assured him that all the necessary steps would be taken to get the permission of the Library Committee and T.U. authorities. I was eager to break this happy news to Vice-Chancellor Shakya, but I could not get an appointment from his office to visit him. I conveyed the information to

Challenges and Unending Struggles

Rector Adhikari and requested him to arrange to fix a partition to mark off the Shingha collection until a separate building could be planned and built. Unfortunately the response to my request was cool. It took more than four years to put the partition in place.

With the approval of the Library Committee, I began to transfer the collection little by little, even without the partition. In the meantime I had already compiled a publication, *Catalogue of Shingha Collection*, to be released and distributed on the inaugural day, with the financial assistance of General Shingha. At last the partition was arranged.

General Shingha never mentioned any intention to donate his beautiful Victorian wooden bookracks with glass shutters and some attractive pillar-like stands. One afternoon when I was talking to him about transferring the collection, I made a suggestion that he might like to donate the furniture as well and took the liberty to use the Nepali proverb, "You give the horse but keep the reins" (*ghoda dinu lagam nadinu*). His eyes sparkled brightly and with a very engaging smile he told me he would think about it. I prayed for his acceptance. I wanted very badly to have those racks in the room of the Shingha Collection — so unlike any other furniture I had ever seen. The next day I got a call from him with news of his acceptance. My few words of appreciation and gratitude for his decision made him quite happy, to judge by his response over the phone.

On July 22, 1977 General Shingha sent his old black Indian Ambassador car to convey me to his residence at Mana Mandir in Thapathali. His purpose was to discuss his wish to have a small but tasteful inaugural function for his collection. I was a little surprised at this emergency-like meeting. As usual, he and his wife welcomed me as soon as I descended from the car — heartwarming hospitality inspiring for a lady librarian. They led me to their small private room. Offering tea to me,

Challenges and Unending Struggles

General Shingha bared his thoughts, telling of an idea of his to request King Birendra to inaugurate the Shingha Collection on T.U. Annual Day. He wanted my opinion before he made such a request. I at once expressed joyful anticipation of receiving the king again in the library, this time to inaugurate the Shingha Collection amid a small gathering of distinguished Nepalese scholars and diplomats.

His asking my opinion was unusual in Nepal; rich people in high position rarely sought out the opinion of poor intellectuals without any power. But here was the general, a living encyclopedia of the Rana regime in his seventies, seeking out mine. He was the son of the most powerful Rana prime minister, Chandra Shumshere J. B. Rana, who was in power from 1901 to 1929, the longest rule in the history of the Ranas. General Shingha had enjoyed every privilege during his father's time. He was an ambassador to Great Britain and an ambassador to India. His many experiences were reflected in his bearing. His love for the nation was great. Listening to him was like reading a book. I always admired his keen memory and loved to hear him salt his conversation with apt quotations and witty humour. He very often used to quote by heart from Shakespeare's *Julius Caesar* while narrating the story of Rana rule and Rana deeds. I can still remember very well his quoting from Antony's speeches: "Friends, Romans, countrymen, lend me your ears: I come to bury Caesar, not to praise him. The evil that men do lives after them: The good is oft interred with their bones." I could well understand why he liked to quote this passage, given his bitter experience after the overthrow of the Rana regime in Nepal, where the present rules men's loyalties more than the past, even if the past contained good deeds. Another quotation he often used was also to my liking:

You cannot bring about prosperity by discouraging
thrift,

Challenges and Unending Struggles

> You cannot strengthen the weak by weakening the rich,
> You cannot establish sound security on borrowed money,
> You cannot keep out of trouble by spending more than you earn,
> You cannot build character and initiative and independence,
> You cannot help men permanently by doing for them what they could do for themselves.

Coming back with the happy news to the library, I immediately called the rector, Jagat Mohan Adhikari, to inform him of the possibility of the inauguration of the Shingha Collection by the king and requested him to convey this information to the vice-chancellor, Surya Bahadur Shakya, as I had no easy access to him.

The next morning, July 23, 1977, a Saturday, General Shingha requested me over the phone to come to his place for a meeting with his grandson, Education Minister Pashupati Shumsher J. B. Rana, to discuss the inauguration. A car was sent to pick me up. We had a very interesting talk for half an hour. The minister asked me to inform the vice-chancellor and the rector of the king's consent to inaugurate the Shingha Collection. I was very happy to hear this. It seemed that General Shingha and Princess Rama had recently had dinner with King Birendra and Queen Aishwarya, during which the request was made. General Shingha looked cheerful now.

I assured the minister and the general that I would immediately inform the vice-chancellor and the rector at their residences, as it was Saturday. When I did, however, I was very much astonished to get a very cool response; the T.U. authorities asked me to wait till the next day.

Challenges and Unending Struggles

The next day, to my great surprise, I got a letter from the University calling for an explanation as to who had given me permission to arrange such an inaugural function. Angered, I immediately wrote back, telling of the meeting with General Shingha and Minister Pashupati. An unnecessary misunderstanding had been created by the university authorities over the inaugural issue. About five o'clock on the same day the rector, as instructed by the vice-chancellor, informed me that the inaugural function would not take place and that Their Majesties would not be coming to the library, that I should not to be childish, and on and on. I was bitterly shocked and for a while lost my equilibrium. What should be my future course of action? I prayed and prayed to God to guide me through this unwanted man-made strife.

It was already late in the evening. My staff was still busy arranging everything in the library, especially the Shingha Collection room, for the inauguration by the king the next day. I was reluctant to break the news that everything had been cancelled, but I had no alternative but to do so. Everyone, of course, was already all geared up for the function. I tried to hide my gloomy feelings but was not totally successful. Many questions were raised, but I could not satisfy their curiosity just then. I told them to forget everything and to enjoy the holiday usually given on Annual Day.

After a brief meeting with the staff, I went with my husband to General Shingha to convey the bad news of the cancellation of the inaugural function. He grew sombre for a while and regretted living in a country where giving presents caused so much trouble, but he soon returned to his usual cheerful mood and urged me not to lament. For a while our conversation was like those in Shakespeare's historical dramas. I wish I had had a small tape recorder to record what General Shingha told me. It was a great solace for me to hear him.

Challenges and Unending Struggles

It was already late evening when we reached back home. My wonderful husband tried to relieve me of my painful thoughts. Even my darling child Pragya seemed worried about me. I held her tight and lulled her to sleep before I had my dinner. Too many disturbing things filled my mind, and I had no taste for food. Sleep was slow to come to me that night. I was restless, but my husband's loving care and his few words on the dark and bright sides of life, based on practical experience gained from working with different people in different offices, calmed me into sleep.

I woke up early in the morning. Even the beautiful dawn looked pale to me, so fed up was I with people. Why had I always to struggle to achieve ideals? I prayed and prayed for a way to screw up my courage. On the advice of my husband, I went not to the Annual Day function but to the library, hoping and praying that the king and queen would grace the inauguration. It was July 25, 1977. At my request the book checker came to open the library. I was alone sitting in the unusually quiet library building while the grand annual function was going on at Memorial Hall. I felt like a prisoner under house arrest. Had I been a poet, I would have written a poem that would have moved God-seeking people to tears. Alas, I had no such talent, but the few hours of my loneliness brought me close to God. I became stronger and happier. While I was paging through some of the books that have changed the world, I heard a car coming down the roadway leading to the library. I went out of my office to see who this sharer of my loneliness was. It was a messenger sent to inform me of the imminent arrival of Their Majesties. I praised God. I had won an unwanted and man-created battle — one of the happiest moments in my life, even if in an empty hall without the presence of distinguished professors, scholars, students, and diplomats, as wished by the donor. Soon I saw from the library

Challenges and Unending Struggles

gate a line of vehicles coming uphill. I was standing with happy heart to welcome Their Majesties and the others who followed them. I wondered who would be coming to attend this quiet function.

The king and queen made a graceful entry. I filled with joy at welcoming them. Their own cheerful mood inspired me to lead them into the library. His Majesty made a sharp-edged remark "Shanti, is smoking still prohibited in the library?" My reply was "Yes, Your Majesty." I was stunned by his memory. He directed me to show some of the sections in the library to the queen, as it was her first visit.

After a brief tour of the ground floor, I requested the king and the queen, General Shingha, his wife Princess Rama, and other members of the royal family to proceed to the first floor of the library, where the Shingha Collection was housed. The king himself unveiled the plaque in front of the donor. No speeches were made by either receiver or donor. The vice-chancellor and rector were standing with hands folded and faces green. Though I wanted to express deep gratitude to General Shingha for such a donation, I purposely did not, as such sentiments fell to the vice-chancellor to express.

The inaugural function was over within a very short time. Their Majesties spent some time viewing the Shingha Collection. I presented the catalogue of it to them and other members of the royal family. It was a great memorable occasion for T.U. Central Library. General Shingha and Princess Rama were in high spirits. The general made a touching remark before he left: "Shanti, my dream to have my collection inaugurated by His Majesty King Birendra has at last come true. I started the collection in 1909 during King Tribhuvan's time, made the decision to house it at T.U.C.L. during King Mahendra's time, and handed it over during His Majesty King Birendra's reign." He added that he already had

Challenges and Unending Struggles

a letter from above — was close to death — and for years had longed to hand over his books before the final letter came.

I could never understand such utterances from him. Later on, after his death in October 1977, I came to know that he had had cancer. Before I left for the UN I went to see him. He was in critical condition, but I never thought that those days would be his last ones. I almost cried when I heard him say, "Shanti, I am extremely happy with your devotion, honesty, and sincerity to your institution and to the country. I have the great satisfaction to know that my collection is in trustworthy hands and being managed better than before, and that it is now more accessible to knowledge-thirsty scholars. It was so good of you to have come today to visit me. Maybe it is our last meeting. We may not see each other again, after you come back from the UN." As predicted, he left this world while I was in the United States. General Shingha was dead, but his collection would remain alive. The Shingha Collection, comprising 5,000 volumes, was unique.

It had become a source of continuous joy and satisfaction for me as the chief librarian to get calls from different Nepalese interested in donating collections ranging from thousands of items to a few valuable ones. Some of the donors were well-known public figures. The late Surya Prasad Upadhyaya was a veteran politician and a former home minister, whose donation I have already mentioned in a previous chapter. The late Kali Prasad Upadhyaya, a lawyer and ex-ambassador to Great Britain, had a small collection of law books and periodicals. I knew him quite well as a lover of libraries ever since I started my career. After his death his collection was handed over to T.U.C.L. It is well preserved and made regular use of by teachers, students, and researchers. I was happy to have his books and other materials but sad to

Challenges and Unending Struggles

have missed the opportunity to express personally my gratitude to him for his and his family members' trust in me.

The late Parasmani Pradhan, a well-known writer and crusader for the Nepali language living in Darjeeling in India, donated his whole collection of the journal *Bharati* to the library even before I met him. I was so happy to have these all but rare issues. I had to wait for a long time — years — to meet him and to welcome him to the library and show him his collection, housed in the periodical section of the library. It was in great demand, especially by lovers and students of Nepali literature.

On the afternoon of June 12, 1975 he and his grandson knocked at my office door unexpectedly. Luckily I was in. I told him of my long-cherished desire to meet him personally to thank him for his donation and trust. Without further ado, he requested me to lead him to the collection. I was at first a little astonished at his abruptness, but he brightened up as soon as he saw his books so well shelved on the racks and easily accessible to researchers. Slowly he bared his thoughts, telling me very punctiliously, "I heard so many bad and disturbing stories about my donation of *Bharati* to your library from some scholars who visited here: that most of the collection had disappeared due to mismanagement in the library. I am extremely happy to find out the truth of the matter." I gave him a tour of the whole library. Back in my office, he rewarded me with a big smile and asked his grandson to take a photograph of him handing over his new dictionary to me. It had turned into a very memorable visit. His love for the Nepali language and literature was unbounded. He had written many books and was awarded the Madan Literary Award for one of them, *Tipan Tapan* (Gleanings), in 1968.

One final collection came totally unexpectedly. The news of the demise of Narendra Mani Acharya Dixit, when it came,

Challenges and Unending Struggles

saddened me. Nepal had lost one of its notable intellectuals. I wanted to go to his place to pay my condolences to his family, as I had known him from the beginning of my career as a librarian. His regards for my profession were genuine, but I knew none of his family, so I suppressed my desire to approach them.

One day, though, I got a call from his son Kumar Mani Acharya Dixit. He informed me of his father's wish to donate his collection to T.U. Central Library. I was deeply touched and at once expressed my wish to see his father's library before we discussed the donation in detail. The next day I paid a visit I wished I could have paid when Narendra Mani Acharya Dixit was still alive. I expressed my gratitude, silently to his departed soul and then openly to his wife Jayanti Dixit and son, for their decision to hand over the collection along with some almirahs. It was rich in literature. Some of the volumes were very rare. Today they are kept in a place all their own in the library.

Chapter 7

Service to Nepalese Women

The year 1975 was designated International Women's Year by the General Assembly of the United Nations in order to focus global attention on the status of women and their rights and responsibilities. Its goal was threefold: to foster harmony between men and women as the basis of equality, to enlist women fully in the task of development, and to give due recognition to the ever growing importance of women in contributing to world peace and in furthering cooperation and friendship between countries.

As the U.N. depository, T.U. Central Library received a good number of documents on International Women's Year. The documents provided me the wherewithal to plan an impressive exhibit on women's contributions to the development of their countries. It had already become the practice of the library to organize exhibitions on subjects targeted by the UN, in the hope of contributing, even if on a small scale, to the success of UN declared years, such as the International Year of the Child 1979, the International Year of Disabled Persons 1981, and International Youth Year 1985. The exhibits on the latter two were viewed by thousands and highly praised. Children's books were donated by different embassies at my request for display. I customarily received many requests from viewers to extend such exhibitions. Happily I was usually able to accommodate them. T.U. Central Library also brought out bibliographies on these subjects to

Service to Nepalese Women

spur further interest and to keep the memory of such years alive.

Being a woman myself, I wanted to have the exhibition on women done in a grand manner, again with the help of different embassies. I circulated a request to all the embassies to send books by and on women from their countries. The timely response of all the embassies and foreign agencies encouraged me to go ahead with my plan to organize a large exhibition in the library to focus attention on the global status of women and their rights and responsibilities, with special reference to Nepalese women.

One day, while I was busy doing research for the exhibit in my office, I got an unexpected call from the personal secretary of King Birendra to inform me that Queen Aishwarya would give me an audience the next day at 12 noon in the palace. I was quite surprised because I had heard that the new queen was not granting frequent audiences. I had not even requested one, yet one came. I looked upon it as a welcomed opportunity.

I was not unknown to Her Majesty. I had met her several times, after being asked by the Publicity Department of His Majesty's Government to write an article on her when she was the crown princess to be published in the special wedding issue of *Hamro Sanskriti* (Our Culture) on the auspicious occasion of Their Royal Highnesses' wedding in 1970. That request had surprised me too, but I enjoyed tremendously interviewing the crown princess, finding her gracious, simple, soft-spoken, and knowledgeable.

Having received her early education at St. Helen's Convent in Kurseong (India) and St. Mary's School in Kathmandu, and having obtained the degree of Bachelor of Arts from Tribhuvan University, she would be an ideal, well-educated queen, I thought. She became the queen when Crown Prince Birendra ascended the throne in 1972 after the death of his father, King Mahendra.

I tried to imagine why I might have been summoned, but I reached no conclusions. On a day in October 1974, then, I went to the palace, reaching there at exactly 11:55 a.m. for the audience at 12 noon. It was my first visit to the palace, so I was quite ignorant of the procedures. There was a person standing at the palace gate with my name slip. As soon as he saw me he welcomed me with joined hands, the *namaste* salute, and led me to the room where the king's personal secretary, Mr. Gehendra Man Singh, was waiting to escort me to the queen's office. I had not met Mr. Singh before. He appeared calm, with a reserved smile on his face, and a very polite, low tone to his voice, so different from all the other palace secretaries I knew. He led me up to the door of the queen's office at exactly 12 noon and went off quietly. As soon as I saw the queen I bowed in respect. She looked more gracious and even prettier than when I had met her as a crown princess six year before. She was sitting in a simple but beautiful chair in front of an attractive table, not as big as the ones I saw in the offices of ministers and high government officials. Her office was nevertheless very impressive. Her presence made it more so.

With a warm welcoming smile she asked me to take a seat next to her. I was overwhelmed. Before she could utter any word I expressed my gratitude to her for remembering me and told her that I could provide her any library and information services she needed, as I knew she was very fond of acquiring new knowledge. All the while she listened with her beautiful smile to what I had to say. Then she in turn spoke and broke the news of the king's decision to nominate me as the member secretary of the International Women's Year Committee Nepal

Service to Nepalese Women

1975, which would be formed in the near future under her patronage; she asked whether I would have time for such work.

For a while no words came from my mouth, and I did not know how to answer. Although I was extremely honoured by the king's proposal — evidence of great trust in me, a librarian, who had yet to be recognized by Nepalese society as an honourable and capable person who could serve the country in any field and in any post — I frankly told the queen that I had no background for such an assignment. Moreover, I was not even a member of the Nepal Women's Organization, having heard none too good stories about it. This might have come as a shock to the self-styled women leaders, I thought. On the other hand, I wanted the challenge of working for our women, who needed organized help and support. After a wonderful and inspiring visit with the queen for more than one hour I accepted the unique offer.

I came back to the library thinking it was a great honour for the library profession. I wanted to prove worthy of Their Majesties' trust. In November 1974 the king constituted a seven-member committee under the patronage of Her Majesty to observe 1975 as the International Women's Year amidst special and befitting programmes all over the kingdom in response to the call made by the United Nations, and provision was also made for including eight representatives of the ministries of Home, Panchayat, Law and Justice, Industry and Commerce, Food and Agriculture, Education, Health, and Foreign Affairs of His Majesty's Government in the committee.

The committee members besides me were Mrs. Punya Prabha Devi Dhungana, the chairwoman of the Nepal Women's Organization, as the chairwoman, Mrs. Kamal Rana, a member of the Raj Sabha, Dr. Kanti Giri, a well-known gynecologist, Mrs. Angur Baba Joshi, ex-principal of the country's first women's college (Padma Kanya), Miss Indira Rana, and Mrs.

Service to Nepalese Women

Inu Aryal. The formation of the committee was announced on the birthday of the queen. For the occasion, the Nepal Women's Organization organized a procession to go to the palace to felicitate the queen. Women from the University, college campuses, schools, and government offices participated in it.

Hearing the announcement, I too went to join the procession. It was interesting to hear women's comments on the make-up of the committee. Women who did not know me were asking one another who that Mrs. Shanti Mishra was who was given a key role in the committee. Most of them were surprised at my nomination. I knew it would be that way.

Women leaders and other women who knew me came up to congratulate me. I saw no sign of pleasure in their faces. They looked very much taken aback, in fact, and hardly able to disguise their humiliation. I didn't let this disturb me, being already committed to my new mission to serve Nepalese women in all possible ways within the stipulated period by conceiving well-planned programmes for well-managed action. I wanted to set an example in this case, too. Moreover, the queen herself was very much interested to see the IWY programmes quickly carried out. This was a great boost for me. I began to work on the programme very carefully for submission to the members for discussion.

The first meeting of the committee was held in the palace in the presence of the patron of the committee. Before the discussion, the queen issued an impressive set of maiden directives for initiating the programme and assigned specific responsibilities to the members, especially to the member representatives of H.M.G. The member representatives present at the meeting were Messrs. Birendra Prasad Shah (Ministry of Home), Janak Thapa (Ministry of Panchayat), Tribhuvan Pratap Rana (Ministry of Law), P. B. Bista (Ministry of

Service to Nepalese Women

Industry and Commerce), Lok Bahadur Bista (Ministry of Food and Agriculture), Dilli Raj Uprety (Ministry of Education), Moti Ratna Tuladhar (Ministry of Health), and Uddhab Dev Bhatta (Ministry of Foreign Affairs). Every member looked cheerful and eager to get started, and vowed as much in humble tones through the microphone arranged for them to use in the meeting. I was given the main task of coordinating all the programmes and providing all necessary office facilities to all seven members. The meeting was indeed a wonderful experience for me. I was encouraged to put my heart and soul into the programmes.

For a short period the committee did not have an office. I was working for the committee with the library as my base. Finally an office was established at Bhrikuti Mandap with the cooperation of the Ministry of Home and the Bagmati zonal commissioner's office.

Until I got a formal letter of deputation from the University, I worked in both places — mornings in the library and afternoons at the committee office. This was not difficult, since I was provided a vehicle by the government to commute from Kirtipur to Kathmandu. A beautiful black Toyota Crown equipped with radio arrived at the library the day following my nomination as member secretary. Every member of my library staff was excited to see such a big car sent for their boss. After using the car for some time for the seven kilometres into town, I found that it consumed more petrol than I thought it should, more than 80 rupees' worth per round trip. I called Mr. Bhogya Prasad Shah, the chief of the Central Service Department of His Majesty's Government, to see if he could provide me with a smaller car. This request caused everyone to wonder about my sanity, but Mr. Shah was kind enough to send me an old Toyota, as no new car was available.

I was quite happy to have made the switch. As a precaution, I told the driver to be very honest with me, having heard lots of stories about the pilferage of petrol from government office cars. But my determination to tame deputed drivers did not work at all; I had to change five drivers within the space of a year. Sometimes I used to be without a driver when important functions called. My husband stood in several times in such cases.

One of the drivers was very outspoken, and I enjoyed listening to him. He told me before he decided to leave that I should not be so idealistic, as pilferage had become an accepted part of a driver's service in the government, given their low salary. The practice was even tolerated by the palace, so why was I being pernickety? What a bold comment, I thought. In one way he was right. The salary was too low to live on. Still, I wondered why someone didn't raise the salary and do away with such dishonest dealings. People should not be pushed to be dishonest, demoralized, and corrupt.

After he left a new driver arrived. The new driver came displaying a gloomy face. He too must have heard about my preaching to be honest in order to be close to God. I understood his feelings quite well. I always hated to see anyone unhappy. I told him he should not worry. If he worked honestly for the committee, I would see that he got a sum of money at the end of the year. His gloomy face changed immediately into a happy and bright one. I was so grateful to God: he remained very honest and served the committee till the end as a wonderful driver. It was a great joy for me to find an upright soul.

All the programmes having been fixed, it became hard for me to work in both the offices, so I insisted that a formal letter of deputation from the University be given to me. I could not understand why it took so long to issue such a letter. The

Service to Nepalese Women

University should have been proud of my nomination. A rumour reached me that the vice-chancellor, Mr. S. B. Shakya, had said that my service was too essential for the Central Library for me to be deputed elsewhere. I went to the king's principal secretary, Ranjan Raj Khanal, to talk about the matter. I had a very memorable visit with him. I found him to be polite, well-read, and administratively skillful. The next day I had the letter, and the truth of the rumour or lack thereof no longer concerned me.

I was extremely happy that I could give my full time towards working for the cause of women. Men and women took equally great interest in the committee's programmes. There was, for instance, a remarkable response from young artists, such as Sashi Shah, Krishna Manandhar, and Batsa Gopal Vaidya, to our advertisement to submit proposals for the symbol and logo of our committee, to be based on the UN logo for International Women's Year. Our selection of the logo, which was designed by young artists, represented the high ideals of Nepalese women and the spirit of internationalism. We also brought out a very attractive brochure on the programme of the Women's Committee.

One afternoon the queen paid a surprise visit to the committee's office at Bhrikuti Mandap. I was extremely moved and encouraged by her deep concern. She wanted to make sure that all necessary facilities were available to the members, including the chairwoman, in our office. I reported on all foregoing arrangements so that everyone could plan well and work to implement the assigned responsibilities. In the following days and weeks I quite often used to get telephone calls from the queen to enquire about our progress. Her genuine concern was a great inspiration to me and all other members of the committee. The programme prepared by the committee was well received. It appears in Appendix II.

Service to Nepalese Women

With the proposed IWY committee's programme list now out in writing, my main task was to see that the items were implemented without any delays and excuses. At the beginning of the work, I had to face some grumbling from women who may have desired to play a larger role in the committee. To defuse the situation I often had to speak in harsh tones with them and thus felt tense and excited sometimes, but I was determined to put my heart and soul into the work.

It was not long before I was astonishing everyone by my grasp of women's affairs in Nepal. Chairwoman Punya Prabha Devi Dhungana, Mrs. Kamal Rana, and Mrs. Angur Baba Joshi were very cooperative. Dr. Kanti Giri and Mrs. Inu Aryal were equally supportive. The government provided additional help in the form of one administrator-accountant, Mr. Bajracharya, who worked very hard and honestly, one typist, and one peon. It was a very small but effective staff.

Everything went very smoothly for some months. Then something unexpected occurred: a violent disagreement between one group led by Mrs. Dhungana and Mrs. Rana and another group led by Mrs. Joshi, the whole thing sparked by a small issue involving an advertisement in the *Gorkhapatra*. The chairwoman of the committee, Mrs. Dhungana, who tended to think that the world revolved around her, reported directly to the queen against what she called an unwise step taken by Mrs. Joshi, who tended to think for her part that she was highly straightforward, intellectual, and could speak and argue on any subject.

One afternoon not many days later, during a meeting with well-known Nepalese women writers and artists to discuss a plan to conduct the first cultural show by women artists and the first exhibition of art by them in Nepal, I got an emergency call that I should go immediately to the palace.

Service to Nepalese Women

Luckily our meeting was almost over. Thanking everyone for their presence and support, I left my office for Narayanhiti. As usual, I was received by the king's personal secretary, Mr. Singh, and he led me to the queen's office. Mrs. Dhungana was also there. I was quick to miss the queen's usual smile. Something was definitely amiss and I kept silent. The chairwoman looked very disturbed; suppressed anger showed all over her face. The queen in her usual low voice asked me to look into the reported matter and see that similar incidents not be repeated in the future. I could not agree more with what the queen said, as I too never liked to see and hear women quarrelling. Actually I was very surprised to find groupism rampant among women who called themselves contributors to the welfare of their Nepalese sisters while working on the IWY committee. It was a great misfortune, I felt.

Gradually I found the differences between the two groups becoming more and more apparent, as if they were together not to agree but to argue with each other. Any programme suggested by the one group, even if geared to the welfare of Nepalese women, was automatically not accepted by the other group. This attitude caused me wonder many times over. Each group wanted me to be in its camp. Since I was determined to take the path of truth, I flatly refused to be in either. I told them that I would certainly support any group's programme if it benefitted Nepalese women.

It was an interesting and hard task for me to balance the two sides during this, my first experience with women leaders. Backbiting, unnecessary critical comments, suspicions, mistrust, and doubts were always in the air, and this was not good for the harmony and undertaking among women who should have been thinking about nothing but women's welfare. In the beginning it was difficult to adjust to these circumstances, but gradually I did. Eventually the women leaders, having come to know my uncompromising insistence on anything but the truth and selfless sincerity, came to support everything I requested. Problems ceased. Mrs. Rana, the diplomatic, politically minded former general secretary of the women's organization, helped to keep the atmosphere in the committee peaceful. Except for her politics I admired her wholeheartedly, especially her simplicity and sociability, these in spite of the fact that she came from the Rana family.

Once I had a long audience with the queen to discuss a number of problems, including finances, the internal strife among the women, and the need for discipline. Her every expression was pure in thought and utterly appealing — so very different from what I was used to hearing about royal family members. She attached great importance to discipline and honesty and avoided spending money for unnecessary show, no matter what the committee members said. This lay close to my own philosophy: no development without peace, sincerity, honesty, dedication, devotion, and discipline.

It was a very enriching experience for me to work for the Nepalese women. Within the set period of one year all the prepared programmes were put into action without any difficulty, thanks to the cooperation and help of all the members and from other quarters. I always found myself throughout the year working around the clock, receiving men and women not only at the office but also at home (though I was always against disturbing people at home, as there was a greater temptation to engage in flattery), writing articles for different newspapers and magazines, and giving interviews for the radio and other media.

I used to wonder why I was so much in demand from every quarter; I was, after all, the same person as before, the chief librarian. Again I thought that it was perhaps due to my closeness to the palace. Some instances I remember very

Service to Nepalese Women

clearly. High officials, including ministers, came to visit me, hoping to get recommended for the king's medals. Some came for promotion, some for transfers. Even the palace secretaries were full of praise for me and quite often said that I had become one of them and even gone a step beyond, being closer to the new queen than they. Some government secretaries, too, talked in the same terms: "Shanti, Nepal should have more women like you to speed its development."

With everyone I tried to be straightforward and frank and to give my true and fearless opinion. When I politely told those who aspired to obtain medals that such things were not given without some notable contribution to the country having first been made, and were not bestowed only upon persons close to the palace, they told me that was not so. Again I insisted that the wrong path should not be followed. After hearing my preaching, some experienced Nepalese advised me not to be such a great idealist, but I always loved to prove my idealism by doing my job and by putting my heart and soul into my work.

Thus I was extremely happy to see more deeds than words sprouting in International Women's Year. At the grand closing ceremony, attended by the king and the queen, Prince Himalaya, Princess Princep, Princess Helen, Prince Gyanendra, Princess Komal, Prince Dhirendra, Princess Prekshya, and other royal family members, the prime minister, ministers, ambassadors, and distinguished guests, I took the opportunity to deliver a report on the International Women's Year Committee Nepal 1975. It appears in Appendix III.

Chapter 8

Planning Social Service - A Dream

I gained a great deal of satisfaction working for Nepalese women during the International Women's Year (IWY) as the member secretary of the IWY Committee Nepal. It was a very interesting and welcomed experience for me, and yet very different from my library work. Before the year came to an end I had a very memorable audience with the queen, during which she talked about her interest in social service and her possible involvement in that field in the near future, and about her wish to have me serve her as a member secretary as I did in the IWY. I was deeply impressed by her desire to serve the poor in order to relieve them from their poverty so that they could participate in the development process of Nepal.

After returning to my work in the University to take up again my struggle for the development of T.U. Central Library and that of the library profession in Nepal, I still quite often thought of social service. This idea was nothing new to me, because my library work had always been service- oriented, and service to readers is service to God, I always thought. Thus social service was naturally very close to my heart. I began to do some research on the subject and acquired additional books and documents on social service from different nations, with the idea of remaining involved in the queen's mission to serve poor men, women, children, and youth.

I began to build a separate collection on social service in T.U. Central Library. I did not face any problem in this regard. Most of the people in top-level positions were most supportive — not unnaturally, given that everyone thought I

Planning Social Service - A Dream

was close to the palace. I always wondered why the same person could change so according to the circumstances. I have learnt a lot about Nepalese ways, and they do not always appeal to me. My philosophy has always been to respect any good, knowledgeable and selfless Nepalese who has the welfare of the country and the people at heart.

Knowing that I might be called at any time to join the task force on social service formed under the auspices of the Jaanch Boojh Kendra, I started planning for the library work to be carried on in my absence. In December 1976 I got a letter from the Jaanch Boojh Kendra informing me of the formation the task force in which I was to be included.

This time I did not have long to wait to receive my deputation letter from the University; it came quickly. In the last week of December, therefore, I again left my library work, this time to join a team whose aim was to plan social services for Nepal. The other members of the task force were Mrs. Savitri Thapa and Mr. Shatrughan Prasad Singh.

The Jaanch Boojh Kendra is situated close to the palace. It is under the direction of the private secretary to the king. Office hours were from 11 a.m. to 6 p.m. I took a 10 o'clock public bus to get to the Kendra, covering a distance of six kilometres from Balkhu, Kuleswor to the palace. Though I hated the crowded buses, I had no alternative. Even in that crowd I could never keep myself from requesting everyone to behave well, so that no bus rider would be crushed, and to give special care to the aged and children. I may not have been heard, but I had to express my feelings.

I was extremely happy to see everyone on time in the office. Quite a number of teams were working on different projects, about which we were not supposed to enquire, I was told. I was rather surprised in the beginning why everything was so confidential.

Planning Social Service - A Dream

An oath-taking ceremony was held in the palace for the three members of the task force. I felt very uneasy, having never been used to such a formality and not seeing why it was necessary. I took the oath simply because I always thought it best to abide by the rules. In doing so, I came to know that it prohibited people who worked in the Jaanch Boojh Kendra from disclosing their projects. For some time I felt very uncomfortable avoiding questions put by friends and relatives about my work in the palace. At times my mind rebelled against accepting such a burden of confidentiality. If every task force was engaged in working for the good of the nation, why keep it all secret? Yet I did obey.

After the ceremony the queen granted us an audience to give us terms of reference and directives under which the task force was to work. These were the guidelines, and we were given only three months to come up with a plan to make changes in the existing social services, which were more criticized at the time than praised. Our team was very hard-working. I provided its members with all necessary documents, which I had collected in the library even before the task force was formed.

We submitted our plan to the queen on schedule. It was very simple but action-oriented, geared to the people who needed such services, and requiring a very small number of committee members, under the chairmanship of the queen, to issue directives and policies to all existing social service organizations. Having submitted the plan, I eagerly awaited an audience with the queen; still impressed on my memory were her words that I might look forward to working as secretary to her if she decided to become the chairwoman of the committee.

Alas, it was not to be. One afternoon Mr. Gehendra Man Singh met me in his office to inform me that I would not be given the post of secretary due to strong opposition from

Planning Social Service - A Dream

different quarters; some other post would be available for me, however, in the Social Service Coordination Committee office.

I was taken aback but not depressed. For a while I lost myself in an ocean of thought, wondering how the queen's desire could have been thwarted. Who had raised the challenge? My straightforward reply to the secretary, Mr. Singh, was that I would like to return to library work if I was not to have the opportunity to serve the nation as member secretary of the Social Service Coordination Committee.

It was a tough decision I made to reject another post on the same committee. The only thing that worried me was the possibility of creating some misunderstanding between the queen and me. Thus I requested an audience with the queen before going back to my library work. The queen was extremely kind to receive me. It was a remarkable and memorable meeting, during which I was able to share my thoughts and feelings about my cherished dream to serve her as the member secretary. She looked very sympathetic and understanding, which relieved me of my aforementioned fear. I expressed a keen interest and commitment to serve her and to make, even if from the outside, the mission of the Social Service Coordination Committee under her chairmanship a great success.

My last visit with the queen was emotion-filled. I could well understand her predicament. Her words and thoughts struck me as being sincere, humane, and selfless. Her voice sounded to me to be as much that of a commoner as of a queen. I often thought that she as queen could change the image of our poverty-stricken country and surpass indeed such famous queens as Sita of the *Ramayana*, the Hindu epic written ten thousand years ago, and Gandhari of the *Mahabharata*, the world's longest poem, written five thousand years ago. It was very hard for me to take my leave.

Planning Social Service - A Dream

My dream to make social service a personal passion and mission remained a dream. After returning from the palace to my library work, I tried to evaluate myself. I believe strongly that a person is one's own best judge. I tried to recall all my activities on the IWY Committee 1975 like a documentary film. I was quite satisfied with the achievements of the committee. The king, the queen, the chairwoman, and the members were all pleased and said so in public speeches. Nevertheless I had been pushed out of the Social Service Coordination Committee.

I realized that I had made more enemies than friends during my term of office by being straightforward and frank and by stating my honest opinion, and by raising my voice against groupism among Nepalese women. I was quite often accused of being too idealistic, but I just replied, "Speak the truth, worship your work; remember God sends us into this world not to be lazy and jealous but to serve and work honestly and sincerely with all devotion. This is the path to God." My own experience reminded me, though, of Shakespeare's lines in *Othello*, "Take note, take note, O world, To be direct and honest is not safe."

Back in the library again, I had more access to documents on global social activities. Whenever I found good and appealing articles I sent them to the queen, the chairwoman of the Social Service Coordination Council after it was constituted by the king in February 1977. Many persons of royal rank, such as the princesses Princep Shah, Shanti Singh, and Sharada Shah, along with the leaders of the two still quarrelling groups of women, Mrs. Kamal Rana and Mrs. Angur Baba Joshi, were made the chairwomen of different committees formed to shoulder the load of the council's social activities. There were too many powerful committees to be useful, I thought. Later on I felt extremely glad to be outside this grand social scene. I thanked God for relieving me from work I would not have

Planning Social Service - A Dream

been able to cope with. A small high-level watchdog committee under the guidance of the queen would have been far better than the present situation. Once the die had been cast, however, it become everyone's duty to provide support, constructive criticism, and solutions. In our society, unfortunately, people in power have a hard time accepting any kind of criticism. They become so engrossed in their own affairs that they do not see the realities around them and have no time to hear simple comments from anyone — a great tragedy.

Although I was out of the scene, I wanted to help the committee by providing information on any social topic so that they could plan and manage better. I wrote regularly to the secretary of the council and to the committees but got hardly any response. Then I thought of organizing a large exhibition of all the books, periodicals, and other related documents on global social services on the council's annual day, but it too failed to materialize due to the very cool response from the council secretary.

Gradually people's attitude towards me changed very noticeably, because they thought that I was no longer close to the queen. The Social Service National Coordination Council used to hold many grand functions graced by the king, queen, and other members of the royal family and attended by distinguished persons of the kingdom of Nepal. Nobody cared to include me in their list of invitees. The same people who used to come seeking me out began to pretend as if they did not know me. But nothing disturbed me, because I had never been away from closeness to God. He was always with me, otherwise I too would have become calculating. I love to study people and their attitudes about different things at different times and to learn something from them. This has been a great boon for me and brought me closer to God.

Chapter 9

Crusade against Corruption

The story of the largest misappropriation of T.U. Central Library funds in its history could be made into a first-class detective novel. I wish I had the skill of Agatha Christie so that I could fictionalize the case, but the simple facts are chilling enough in themselves. The main character was Ram Prasad Poudyal, and his supporters, according to the Special Police Department, were his brother Shankar Prasad Poudyal, his brother-in-law Shankar Prasad Rimal, and others who tried to cover up his dark deeds in the library. The chief perpetrator was almost incomparable to any corrupt person of any corruption case I ever knew of, utterly knavish and cruel.

After my involvement in 1975 in the International Women's Year Committee Nepal, and in the planning of social services for Nepal, I continued to be in and out of library work for a few years. I was happy to be involved in other activities, as I was not getting the support I needed to advance my plans for T.U.C.L., and by my nature I could never remain idle. Assistant Librarian Purna Prasad Amatya always looked after the library as directed by the University in my absence. His loose administration played into the hands of those staff who were undedicated, and I used to complain to him about this when I came back from my outside duties. He loved to gain cheap popularity by supporting university authorities and others even at the expense of harming the library profession, and also by not reprimanding the staff for undisciplined and non-professional acts — the source of much trouble for the library. I very often used to warn him of the bad consequences of such behaviour.

Crusade Against Corruption

I could never understand him. I always had regards for him because he was the first person from Nepal to get a diploma-level degree in library science from India, in the early 1950's. I tried very hard to change his mental attitude so that he would support the struggle for T.U.C.L.'s development and the library profession in Nepal. Hoping he might change by seeing the situation abroad, I recommended him for training at the National Library of Australia upon an invitation forwarded to me from the British Council. Alas, he never changed. He remained the same inbred product of Nepalese culture.

Some calculating staff members didn't want to see him change to fit my expectations of being devoted to duty and true to the profession. In my absence, it seemed, he had been very much exploited by some of them, especially Mr. Poudyal, a cunning devil if ever there was one.

Poudyal joined the library as a sub-accountant, having left his job in the government. He had a host of good qualities: discipline, punctuality, and the ability to work hard. I never had had any complaint with him. No one could have suspected him of any dark deeds. Even Scotland Yard would have had a hard time uncovering his skulduggery in the library, I thought, when I went back over the investigation of the case, so well conceived and hatched was it. He planted the seeds of his crime during my absence and before he was appointed an internal auditor of the University. He nurtured things along gradually, after gaining access to the budget of the library, which was kept not in the library but at the Financial Administration Section of the University at Tripureshwor in Kathmandu, where he had his office.

I had no administrative power over the library budget, which was handled entirely by the centre at Tripureshwor. The library could not spend more than Rs. 50 at a time from the petty cash given by the centre to meet its contingencies, so I could hardly imagine any misappropriation taking place in it, not even after breaking the case myself.

The month of May was always a busy one for me: checking the budget, reallocating budget items, preparing the annual report, planning library activities for the next fiscal year, and more. In the last week of May I received a letter, dated May 1980, from the chief fiscal officer, Mr. Suresha Raj Sharma, that I should not forward any more bills to the Financial Administration Section for payment, as the money budgeted for books had already been exceeded. I was quite surprised, because in that particular year the library had not spent much on the purchase of books, some of the teaching departments having been slow in submitting their lists of books needed for teaching and research. The library had already adopted a book purchasing policy approved by the University. According to it, I had no authority to purchase books needed for subjects taught on campus without the recommendation of department heads, only authority to select and buy reference books and books on Nepal. I always felt it proper to involve teachers in book selection; this strengthened the bond between them and the library.

Our teachers were also cooperative in ways of their own. Whenever I got a chart of the library budget from the centre, I called a Library Committee meeting to allocate funds to the departments. Then I sent a circular to all the department heads requesting them to prepare a list of books for their departments. I established a book selection corner in the library with book selection tools to help the teachers in making their choice. Due to lack of funds, I never managed to assemble all the tools I felt were needed. A few important ones, though, I got regularly from the British Council and USIS as gifts, for which I was grateful. Without them my mission to obtain the best books for the library would not have been a success.

Crusade Against Corruption

In a developing country, such selection has always been a great problem. There is a lack of good and timely information on new resources. Every library usually waits to spend a good portion of its budget at the end of a fiscal year, and then it cannot give due attention to selecting the best books. Clever book dealers also try to take advantage of the situation by selling old stock at large discounts not mentioned on the bills. Most libraries in this part of the world fall prey to this, an evil practice that needs to be eradicated if libraries are to play their proper role in education. I disassociated T.U.C.L. from such book dealers.

Well-known book dealers from India and our own local book dealers were very appreciative of my selection techniques. I always got good help from them in procuring the best books for our needs, at set discounts mentioned on the bills. Whenever I heard about underhanded discount practices in other libraries from professional staff transferred to T.U.C.L., I called a meeting of local booksellers to discuss the matter and tried my best to convince them to do away with such practices for the sake of the library, a temple of Saraswati (wisdom) where knowledge, truth, and sincerity should prevail. They never disagreed with me, but they told me many shocking stories about the pressure they were under — unthinkable, unbelievable stories. They said, "Corruption has already become a part of life, so it's useless to talk about it and better not to pay it any heed." I understood them well. They promised to help me to get books that were recommended by department heads, knowing well that our library bought neither only books stocked with them nor multiple copies of the same title oblivious of the needs of university teaching and research.

Quite often I faced problems with authors, teachers, and writers who wanted to sell multiple copies of their own publications to the library. I had to explain to them that books

Crusade Against Corruption

are not written to be dumped in one place but to be disseminated far and wide; if a real demand arose among teachers, students, and other library users we would definitely add to the number of copies. Moreover, the library never had a sufficient budget to purchase even single copies of needed books and periodicals, and it was against library policy to purchase multiple copies that weren't needed. They retorted by pointing out that other libraries and research centres bought multiple copies, so why not T.U. Central Library. Sometimes very unpleasant situations arose in my office when I tried to run the library according to rules and regulations. Out of this came more foes than friends, but my greatest guide, God, was ever with me, leading me along the path of truth and right.

Having received the letter from the fiscal officer, I immediately called in the person in charge of such matters, Mr. Raj Bahadur Shrestha, junior librarian, to check the library records properly, telling him that if my memory did not betray me, there must be quite a bit of money still left for book purchases that year. The library always kept a record of the amount mentioned on bills forwarded for payment in order to be able to check current balances of money allocated to the different departments.

After about half an hour Mr. Shrestha reported to me that I was right: more than half of the book budget had not yet been spent. I asked him to bring the record book so that I could check myself. His figures added up. Wondering where the mistake could have been made, I asked him to go himself to Tripureshwor to compare our record with that of the Financial Administration Section.

It was late in the afternoon of May 29, 1980. I was waiting for Mr. Shrestha to come back to the library with the report. It occurred to me that mistakes might have been made in recording the amount. Mr. Shrestha returned with a whole

Crusade Against Corruption

assortment of unknown and unforwarded bills, with what could only have been forged signatures discovered while checking the files of the bills he had sent for payment. He looked pale and astonished. Without any word he handed over the fake bills to me and after some moments told me how he had discovered them. I, too, was extremely astonished to see such bills, which were made out by one Rastriya Patrika Agency.

I called in my senior staff. They had heard nothing about such a book dealer before. Then I called my husband, who after leaving the library profession had become the deputy registrar of the University, to come to the library as soon as possible. Surprised to receive this emergency call, he arrived in record time.

I showed him the bills. He seemed more concerned and worried than me, already envisaging the possible implications. We decided to report the matter to the vice-chancellor, Dr. Mahendra Prasad, and to request him to hand over the case for investigation to the Special Police Department of H.M.G., having often read news reports about their investigations of suspected fraud and corruption. We thought that they would surely find the culprit quickly. We were anxious to find out who could have used the library money so foully. With fake bills in hand, I took my place behind my husband on our 50cc motorbike, which we had acquired at a very cheap price through the kindness of my good German friend Dr. Liane Nitschke, a well-known pediatrician who contributed many services to the children's ward at Shanta Bhawan Mission Hospital (now Patan Hospital). The small motorbike chugged along at what seemed like a snail's pace, but somehow we managed to reach the office before the vice-chancellor left it. It was closing time.

We first went to the registrar, Mr. Yubaraj Singh Pradhan, the administrative head of the University, to inform him of events. He, too, was taken aback to see the bills with forged signatures. The three of us went to the vice-chancellor, whose interest in my report was no less keen. I requested him to hand over the case to the Special Police Department immediately, worried that the culprit might abscond; news of the fake bills had already spread within the library and Financial Administration Section. The vice-chancellor telephoned the chief of the Special Police Department to ask him to come to his office. It was already past office hours, so it was decided to meet the next day at 12 noon.

Back home, my husband and I looked at the bills again and again. The forgeries of my own signatures and those of my staff looked unbelievably real. According to T.U.C.L. practice, whenever new books came in they were checked against their bills and then entered into the library accession register by the staff of the Acquisition Section. An accession number was put on the book, and the bills were stamped with the words "Entered Into The Accession Register" and signed. The bills were then signed by me and sent to the Administrative Section of the library, to be forwarded to the Financial Administration Section at Tripureshwor for payment.

All these procedures seemed to have been followed in drawing up those fake bills, so we thought that the culprit must have been someone who was well acquainted with library practices. But whom to suspect? I did not distrust anyone on my staff. Placing my hopes on the Special Police Department, I went to bed. The night was long, and the next morning I got up still restless to find the doer of the deeds. Once in my office, I kept looking at my watch, waiting for the minutes to tick away till noon. I reached the vice-chancellor's office on time.

The chief of the Special Police Department, Mr. Shailendra Prasad Singh, came with his joint secretary, Mr. Kul Raj

Crusade Against Corruption

Pandey. The registrar and the chief legal adviser of the University, Mr. Sambhu Prasad Gyawali, were also present during the meeting. I reported everything in detail. Everyone present seemed attentive.

Mr. Singh put a few simple queries to me regarding our payment procedure and then requested the registrar to summon the person who issued the check to the Rastriya Patrika Agency, Mr. Dhyan Kaji Shelalink of the Financial Administration Section. I was quite impressed by the way Mr. Singh questioned him. Without any fear and hesitation Mr. Shelalink openly told us that the internal auditor of the University, Mr. Ram Prasad Poudyal, quite often used to press him to issue the check quickly. He could also identify the person who came to collect the checks. Everyone present at the meeting thought that his story might contain a clue. I gave information on Mr. Poudyal's previous record in the library as sub-accountant before he became the internal auditor. It was hard for me to think of him as a criminal, but I remembered later the proverb "You can't judge a book from its cover." After the meeting I was asked to write a letter to the registrar formally informing him of the case. This I promptly did.

On June 1, 1980 I was apprised that Mr. Poudyal had been arrested by the Special Police Department for investigation. I admired the authorities for their quick action and waited for the truth to come out. The news item was published in *The Rising Nepal* and the *Gorkhapatra* newspapers. The culprit, it seemed clear, was Ram Prasad Poudyal, who had indeed confessed to the black deeds. I was on the whole happy and thought that the Special Police Department might have surpassed even Scotland Yard standards.

I was relieved. I thanked God that the guilty party had been found. I was full of hope that he would be sent to jail and the library money would soon be recovered. But things did not turn out that way. Within a few weeks, all kinds of unexpected and awful rumours were being spread, behind which seemed to be a plot to incriminate my innocent staff and to get the devil off the hook. I could hardly believe it; even a low-ranking member of the Special Police Department was creating baseless stories to shift responsibility on to the guiltless. What was happening was next to impossible, I thought, but I was wrong. To esteem the Special Police Department so highly was a great mistake, I was warned by experienced well-wishers of the library. Some, including the rector, told me that the case should not have been handed over to them.

I was still reluctant to believe this, but I had to rethink things when they started questioning the unquestionably honest T.U. Financial Administration Section and the library staff whose signatures were forged. Most of them were issued summonses, seemingly at the request of Mr. Poudyal and with the connivance of the acting District Superintendent of Police (DSP), Mr. Gopal Bista, of the Special Police Department, a seasoned foul player. Mr. Padmananda Shakya from the library and the aforementioned Mr. Shelalink were taken into custody along with Mr. Poudyal, turn by turn, so that the latter could try to convince them to write confessions shifting blame from him either onto themselves or onto me.

It was sobering to hear from them of the threats and harassment they were subjected to day and night. Padmananda Shakya of my staff, whom I always referred to as a rare gem of honesty, almost lost his sanity after the continuous bullying and torture inflicted upon him by DSP Bista. Mr. Shelalink and Bal Bahadur Shrestha, another employee of the Financial Administration Section, also told me with tears in their eyes how they had been harassed, threatened, and tortured by Bista until they broke down and wrote dictated replies. They repeatedly apologized for writing such baseless accounts.

Crusade Against Corruption

Now I became dead sure that some kind of conspiracy had been hatched. I told my husband all I had heard. He took it more seriously than I did, being a man of farsightedness and knowledge of the law.

I decided to go to the chief of the Special Police Department, Mr. Shailendra Prasad Singh, to complain about the inhumane treatment, which was completely uncalled for, especially after Poudyal's confession had been extracted by his own office. I called him to fix a time to visit, as I always hated to go anywhere without an appointment and then have to wait hours to get called in.

At 11:30 in the morning of July 3, 1980, my husband and I stepped into the office of Mr. Singh. He received us with lulling phrases. We felt at ease to talk openly, especially with reference to DSP Bista. Our words were almost a warning to him, too. I was thus surprised to find him neither arguing against nor accepting what we said. If I had been in his position, I would have at least assured us that I would take my subordinates to task if they were found to be involved in such unlawful acts.

Mr. Singh began to turn to his pending files as if to indicate that the meeting was over, but to our great surprise he presently mentioned that my signature had been sent for examination. I immediately questioned him why such an examination was necessary, given that Mr. Poudyal had already confessed. He had no answer to satisfy me.

After the visit I kept myself busy with my library work, as I did not want services to be disturbed. It was even a kind of relaxation because I truly loved my job. Once I got absorbed in it I forget the rest of the world.

One day the ringing of my telephone drew me away from my work. It was a call from an editor of a well-known newspaper. I was happy to hear from him, but his news of a

Crusade Against Corruption

circular put out by some evil-minded person bent on defaming me and the library was very unpleasing. He did not wish to mention the writer's name over the phone, but he assured me that he would never publish such libel in his newspaper. I thanked him for his support and information.

Some other friendly editors also informed me of the same thing. One to whom I was close came to my place to show me the original circular but made me promise not to disclose his name, as his action had been a breach of journalistic ethics. The circular had been written by S. B. Thakur, the notorious troublemaker who could invent anything and slander anyone at random. Going through his circular, I became so furious I could have bitten him, and at the same time I almost decided to bring suit against him for trying to assassinate my character and defame the library. In the end what I did was to immediately report the matter in writing to the registrar, attaching a copy of the deplorable circular of July 10, 1980 for necessary action. I prayed for strength to tolerate such things, which were beneath contempt.

I was happy that none of the well-known newspapers of Nepal published the circular. A few Nepali papers, such as *Naulo Nepali* and *Katibaddha*, under the editorship of Khem Koirala and Bhabook Ghimire respectively, published the information contained in the circular without doing any investigating of their own. I had always expected great things from editors as searchers after truth and discouragers of baseless stories. Now, though, they had failed to measure up, and so I wrote two critiques of the circular, giving a true account of the misappropriation case and Mr. Thakur's hideous circular, and sent them to all the editors of well-known newspapers and to various lawyers. Most of these papers — *Naya Nepal, Matribhumi, Nepal Post, Jagriti, Pratigya, Asiali Awaj, Naya Kiran, Jaruri, Charcha, Jwala,*

Crusade Against Corruption

and *The Commoner*, under the editorship of Govinda Prasad Pradhan, Govinda Biyogi, Devendra Gautam, Shakti Ram Bhandari, Viswanath Luitel, Nirmal Kumar Aryal, Narendra Vilas Pandey, Bhim Narayan Sharma, Nepal Bhooshan Neupane, Gopal Siwakoti, and G. D. Shrestha respectively — published my statement, and this boosted my courage to fight for the truth with God in my heart. I have remained always grateful to them for their moral support.

Having strongly complained about the actions of some of the staff of the Special Police Department to its chief, Mr. Singh, I was eagerly waiting to hear of some appreciable steps against those persons, of whom Gopal Bista was the ring leader, according to what I learned from other staff of the department itself. Instead I received information that Mr. Bista was being recommended by Mr. Singh for a medal given on the occasion of the king's birthday. This was utterly incredible, and if true should have been strongly deplored.

On July 10, 1980, one month after Mr. Poudyal's confession, I was asked to appear in person at the Special Police Department to answer questions. I was shocked and furious and at first intended to refuse to go to give my statement unnecessarily, but I changed my mind, seeing this as an opportunity to fight evil. I feared no one, as I was always under divine guidance.

The long list of queries prepared by the department on the initiative of Mr. Bista enraged me at first, and I felt like throwing it in his face. The DSP had a wicked look and hinted that his chief had already told him of my strong complaint against him; he seemed quite determined to invent anything to trap me. This war — a war between good and evil — went on for a few days. With full confidence and conviction, I gave my written statement in response to the queries, wanting to put a stop once and for all to the anti-Shanti move. The whole thing was like something out of the Inquisition. I wish I could publish it.

In between I went to meet Prime Minister Surya Bahadur Thapa — the Special Police Department was directly under him — to give him my complaint in writing. It was early in the morning. Many visitors from different districts of Nepal were waiting to meet him. When I saw the crowd, I thought there might be some important function going on. It was my first visit to the prime minister's official residence. I asked his P.A. what all the people were doing there. He looked at me with great surprise and with a smile set me straight. That day, in fact, there were fewer visitors than usual. I wondered how the prime minister could deal with so many visitors so early in the morning — not at all a good practice, I thought.

I requested the P.A. to take my name slip to the prime minister as an emergency case, which it was. Immediately he returned to take me and my husband into the residence. The eyes of dozens of fellow visitors followed us as if we were from a different planet. I felt for them for having waited so long. I was against the *chakadi* system to which they were enthralled. Social change was more important than political change, I thought, but who would bring it about? Aptly it has been said that everyone thinks of changing the world, but no one thinks of changing himself. So very true of our people.

The P.A. led us through two waiting rooms full of seated visitors to an upstairs room, where Prime Minister Thapa came to receive us with his usual welcoming smile and lead us to a well-decorated drawing room.

I expressed my deep gratitude to him for giving us his valuable time without an appointment beforehand. I told him briefly why I had come and handed over my letter of complaint about the deplorable methods of investigating my staff and me. He took it very seriously and showed very admirable concern and sympathy to me. His assurance that he would enquire into the case made me feel very relieved. He was one of the prominent prime ministers of the Panchayat period; I admired him no less than Prime Minister Dr. Tulsi Giri for his statesmanship and shrewdness.

My hopes and expectations were high. For a few days nothing was heard of from the Special Police Department. Everything looked bright. Finally I was called to come down to their office.

I went to see the chief first. He looked very nervous. With a forced smile he tried to be ingratiating and requested me not to care about what DSP Bista said and did. It was obvious that the prime minister had talked to him. I almost lost my patience with all this innuendo, as I wanted to know why I was being called down again. He pretended not to know and asked me to see his joint secretary, Mr. Kul Raj Pandey, as he had to go out to attend an important meeting. I smelled that something was up but did not try to corner him.

As usual, Mr. Pandey received me respectfully and requested me to wait for a while, as he had some other visitors. Mr. Pandey seemed to be a first-class civil servant of a simple, gentle, and religious nature. Alas, he turned out to be just the opposite, a man of no principles and responsibility and easily moved by evildoers.

When the visitors left the room, he lowered his face to the table and politely requested me to find someone ready to stand security for me, hinting indirectly at the report of the handwriting expert. Even before he finished speaking I began to attack him sharply, mocking what he said. He kept quiet, but I kept on repeatedly asking him the reason for these accusations. I almost lost my senses, and my temper was beyond control. If Mr. Pandey had not kept silent, I don't know what I would have done to him, as I never expected to hear such things either from him or from his department. One occasionally heard, from credible sources, of people in Nepal hesitating to report cases of murder, robbery, or corruption, since the informant had to reckon with unpleasant consequences, including jail and punishment — the fruits of corruption.

After my exchange with Mr. Pandey I immediately went to see Chief Singh to challenge him with regard to the baseless report about my forged signature. He turned blue as soon as he saw me. I had some fiery words for him: "Down with your expert's views — a devilish, corrupt expert! How could you deceive me and require security from me on the basis of such a false report?"

He was unexpectedly demure. He told me very politely that he was planning to seek an expert's view from the outside and to appoint a panel, so I should not feel deceived. He requested me to have patience and be cooperative.

I went to consult again the prime minister and other high-ranking officials regarding what had transpired. Their advice was to abide by the rules of the Special Police Department; there was no harm in putting up security, they said, which would be given back as soon as the final investigation was over. In the end I decided to act on their advice, swayed perhaps by the importance I myself attached to the written rules and regulations of any office.

I had nothing in the way of significant property I could use as security, so I went to my father and brother. They received the news glumly but agreed to draw up a paper on their own property. I remained ever grateful for their support in such a critical hour. If I had failed to produce such security, who knows but what I would have been taken into custody in order to assassinate my character and the reputation of the library.

Crusade Against Corruption

With a strong determination to begin this unwanted struggle with the Special Police Department, I returned to the library to plan my strategy of truth. I knew it was not to be an easy battle. Some of my friends told me not to take the risk of challenging the police staff, but nothing could stop me, as I had already been guided by my divine urge. I was not against the police, having a high regard for the service of policemen who are able to fight evils and provide for a peaceful environment in the country. I knew I would have their support.

During this period I contacted many chiefs of different departments and offices of the government, including the Intelligence Department, to find out why I had been asked to put up security. At last I got access to confidential information that my adversaries had succeeded in getting a report issued stating that my signature was not forged but real. What a pretty state of affairs!

My husband and I visited and revisited many dignitaries and well-wishers during our own investigations. They were so kind as to find out the name of that expert. It was Ram Bahadur Thapa. He worked in the police headquarters as a DSP and also as a handwriting expert. At first I could not believe that a DSP from the head office could be so lowdown and corrupt, but I quickly learned better.

As soon as I got confirmation of DSP Thapa's complicity from other sources, I made a list of concerned authorities and persons to visit to inform of the devilish goings-on in the Special Police Department, hoping that the conspirators would be put on trial so that honest people would not have to suffer in future.

Since the so-called handwriting expert was from police headquarters, my husband and I went to see Inspector General of Police (IGP) Mr. Durlav Kumar Thapa, having fixed an appointment beforehand, on July 21, 1980. We were extremely impressed with his response. It was a long visit, about two hours, during which we discussed many things: honest investigation, corruption, and threats and harassment directed towards honest people, in particular the report on my signature by DSP Thapa. I demanded the latter's immediate dismissal.

IGP Thapa seemed well acquainted with the deep-rooted corruption everywhere in the country. Naturally he could not promise me anything without first enquiring into the matter, which he politely assured me he would do. He stated indirectly that the Special Police Department did not have to depend only on the report submitted by DSP Thapa, who was not really an authorized expert. Before leaving I urged him to act in accordance with the principle of rewarding honesty and punishing dishonesty and corruption — the best way to ensure development and peace for Nepal.

On the same day, my husband and I visited Attorney General Ramananda Prasad Singh, who had been a good friend of T.U.C.L. ever since I started my career as the librarian. I had always had high regards for him, and I wanted to inform him of the rot within the Special Police Department and to seek his advice and suggestions. He showed appreciable concern and tried his best to calm me, telling me not to worry about the false report and saying that no injustice would come to a dedicated, honest person like me. What a relief to hear such words from him. I requested his support in my battle, and knew I had it.

Late in the evening of August 2, 1980 I went to confer with Superintendent of Police Lekh B. Pandey of the Intelligence Department. As usual, my husband was with me. The main purpose of our visit was to enquire whether the Intelligence Department could help me in finding the truth behind the devious actions of the DSP in the police headquarters and the DSP in the Special Police Department.

Crusade Against Corruption

Having listened to my account, Mr. Pandey told us a number of interesting stories based on his intelligence work. I strongly urged that the Intelligence Department dig into the matter, wanting backup proofs before anyone was punished. He seemed more than willing to help me. I was quite happy to have discussed with him in detail how to go ahead with my painful efforts to fight against the devils. Being merely a superintendent, he suggested that I report to his boss, the chief of the intelligence department, Mr. C. B. Rai. I knew very little of Mr. Rai, so I kept my visit pending for some time. If needed, I would go to visit him in future, I thought.

In the meantime some of our close friends came to the library to suggest that I seek out Mr. P. L. Kafle, a handwriting expert on the staff of the Karmachari Sanchaya Kosh (Provident Fund Department). It was not long before I, in fact, went to see him with my husband. When he heard my name, he looked as if he was trying to recollect something. I began to outline the case, but before I had finished, he suddenly interjected with a broad smile that he had already examined my signature at the Special Police Department and given a verbal report that all my signatures were definitely forged, a fact that was clear to the expert even without using precision techniques. He seemed very convinced that what he said was one hundred percent correct, even before hearing my side of the story.

Oh, it was a great source of joy to hear someone speak the truth! Before leaving I put one last question: Why did he not give his report in writing? His answer was that he could not do so unless the Special Police Department requested. He would be called back if they wanted such a report. He further assured me of his professional help if needed and gave me the address of forensic science laboratories run by the government of India and the addresses of private and government consultants.

Crusade Against Corruption

I was also advised by my well-wishers to go to visit the king's principal private secretary, Narayan Prasad Shrestha, who could, if he wished, order Chief Singh to conduct his investigation honestly, as Mr. Singh never said no to him, having once been appointed zonal commissioner by the king at his strong recommendation. Though I knew him well as a professor even before he joined the palace, I never felt at ease visiting him, as mentioned previously. His thoughts were ever elsewhere. Maybe he had more responsibilities and burdens than he could handle. Ever since I had received information about the false report on my forged signature, I too became like a fish out of water. The whole of Nepal seemed like a can of worms, and I began to suspect everyone. To fight the evil I had to go everywhere, whether I wanted to or not.

I went with my husband to Secretary Shrestha early one morning during his visiting hours. I thought it would be too early, yet quite a number of people were already waiting to see him. He was playing badminton with his friends, who obviously were enjoying basking in his presence. Other visitors with problems on their minds and worries on their faces were forced to watch the match. Some sycophant would comment, "Oh, Mr. Secretary, how well you played; what a shot!" It was first-class entertainment.

I was standing a bit off to the side. Luckily the game was soon over. The cynosure of all eyes was dripping like a rain forest. All his visitors made an instant display of respect with folded hands. He seemed a bit uneasy to see me waiting amid so many visitors and was kind enough to call me first to his visiting room, where his beautifully dressed wife was waiting with a thick towel to wipe his sweating body. I felt somewhat awkward entering the room, but he requested me to do so, so I did.

Crusade Against Corruption

As usual, he was in a great hurry. I got to the point, telling him that he should call Chief Singh and order him to be honest and conduct a proper examination of my forged signatures. I quoted Confucius — "To know what is right and not do it is the worst cowardice"- having faith that the secretary would never distrust me or doubt my honesty and sincerity. But he had neither proper answers nor assurances for me, only a peculiar and unexpected silence, and this from a friend whom I trusted greatly.

My next move was to consult with well-wishers. I made a list of powerful palace secretaries to inform of my strategy for dealing with the Special Police Department. I wanted in particular to test how far these powerful agents of the palace were true to their duties to keep the spirit of *nyaya magnu gorkha janu* (go to the palace for justice) alive.

Accordingly my husband and I went to Principal Secretary Ranjan Raj Khanal one day early in the morning during his visiting hours. His residence was a blend of the traditional and modern. Well-fed and -tended cows were in evidence, as befitted a traditional Brahmin household. There was an abundance of trees and flowers. Shoes were not allowed into his modern chair-lined living room. I was at first rather surprised to see so many pairs of shoes outside, as if some sort of *puja* (ritual) was going on in the room. A few people were outside, as all chairs inside were taken. Knowing nothing about how Secretary Khanal received his visitors, we asked those who were standing. They told us that people were usually received in a small room adjacent to the living room in the order of their arrival.

A few visitors left while we were talking outside. Some chairs became empty. We went into the room after removing our shoes — a good practice, as our roads were full of nasty things.

Crusade Against Corruption

It was already 10:30. Palace office hours started at 11 a.m. I wondered how the secretary would be able to meet so many remaining visitors before having his morning meal and setting off for work. I posed this question to the waiting visitors. They told me that the secretary would manage; he always managed to find time. They were all praise for him.

Then the door of the adjacent room was opened by the secretary himself, and he smilingly ushered the visitor out. He did not look in a hurry at all. When he saw us he gave us a very welcoming smile and requested us to enter the room. We could have used more such welcomes.

He told me that he had been shocked when he learned from newspapers about the case. He offered many interesting quotes about how sincere people in our sacred books had to suffer at the hands of devilish figures and recalled how he had once been the target of corruption charges and baselessly harassed himself. "Pray to God. He will never disappoint people of good will like you," he repeated several times. What a solace for me to hear him. I reminded him of his waiting visitors. He smilingly told me that his visitors were his god, as written in the sacred books (*atithi devo bhava*). Thus he never felt in a hurry to see them off. I could not agree more with what he said, believing strongly in the saying, "You will never 'find' time for anything. If you want time you must make it."

Secretary Khanal's every pious word made me feel good, yet I did not praise him in words, because in our country there are many people who can speak captivatingly but whose actions always prove disappointing, almost the reverse of what they say. Thus I decided to wait to express my admiration to him until the proper time came.

Before leading me out of his room, the secretary made the suggestion to visit both the well-known astrologer Prof. Mangal Raj Joshi and a hermit at Balaju. The latter, he said, would not

Crusade Against Corruption

respond to any evil-minded person and would not ask any fee for helping anyone to rise out of their troubled waters. Before going to the yogi we read the description of yogis by Abbé J. A. Dubois in his classical study *Hindu Manners, Customs and Ceremonies*.

Although my husband and I never particularly believed in such predictions and astrological readings, we decided to follow the secretary's advice in order to calm our mental agitation. I realized how people in their dismay and under critical pressure became disposed to believe in such supernatural things. I myself gave way and began to think that there was no harm in visiting the hermit and the astrologer.

My husband and I set out early in the morning of January 30, 1981. It took a while to locate the hermitage. People living near the place directed us towards a dwelling with a red flag hoisted on top of it. This was the first we had heard of the holy man and his *kuti* (hermitage) where, according to the villagers, *akhanda homa* (continuous sacrifice to fire in honour of the planets) was being carried on day and night for the welfare of humanity. The people told us that the hermit, Nijananda, had foretold many incidents, so that many high officials, politicians, and poverty-stricken villagers came to visit him for consultation. It all seemed to us like a mystery.

We took the muddy path to the place, consisting of some small thatched houses grouped together. Smoke was issuing forth from one of them. A woman came out to receive us when words of our coming were conveyed inside. Later on I came to know that she was the yogi's chief attendant. She took us to the platform of the house where he was resting. He was dressed in red and looked old and weak. We doubted whether he could really see us with his extraordinarily thick glasses. He caused us some surprise, asking some relevant questions about our visit even before I could disclose anything about the case. He immediately requested us to sit right next to him and showed appreciable affection towards us. From the first we felt that we were in a place apart — so very different from all the places we had visited so far with the story of our tribulations.

The yogi seemed moved by my narration but said that I should not worry; it all happened due to bad stars only. He would do the necessary *puja* and *homa* to counteract the bad stars and bad omens. During our visit the yogi unexpectedly asked us whether we practised any mantra. My husband told him that he practised the mantra Gayatri, which gave birth to the Vedas. My own answer was negative, because women are not given that particular mantra; only men were enjoined to keep it secret and recite it every day in a low voice so that no one could hear them. The yogi immediately asked my husband how he could recite the Gayatri, thinking him to be a Kshatriya. My husband told him that he was a Brahmin. Then the yogi began to explain in a very impressive way that the Gayatri should not be the monopoly of Brahmins; it could be recited by all God-loving people who wanted to be closer to Him. He was sorry that I did not know the mantra. He asked me to note it down and taught me how to recite it properly.

I was thrilled to have the Gayatri mantra. He also gave me a new name, Mahasati Anusooya, a lady in the Hindu epic renowned for her inviolable chastity and for her devotion to the gods and for her tender compassion for the unfortunate. We were very much impressed by the yogi's broad outlook and his profound explanation of Hinduism and nature — for instance, his explanation that karma arises from dharma and vice versa.

It was already late evening. Agreeing to come back on the appointed day for *puja*, we left his abode after first visiting the holy ritual site where he would perform the *homa*. Everything there had such an otherworldly and mysterious air that we

Crusade Against Corruption

could not help accepting what the yogi said. That the holy man trusted us gave us peace of mind.

On February 5, six days later, we went back to the yogi. We took our nine-year-old daughter Pragya with us to show her how *homa* and *kumari puja* (worship of virgins) is performed. Though small, she was a very bright child. Her few words during the crisis written in English on a small piece of paper displaying Lord Krishna and his consort Radha and placed on my pillow show this:

> Dear mother, Do not be afraid. God will help us to send that man to the jale. God, Please Help US To Send That Man to the Jale.
> Love From Pragya
> 25.7.80

I cried when I read it, knowing how worried and concerned she, a girl of nine, was; I felt her words were manna from heaven. My daughter surprised the yogi by reciting the *Durga Kawach* in praise of the goddess Durga with perfect elocution. It brought tears to his eyes.

It was a new experience for us to watch the *homa* and the worshipping and feeding of the *kumaris*, five virgins called from a nearby village. The *homa* was performed by the yogi and his assistant by kindling a fire of big logs and small chips, throwing into it some grains of rice, barley, and sesame seeds that had been soaked in ghee, and reciting mantras. It seemed that the whole day was spent in such performance, which was repeated several times every day for six days on my behalf. The yogi told us that the *homa* is the most meritorious sacrifice of any, and feeding the *kumaris* adds still more meaning to it.

We were asked to throw the above offerings into the fire. Most of all we enjoyed watching the virgin girls partake of the offered food — curry, beaten rice, curds, and some sweets. We were also given *prasad* (blessed food) to eat in the yogi's dwelling. We looked upon it as a spiritual picnic; so relaxing was it that I actually forgot the battle I was fighting.

Expressing my deep gratitude to the yogi, I left with my family for home. I took pleasure in remembering the yogi's selfless method to relieve me of my anxiety. He did not ask for any *dakshina* (sacrificial fee). We spent Rs. 600 for buying all the things — grains, firewood, beaten rice, fruits, towels, sweets, curds, etc. — needed for the *puja* and feeding the *kumaris*.

Since we loved his preachings and teachings, whenever we had time we visited him, and he always showed appreciable concern for what I was going through. Once I told him how I had to struggle to get due status for professional posts, including my own, at the University. Before I could finish my story, he interjected in a joking and cheerful tone, telling me that I should give him ten percent of the increased salary I received from the University for sacred acts. I very willingly accepted his demand; if calculated from what I received it came to Rs. 500.

With peace in my mind I went quietly about my library work, in spite of my continuous struggle to expose the plots and conspiracies. It took me longer than anticipated to find time to visit the yogi and to offer the Rs. 500 to him. One evening I decided the time had come. I went with my husband, who kept the Rs. 500 ready in his pocket. We reached his hut with our usual expectations but were surprised at the cool response from our host and especially from his caretaker, an old lady. We were not asked to attend the *homa* or given any *prasad*. Silence prevailed. I therefore gestured to my husband that we should hand over the money and leave. My husband gave the money to me to offer to the yogi. I took it and did so with the apology for not having come earlier. Then, totally unexpectedly, the yogi, and more so the lady, flushed with delight and with very tender words came to welcome us with *prasad* and the request to visit the *homa* as before. It was very hard to believe such behaviour possible. After this we never went back to the old yogi. I have no idea whether he is still alive.

Before our last visit to the yogi, my husband and I went to Prof. Mangal Raj Joshi, a well-known astrologer, who had also been suggested by the principal secretary, Mr. Khanal. Prof. Joshi had been known to us for years as a professor of geography at the University and also as a friend of T.U.C.L. Thus we felt no inhibitions to consult him, though we had never consulted any astrologer in our lives. This was unusual, because Nepalese usually seek out an astrologer before marriage, naming their children, buying land for houses, and so forth. But we had never believed in astrology, though it did at all times exercise a great influence over our parents and other close kin. In this case, however, as I have said, I was ready to consult anyone — yogi, astrologer, or any other person — for my peace of mind, no matter whether I believed or not, because my battle against the devilish forces was not an easy one, being full of knots from top to bottom.

Mr. Joshi lived in a traditional type of Nepalese house in Patan, one of the scenic cities of the Kathmandu Valley. As soon as he saw us from his window, he cheerfully directed us to come upstairs to his room. Some horoscopes were scattered about on his small table. He sat cross-legged in front of his small table and told us how sad he was to hear about the library case. He tried to convince us of the validity of astrology and very beautifully explained how rogues might have the upper hand temporarily when a bad planet like Saturn influenced a person, so that I should not worry even if one was influencing me. It would be a passing matter.

Crusade Against Corruption

I immediately requested him to see whether I was under Saturn's spell and if so to tell me the way to get out from under it. He opened his chart on the table and threw some rice on it. Asking me my date of birth, he plunged into study. After a while he told me that I was suffering from the *sarhesat ko dasa* (7½-year cycle) and so was caught in the case unnecessarily. He suggested some rituals I was to have a pandit perform to get loose from the bonds of Saturn. I was asked to recite every day a prayer: *om rim batukaya apad uddharanaya kuru kuru batukaya rim* (O God Batukaya, relieve me from my troubles). I was also to visit regularly two temples, Batuk Vairab and Bagalamukhi, both in Patan. He would send a pandit to offer *puja* and recite mantras to the goddess Bagalamukhi, who destroys one's enemies.

We let ourselves believe what he said and agreed to carry out his suggestions. He gave us a tour of the rooms where all his books and old Nepali calendars were kept for his research and study of the influence of the stars on lives of peoples and nations. During the tour he told us some of his predictions and forecasts for the royal family; they came true, so he was regularly being consulted by the palace. If an astrologer could be that effective, Nepal should one day be free from corrupt politics and social evils, the main obstacles to development.

The next morning a young well-dressed pandit came knocking at our door, apparently sent by Prof. Joshi. He did not look like a traditional pandit at all. We took him to our verandah, where we had assembled the necessary materials. Since we were entirely ignorant of such rituals and *puja*, we asked him to tell us how much we should give him as *dakshina* to perform the *puja* at the temple of Bagalamukhi. He gave us a surprised look. I could guess he was thinking that I was pretending to know nothing. When I repeated the same question he mumbled a few incomprehensible words. I was

Crusade Against Corruption

taken aback at his peculiar behaviour. We gave him about Rs. 40. He was supposed to bring *prasad* to us after the performance of *puja*, but he never came back.

During this period I received disturbing information that the Special Police Department was trying to get another report from the same collaborating expert to cover their conspiracy. My heart ached and my head spun, as if I would lose my balance at the prospect of having to fight on alone. I prayed and prayed for strength. I was beginning to think that I should go to Princess Princep Shah, although I never liked to disturb members of the royal family if I could get things done myself. I found no other way out, though. With my husband I hastened to Tahachal Durbar to appeal for justice, sure that the princess would listen to and help me as she had always done in critical situations before. Alas, she refused to see me. The message was brought by her favourite assistant, Ram Lall Shrestha. If I wished, though, I could leave a message in writing. I did leave a brief note stating why I had come to see her.

It was one of the greatest shocks in my life. I almost burst into tears, but I prayed for control over myself, sensing that something was wrong: maybe the princess had been given false reports on the case, as quite often royals are forced to depend on limited sources of information. I hated to blame the princess, because she had been so wonderful to me. I shall never forget her noble character as long as I live. After that I never went back to her. Unfortunately she passed away just after my troubles were laid to rest. I was later told by a close confidante of hers that she lamented all the painful things that had happened to me unnecessarily. I was extremely happy that she had not mistrusted me; I shall never stop praying for the eternal peace of her departed soul.

Now I did not know where to go. I was tired of fighting for the truth, but I did not want to give up either. I thought and rethought things out. I remembered how highly placed persons talked about day-to-day politics in Nepal. Some of them told me I should seek out Prince Gyanendra, who was easily approachable, for help, and if I was not given an opportunity to see him I should go to Mr. Damodar Shumshere J. B. Rana, a well-known staunch supporter of the Panchayat system.

Accordingly I went several times to Jeevan Niwas, the beautiful and architecturally noteworthy residence of Prince Gyanendra, to seek an appointment with him. I met an army man named Ganesh whose surname I no longer recall. He was on duty. Although he was of low status, he talked uninhibitedly and responded to me in such a heartfelt manner that I began to share with him my woes. A person's status hardly mattered to me anyhow. If I scorned anyone, it was people who made an excuse of their status to act shabbily.

I returned several times, and Ganesh always raised my hopes by telling me of his efforts to find time with the prince to convey whatever he heard from me. Poor fellow that he was, however, he could not manage to fix an appointment and said that the prince wanted me to contact his ADC Mr. Prakash Shah to arrange things. I visited Mr. Shah several times. He looked very sympathetic and concerned while listening to my story. Alas, the meeting with Prince Gyanendra never materialized.

Then I went to visit Mr. Damodar Shumshere J. B. Rana at his Rana mansion close to the palace. His quarters looked grand, but poor maintenance had taken its toll. The upper roof section was a safe place for flocks of wild pigeons to dirty the verandahs, where a large number of people seeking help — reporters, students, teachers — were waiting for him. I was truly surprised to see such a crowd at his mansion, because he was at that time without any portfolio in the government. In our culture, people do not go to those who have no power and position. Maybe what I had heard about Mr. Rana's influence was true.

By nature I never had any patience to wait long for anything, so I requested his man on duty, Mr. Bharat Rana, to inform his boss, whom he addressed as raja, of my wish to see him if he had time; otherwise I could come back another day. Among the Ranas, men are usually addressed as rajas and women as ranis. I always enjoyed hearing such etiquette.

Within a short period Mr. Rana, dressed in snow-white attire, came himself to receive us amid the crowd and led us to a small, darkish room, where he told me and my husband that he had already heard about the case. I was surprised to hear this, as it was my first visit to him. I requested him to do what he could and left his mansion, expressing my deep gratitude for his assurances of help. He told me to feel free to come to see him whenever necessary. I did in fact visit him several times.

In the meantime I received an invitation from the IFLA (International Federation of Library Associations and Institutions) to participate in an international conference which was to be held in Manila. I was extremely honoured, but I was also in a dilemma whether to go or not during such a critical period. Consulting some of my well-wishers about the problem, I was advised to go to visit the palace general Dan Gamvir Singh Rayamajhi at his residence. I did not know him personally but had seen him several times at parties and also in the library during King Mahendra's visits there. I immediately decided to see him.

On August 4, 1980, at the prearranged time of 8:30 a.m., I set off with my husband to the general's place, which was close to the Chinese embassy. It did not take long to find his modern bungalow with a well-kept garden. It was unusually quiet. There were not the visitors there were at other powerful palace secretaries' residences. Some army men were on duty at the gate. I requested the guard to take our name slip to the general. After a while he came back to lead us to a nicely decorated room and requested us to be seated. Before we could do so the general appeared from within with Mr. L. B. Pandey from the Intelligence Department, whom I had already met and asked for help. This was a pleasant coincidence, but after a simple greeting we were alone with out host.

At first I felt a bit uneasy, as it was my first visit to a palace general. Though not that tall, General Rayamajhi had a commanding personality that would have immediately been felt by anyone. He listened attentively to my story. His few comments set me at ease. I found him shrewd and farsighted. I wished that the palace had had more such persons in its employ. During the crisis he met with me many times despite his busy schedule. He became the greatest source of encouragement to me in my fight against my adversaries and for the truth.

It had been quite some time since I had visited the chief, Mr. Singh, and the joint secretary, Mr. Kul Raj Pandey, of the Special Police Department. I wanted to see them and sound them out before I made a decision to go to the IFLA conference. My husband and I went to see them on August 5, 1980. As soon as the seasoned troublemaker DSP Gopal Bista saw us, he let out with a barrage of words, swearing his innocence by touching the fire of his cigarette and calling on different gods and goddesses as witnesses that he was doing his best to investigate the case properly. I was rather surprised at his changed attitude. I made no comment but silently thanked God for the new tone he was taking.

After a brief meeting with Mr. Pandey I went to see Mr. Singh. He, too, seemed quite different that day: far from putting me off, he prolonged his conversation with me, during which he even mentioned that someone had offered Rs.

Crusade Against Corruption

100,000 as a bribe to him and Rs. 150,000 to Mr. Pandey in the library case; but neither Mr. Pandey nor he had accepted.

I was utterly stunned. In an unbroken flow of words I said, "How could the devils dare to offer you and your deputy bribes? You both were appointed to stamp out crime, including bribery. You are both utter hypocrites. Why didn't you arrest them and put them in jail?"

His reply was even more surprising. Grinningly he said "How could I arrest my own people?"

He told me I should go to Manila to participate in the conference, about which he had heard from the vice-chancellor. My surprise at all the things the chief said that day knew no bounds. Before leaving him I again urged him to punish the devils and be watchful while I was away. He promised to be as fair as he could. I could never judge him properly; his face seemed not to be the mirror of his mind. I was always suspicious of him because he had prolonged the case even after so politely expressing his determination to support the truth. If he was really honest, the case could have been laid to rest within a very short time; he had all the proofs needed to punish the culprit Ram Prasad, who had already confessed to the black deeds and the involvement of his brother, brother-in-law, wife, and others of his own people.

There was thus reason to continue visiting people in power. After the International Women's Year 1975 was over, I no longer had easy access to the palace. An audience either with the king or with the queen would have meant much, but kowtowing was not in my blood.

Suddenly the thought came to my mind that I should visit the queen's parents, General Kendra Shumshere J. B. Rana and Rani Rajya Lakshmi Rana, whom I knew well as very staunch and devoted supporters of the Nepal Red Cross Society from the beginning, before their daughter became queen. I went to see them, sensing that they would react sympathetically to my woes and inform the queen.

It was late morning when my husband and I reached Kendra Niwas, which was surrounded by beautiful bushes and other plants, all making for quiet and pleasant surroundings. I had thought that they would have a fair number of guards and servants in the compound, but we found no one to convey news of our presence to them. I liked the place the better for it. After a while, though, a person approached us and took in our name slip. Shortly thereafter General Kendra and Rani Rajya Lakshmi came to receive us, leading us to a cosy room decorated with indoor plants, many of my favourite ones. We were extremely impressed by their hospitality.

I began my story. Both of my listeners showed great concern and sympathy; Rani Rajya Lakshmi in her extraordinarily soft-spoken way, bade me not to worry and cry; truth would surely triumph — affectionate and touching words. I requested them to convey news of my situation, if possible, to the queen, so that Nepal could be made free from the clutches of evil. It was my strong conviction at that time that the palace was for justice and truth. I had high expectations and hopes.

I revisited the general and more especially Rani Rajya Lakshmi several times. I have never forgotten and would remain grateful to Rani Rajya Lakshmi for her affection and care for me. I admired her not because she was the mother of the queen but for her few consoling and caring words, which mattered a lot to me, especially in a society like ours where jealous people always find ways to make honest people suffer.

During this crisis many people avoided me and I heard many absurd things. One thing I could never forget and could hardly believe was that Dr. Panna Lall Pradhan, one of the seasoned *thekedars* (smooth operators) of the University, told

Crusade Against Corruption

Vice-Chancellor Dr. Mahendra Prasad that the forged signatures were real. I could not understand how Dr. Pradhan, not being a handwriting expert, would dare to make such a comment. Though he had a Ph.D. in psychology, it was sad that he had such a poor understanding of someone who had given her sweat, energy, and time to develop T.U.C.L. as a model in Nepal. Maybe he wanted to please the VC. I knew that he used his professional expertise to advance his own cause with university authorities, no matter who came to the top posts. His keen interest in memorizing educational statistics and important dates in educational development, along with his ability to draft anything in Nepali and English, laid its spell over them. Sometimes he might have been pitied for not getting any top post himself, but when I thought of his salary, which was higher than that of the VC, his ambitions seemed misdirected.

Another shock was when one of my well-wisher told me that Mrs. Angur Baba Joshi, the ex-principal of Padma Kanya Campus, rose at a meeting against my nomination to a committee in view of the case against me. I could not understand why she should do so. I expected the moral support of one who pictured herself as a leader in the fight to uplift trouble-stricken women. Moreover, she could have studied the documents and seen that the whole thing was a frame-up.

Days and months passed with no news from the Special Police Department. Then I heard during a big reception that the villainous DSP Ram Bahadur Thapa had been asked by the department to re-exam my forged signature. I discussed with some officials how he could be trapped for his misdeeds. General Samrajya Shumshere J. B. Rana, an ADC to the king, kindly asked me to visit him. Accordingly I went to Shah Mahal, where I had once gone for many years to tutor his daughter, Netra, and had a long talk with him and his wife,

Crusade Against Corruption

Rani Saraswoti Rana. They took admirable interest and assured their support. The general took great pains to enquire in different departments about the case but to no avail. It seemed that no one paid any heed to him; he was not the normal powerful palace general. Nevertheless I was grateful to him for his unending efforts to give me some peace of mind during this critical period. He never tired of reviewing the matter with me and my husband, often on his own initiative.

Then came a big blow: News of the release on bail of the chief culprit, Ram Prasad Poudyal, was published in the *Gorkhapatra* (the government daily). I was astounded and felt like strangling the whole staff of the Special Police Department involved in the case. The department was said to be carrying out a thorough investigation to ensure that the guilty parties would not escape justice. What outright hypocrisy! My anxiety increased; I had totally lost faith in the chief of the Special Police Department and was suspicious of his every sleek word. I felt helpless, not knowing whom to trust and where to go. Would I lose my battle against the abuse of power and widespread corruption in the country? No, I told myself. By all means truth would win out. I prayed and prayed day and night for strength to continue. After a few days I resumed my visits to officials.

As advised by some, I went to the office of the Adhikar Durupayog Nivaran Ayog (Commission for the Prevention of Misuse of Authority) to fix an appointment with Chief Commissioner Anirudra Prasad Singh, but he was in his office, and as soon as he saw my name slip he kindly called me in. I repeated my same sad tale, about which he had already heard. He, too, felt sorry for me, he said. In benevolent tones he tried to convince me that I should not worry about the forged signature at all, because there were many offices to verify it by using various modern techniques. He assured me of his support

Crusade Against Corruption

if needed and repeated his suggestion to enquire about handwriting experts in India. I was very grateful to him.

Since the Special Police Department was directly under the prime minister's office, I thought it would be useful to see the chief secretary of H.M.G., Mr. Krishna Bahadur Manandhar. An appointment was fixed for August 31, 1980. I had known him as education secretary before he was promoted to the post of chief secretary. He showed deep interest in my plight and advised me to write a brief report. I happened to have a copy of such a report with me, so I surprised him with it. It was the report I had prepared to be circulated to officials just after I was summoned by the Special Police Department. Though he looked quite sympathetic, I did not expect much help from him, as I had heard about how he tended to shirk responsibility. I had the same feeling from talking to him, but I was nevertheless grateful to him for taking and looking at what I had written.

On my way back I was standing on the zebra stripe waiting to cross the road in front of Singha Durbar (H.M.G. Secretariat) when suddenly a taxi stopped next to me and a friendly voice called out, "Shanti, where are your heading? I was so sorry to read the news." I looked around and saw ex-Prime Minister Matrika Prasad Koirala. The light had turned, so I hurriedly told him I would go to his place the next morning. These few words of concern from a distinguished person like him made me really happy. I had known him since my student days in the United States, at which time he was Nepal's ambassador. Whenever I went to Washington he and his wife always poured out their hospitality, letting me enjoy Nepalese food and feel at home at his residence. It was always a joy to visit him and hear of his experiences as prime minister and get a feeling for his deep concern for the future of Nepal.

Crusade Against Corruption

He always struck me as being very knowledgeable and diplomatic — the consummate politician.

The hours of the night ticked by. Early in the morning I set out with my husband. The number of cars in front of the ex-prime minister's place indicated that some kind of meeting of dignitaries was going on. Before I entered his drawing room, Matrikababu came to the door to receive us and led us to the room where a host of top politicians were assembled: ex-Prime Minister Kirti Nidhi Bista, ex-Prime Minister Dr. Tulsi Giri, ex-Chairman of National Panchayat Kamal Raj Regmi, ex-Minister Shailendra Kumar Upadhyaya, ex-Minister D. P. Adhikari, member of the National Panchyat and well-known lawyer Krishna Prasad Pant, and ex-Finance Minister Dr. Yadav Prasad Pant.

What an impressive gathering! It was as if a parallel National Panchayat was in emergency session. I was delighted to be there for the occasion — the perfect opportunity to inform all present about my devil of a case. While I was telling my tale, everyone of them (except Mr. K. P. Pant, who left beforehand) looked utterly sympathetic and astonished. They all said in the same encouraging tones that I should not worry. This was balm to my soul, and I in turn encouraged them to give their urgent attention to the deteriorating situation in the country, where many other sincere and dedicated people, not just me, had suffered and were suffering for things they did not commit. Justice delayed and corruption had taken deep root.

I had tried to convince Mr. Pant to stay and listen, but he refused politely, telling me frankly that he had agreed to be Ram Prasad Poudyal's lawyer. I was extremely surprised to hear this. I asked him pointblank why he, who at the time was raising a storm in the National Panchayat against the army for its corruption, would want to touch such a case. For some moments he was dumb, with a forced smile on his face, but then he told me to understand the spirit of his profession, the ethics of which required him to help any person. I came back at him that I did not care to hear about such worthless ethics and requested him to drop the case and let a lesser man take it. He, being an honourable member of the National Panchayat, should not speak for the devil against the truth. I was glad he did not argue with me, because otherwise I would have given full vent to my temper; I already had heard that his sister, Mrs. Angur Baba Joshi, had raised her voice against me, as I have mentioned before. Mr. Pant had taken the devil's case. Oh, how I hated to think that they were against me, pouring butter rather than water into the blazing fire. I had always had high regards for the family.

When I was almost on the point of shouting, everyone else seemed to start paying attention to our conversation, though they didn't intervene as I over and over requested Mr. Pant to renounce his commitment. Later, having had my say and expressing my deep gratitude to all the dignitaries for their kind concern, I left.

I was tired both mentally and physically. I hardly could recall how often I had visited different temples and influential persons. I tried very hard not to forget to recite the prayers I was told by Yogi Nijananda and the astrologer Prof. Mangal Raj Joshi. Alas, nothing seemed to move the stumbling stone erected by the devils to deny access to the truth. It had been more than six months. If God had not nestled me closed to his bosom, I would have gone mad. What a torture it was to wait day and night for justice so long!

The crass complicity of certain staff members of the Special Police Department, the complicity of the handwriting expert, and the utter inhumanity of the chief were something out of a nightmare. If I had had the power to, I would have put them together in a cell where they could lament their past deeds and

Crusade Against Corruption

see how an innocent person was being reduced to total despair for their convenience.

On November 12, 1980 I saw the chief of the Special Police Department, Mr. Singh, at the airport where all the special classes of His Majesty's Government and the University were present to see off the king and queen on their state visit to the United Kingdom. As soon as Mr. Singh saw me, he became nervous and tried to avoid me. I was curious to find out the reason for such a changed attitude; he always used to be bold and forthright. He was going about his duty of tactful *namastes* to high officials when at last I maneuvered right in front of him. He threw an irritated wordless look at me. Before he could get away I asked him whether he had received the promised report from outside on my forged signature. His angry reply was that this was not the right place to be discussing such things. I became furious and tried to cut into him with sharp words. He then disappeared from the scene. I was ready for a big fight even amidst the highest dignitaries of Nepal, who immediately came to express their concern to me.

I returned from the airport distraught, my head spinning. Things would get tougher but I was not a bit worried because I knew God was with me. I felt immune from all evil plots and conspiracies with God as my saviour.

My well-wishers advised me to keep low for some time, so I did. But then something dreadful happened. It was the middle of the morning, about 9:30, November 14, 1980. Two unknown persons in *daura, suruwal* and caps (the national dress) came knocking at my door with an unbelievable and astonishing message. They both looked out of the ordinary — not pleasing at all. I became very suspicious of them and informed my husband. I told him to be very careful before letting them into our house; we had already heard different things about the plans to send gangsters against us.

Crusade Against Corruption

My husband slowly opened the door. Both of them performed a *namaste* in a very respectful manner. I was watching from upstairs. After a brief conversation, they were brought into our living room, having requested entry to deliver a message regarding the ongoing case — a highly confidential message. I came down to meet them. They showed respect for me as if they were minions, but I was not happy with their visit at all.

I straightaway asked them what the confidential message was and who sent them with it. Both of them looked nervous, their eyes moving all around, as if even the walls could hear. The message was from the same crooked police official; if I gave him some money, arrangements could easily be made to change all the papers, prepared by Ram Prasad Poudyal, blaming me for the black deeds. No questions about my forged signature would be asked.

It was a cruel and unexpected turn indeed — illicitly asking for money from a person who had always raised her voice against such evil practices. I was too furious to listen any further, but my husband tried to dig deeper. Finally I could no more control myself and told them, "Why should I give money? I didn't do anything. Go and ask money from the real culprit, or better yet, stop working as agents for the devils." Both of them stared at me with great surprise.

At first no words came from them for a while, but then one of them slowly opened his mouth and politely explained to me that I should not take them amiss; they had come to help me escape from the trap with all good intentions. Although they looked dull-witted, their method of approach was that of trained and experienced agents, so I was on high alert, more than they could guess. I wanted to tape their visit but it was so sudden and unexpected that it would have been impossible, so I did not prolong my dealings with them. Studying my bad mood, both of them requested with folded hands that I think over their offer; they would come back. If they did, I would have my tape recorder ready for them. Before they left, though, I reiterated my negative reply: I would not give even a single pice. Without comment they left.

Oh, I was relieved to see them go, because their every word was poison to my ears. I discussed with my husband for hours how best to get them arrested along with the villain who sent them. We wished we knew some tactics used by detectives, but unfortunately we had very little such knowledge, so we decided to visit the chief of intelligence of H.M.G., Mr. C.B. Rai, for his advice and, if possible, help.

The next day, on November 15, 1980, at 3 p.m., my husband and I went by appointment to Mr. Rai's residence. He was very kind to receive us on such short notice at his simple bungalow. His modest bearing and open hospitality encouraged me to speak my mind freely. I told him first briefly about the origin of the case, subsequent developments, and finally about the most recent event. Mr. Rai, seasoned in these matters, did not take long to understand how things stood. I was impressed by his analysis of the plot and the attempted extortion.

He had a plan. He would provide us with some of his staff equipped with tiny modern tape recorders and a telescopic camera to take photographs of the unknown visitors. He requested me to inform him as soon as they came back to my place as they had promised they would. Thanking him for his assurances of help, we returned home.

The next day, as usual, I went to the library and took the opportunity to do some research on detectives so that I, too, could be better prepared for the task at hand. I took two books on the subject home to share with my husband. In the meantime I wrote a few letters to the handwriting specialists in India to enquire about their methodology in case I needed their expertise.

Crusade Against Corruption

After the visit of the two unknown agents, I tensed up whenever there was any knocking at our door. Each knock seemed worse than the last. I wanted to stamp out the evil of extortion by severe punishment if I could, but I knew quite well by this time that this might be impossible to accomplish easily. My determination, though, was strong.

My husband and I again visited Prime Minister Surya Bahadur Thapa, Home Minister Nava Raj Subedi, Palace General Dan Gambir Singh Rayamajhi, ADC to the king Shanta Kumar Malla, Palace Principal Secretary Khanal, and General Samrajya to inform them about recent developments. General Rayamajhi and Principal Secretary Khanal, as always, took keen interest and told me to secure the tapes if possible. I was quite emboldened to screw up my courage and fight the devils as directed by my conscience and my God. I knew it would be hard to inflict a direct open blow upon the cynical police officer who was in charge of the case, but there was no fear in my mind; I was determined to hit hard, assured of divine help in my fight.

Braced now to start my real war against the devils, I urgently wanted the agents to come back. Days had passed and there was still no sign of them. Perhaps my fiery words had scared them off. About a week later, however, on November 20, one of them returned. It was 10 a.m. and I was getting ready to go to the library. I went to open the door, and my husband hurriedly went to turn on the tape recorder.

For about one hour we carried on a conversation with the man. He told us that his name was Krishna Bahadur and that his friend's name was Bhaju Bir, a friend of DSP Gopal Bista of the Special Police Department. My husband found an excuse to go to our neighbour and requested that a photo be taken of our guest on the way out. He came back so quickly that I was doubtful whether he had been successful. Presently, though, he

243

gave me the high sign with his look, so I brought our conversation to an end. The man was escorted out, and our neighbour, Mr. Shakya, managed to take the photo without being noticed.

Our man seemed to have fallen into the trap. He promised himself to help us, saying that he and his friend would come back with a clear message. It was equally important for us, of course, to record his friend.

We hurriedly went to turn off the recorder, but to our great dismay we found that nothing was on it, as the wrong bottom had been pushed. We spent useless time blaming each other. What a shame, I thought. I prayed for the intermediaries' soon return.

Bhaju Bir and Krishna Bahadur kept low for almost a month. They were cunning and of course did not tell us how we could contact them. But finally, early in the morning of December 8, they returned.

When the doorbell rang I felt it must be them, and I went to peep out from my room. There they were, standing at my door. My husband was still in the prayer room, performing the daily worship. I did not open the door immediately; with great care we set the tape going.

My husband went to receive them. Since it was early they wanted to go to a nearby tea shop before getting down to business. My husband readily agreed. They would come back after twenty minutes, they said. What a wonderful chance for me to call Chief Rai of Intelligence for his help, as he had suggested I do. He could send his staff with a small but powerful recorder and telescopic camera. I got through to him, but his response was quite different from what I expected. His staff, he said, were already out on duty, but if anyone came back he would definitely send them. In any case, we ourselves were ready to tape and film.

Crusade Against Corruption

The doorbell rang after about half an hour. We quickly pushed the button to start the tape — this time the proper one — and then went to receive them. We led them to where we entertained guests and got them to sit on seats close to the recorder. They looked more at ease than before. I too tried to act as if I had changed my attitude totally and was ready to do a deal with them. They lighted up, thinking their mission a great success and anticipating a lump sum of money as their share. I was pleased with myself that I could put on such an act that the agents felt free to discuss things with us without any fear and suspicion.

Forty-five minutes passed. I was worried how to change the tape. Just then my friend Robert Palmer, the Fulbright librarian working for me in T.U.C.L., appeared at my door as if God had sent him. We told the agents to step out for a while under the pretext of having something special to talk about with our foreign friend. Without any hesitation they agreed. Bob knew about the first visit and how we had bungled the tape. He proceeded to put on a new tape more quickly than we ever could have. That done, I requested him to take photographs of them. We went outside and told the agents that my friend was very interested in taking photos in their national dress. They were happy to oblige. Bob took some shots, expressed his thanks in broken Nepali, and headed on to the library. We took the agents back inside to resume our conversation. The tape was running. They left after an hour; altogether they were with us for more than two hours. My husband and I framed our conversation in such a way that there would be real proof of the plot hatched against me.

We spent two hours listening to the tape we recorded. What a foul business! It was unimaginable that humans could be so depraved, all the more so given that they were people whose responsibility it was to punish wrong and reward honesty.

Crusade Against Corruption

I was extremely happy that I had achieved my goal to collect irrefutable evidence. I felt I had won the battle. Soon I was again visiting high officials and dignitaries to inform them of the success of my mission. Everyone told me to preserve the tapes very carefully; if need be, they would ask me to make copies. Requesting their confidentiality, I returned home in a happy mood.

On December 12, 1980 my husband and I went to see the chief of the Special Police Department to enquire about further developments in the investigation of the case. Before going to the chief's office, though, we dropped in to see DSP Gopal Bista and feel him out regarding the agents sent to us to get money. As soon as he saw us he turned blue and let out his feelings. "What do you gain by making allegations against a lowly officer like me? You'll certainly be in for more trouble. I have not been further concerned with your case." Bista's comments did not surprise me. Immediately I remembered the Nepali proverb "A thief when accused protests loudly" (*jo chor usaiko thulo shor*). Without giving him further opportunity to prolong his nonsensical comments, I walked out. His remarks alone were enough to cast suspicion on him.

Since the chief was not in his office, I went to Mr. Pandey, the joint secretary, to ask him why Bista was behaving so. As usual Mr. Pandey received me politely. He was quick to tell us that the chief had asked Bista whether he had sent any of his men to ask for money. That had doubtless vexed him. He told me that I should come back in two weeks. I left to rejoin my husband, who was waiting downstairs close to DSP Bista's office. On the way down I heard the loud quarrelling voices of my husband and the DSP. I ran to the spot and saw Bista positioned like a black fighting cock, mouthing obscenities, and ready to hit my husband in mock defence of his dark deeds. My husband also seemed about to lose control of himself. His

Crusade Against Corruption

fiery words against the DSP made the latter even madder. I could sense only trouble, so I pushed my husband by force from that unsought battlefield. Who knew but whether DSP Bista, more powerful than his bosses, might take my husband into custody on the basis of false allegations as he had just threatened to do. We were lucky, though, that most of the staff of the Special Police Department showed a real spirit of impartiality.

In the meantime Chief Singh had come to his office. My husband and I made our way there. It seemed he had already heard about the tug. To our great surprise he asked us to give proofs of the attempted extortion by DSP Bista. We straightaway refused and told him that he had not performed his duty properly: he should not have disclosed the matter to Bista without having conducted an investigation. The ruse was up; no one would come back again for money. I really got terribly mad at him and told him to get the proofs from the person who had disclosed the matter to him. I could not right away guess who might have told him, as we had visited so many officials.

When Mr. Singh saw me in high temper, his attitude seemed to change. He pushed his calling bell, and an attendant appeared. The latter was asked to summon Mr. Pandey and DSP Bista. Mr. Singh was visibly blushing, so I refrained from further comments. His usually calm face had taken on a lamentable look, and I was inwardly enjoying seeing him that way. After a while Mr. Pandey and DSP Bista came with joined hands in a gesture of respect to the chief, as is the custom in Nepal's offices. No sound was uttered for some moments. I wanted to affect the scene with my own silence, which could speak loudest in such a situation. Mr. Singh began to reprimand the DSP for uttering obscenities to my husband

and ordered him to remove himself from the case from that day on.

Oh, what a joyous relief for me and my husband to hear the chief's decision! With deep gratitude to God, my husband and I returned home and stopped worrying for a while what would happen next. But one thing still pricked me: the identity of the person who told Mr. Singh of our plan to catch the devils red-handed taking money from me. I was dead sure that the agents wouldn't come back, and in fact they never did. I smelt the stench of the devil everywhere. Most of the people in power and position had come to seem more like hucksters than patriots, and the tools of their trade were wealth and connections.

When my tormentors failed to squeeze money out of me, they hatched another plot to harass me with the connivance of the same culprit, Ram Prasad. S. B. Thakur and some of the auditor general's staff were behind this plot. Their idea was to raise the question of physical verification of the library stock in T.U. Central Library in order to divert attention to the issue of loss of books. In any developing country this has always been a burning issue. Some top people in the administration have always tried to make library staff responsible for any book losses — an unreasonable and unprofessional attitude bound to discourage any sensible person from joining the library profession. Ever since I started my career I had been slowly working with the administration to solve the problem in such a way that the library staff would be held responsible only for losses due to their own negligence or dishonesty. It was unjust to have honest people paying for others' crimes. The University still had failed to redefine its policy regarding the loss of books despite my draft proposal. One of the clauses stated that all library staff, including the chief librarian, would

Crusade Against Corruption

be punished as thieves if they were found guilty of stealing books. There was no excuse for such dereliction of duty.

On January 11, 1981 I heard from my staff that an unknown person named Sagar had come from the Office of Auditor General to meet me. I had not been in the library that day. I immediately asked my assistant to call the man and fix a time to meet him in the library. To my great surprise, though, he avoided meeting me in spite of several calls. Then I contacted several high officials of the auditor general's office in order to inform them of the attempt from the outside to harass me and also to give them a brief idea of inventory or stock-taking as practised in developed countries, where the library profession has been duly recognized. Whenever I talked with them, either over the phone or in my own office, they had neither questions nor criticisms. I always found them to be silent listeners. For weeks no one except a person in a yellow shirt, a disciple of Rajneesh, came to the library from the staff of auditor general's office to talk about the inventory. I was satisfied that they understood my point about the unnecessary auditing of every book.

One afternoon, on March 16, 1981, I decided to go to the registrar to inform him about the suspected foul play relating to the inventory instigated by Ram Prasad, who had told Dhyan Kaji that he would create just such a problem for me when they were put together in custody. I also mentioned S. B. Thakur and my recent contact with the officials of the auditor general's office. To my great surprise, when I entered the registrar's office I found a group of officers — Mr. G. P. Gorkhali (a financial adviser), Mr. S. R. Sharma (the chief), Mr. Ganesh Pradhan and Mr. Min Bahadur Shrestha from the Financial Administration Section of the University, and one Purushottam Bahadur Shrestha (director of the auditor general's office) — discussing the very topic of stocktaking and

Crusade Against Corruption

inventory in T.U. Central Library. I was furious that they had arranged to have such a meeting without me. I always remembered what the great librarian of India Dr. S. R. Ranganathan wrote in his *Library Manual for Library Authorities, Librarians and Honorary Library Workers*:

> Sometimes an unscrupulous person uses the inevitable loss of books in a library as a stick to beat the librarian against whom he has developed a grudge for some reason or other. In some libraries, such a top management man even deliberately concocts false loss to wreak his vengeance on the librarian. These antisocial persons are a menace to society. Public opinion should grow strong enough to eliminate such persons from positions of power.

I quietly listened to their discussion. The registrar asked me if I wanted to say something. I felt like bursting out, "And how!" But I just nodded my head. The registrar gave me the floor. It was a good opportunity to make a speech on conducting inventory and who should be involved in the work — the answer to which was definitely not the auditor general's office. A library is not like a bank, and books are not to be counted like money. Money is kept under lock and key, but everyone should have free access to book collections, according to the modern concept of library science.

After my brief speech I posed some pertinent questions to the official from the auditor general's office, such as why after decades the question of inventory should suddenly be raised for the first time in the history of the library. Was the idea to help the library to adopt some good measures to prevent future loss or was it to defame the library and its staff by distorting the matter and to harass it by threatening to make them pay for losses from their salary.

I could have asked many more questions, but instead I explained how I conducted physical verification of some of the important sections of the library to provide better services to the users, even before anyone thought to take inventory. I told them that the library followed the general procedures listed below, as spelled out by well-known librarian Guy R. Lyle in his book *The Administration of the College Library.*

1. Arranging the books in correct order on the shelves,
2. Comparing the shelf-list cards in their order with the corresponding books on the shelves and noting any books not found there,
3. Checking the record of books not located with the circulation records and other records which might account for these books,
4. Making a periodic search for missing books,
5. Replacing lost books which are needed by the library, and
6. Cancelling or withdrawing catalogue records of books not found or replaced.

Since so many professional procedures were already involved, no inventory seemed called for from the auditor in the first place. That the question was being raised under the present circumstances made me all the more suspicious.

I was pleased that everyone seemed impressed by my presentation. They themselves decided to drop the matter for the time being. I had, I thought, been able to convince them of the possibility of foul play. Still, things did not evolve as smoothly as I expected. On April 1, 1981 a confidential letter from the vice-chancellor's office was delivered to me, marked urgent. It sent my blood pressure soaring, containing as it did the vice-chancellor's order to let the staff of the auditor general's office carry out the inventory in the library. For days I had no peace. I was not against the inventory, but as a professional I was deadly against the methodology sure to be used. To unburden myself of my rankling fears, I wrote a long letter to the vice-chancellor — a veritable thesis on inventorying with examples from other countries — and in the end got around to the question of the behind-the-scenes intriguing by my tormentors.

On April 6, 1981 I sent copies of the letter written to the vice-chancellor to the rector and the registrar. Whatever its effect would be, it was at least a record of the truth based on professional criteria. I knew quite well that the auditor general's office could not do the job properly in the stipulated period. Some of the people involved I suspected of being tools of my adversaries, but this was not my headache. I was determined to provide all the facilities and help they needed to do their job, that of auditing the library collection of more than 150,000 items.

The team from the auditor general's office along with some staff of the Financial Administration Section of the University started their work in May. At their request I closed the library to facilitate work. After some months they told me they had finished the job but had to work some more on the outside before preparing a report on the inventory.

With keen interest I waited for their report. Who knew but whether they might have miraculously really done their job. If so, well and good. Eventually a very thin report did come out, but to my great surprise the auditor general's office had included a brief paragraph on the inventory system of the library, putting all the blame on me and making me the scapegoat for their inability and failure to complete the inventory in their traditional way within the stipulated period.

Crusade Against Corruption

I was utterly furious by the time I reached the end of that deplorable paragraph. It was becoming almost impossible to cope with all these things one after another. I talked with God, and being close to Him brought me new strength. I was determined to challenge the auditor general's office for releasing such a baseless report — another battle in the prolonged struggle for truth.

I went to the newly appointed registrar, Mr. Netra Bahadur Basnet, to arrange for me to comment on the report before all the Financial Committee members of the National Panchayat. Registrar Basnet, a good friend of T.U. Central Library was himself not happy about the turn of events and promised me that he would invite me to speak after fixing the time with the chairman of the committee, Mr. Bhagawati Das Shrestha, who also showed sympathy when I later met him.

I was invited to speak. All the members of the committee along with a top official of the auditor general's office, Mr. Gehendra Nath Adhikari, and the registrar, Mr. Basnet, were present for the meeting. I took more than one hour to refute all the charges laid by the auditor general's office in their report and to explain in brief the professional methodology of inventorying practised by libraries in other nations. Although I tried to control myself, I must have sounded on edge.

Mr. Adhikari, who had agreed with what I had told him when he came to the library before the taking of the inventory, now looked blue in the face. He took the floor to defend himself but did not sound convincing. It is always easier to speak the truth than to concoct baseless stories.

I expressed my sincere thanks to all committee members present for their attention. Some of my friends told me later on that I did not do the right thing in challenging such a high governmental body. My reply to them was very simple. My comments were not a made-up story against the auditor general's office but based on fact, so I had to speak out. So long as God was with me I feared no one.

Some well-wishers advised me to go to Mr. Ram Prasad Joshi, the auditor general. Mr. Joshi was unknown to me, and I was not that bent on visiting him, yet my friends' insistence weighed heavily.

The signs were not good. As soon as I reached Mr. Joshi's office, it started to rain heavily. Mr. Joshi came to receive me without a welcoming smile on his reserved face, as if he was not pleased with my visit. I myself was not at ease at the beginning of the meeting. I slowly began to tell him the reason I had come. He seemed to have been fed so many stories by his staff about the library and me that he had no room left for the truth, but I did not worry. If he was a man of principle, truth-loving and humane, he would succumb to the force of my argument. Gradually I noticed a change come into his face and whole attitude, which gave me a thrill. The rain helped to prolong my visit so that I could say the things that were required to clear up the misunderstanding in his mind.

He offered me a cup of savoury tea and began to tell me of his different duties and activities — a brief curriculum vitae: He had been a school teacher and then a finance secretary of H.M.G., had been dismissed from the secretarial post in 1962, had found a job at UNDP, and had eventually become the auditor general. It was a very inspiring story, I told him.

At the end of my visit he assured me that he would enquire into the matter as soon as Mr. Adhikari was back from Australia. I told Mr. Joshi that I knew Mr. Adhikari and that he had never failed to show his regards to me whenever I happened to meet him, so I always thought that he had high regards for the library profession too. It was beyond comprehension how his mind could have been poisoned against me. Our culture does not encourage mutual trust, and I was a

Crusade Against Corruption

fool myself to trust people. In any case, I was happy that I had visited Mr. Joshi. He seemed to understand me and my professional approach to inventories quite well — a good omen not only for T.U. Central Library but for all the libraries under government control as well.

Shortly thereafter a divinely guided thought came to my mind, namely that this was the right time to push the university authorities, with the support of the Library Committee, to approve the draft on inventory policy I had submitted long back. With the permission of the chairman, I called several meetings to discuss the matter. In spite of some heated arguments and unnecessary amendments, the practice of taking inventory in the Central Library and the campus libraries of the University in the standard professional way became approved policy, as of November 27, 1984.

It had been more than eight months, and still there was no news from the Special Police Department. I kept recalling the chief's promises to get my forged signature examined on the outside and wondered how much longer I'd have to suffer mental agony. Quite often questions to God arose in my mind: Why did I, a fighter for the truth and for the development of the institution, have to undergo all this? Whatever the answer, I never stopped praying.

It was on February 26, 1981 that I got a call from the joint secretary of the Special Police Department to come to his office. My husband and I set off posthaste, hoping to hear the true report on my forged signature. Alas, I was merely asked to put my signature ten times on each of six pieces of white foolscap. I wondered why they were gathering specimens after so many months; they should have taken them long before involving the handwriting expert in Nepal. Once again this whole drama was going off on a tangent, and I failed to understand why. Without any argument I signed.

Crusade Against Corruption

Mr. Pandey seemed eager to prove that he was trying to send the case to court as quickly as possible. He politely asked me not to worry and to phone him after a week. That week seemed never to end. When it finally did I called him, but to my great dismay he had no news. Incredibly, I had to wait another two and half months to hear anything. I don't remember how many times I went downtown to enquire. My expectation of hearing the truth kept me going during that critical time.

It was two o'clock in the afternoon of May 1, 1981, and I was on my way yet again to the joint secretary of the Special Police Department. I found him in his office with not a word on his tongue. After a while I broke the silence by putting the standard question to him: Had the report come and was any date fixed for the court case? Without even the hint of a smile he gave me the long-awaited happy news. I was freed from the charges: the Central Bureau of Investigation (CBI) in India had proved that my signature was forged by the devil Ram Prasad Poudyal himself. Thus I would get back title to the property offered as security.

I literally jumped for joy. It was the end of my eleven months of mental torture and unnecessary harassment. I felt the hand of God and wanted to offer my gratitude for His never-failing guidance, having sensed His presence everywhere blessing me. On that day almost every staff member of the Special Police Department seemed cheerful; they were prompt to prepare the necessary documents releasing my pledge. Oh, what a relief! Everything looked so gay and bright.

I returned home to tell my ten-year-old daughter that I was free from the clutches of the devils, but as soon as she saw me she herself told me tenderly, "Muma (mother), perhaps you won the battle because when you went to the police I was alone in the room praying and praying." Her words surprised us beyond belief; how had she guessed the truth? Tears of joy rolled down my cheeks, and I embraced her, saying, "Yes, darling daughter, with the grace of God I won the battle."

Exactly one month later, on June 1, 1981, the case was filed in the Bagmati Special Court against the architect of the misappropriation of Rs. 429,874.68 of funds from T.U. Central Library, in particular for having submitted forged bills to the Financial Administration Section of the University without supplying any books and periodicals to the library. Now my great concern was to get the money back. Alas, it took more than ten years, up to 1991, and then it was only the original amount. It was a defect of the law not to have charged interest, and I went to complain to the Kanun Sudhar Ayog (Law Reformation Committee). Up to now I don't know whether any useful changes have been introduced into law to punish such criminals properly.

This library case was an eye-opener to me concerning the real state of the country. From an investigation conducted by the Special Police Department upon the forged letters, their registration, and the non-existent book accessions, nothing amiss was found within the library: no involvement on the part of the chief librarian and staff members was discovered, and no money was found to have been drawn from the library; it was, in fact, the library that initiated the investigation. There were dozens of such arguments, and it was, ironically, only because of a forged signature that I, as chief librarian, had to suffer for such a long time. I came out of the bitter and horrible experiences hardened and wiser. It is a great tragedy that people in power often blunt their sense for what is right. Everyone enjoys shifting responsibility and no one pushes for the truth. Temporizing is everywhere in evidence; otherwise it would not have taken more than ten years to get the money back from the culprit. O God, only you can save Nepal!

Chapter 10

The UN General Assembly Thirty-second Session

It was a long-cherished desire of mine to go to the UN General Assembly as a Nepalese delegate. Every year one woman is included in the Nepalese delegation, not so much on the basis of her contribution to the nation's development but because pressure and influence has been brought to bear. Not wishing to employ such means, I had never had an opportunity to represent my country before that forum. Delegates to no matter what conference, seminar, or symposium should be selected among honest, dedicated, and knowledgeable people who have contributed to the development process of the nation and who can truly represent it. But in developing countries, things always tend to take a different turn. I had once, in fact, expressed my opinion on the subject to the queen, as I was always being encouraged at that time to comment on anything I found amiss.

It was in the month of August 1977. To my great surprise, the king's private secretary, Narayan Prasad Shrestha, suddenly appeared with his impeccably wife in T.U. Central Library and informed me in a somewhat offhand fashion that my name had been proposed to be included among the Nepalese delegation to the UN. No comment seemed called for from me because it was all so vague. He left the library as quickly as he had arrived. I was elated to hear of the proposal but could not decide how to follow up on it. The only thing to do was to keep praying that it be true.

Later I got a call from the king's personal secretary, Gehendra Man Singh, informing me that, as commanded by

The UN General Assembly Thirty-second Session

Her Majesty the queen, he had instructed the Foreign Ministry to include me among the Nepalese delegation to the UN. I requested him to convey my deep gratitude to the queen for giving me this opportunity. My long-cherished desire to go to the UN was being fulfilled. I was thankful to God. As a librarian, I would normally have never got such an opportunity, as Nepalese society was not yet ready to accept librarianship as one of the top professions needed for building the nation.

I very eagerly waited for a formal letter from the Foreign Ministry. I did not disclose news of my forthcoming trip to the UN till I got the letter, having learnt by many bitter experiences that words are often one thing and deeds another. It was already very late to be preparing myself for such global meetings, I thought, yet I dared not ask for the formal letter outright. To prepare or not to prepare? I decided to go through different documents published by the UN, especially ones concerning developing countries and key donors to the UN, so that I could make some contribution to the committee sessions, even if only a modest one. I wished that my voice, projecting the views of a small but beautiful country, might be heard.

I was quite fortunate to have the UN collection in the library, which had been recognized in 1965, upon my initiative, as the UN depository for Nepal. I always took great pride in telling our distinguished visitors that the library was a UN depository and that it had done much to disseminate the information provided by the world body to help all nations, especially developing ones, to speed their development and to avoid committing the same mistakes made by developed countries regarding the environment, the preservation of culture, and the like. Exhibitions devoted to UN activities, its agencies, and publications were organized to mark important occasions, with or without support from the United Nations

The UN General Assembly Thirty-second Session

Development Project (UNDP) of Nepal. UNDP, Nepal was very cooperative in the beginning (the 1960's and 1970's). Resident representatives — Herbert Grantham, Andrew Joseph, and Jacob J. Joury — were praiseworthy supporters of T.U.C.L. Mr. Tulsi Nath Dhungel and Mr. Shankar Mani Poudyal of the UN Nepali staff were also faithful supporters. With the help of American Peace Corp and Japanese aid volunteers, I brought out such publications as *United Nations Depository for the Kingdom of Nepal: An Introduction to Periodical Publications,* compiled by Barbara Haven (1974), *Catalogue of Reference Books in the United Nations Collection of Tribhuvan University Central Library,* compiled by Nobue Yamada (1982), and *Catalogue of United Nations' Periodicals,* compiled by Yuriko Yanaka (1984), and distributed them to palace secretaries, planners, policy-makers, teachers, and friends of the library, hoping that they might benefit from the thoughts of UN experts.

At last, on August 26, 1977, just seventeen days before the delegation was to leave for New York, my letter came from the Foreign Ministry. It was a copy of the letter, written to the vice-chancellor of the University, requesting that I be deputed to join the delegation according to the decision of H.M.G. It was now certain that I was going to the UN as a delegate to the Thirty-second Session of the UN General Assembly, which was to start on September 20, 1977.

Although I had easy access to UN publications, I still knew very little about the procedures followed in conducting UN committee meetings. I had many queries to make at the UN section of the Foreign Ministry. A brief introduction to such procedures and to the role the delegates were expected to play in that global setting, along with a meeting with high officials of the ministry, would have been very helpful, I thought, but nothing was arranged.

The UN General Assembly Thirty-second Session

I got another letter authorizing me to collect my travel allowance and daily allowance (TADA). When I went to collect it I was informed by Dr. Jagadish Sharma, another delegate, that I was not being given the allowance according to my status. I expressed my gratitude for the information. My status at that time was equivalent to that of a joint secretary. I was confused and began searching out the truth. I wondered how the ministry could justify reducing my status and giving me a low TADA. Maybe they thought that a librarian could not be the equal of a joint secretary because in government libraries most of the librarians are non-professional persons occupying clerical posts.

I went around to all the concerned high officials and put the question to them flatly what right they had to lower my status. It was a fact that government officials were always uneasy with university teachers and staff and that they never liked to accept them as their equals. Many unpleasant arguments took place on the subject between such officials and me. In the end I was assured that in the near future I would receive a TADA commensurate with my status, with the unpaid portion being forwarded to my address in New York. It was not so much the money, however, as the status I was fighting for. I was requested to accept the money given to me according to their own determination of what my status should be: that of an undersecretary. I accepted the check, as they knew I would, there being no time to fight the battle through to the end. Occasionally I felt I should have taught them a lesson by refusing to join the delegation, as my own dignity and that of university teachers was at stake. Material gain was the last thing I cared for.

Having marshalled what assurances I could, I got busy collecting documents on Nepalese women, youth, social services, foreign relations, and like topics to carry with me so

The UN General Assembly Thirty-second Session

that I could represent my country well. My small suitcase was full of such material. I did not carry many saris, having been told that they could be bought cheaply in New York. For that matter, I never cared much for fashion anyhow. I always loved to look like a simple Nepalese lady with sari and blouse. When I opened my suitcase at airport customs, the checkers seemed surprised to find so few dresses and so many documents. I gave them a big smile. They closed the suitcase.

I left Kathmandu for New York with a Nepalese delegation consisting of Mr. K. B. Shahi, Dr. Jagadish Sharma, and Mr. Kumar P. Gyawali. Foreign Minister Krishna Raj Aryal, the leader of the delegation, was to come after some days.

I was so happy to be back in the States after more than fourteen years. The delegation was received at the airport on September 18, 1977 by the staff of the Permanent Mission of the Kingdom of Nepal to the United Nations. My friend Nancy's parents, Mr. and Mrs. Robert S. Winter, were also waiting to welcome me. It was a great joy for me to see them, as they were always so affectionate and loving. I had thoroughly enjoyed the trip by Lufthansa from Frankfort to New York. I always loved to take Lufthansa, which I think one of the best airlines in the world. Whenever I go by it, I'm always taking note of things Royal Nepal Airlines might imitate to make their services even better.

By the time I reached Hotel Sutton it was late afternoon. Everything had been arranged by the Permanent Mission. All male delegates shared a flat close to the UN building. My hotel was far away, yet I liked it: it was quiet and comfortable, if expensive, and I had no one to share it with the way male delegates did. I preferred to be by myself in peaceful surroundings. All in all, I was quite pleased with the arrangements.

The UN General Assembly Thirty-second Session

It was Sunday, so most of the shops were closed. Nor was I in a mood to go sightseeing. I slept without taking dinner, eating only some fruits and thinking of my husband and our six-year-old daughter.

I woke up to a beautiful morning with unusually bright sunshine. The sun's rays were all the more beautiful for filtering down between the tall buildings of New York. I went out to take a morning walk, stopping along the way at a nearby grocery store to buy some milk, bread, fruits, and eggs in preparation for a good breakfast. When I was in the States as a student I always loved to do shopping at the grocery, where you have your whole domestic world in front of you — everything you need for running a household. It was very fascinating, though I always had problems deciding what to buy — a very different situation from the shopping system in Nepal, where you go from one place to another to buy things.

Having returned, I prepared a five-star breakfast in my hotel. I enjoyed it all the more for not having had dinner the previous night. After breakfast I went to our mission to attend a meeting called by Mr. Shailendra Kumar Upadhyaya, the permanent representative of Nepal to the UN. I had seen him several times at parties in Nepal but had never been introduced to him. Now I had the chance to be. He looked quite different in his diplomatic suit — very tiptop. He tried to look younger than his age, I thought. He looked, in fact, as much like an aristocrat as a diplomat.

Mr. Upadhyaya presided over the first meeting of the Nepalese delegates in an impressive way. All the delegates were given the responsibility of representing Nepal on different committees of the UN. I was given responsibility for the Third and Sixth committees. If I needed any information I could consult Dr. Mohan Prasad Lohani, the deputy permanent

The UN General Assembly Thirty-second Session

representative of the Mission. Another staff member of the Mission, Mr. Gopi Nath Dawadi, was kind enough to acquaint me with all UN procedures and to accompany me to the committee meetings.

I was extremely anxious to watch the opening of the Thirty-second Session of the General Assembly. It was first announced that the meeting would start at 3 p.m., but 3 p.m. turned into 5 p.m. — so much like Nepalese time, I thought.

I was extremely proud to be representing my country in the Assembly. Next to me was a delegate from the Netherlands. I set about introducing myself to the delegates from that country, but then the function started in a very grand manner in that most imposing historic hall, with all the delegates from all the different parts of the world wearing their national costumes. The whole assembly looked like a great map of the world decorated by the delegates themselves. It was utterly unique. I silently expressed my deep gratitude to those who had worked for Nepal's admission to the United Nations in 1955.

It was a memorable evening for me. After going back to my hotel I got a very loving call from my friend Patty Glass. I enjoyed talking to her over the phone after such a long time. She had first been in Nepal as a Teach Corps volunteer and then taught at the Lincoln School in Kathmandu. She was introduced to me by Nancy as her bosom friend before Nancy left Nepal in 1972. Pat remained on to cheer us up whenever we missed Nancy and her family. We all, especially my daughter, always enjoyed her regular visits. She was a great admirer of Dr. Bethel Fleming's contribution to medical services in Nepal. Many sweet memories came back to me. She promised to visit me in New York while I was in the States.

It was already late, yet I could not sleep so I turned on the TV, but the shows were not to my liking. I turned it off and began to read the agendas of the meetings which I got that morning from the office. Going through them, I wondered how I could digest their content within such a short time. I should have received them months before so that I could coolly think, consult, and discuss with experts about the different topics before coming to the UN. I could have presented some new resolutions on behalf of our delegation, I thought. Why did it all have to be so confidential up till the last moment before departure? I failed to come to any conclusions. I prayed for divine guidance so that I could represent my country and contribute, even if in a very small way, to the noble objectives of the meeting of the UN. These thoughts lulled me to sleep.

The next morning I woke up quite early. I prepared my breakfast with toast, egg, juice, and a glass of cold milk — my favorite combination. Usually I avoided bus rides, preferring instead to walk. It took about forty minutes to reach the UN building. This day I reached my destination at exactly 10:30 a.m., just in time to participate in the flag-hoisting ceremony organized by the UN to admit Vietnam as a new member. I enjoyed this function. Afterwards I went up to congratulate and chat briefly with the vice-prime minister and the permanent representative of Vietnam.

Mr. Krishna Raj Aryal, the Nepalese foreign minister and the leader of the Nepalese delegation, had also come. He was a good friend of T.U. Central Library and the library profession. I had known him ever since I began my career as the chief of T.U.C.L. As the founder principal of the private Ratna Rajya Laxmi Campus, he used to consult me regarding the management of the college library. I admired his interest in library service — an interest growing out of his knowledge that without a library no college could raise the quality of education. He wrote a book on education entitled *Education for the Development of Nepal* (Kathmandu, self-published, 1970), which attracted wide attention. Though very busy as a

The UN General Assembly Thirty-second Session

principal, he visited me quite often in my office in the library to discuss his concerns.

I got a call from him a day or two after his arrival and was invited to visit him in his hotel close to the UN complex. His hotel looked very impressive and grand by Nepalese standards, but I found out later on from him that foreign ministers from other countries stayed in even more luxurious hotels. I had a long and memorable visit with, during which we talked about politics, foreign relations, and social and cultural problems, exchanged stories about former prime ministers Dr. Tulsi Giri and Mr. Kirti Nidhi Bista, and then veered off into palace politics, especially with reference to such powerful secretaries as Narayan Prasad Shrestha, Chiran S. Thapa, and ADC Tara Bahadur Thapa — all in all a very informative and interesting talk, through which the thread of the problems of the development of Nepal ran. I felt happy that he trusted me enough to share such experiences with me. Usually in Nepal people change as soon as they get position and power, but I was pleased to find him unchanged in his behaviour towards me, a librarian.

Since I knew personally very little about Mr. Shailendra Kumar Upadhyaya, I wanted to pay a visit to him, too, so that I could tell him about T.U. Central Library as the UN depository for Nepal and to sound him out on his attitude towards the library profession. I had met him several times in the staff meeting and found his response to me a bit too cool in the beginning. He did not know anything about the library's role as the UN depository. I briefed him in detail about T.U. Central Library and its efforts to help the nation and about my involvement in the International Women's Year 1975. He took very encouraging interest in my story.

After the visit I judged him to be a different man, able to establish a warm, engaging rapport with others. During my

The UN General Assembly Thirty-second Session

three months of faithful participation in all the meetings, he for his part found me to be very hard-working and willing to take on the tough responsibilities assigned by him. He became a great admirer of my contributions to the different meetings. I was asked to present two papers, one on the elimination of all forms of racial discrimination and one on women, to the Third Committee. I did not like having to confine myself to these two topics. There were so many others on which the delegates could make statements informing the committee about their country's views of its own situation and its stand on various issues. I thought I should not miss such an opportunity to make as many statements as I could prepare on different topics. The resources available for consultation were vast. The Dag Hammarskjöld Library of the UN was well managed under the able direction of Mrs. Natalya Tyulina, a very beautiful and charming lady. I had a long meeting with her. She expressed her extreme joy to see a librarian delegate from Nepal — perhaps, to her recollection, the first librarian to represent his or her nation in the General Assembly.

She introduced me to her senior staff and hosted a lunch for me. I enjoyed sharing this time with her. I got tremendous help from the library staff to find the information I needed to write my statements. Besides racial problems and women's rights, I prepared three more statements on youth, the elderly and the aged, and the elimination of all forms of religious intolerance — altogether five statements. Dr. Lohani was kind enough to go through my drafts, for which he had high praise. I was appreciative of his comments. Our permanent representative, Mr. Upadhyaya, also had the ability to express approval of good, hard work, an unusual trait among Nepalese, who enjoy coming down hard on others' efforts. I was thus surprised to hear him appreciating and praising my active role in the committees. He later told me that he had sent a good

The UN General Assembly Thirty-second Session

report on my activities to Secretary Chiran S. Thapa and to the king. His words encouraged me greatly.

I became known to most of the active representatives of the different countries. With all the contacts I made, I soon found myself attending luncheons, dinners, and receptions hosted by individual countries. I enjoyed these courtesies, sometime four or five parties a day, immensely. During the three months I hardly ever ate at my own expense. Dr. Lohani quite often asked half in jest, "Shanti, how many parties do you have to attend today?" I was certainly in great demand. It was a great source of pride not only for me but also for the delegation of Nepal, I thought. I became quite close with Indian delegates, especially with Mrs. S. Kulkarni, who was so much like my own sister; her love and care for me is still fresh in my mind today. I enjoyed my brief visit to the external affairs minister of India, Mr. Atal Behari Vajpayee, who made the first statement ever in Hindi before the UN General Assembly. He sounded beautiful. His command of Hindi was superb. He read his statement so majestically that I wished he would never finish. I told him so afterwards. He lighted up at my remark. He was a great patriot and lover of his own language.

It was October 3, 1977. I was to deliver my first statement to the Third Committee, on the elimination of all forms of racial discrimination. I was very excited and could feel my heartbeat picking up. I prayed for a sense of calm. My name was called by Chairwoman Lucille Mair (Jamaica) to present my paper. Mrs. Mair had a very dynamic personality and a satin voice. Her call harboured a sort of pleasing appeal to present my statement forthrightly. I presented my statement (Appendix IV) with great confidence, summoning all the delegates to put my words into action.

Mr. Shahi, a member of the National Panchayat, and Mr. Dawadi were with me during the deliberations. Mr. Shahi

The UN General Assembly Thirty-second Session

expressed his appreciation of what he called a good and impressive presentation. Many delegates came up to me to congratulate me. Even Mrs. Mair told me personally that my statement was one of the best she had heard and asked me to lunch with her. Oh, what a tremendous joy it was for me to hear such inspiring comments from one and all!

That same month the American president, Jimmy Carter, was to address the UN General Assembly. I was very eager to hear him. I reached the Assembly Hall twenty minutes earlier than the scheduled beginning of his address, and twenty minutes seemed a long time to wait. Finally he came dressed in a handsome blue suit. There was no escort to accompany him to the rostrum, no one to carry his speech. He carried his own speech in a thin folder. So out of the ordinary, so informal, but very human, I thought, compared to other presidents and heads of the developing nations, who were seen always with bodyguards or escorts to carry their speech and even to turn the pages during its delivery before the Assembly. President Carter's speech was very well thought out and appealing. It was not too long, and it was not too short either. I enjoyed every word he uttered.

I liked his personality, which reminded me of the late President John F. Kennedy, my favourite U.S. president. During my student days in the States, I tried not to miss seeing and hearing President Kennedy on television. His speeches stuck close to realities and were based on truth. I loved his saying, "Ask not what your country can do for you but ask what you can do for your country." Without knowing much about world politics, I became a great admirer of a few leaders of the time, such as President Kennedy, Martin Luther King Jr., President Sukarno of Indonesia, President Khruschev of the USSR, Prime Minister Jawaharlal Nehru of India, and Prime Minister Chou En Lai (Zhou En Lai) of China.

The UN General Assembly Thirty-second Session

President Carter was applauded warmly after his twenty-minute speech. I greatly wished to congratulate him personally, but I was too far away to reach him.

As arranged by the Home Hospitality Center, I left New York for Vermont by plane on October 6, 1977, with a group of other foreign friends. I was given a list of states to select and chose Vermont, as I had long heard many beautiful things about it. My host was Messi Williamson, a tall, attractive, and well-dressed lady with a pleasing personality. I thought she must have been easily the equal of my other friends' hosts. I enjoyed the ride from the airport to her beautiful residence, located in a scenic spot far from distracting crowds. She drove very leisurely, pointing out the leaves on the trees, which were changing colours. It all looked like a framed picture.

There were quite a number of interesting programmes planned for me for the next three days, according to the printed schedule. After a good American-style dinner and table talk on Nepal with my hostess, I retired to a well-decorated bedroom. Soon I was asleep amid very different surroundings from a hotel in New York. I felt very much at home.

I woke up quite early in the morning and filled my nature-loving eyes with the beauty of the place. Looking outside the big window, I remembered my husband and wished he could have been with me to enjoy the scenes that Woodstock had to offer.

My hostess took me to an old apple cider mill run by a member of the state legislature. I was astonished to find a legislator doing everything by himself without any helpers. What a spirit of self-reliance there was there, unlike in Nepal, where labourers, and even children, were everywhere being exploited. I enjoyed talking to the owner of the mill and tasting his apple cider — my favourite drink.

The UN General Assembly Thirty-second Session

Afterwards we drove to a cattle farm. I had great fun watching sixty-two cows and their calves playing around them. The cows' udders were larger than what I was used to back home, and I could hardly believe that only two people were taking care of everything. The farm owner made me believe, though, by showing me the milking machines and how milk was channelized to a tank. It was incredible. It was such an interesting experience for me to be out on such a well-managed farm.

Wherever I went I thought of my homeland, where all the traditional ways of tilling and raising cattle are still backward and no one in power and position seemed to have the time or inclination to plan reforms to alleviate poverty. Although Nepal is an agriculturally based country, no good plan existed to help the traditional farmers and cattle owners to increase production. Having visited the farm in Vermont, I became sympathetic towards our cows, which were not taken care of so well as in the States, even though they are worshipped and the killing of a cow is a punishable offence.

After this memorable outing I was treated to a good lunch at Woodstock Union High School, where public education was being provided. The high school, set in scenic surroundings, looked far better than any college in Nepal. It was easy to become envious of all the facilities available in it. After lunch I visited some of the classes and its well-managed library. Sad thoughts on the bleak situation of the schools in my country made me dizzy, and I prayed for better educational planning for Nepal.

On October 3, a visit to the public library in the same lovely town was arranged for me. Being a librarian myself, I obviously looked forward to this. The director of the library was there to receive me and give a quick tour of his finely organized collection. He inquired about the public library

The UN General Assembly Thirty-second Session

system in Nepal, but I had to disappoint him by saying that Nepal didn't have any. I told him not to give up on us, though. A public library system would surely one day come into being. I had, in fact, already submitted a plan to the Education Ministry in 1967 that entailed not only setting up a public library system but also improving the condition of Nepal's so-called National Library and college and school libraries. He brightened up at that.

I was very much impressed by the local library services to the whole community; they were its university. My three-day visit to Woodstock revitalized me, and I cherish the memory of my time there even now. Expressing my deep gratitude and appreciation to Mrs. Williamson, I reluctantly left Vermont.

It was back to participating and attending meetings, including ones other than of my own committees, in order to gain more information, meet new delegate friends from different countries, and produce some impact on the world's picture of Nepal. During this period I met two veteran diplomats: Mr. H. S. Amerasinghe of Sri Lanka, and Mr. Jamil M. Baroody of Saudi Arabia — together a living history of the UN. Each represented his country on different committees. To be with them was to imbibe automatically the wisdom of a lifetime spent in the League of Nations and the UN. The two men were very kind and gave of their valuable time whenever they met me. The regard shown to me became a source of inspiration and encouragement to me to make my activities as a Nepalese delegate during the Assembly session fruitful in all the ways I could. I felt flattered when they recommended during a dinner party to our foreign minister, Mr. Aryal, and representative, Mr. Upadhyaya, that I be made a permanent member of our mission. That both the latter took pride in me was evident from the smiles that they greeted this suggestion with.

The UN General Assembly Thirty-second Session

Once I had a long visit with those veteran diplomats separately and asked them some of the questions floating around in my head ever since my participation in the different committees began: Why did the UN have seemingly always to be a platform for block politics — American and Russian? The Russians in particular tended to be manipulative and assertive of block interests, and most of the Third World countries, especially African nations, liked to dance to their tune. Why? Why could not the UN be free from such machinations? Why could it not be just a platform for the discussion of global problems so that sustainable peace and prosperity might be promoted among all its member nations?

They had different answers to my queries, based on their practical experience. I always loved to listen to these experiences. In the end, I remained convinced that if every delegate had aspired to nothing but the welfare of all humanity, the UN would be a holy place in the world under the grace of one God.

It had been a long-cherished desire of mine to see and listen to Foreign Minister Moshe Dayan of Israel. I had heard a lot of good things about his contribution to his nation. Since visiting Israel with my husband, I had become a great admirer of that unique country. Thus it was not unnatural for me to be quite excited when I learned that he would address the Assembly on October 10.

He delivered a very impressive speech. I was introduced to him by Israel's permanent representative, Mr. Chaim Herzog (the current president of Israel), when I went to congratulate him. I already had met Mr. Herzog at several parties, so he knew me as a good friend of Israel. He struck me as a shrewd diplomat with strong convictions. Years later it was a tremendous joy for me when I heard that he had been elected president of Israel — the right person in the right position.

The UN General Assembly Thirty-second Session

It had become a sort of routine for me to visit our mission before going to the UN, even when no staff meeting had been called. The real reason was that I got almost every alternate day a letter from my husband sent to the mission's address. It was nice to hear the staff member of our mission say upon handing over the letter, "You have a very faithful husband." These loving letters gave me such a boost that I never felt tired on the job.

The mission staff all tried their best to make us feel at home, inviting us to come for lunch and dinner at their houses turn by turn. I enjoyed the excellent Nepalese food prepared by the wives. The permanent representative, Mr. Upadhyaya, also used to be asked out. For fun and relaxation, everyone loved to play cards, particularly a game called *paplu*. I was the only delegate who didn't know it. While they played, I either watched TV or read articles on the UN.

I found the whole mission staff to be like a happy joint family. I always enjoyed visiting Mrs. Sudha Lohani, Mrs. Shanti Rana, and Mrs. Rupa Dawadi whenever I had free time. Mrs. Lohani and Mrs. Dawadi helped me tirelessly in my shopping, thus contributing their part to the well-being of our diplomatic mission.

Besides our mission staff, there were other Nepalese working in New York who were eager to help visiting fellow countrymen. One such was Nirmal Shrestha and his family. His pretty wife Sudeshna and son Sabin made me feel right at home in their nicely furnished house. They even insisted on inviting some of my close foreign friends who had at one time worked in Nepal in different capacities. David Smith (an ex-deputy resident representative of UNDP Nepal) and his wife were stylishly entertained by them, for example. Nirmal helped me often in various ways during my stay in New York, with a generosity of spirit I gratefully remember.

The UN General Assembly Thirty-second Session

Two other persons I haven't forgotten are Mr. M. Sharif and Mr. Shail Upadhyaya, who held good positions in the UN. Mr. Upadhyaya invited me to dinner more than once in his flat, where I met his aunt, Bijaya Lakshmi, who was married to a Pakistani diplomat. Having met them, I came to know that she was the sister of Congress Party leader B. P. Koirala and that Shail was his nephew. I heard lots of sad stories about the cat-and-mouse games that went on between the king and the politician, which were ruinous to the policy of reconciliation being sought by the latter. I was left deep in thought and wished I could have met Mr. Koirala. Later on I was warned not to get close to his circle, but I had my own philosophy not to hold aloof from people of good will.

Mr. Sharif was kind enough to provide me some good materials on the world's youth before I made my statement on the subject. He told me of some of his experiences in the UN, and of his working and writing speeches for Helvi Sipila, a top lady official in the UN (she was appointed secretary-general of the International Women's Year 1975).

It was on October 17 that I was to make my statement on women. Mr. Lohani told me flatly that my statement was too long. I did not want to make it shorter, though, so I decided to deliver it as it stood but to read faster than I had my address on the elimination of all forms of social discrimination, forgetting that the interpreters would have to keep up with me. When I began to rattle off my statement, a note was handed to me asking me to slow down. Then only did I realize what constraints I was under. I immediately shifted gears.

Our representative (Mr. Upadhyaya), Mr. Prabal Rana, and others were in attendance, and I was proud to make a detailed statement (Appendix V) on activities being carried out in Nepal for the welfare of Nepalese women, especially with reference

The UN General Assembly Thirty-second Session

to the International Women's Year 1975, of which I had been the member secretary for Nepal.

My old American friends from Nepal kept me busy by inviting me to lunch, dinner, tea, and talks. One of the memorable talks I delivered was at Barnard College, Columbia University. It was arranged by Robert Palmer, the director of the college library. He had come to T.U. Central Library on two separate occasions at my request as a Fulbright fellow to help my senior staff to learn how to select the best reference books and to provide better service. I had to do some hard convincing before our university authorities allowed him to work in the library. He was the first Fulbright librarian the University ever had. Whenever I introduced him to our people as such, I noticed a surprised look in response, as if to ask how a Fulbright scholar could be a librarian. I was personally extremely glad when the U.S. Education Foundation entertained my request for such a librarian and grateful to the directors, Terence R. Beck and J. Gabriel Campbell, for their cooperation and help.

The topic on which I had to speak was women in Nepal. My talk was well received and applauded by the audience. Very interesting questions were asked afterwards. I actually preferred the question-and-answer format to delivering a formal speech. It was, in any case, all very enjoyable.

Another memorable highlight during my three-month stay in New York was my visit to my best friend Nancy at her beautiful house in Cortland, New York, after first stopping to see her wonderful parents, Mr. and Mrs. R. S. Winter, at their own lovely residence not far away from New York City. I was fascinated to see their motor-home with all the facilities needed for a tiny one-bedroom house — kitchen, bath, bed, and what not; it was something I had never seen before in my life.

The UN General Assembly Thirty-second Session

It was good to see Nancy, Doug and their three daughters — Shanti, Kamala, and Allison — after five years. Nancy had left Nepal with her family in 1972. Their dedicated service as Peace Corps volunteers, I knew, was still alive in people's minds. The girls had changed a lot. Shanti, born in Nepal in 1970 and named after me, had grown so big and looked so beautiful. Kamala, already a blooming flower of seven months when plucked by Nancy from the Bal Mandir (orphanage) in Nepal, had turned into an even prettier flower and could hardly be recognized. I was thrilled to see her growing so fine. Allison, born in the U.S.A. after Nancy's return there, was still a crying but lovely baby. I embraced all three girls as soon as I saw them. Nancy also joined in our circle — a circle of love and friendship. Joyous tears rolled down our cheeks. It was a great blessing for me to be with the Hatches for those few days.

During my visit Nancy took me to many different places. I really fell in love with Cortland and its scenic environment, the very opposite of New York City's concrete jungle. When the time came, it was hard for me to part with Nancy and her happy family. The children had grown close to my heart. They even quarrelled with each other over who would sleep with me. Kamala, of course, claimed more nights with me than the other girls, who very willingly let her enjoy that privilege. I admired all of them.

By the end of my visit I had shared lots of moments with Nancy, my great friend and support during the early days of my married life. Even before we met in Cortland she made me feel right at home, making regular long-distance calls to me in my hotel in New York to enquire about me and my work at the UN — a living example of true friendship. We both cried openly when I left Cortland for New York. At the end she promised to visit me there before I returned to Nepal. Her

The UN General Assembly Thirty-second Session

promise solaced me, and I went back to New York with the assurance that I would see her again soon.

Although I felt lonely, I continued to be as busy as ever at the UN. During the month of December I got a call from my good friends Dr. Frederick H. and Mrs. Austra Gaige asking me to dine with them. It was good to be with them, even for a short visit. They, too, were lovers of Nepal and Nepalese. I had met them in Nepal at the beginning of my career as a librarian. Austra Gaige worked for the Planning Commission Library at Singha Durbar in Kathmandu. She was a very dedicated professional. I always enjoyed sharing with her memories of those days. Fred Gaige had been a Fulbright scholar doing doctoral research on the Terai region, the results of which appeared in his well-received book entitled *Regionalism and National Unity in Nepal*, the first systematic and interdisciplinary study of the Terai region published in English (Berkeley, University of California Press, 1975). During our dinner we shared many thoughts relating to the development of Nepal. My hosts were full of gracious remarks and comments on my having been sent as one of the delegates to the UN.

A special request was made by the chairman of the Third Committee to have me deliver my statements on both youth and on the question of the elderly and the aged on the same day, December 6 and on elimination of all forms of religious intolerance on December 9. Usually only one statement was made by a delegate on any one day. I very willingly accepted our chairman's request and proudly delivered the statements to the committee (Appendices VI, VII, and VIII). I was quite satisfied with my presentation and was congratulated by delegates from different countries. They seemed to appreciate especially my statement on the question of the elderly and the aged. Some came asking for permission to publish my remarks

The UN General Assembly Thirty-second Session

in various non-governmental publications. I thanked God for such a positive response.

December 6 was a very busy day for me. At 1 p.m., after my delivery of the two statements, I went to attend a grand luncheon, hosted by the president (Mrs. Francis Sawyer) and the members of Women United for the UN. I enjoyed this meeting of prominent women, all glamorously dressed in their different national costumes.

That same evening I was invited to a dinner hosted by the foreign minister of China at the Chinese mission at 7:30. The dinner was quite different from other dinners I had attended before in missions. The dining tables were stylishly decorated and contained all variety of tasty Chinese dishes. Loving Chinese food as I do, I was very much impressed. I again took the opportunity to meet and talk with diplomats gathered there, and they showed a lively interest in my country.

The United Nations General Assembly Thirty-second Session was coming to an end. On December 14, just a few days before the closing of the session, I was invited to lunch by Mrs. Helvi Sipila, the United Nations assistant secretary-general, the topmost lady in the UN. It was a quiet affair — only the two of us. We could very freely discuss the many festering problems faced by the women of the world, especially with reference to Nepal.

I had met Mrs. Sipila for the first time in Nepal in February, 1977, when she came to attend the United Nations Regional (Asia and Pacific) Seminar on the Participation of Women in Political, Economic and Social Development held in Kathmandu. Since my first meeting with her I had become a great admirer of her personally and of the ideals she espoused concerning the welfare of women all over the world. In particular, I shared her deep concern about the disturbing situation of women in South Asia. She agreed with my idea that the equality of women is something not bestowed upon but earned by women, who prove by their ability and efficiency that they are equally, if not better, equipped than men are to make this world a better place to live in. I told her that I liked her opening remarks expressed during a meeting, organized on March 7, 1975 at the UN headquarters, to discuss the topic Women and Men: The Next 25 Years in celebration of International Women's Day:

> If progress to implement the principles of equality between men and women had been even remotely as positive as that achieved in other sectors of the social field, we would not need International Women's Year. As it is, the status of women is generally inferior to men's in the educational, economic, legal, social and political arenas. Whatever progress has been achieved in recent years has been very slow and sporadic and the problems of women have generally been tackled in isolation, as though they concerned the female population only. Women's rights are still spoken of independently of human rights.

During the UN Session I met Mrs. Sipila several times at different parties and once in her office. I was pleased that she had time to talk with me when I stopped by for a very brief visit out of a desire to meet her in private and to profit from her long years of working for women. Being with her was a learning experience.

Now, on this later occasion, I was extremely happy to be sitting with her at the lunch table discussing issues and hearing her accounts of different conferences, including the World Conference of the International Women's Year held in Mexico in 1975 (attended by the representative of 133 countries), the Declaration of Mexico Plans of Action Decade (1975-85) for women and development, and the World Congress for

The UN General Assembly Thirty-second Session

International Women's Year held in Berlin in 1975, to which the IWY Committee Nepal 1975 sent representatives. She told me that it would have been nice had I attended those important meetings. I told her that I intentionally had avoided such meetings, having preferred to concentrate on the work inside my country as the member secretary; I had wanted to make the year a great success. She gave me a warm smile and even hinted that if I was interested I could become involved in women's issues in the UN, as there was a need for active women. I thanked her for the time together and told her that I wished I could have more such opportunities.

Later on I was also invited to lunch by the chief of the UN recruitment division, Mrs. Tamar Oppenheimer, who offered her support if I should become interested in UN service. But I was not yet ready for any service outside my country, which desperately needed more women like me to contribute to its development.

That same evening I had an invitation to attend a reception hosted by Coretta Scott King at the U.S. Mission at 7 p.m. Ever since my student life in the States I had been a great admirer of her husband, the late Dr. Martin Luther King, Jr. I loved to read his speeches, all so eloquent and appealing. Naturally I was overwhelmed. The grand reception was crowded, yet I got an opportunity to have a few words with Mrs. King, who showed appreciable interest in Nepal. Her few polite and meaningful words are still fresh in my mind.

When I returned from the reception to the hotel, a thick letter was waiting for me in my letter box. I was eager to open it and took the lift to reach my room quickly. Opening the envelope, I found a beautifully planned programme for a month for me to visit different universities and libraries in Washington D.C., Nashville, Chicago, Los Angeles, and places in Florida, California, and Hawaii under the USIS International Visitors

The UN General Assembly Thirty-second Session

Programme (IVP). It was just like a wonderful dream and hard to believe. I was extremely happy to receive such a thoughtful and highly appreciated invitation, which had been initiated by a great friend of T.U. Central Library, Diane Stanley, the director of USIS, Nepal. It would be difficult to enumerate all of her contributions to strengthening the cultural and educational ties between Nepal and the U.S.A.

According to the programme, so well planned by Vincent W. Allen, programme officer of the Institute of International Education (IIE) in Washington, I was to leave New York on December 17 for the capital. In the afternoon of the appointed day, with very fond memories of my three months of participating in the UN, I left New York to start my tour, about which to write only a few things would be doing an injustice to the IVP programme. A whole book would be needed to describe my visits to so many wonderful and beautiful universities and libraries — a great seeing and learning experience. It had been a long-cherished desire of mine, ever since I was a student in George Peabody Library School, to visit such universities and libraries. I was grateful to God for making my dream come true. Every visit was very memorable and fruitful and enriching.

Chapter 11

Mission to Bhutan

Small nations of the world have always fascinated me. I love to read about them. Maybe my fascination grew out of the fact that I am also from a small but beautiful country, a Shangri-la for foreigners. Bhutan, Sikkim, and Tibet are all of great interest to me.

I was drawn to Tibet both before and after it was taken over in 1959 by China, which claimed that it had been an integral part of itself since the 13th century, ignoring the cry of the Dalai Lama (the receiver of the Nobel Peace Prize in 1989), its spiritual head. Sikkim came under the control of India when its people rose against their ruler, Chogyal (Maharaja) Palden Thondup Namgyal, who was forced to leave the country with his American wife, Hope Cooke, in 1974. These political dramas were well staged to avert too great a public outcry.

Bhutan was a less talked about nation, and I used to wonder how that country was developing. My thirst to know more about it was somewhat relieved during my participation in the different meetings at the UN in 1977 as a delegate from Nepal. Nepal and Bhutan had been working quite closely at the UN ever since Bhutan joined the organization in 1971, sixteen years after Nepal's admission in 1955. In 1977 Nepal and Bhutan were as close to one another as ever. We consulted each other quite often when votes were called. I enjoyed talking and meeting with Mr. Dago Tshering, Bhutan's representative, and Mrs. Tshering Lhamu Dorjee, one of its delegates at that time. I used to tell them that I would one day visit their country, the land of the Thunder Dragon, but I could not predict when.

Mission to Bhutan

I believe strongly that if one wishes for something with all one's heart, it will happen, like a miracle. And so it was the case with my library mission to Bhutan, when my long-cherished dream came true.

One fine afternoon I received a registered letter, dated May 26, 1983, from Mr. K. R. Pandey (chief ai of UNESCO's Asia Section, Operational Programmes Division, Education Sector) informing me of their search for prospective candidates to carry out a consultancy mission to Bhutan and requesting me to inform them if I was interested and would be available for a period of one month. It was indeed a happy and unexpected surprise for me. Such offers, I had heard, were made to those with a good reputation in their particular field of endeavour who constantly kept in touch with people working in the same field in UNESCO. Establishing such contact was far from my mind, as I was involved enough as it was in developing T.U. Central Library into a model for the country and in boosting the library profession in Nepal. What admirable trust UNESCO bestowed upon me!

Before sending the offer, the concerned section of UNESCO may have consulted Nepal's ambassador to France at that time, Mr. Krishna Raj Aryal, regarding my contribution to the library development in Nepal. He was representing Nepal in UNESCO, too, as I understood it. Moreover, being an educationalist, he was one of the best friends of the library profession Nepal had. But why, without my own request or the customary kowtowing, would he have made his recommendation. Whatever lay behind it, the offer came to me during his tenure of office in Paris. I remained grateful to him.

The letter bearing the offer was signed by Mr. Pandey, who joined UNESCO from a post in His Majesty's Government of Nepal. Since he had been away so long, I knew very little of

Mission to Bhutan

him personally, but I nevertheless appreciated his trust in me for such a mission, which I was quick to accept.

Soon I was busy getting needed clearance from the UNESCO section of the Education and Culture Ministry. It was an unexpectedly and unnecessarily slow procedure, which at times irritated me so, that I had to resort to sharp words. Instead of speeding things up, the authorities seemed to slow things down. I told the chief of the section that every Nepalese should be proud of such an offer; I was representing my country and the library profession. I could well sense that my words did not please him. Things came almost to a halt. This was my first bitter experience in the ministry. I was told, though, that they were usually slow.

It took a few months to get all the needed documents to be forwarded to UNESCO, once the process got going. I sent my date of availability to UNESCO and was duly informed that they had been waiting for the approval of the Bhutanese government; this was the normal procedure, which I found quite interesting.

While waiting for the approval, I was kept busy arranging for all the work in the library to be carried on in my absence. A telegraph, dated June 1, 1985, from Mr. J. Murdoch of the Division of Higher Education and Training of Educational Personnel at UNESCO in Paris, was delivered requesting me to plan to arrive in Samchi on June 11 via Patna and Bagdogra; the Royal Government of Bhutan had selected me over other candidates for the library consultancy mission to Bhutan. In pursuance of this request and as advised by Mr. Toshiyuki Niwa, the UNDP representative in Nepal, and his knowledgeable wife Jean, I left Kathmandu in June for my destination.

I reached Bagdogra on June 11 and was met by Miss C. K. Gurung, the principal of the National Institute of Education

Mission to Bhutan

(N.I.E.), the body overseeing my mission. The surroundings looked different from what I had expected. Amid all the heat and dirt I did not feel at all at ease. Thus I was happy to have someone at least to orient me.

It took about four hours to reach Samchi. The ride from Bagdogra went through villages and past tea gardens. Miss Gurung, good guide that she was, pointed out the sights.

Samchi, too, looked quite different from what I had imagined: rather less mountainous and cool but still beautiful. I was glad that I had not brought warm clothes. It was quite a pleasant evening by the time we arrived. Miss Gurung was kind enough to take me to her home for dinner. Her hospitality made me feel very much at home. After dinner she took me to the beautiful royal guest house, close to N.I.E., where I was to stay during my mission. The colourful patterns covering the building and its peaceful surroundings were utterly captivating, but I was all alone in that huge edifice; no houses were around. All was quiet, lonely, and a little bit frightening. Nevertheless, I was already tired and slept soundly.

I always love to wake up early and get out to enjoy the morning air, no matter where I am. It was a particularly beautiful morning when I woke up on June 12. The landscaping about the premises was extremely well planned, and untouched nature was close by, where I could feel the presence of God. While I was strolling around the garden, though, a man came to warn me of poisonous snakes in the area. That was unwelcome information indeed; I wished he had not told me. Later on I came to know that he was there to help with marketing, cooking, and the like. I never could stand even non-poisonous rat snakes, so his warning caused great alarm in me. I was determined to see if there was another place close to the teachers' quarters where I could stay.

Mission to Bhutan

At about 9:30 a.m. a shining Landrover came to pick me up. I was quite used to doing consultancy work in different fields in Nepal for shorter or longer periods, but I had never gone to any foreign country in that capacity. It was my first such consultancy. I was happy to enjoy such a privilege in a small country so close to my heart and was determined to do as well as I could to make UNESCO's contribution to the development of education in Bhutan a great success.

I was graciously received by Mr. Pema Thinley, the director of the National Institute of Education, and his staff. Mr. Thinley immediately arranged a meeting with Dr. A. Raoof, the chief technical adviser, and Dr. J. C. Goyal, a specialist in curriculum development. We discussed the job description sent to me by UNESCO before I came to Samchi. During the meeting the director recounted in brief the history of N.I.E. Afterwards the director and the principal gave me a quick tour of the existing N.I.E. library. I was taken aback upon seeing the horrible condition the library was in, and though I felt like bursting out at the negligence on the part of educationalists and UNESCO advisers, I did not express my feelings during the tour.

The National Institute of Education is located in the southern part of Bhutan in as picturesque a setting as one could hope to find. The founding members chose the site well when, in 1968, they established it and began the job of preparing teachers to teach in the schools of Bhutan. Having begun as the Teacher Training Institute, it immediately assumed a leadership role nationwide in its field. Its limited curriculum was soon expanded, and in 1983 it met the need for rising educational standards by offering a three-year programme, being upgraded to the National Institute of Education with the assistance of UNDP/UNESCO. The institution had come a long way since it prepared its first batch of 33 teachers in 1970. In 1971 there were 63 students enrolled, and in 1985 37 students were in the primary course and 32 students were working towards a B.Ed. It has been estimated that by 1995 the institution will have an enrolment of 160 students.

The library is housed in the N.I.E. building. It had yet to be recognized as the heart of the institution. The library had the unusual distinction of having had just one clerk-cum-librarian in its entire history. It had been growing haphazardly under this non-professional and looked like a run-down secondhand bookstore.

I came to know from the clerk that the library was established in a small room 30 feet by 20 feet with just 98 books in 1968. It could hardly serve more than a dozen users at a time. For 17 years after the institution had come into being, the library remained near the bottom of the academic community's scale of priorities. Leadership and management of the library were entrusted to no one, but the way the library operated it seemed that the administration retained overall responsibility for supervision and delegated responsibility for internal administration to a clerk in the institution's main office. I was surprised to find that after 17 years the collection of the library comprised less than 5,000 volumes of unequal worth. I used to spend some time in the library just noting how many students came to use it. On the average it was 25 students per day out of an enrollment of around 69.

After a brief period of study and research on the institution and its library, I began working very seriously day and night. The allotted time was too short for the task. It was a challenge to which I responded wholeheartedly. The library situation in Bhutan would have made a library expert from a developed nation throw up his hands, but for me it was nothing unusual; throughout my career I had been facing such situations wherever I went in my country. UNESCO and the Royal

Mission to Bhutan

Government of Bhutan were wise to invite me, I thought. No one had to provide me with shock treatment. I could feel things out for myself and plan my mission in such a way that it would have a good impact on the country's planners. Moreover, the place was like an ashram far from outside disturbances and the perfect place to become lost in work if you wanted to. Everything was very traditional and even primitive. Once a week vegetables and other edibles were on display in an open place for local people to buy. I enjoyed visiting such places in my free time.

During the two weeks of June 12-26, when not attending the regular meetings with the chief technical adviser and the director, I spent most of my time examining all aspects of library operations, consulting with the engineer and contractor, holding interviews with a large number of teachers and students, measuring the library rooms in the new N.I.E. building for furniture, making drawings of the furniture, equipment, and supplies required, making the existing library more attractive with simple things like flowerpots, selecting reference books, and conducting in-service training in librarianship for Mr. Lama, the clerk-cum-librarian.

No counterpart was formally designated. I was very grateful to Dr. Raoof, Mr. Thinley, Miss Gurung, and Dr. Goyal for helping to make my mission a memorable success. All the teachers, students, and the staff of N.I.E. were also very cooperative. By the time I left Samchi, I felt I had become a part of N.I.E. and wished I could have stayed on to see the library develop according to my plan.

In my last meeting with the technical adviser, the director, and the principal, I pointed out a few things I noticed there during my two-week stay to which they might profitably give some attention so that UNESCO money and efforts would bear fruit. Much modern equipment bought with money from the

Mission to Bhutan

UNDP/UNESCO project was unnecessarily left standing unused. Why had such equipment been bought for a place where even a tap could not be repaired due to the lack of trained manpower? The money spent on it could have been spent on the library itself, I told them in the meeting. They listened very attentively to my remarks without reacting. I could not tell whether I was getting through to them or not, but I had the great satisfaction at least of laying things straight.

I was given a touching farewell party by teachers and N.I.E. staff one day before I left Samchi. Early in the morning of June 27 I set off. The director of N.I.E. along with Dr. Goyal and Mr. Akhatar was kind enough to accompany me to Thimphu, the capital of Bhutan. It took almost ten hours to reach there. The trip was quite enjoyable, though in some places horrendous landslides had occurred. I thanked God that I was not travelling alone.

It was already late evening when I was told that we were approaching Thimphu. I was looking forward to a good room in a stylish hotel. The peaceful atmosphere surprised me; I had not expected a capital city to be that way. How nice it would be if the capitals of all nations were as serene.

After a pleasant dinner I had a brief discussion about my programme with Mr. Nima Wangdi, who came to welcome me. Though the journey was quite long, I did not feel all that tired because I had so looked forward to being in Thimphu. Even that first night I felt fresh. The climate of Thimphu was quite to my liking — not as hot as in Samchi. The night seemed too long; I wanted to see what the place looked like.

The next morning I was ready hours before the appointed time for a tour of the town. It was a Bhutanese holiday. The director of N.I.E. was so kind as to conduct me around. I enjoyed every new view of the quiet and scenic city, which is situated at an altitude of 7,600 feet in the broad, fertile valley

Mission to Bhutan

of the graceful Wang Chu River. An estimated 20,000 people live in the town. Tashichhodzong (Fortress of the Glorious Religion), Bhutan's administrative and religious centre, was built in the 13th century on the bank of the river and is surrounded by weeping willows and lovely terraces of rice paddies. It has more than a hundred spacious rooms, including the king's throne room, all the government departments and ministries, the assembly room of the Tshogdu (national assembly) and the nation's largest monastery (the summer headquarters of the Je Khempo and his two thousand monks). All the unique decorations of the place, full of tantric symbols, and constituting Bhutan's finest religious art, charmed me beyond words. It was on June 2, 1974 that the present king, Jigme Singye Wangchuck, the world's youngest reigning monarch, was crowned, an event attended by 156 dignitaries from all over the world.

I also enjoyed my visit to the royal palace at Dechencholing, the residence of royal family members. A three-storey building in the traditional style, it is elegantly surrounded by sweeping lawns, ponds, and willow trees. I luxuriated in the natural beauty of the place far from the hustle and bustle of modern cities. On the way back my guides seemed astounded to hear me admiring the city so profusely, but it was really a fact that the buildings, the monasteries, and even the forts built on the hilltops around all looked like something out of a perfectly preserved past.

At the end of our tour I told my companion not to commit the mistakes committed in Kathmandu, which has already lost its otherworldly characteristics — a paradise whose return everyone yearns for but to no avail, as the people at the top do not practise what they preach on environment. They agreed wholeheartedly.

Mission to Bhutan

After this pleasant interlude, I awaited the arrival of Ms. Brigid Mayes from UNDP, Bhutan. She came at the exactly appointed time with a warm smile on her face. We discussed in brief my ten-day programme in Thimphu. After she left I went to my room to view the city at night from a window — a peaceful and tranquil scene. The moonlight looked brighter in the absence of excessive lights. There were no garishly illuminated tall buildings, no bright advertisements, and no traffic lights. There was no noise of buses, trucks, ambulances, or cars. I prayed that Bhutan would remain that way: rich in its heritage and firm in its values.

The next morning, June 29, I was to have a meeting at their office with Dasho Nado Rinchen, the director general, and Mr. Zangley, the deputy director of the Department of Education. As usual a vehicle came to pick me up. The department was not far from my hotel. The director general impressed me very much as being in full command of his subject. I was so pleased to find that he spoke Nepali and was keenly interested in Nepal. I had a very useful discussion of my library mission and the library situation in Bhutan with him and his deputy.

After my long meetings I wanted to look into some of the other offices in the Department of Education. The deputy director was kind enough to give me a quick tour. I soon felt as if I was in India, because almost all offices in Bhutan were run by an Indian staff whose members came either from West Bengal or from South India. Only the top posts were filled by Bhutanese.

I was equally astonished to find English as the medium in the office, even though Dzongkha is Bhutan's official language. It is similar to Tibetan. I was told that English was the medium of instruction in secular schools, Cheokay, or classical Dzongkha, was widely used in traditional and monastic schools, while Nepali was spoken in the south. All the top

Mission to Bhutan

officials looked dapper in their national costume, the *kho* (worn by men) and the *kira* (worn by women). Even the king wears this same distinctive dress.

Other memorable meetings were with Mr. Raj Kumar Dar, the UNDP resident representative, and Sarah J. Papineau, the assistant resident representative (Programmes). Mr. Dar showed very appreciable interest in information systems with special reference to Bhutan. After our meeting he showed me the UN collection housed in his office. It was well stocked but needed organizing. I tried to be as frank as I could in discussing the neglect shown to libraries in Bhutan — a matter UNDP should have given priority to.

Sarah was a very energetic lady. She agreed fully with me on this point and on the similar situation with regard to the media. During my short stay in Thimphu we became quite close. I enjoyed sharing with her the results of my investigations and mission. She organized a very interesting and informative meeting in the Planning Commission conference room on July 4. The participants were Sarah herself, Mr. Zangley, Mr. Sangay (a training officer in the foreign ministry), Mr. Shiva Pradhan (a manpower development officer), and Ms. Tshering Dem (a training officer in the Planning Commission). I was truly gratified to see all of these important people who could do much to improve the library situation in Bhutan.

It was a formal meeting. After welcoming remarks by the representatives of UNDP and the Department of Education, I presented excerpts of my 55-page draft report of the library mission, explaining that the library at the National Institute of Education at Samchi had more or less been neglected or at least received very low priority in project activities over the last decade. I wanted to draw their attention to the main problems, not only of N.I.E. but of Bhutan as a whole, and to outline

Mission to Bhutan

what steps should immediately be taken to improve the situation, especially with reference to skilled library manpower. Everyone present reacted favourably. We spent more than two hours on the report. Almost all recommendations I made in it were endorsed. I was extremely happy and felt that my mission had been a great success on hearing them thank me with words of praise for having carried it out with such thoroughness during such a short period. I expressed my deep appreciation to Sarah.

The next day I went to present my report and had a long visit with Mr. Dar in his handsome office, which looked out on scenic surroundings. We discussed UNDP's different projects in Bhutan. He appreciated my spirit, and I too thanked him for the keen interest he took in my work.

On July 6 I had a final meeting with Dasho Nado Rinchen. I presented my report to him. He seemed quite glad to receive it and stated his appreciation for my work. We had a very interesting and useful discussion of Bhutanese educational development and also of the Nepalese educational system. Before leaving I expressed my gratitude for the help and cooperation that I had received in my mission from him and his deputy, Mr. Zangley.

Afterwards I went to visit Dasho Dr. T. Tobgyal, the foreign secretary at the Department of Foreign Affairs, as I had heard lots about him while I was in Thimphu. Moreover, wherever I went I took pride in representing my country as an informal ambassador and in discussing how to further strengthen existing relations.

Dr. Tobgyal gave me a very warm welcome. My short visit with him was highly memorable. I came away feeling that he had genuine a desire to see relations with Nepal deepened.

My mission came to an end on July 8. I was given a very fond farewell. The Department of Education gave me a *kira* and the book *History of Bhutan* by Bikram Jit Hasrat as gifts. I left beautiful Thimphu for Paro to catch a small plane back to Nepal. The airport at Paro, itself small, displayed the same traditional type of colourful buildings. Up to the last moment of my stay I was shown great affection by the Bhutanese friends I had made during my short visit. They are indeed a smiling and amiable people.

I flew back home with very happy memories of my mission in Bhutan.

Chapter 12

Honour from Without

From the very beginning of my career as the chief of T.U. Central Library, the moral support, encouragement, and inspiration I constantly received from my foreign friends kept me always going forward, never backward. I never aspired to receive foreign financial aid to further the development of the library so long as I could manage within the allocated budget, not being in favour of depending overly on outside money. I prefer to have ideas that will change what needs to be changed in our deep-rooted tradition, giving more emphasis to our own values than to money. Huge amounts of money and cash donations in developing nations do more harm than good, as exemplified particularly by Africa. It makes people of poverty-stricken countries dependent, lazy, money-minded, materialistic, and at times corrupt. Shared wealth doesn't create wealth. Moreover, development doesn't start with donations alone; it starts with people and their education, organizational ability, discipline, dedication, honesty, and sincerity. Without these, whatever material resources there are are as good as untapped. My foreign friends also used to agree with my philosophy. Even without any financial aid from foreign donors, due to the grace of God and with the moral support of my foreign friends, I was able to achieve my main goal to make T.U. Central Library a model in Nepal, according to our standards, within a decade. Actually I did not realize this fact till I read the following press conference report of the British Book Development Mission to Nepal, published in the daily English-language newspaper *The Rising Nepal* on November 13, 1969.

Honour from Without

British Council to Help T.U. Library
Kathmandu, November 12

Representatives of the British Book Development Council Mr. Rayner Unwin, Mr. Andre Deutsch and Mr. Charles McGregor left here today for New Delhi after a five-day sojourn here, reports RSS. At a press conference held here today at the British Embassy, one of the members of the team, Mr. Andre Deutsch, said that they were highly impressed by the Tribhuwan University Library. Summing up their impression of the library as very excellent, Mr. Deutsch said that the library was almost unique in Asia. He said that the British Council would like to help and support the T.U. Library.

Our culture does not encourage people to appreciate good hard work, and envy and jealousy are usually the cause. I only infrequently heard any words of appreciation and songs of praise for my work from my own people that I can recall. As the *Bhagavadgita*, the Song Celestial, teaches us, however, "Your right is to work only, but never to the fruit thereof. Let not the fruit of action be your object, nor let your attachment be to inaction." I have always tried to follow the preaching of the *Gita* by strictly practising *karmayoga* (yoga of action) and *sankhyayoga* (yoga of knowledge) so that I could reach the truth which leads to supreme bliss.

Despite my unending struggle to develop the library, I kept my spirits always high, pursuing my work by all skilful ways and means. I never gave a thought to focusing my library activities outside Nepal. I was thoroughly happy within the four walls of the library, keeping myself occupied with the needs of teachers, students, researchers, and scholars. I used to get lots of information on library seminars and conferences held in different countries, but I was loath to leave the library until it became the pride not only of the University but also of the nation. It was my ascetic calling as a *karmayogini*. These days it has become an inbred part of our system to seek opportunities to make trips to foreign countries and to aspire to nice-looking cars as soon as good and respected posts have been secured. Developmental work comes last, not first. If we love to work for the institution and the country, we must change such attitudes, I have always thought.

My First Official Visit to the United Kingdom, 1970

While I was thus deeply involved in my library work, I got a call from the representative of the British Council Nepal, Robert Arbuthnott, to fix an appointment with me to discuss the possibility of my visiting Great Britain on the recommendation of the British Book Development Council Mission to Nepal from November 8 to 12, 1969. I was curious to read the mission's report and learn of their recommendations. Moreover, I always enjoyed having Robert visit the library, as his every word of support for the library had always been a source of inspiration to me and my library staff.

He brought me the report. I was extremely touched to read in it as follows:

Visit to the remarkable University library, specially opened for us [during the Dasai Festival] by its dynamic and charming librarian, Miss Shanti Shrestha [maiden surname]. Undoubtedly this is the best library in the country and, as the Public Library System is rudimentary, it is available also to non-university readers.... We recommend Miss Shanti Shrestha,

Honour from Without

Librarian of Tribhuvan University, be enabled to make her first official visit to the United Kingdom soon. Her library will probably become the main training centre for librarians as the school and college library systems in Nepal grow more rapidly; it is essential she be introduced to the British Library World now, so that appropriate assistance may be requested and provided from Britain...

I really took this as a great honour for me and my work. I have already described in Chapter 5 my visit to the United Kingdom in 1970, when I left the library for the first time since I joined it as its chief in 1963. I remain ever grateful to the British Book Development Council and British Council for the honour.

The One Asia Assembly 1973, New Delhi, February 5-8

The year 1973 was not a happy year in the history of T.U. Central Library. The ten-year golden period had ended with the advent of the New Education System Plan. I was now more concerned for the library's very survival than for its development. Chapter 6 contains the whole story. It was very shocking that nothing was mentioned about library services in the plan, but I kept my hopes as high as I could, working on a plan to be included as supplementary to the original one. While I was pushing forward day and night with my husband to complete it, a letter dated January 2, 1973 came to me as a happy surprise from Mr. Chanchal Sarkar, the director of the Press Institute of India and the programme director of the One Asia Assembly 1973, inviting me to participate in the One Asia Assembly to be held in Delhi from February 5 to 8. I knew I really needed a break from the stress of my pressing problems.

Honour from Without

Moreover, I regarded the invitation as a special honour bestowed upon me by our Indian friends without their having been approached by anyone from my side — so unusual in this part of the world.

I immediately sent my acceptance, expressing appreciation to them for inviting a librarian. They thereupon requested me to send a 300-word biographical sketch to be circulated during the conference. I enjoyed making such a description of myself for the first time.

The whole programme sounded well planned. High officials, including Indian Ambassador Raj Bahadur, seemed quite pleased that I had been invited, and Vice-Chancellor Sardar Rudra Raj Pandey, too, was gratified that the librarian had been given this privilege. Besides me, the late Ram Raj Poudyal (editor of *Gorkhapatra*), Mr. Gopal Das Shrestha (editor of *The Commoner*, the oldest English daily published in Nepal), and Mr. C. L. Jha, editor of the Nepali-language *Nepal Times*, were also invited.

With buoyant feelings, I left Kathmandu for Delhi on February 4. The arrangements were excellent: I was given a very beautiful room in the five-star Asoka Hotel. The One Asia Assembly was to be inaugurated by Dr. Kurt Waldheim, the secretary-general of the UN, and the president of India, Mr. V. V. Giri was to address the inaugural session. The members of the Programme Management Committee were busy down to the last minute. The hall looked magnificent. I was told that they had had a very successful One Asia Assembly in 1970 in Manila, when it was inaugurated by Mr. U Thant, the previous secretary-general of the UN.

On February 5 Kurt Waldheim reached the hall at exactly 10 a.m. and was welcomed with applause. He presented a very impressive speech on the theme of the Assembly: Why Asian societies, even though endowed with power and the capacity to make decisions, had still not been able to raise significantly the living standards of their people. After the inaugural function I went to congratulate him on his speech, which would be the basis of conference debate.

The four-day conference was divided into eight topics, each one addressed by distinguished academicians and scientists, such as Prof. Gunnar Myrdal, Alva Myrdal, Prof. Abdus Salam, Raul Prebisch, Mrs. Shirley Williams, Dr. K. N. Raj, Dr. S. Swaminathan, Dr. B. D. Nag Chaudhury, and several senior statesmen from Asian countries. After the colourful and impressive inaugural function, the assembly dissolved into nine committees.

The committees were each formed with 20 to 25 members from the participants. I took part in two committees, Stewardship of Mass Media and the Future of Education. All the deliberations were very interesting and useful. I was very much impressed with the documentation services provided during the conference and equally so with the untiring assistance provided by the link person (Ms. Leni Gavinio) between committee chairmen and members.

Besides the meetings, conferences, luncheons, and receptions with dignitaries and scholars, evening socials were also planned to make our stay not only academically fruitful but also enjoyable and relaxing. One of the social events I still remember was a grand reception hosted by President Giri in honour of the participants at the beautiful Rastrapati Bhawan Mughal Garden. I took the opportunity to introduce myself to him, and he expressed a very affectionate warm welcome. He astounded me with his keen interest in Nepal and Nepalese. I met quite a number of other distinguished Indians also at the reception, which was quite different from any reception I had ever attended.

Honour from Without

On the evening of February 6, the Rama Leela (a dance drama) was staged in Kamani Hall in honour of the participants. I enjoyed it from beginning to end, so much that even now it gives me great pleasure to recall it. I saluted silently all the skilful and talented artists of the play and wished our Nepalese artists had the same opportunities to pursue their profession, knowing that they can do much to brighten the cultural image of the country.

Another event I would always treasure in my memory was the *Son et Lumière* at the Red Fort, a recreation in sound and light of Indian history.

One of the highlights of the conference was a talk programme by the prime minister of India, Mrs. Indira Gandhi. She came at the exactly appointed time. I was so happy that she knew the value of time as much as any prime minister of developed countries. She was very gracious and radiated a delightful personality in her beautiful national dress. Even before I saw her personally I had become a great admirer of hers. I had always taken great pride in such women, regardless of their nationality, and always celebrated silently whenever women came to occupy positions of trust. The list includes the late Israel premier Golda Meir, Prime Minister Margaret Thatcher of Great Britain, Prime Minister Sirimavo Bandaranaike of Sri Lanka, Prime Minister Edith Cresson of France, Prime Minister Gro Harlem Brundtland of Norway, Prime Minister Hanna Suchocka of Poland, Prime Minister Benazir Bhutto of Pakistan, and Prime Minister Khaleda Zia of Bangladesh. I always prayed that Nepal be given such women also.

Prime Minister Gandhi was extraordinarily eloquent. I thoroughly enjoyed her speech and her admirable facility in responding to all the questions during the session; she displayed a high command of a wide range of subjects of

Honour from Without

national and international importance. After the session I took the opportunity to thank her for having shared thoughts so pertinent to the basic problems and needs and the future development of Asia and its people, and also to express my profound happiness at her upcoming visit to Nepal. Her warm response caused me great joy; I thought that Asian countries should have more women like her.

With these happy memories of four days of the One Asia Assembly I flew back home, feeling that my time had been well spent.

International Summer School, Sheffield, England, 1975

The year 1975 kept me quite busy with different activities geared to the welfare of women in Nepal. It was International Women's Year. Every nation of the world was called upon to focus attention on the problems of women and seek out ways to ensure that women be allowed to contribute their share to global development. From the beginning of my library work the British Council had been supporting me in all ways it could. Mr. D. M. Waterhouse, representative of the British Council in 1975, wanted me to participate in the International Summer School organized by the Postgraduate School of Librarianship and Information Science at the University of Sheffield in the U.K.; the director of the school, Prof. W. L. Saunders, had informed him about my selection to the course by the screening committee. I too got a copy of the letter, dated January 3, 1975, announcing my selection. It was a great privilege for me to be chosen without any initiative on my part.

I immediately sent a letter of appreciation to Prof. Saunders. Mr. Waterhouse came to my office to discuss the matter. I was in a great dilemma whether to accept or not, being already involved in the International Women's Year programmes in

Honour from Without

Nepal. I was used to feeling bound to any work I took responsibility for and so did not see how I could go. The temptation to participate was quite strong because I love my library profession, yet I decided not to accept. I very politely told Mr. Waterhouse and wrote a letter to the director informing him of the reason for my decision, while at the same time expressing my appreciation for his efforts to bring librarians from different parts of the world together.

The Seminar on Libraries in National Development, Bangladesh, July 23-25, 1976

After the emergence of Bangladesh in 1971 as a new star on the Asian horizon, I was told that many Western countries took interest in opening embassies and offices to help it to achieve its goals as an independent country under the late Sheikh Mujiber Rahman, its founder. The Asia Foundation also set up an office there, about which I was glad to be informed, having been sad when their office was ordered to close in India. The representative of the Asia Foundation in Bangladesh, James M. Dillard, kept closely in contact with T.U. Central Library so that our library could continue to get books that were needed for study, teaching, and research. Whenever Mr. Dillard came to Kathmandu, he visited Kirtipur, allowing me to share with him my library-related problems. I was happy to hear that the Asia Foundation was taking a deep interest in helping to ensure that libraries in Bangladesh would have an important role to play in education.

It was the last week of June 1976. James L. Woodcock, the acting representative of the Asia Foundation in Bangladesh, came to the library with an invitation to me from the president of the Library Association of Bangladesh, Muhammad Md. Shahabuddin, to participate in the seminar on "Libraries in

Honour from Without

National Development" to be held in Dacca under the sponsorship of the Asia Foundation. He also told me that if I accepted the invitation, the foundation's headquarters in San Francisco would authorize its Bangladesh office to take care of all necessary arrangements. I was honoured, of course, and I expressed my deep gratitude to the Asia Foundation and to Mr. Woodcock for bringing the invitation personally, yet I could not immediately accept because I was engaged in a fight for the library at the time and was sceptical that I would readily be given permission.

I was happy to meet Mr. Woodcock who, like Mr. Dillard, assured me of continued cooperation in the development of libraries and librarianship in Nepal. After receiving follow-up enquiries from him, I began getting the necessary documents together to go to Dacca. Because the foundation had no permanent office in Nepal, it had written to the USIS public affairs officer in Kathmandu, Mr. Kent Obee, and Dr. Devendra Raj Pandey of the Ministry of Finance to ask for their help in arranging my trip to Dacca. In the meantime I received a copy of a letter signed by Mr. Rahman, the second secretary of the embassy of the People's Republic of Bangladesh in Kathmandu, requesting our Ministry of Foreign Affairs to confirm my acceptance to attend the seminar. I was pleased to note everybody's appreciable interest in my participation. No problems arose.

In order to be in Dacca for the beginning of the seminar, I took one of my favourite airlines, Thai International, on a flight leaving Wednesday, July 21 and connecting in Calcutta with an Indian Airlines flight to Dacca. As soon as I reached Dacca airport I felt I was in a familiar place: everyone spoke Bengali, just as in Calcutta. I was thus not worried whether anyone had come to receive me, but while exiting through the terminal I saw Mr. Rakib Hussain of the Library Association of Bangladesh and Mr. Syed Manjur Hussain of the Asia Foundation waiting with warm welcoming smiles. They took me to a very nice hotel in Dacca.

The next morning I got up quite early to see and feel the morning beauty of the city. When I went out for a short walk, however, the city did not look cheerful. The army was on patrol. Hardly any women could be seen in the streets, though naked children roamed here and there. I was rather surprised and astonished at the sights. It was just one year after the assassination of Sheikh Mujiber Rahman and his family members on August 15, 1975, which shook the whole world.

When I reached Dacca I had a great urge to learn more about that evil deed, but to my great dismay people did not seem willing to discuss it. The only person with whom I could talk about it was Prof. Neelima Ibrahim, the chairwoman of the Department of Bengali at Dacca University and the president of the Bangladesh Women's Committee. She was extremely kind to me. I had met her for the first time at the One Asia Assembly in Delhi in 1973, so I made a point to seek her out during my stay in Dacca. One afternoon she drove me in her car to show me the house of Sheikh Mujiber. I was sad to see it under army supervision; it looked utterly deserted. It should have been a historic landmark, I thought. She told me the whole sad story of Sheikh Mujiber. I prayed for his eternal peace.

The seminar was held at Dacca University. It was inaugurated on Friday, July 23. Abul Fazal, a member of the President's Council of Advisers, was the chief guest. After an impressive welcoming speech by Mr. Shahabuddin, Ahmad Husain presented a paper on "The National Library: Its Role in National Development."

The seminar lasted three days and consisted of seven sessions. Every session had a dignitary as its chief guest. I was

Honour from Without

impressed to see so many members of the President's Council of Advisers: Dr. M. N. Huda, Dr. M. Ibrahim, Secretary Haq Mugibul Haq of the Ministry of Education, and Dr. A. Rasid. This was a good sign for the status of Bangladesh libraries.

The seminar as a whole was quite interesting. At the end of it I was requested to speak a few words. This I did with reference to the problems of libraries and the library profession in South Asia and was warmly applauded.

A few days in Dacca with professional colleagues gave me a real picture of the library situation and profession in Bangladesh. If all the dedicated librarians could unite together, the situation could greatly be improved, I thought. With happy memories of Bangladesh I returned home to my normal library work. My work kept me so involved that I found myself postponing writing a thank-you note. It was a great joy for me to get a letter from Mr. Dillard even before I sent mine. Two sentences in it made me particularly happy: "You will be pleased to know that on several occasions we have been told by the Bangladesh Library Association that the success of their seminar was partly due to your participation. Your advice and suggestions will definitely assist them to work more efficiently for the development of the library field in Bangladesh."

International Visitors Program, Bureau of Educational and Cultural Affairs, U.S. Department of State, 1977

My long-cherished dream since my student life at Peabody to visit libraries in different states from the east to the west of the United States came true after fifteen years at the initiative of the USIS director in Nepal, Diane Stanley, who promoted educational and cultural ties between Nepal and the U.S. by many skilful means. I used to marvel at her diplomatic finesse, which made her one of the most affectionately remembered directors the USIS has ever had. The invitation came to me at the end of my participation in the U.N. General Assembly, about which I have already mentioned in brief in Chapter 10 of this book.

International Women's Delegation to Iran, 1978

In 1978 a telegram dated March 15 reached me stating that "de Beauvoir leading international women's delegation to Iran. Leaving Paris Sunday March 18. Can you come? Please call Claudel Servan Schreiber in Paris... or me in New York.... We need you." It was sent by Gloria Steinem, the famous political activist, writer, and co-founder of *Ms.* magazine. She had also been one of the commissioners appointed in 1977 by President Jimmy Carter to the National Committee on the Observance of International Women's Year. It made me feel good to know that a women leader like her, whom I had met during the UN sessions, remembered me so well and thought enough of me to ask me to join the delegation. Unfortunately circumstances did not permit me to do so, and I was sad to have missed the opportunity.

The Inauguration of the New Facility of the American Library, 1979

It was a happy surprise for me to get a letter from Diane Stanley inviting me to inaugurate the new American Library and to propose a toast afterwards — surprised because, in this part of the world, librarians are not usually invited to functions of great importance from a professional point of view, not to mention extended such a privilege as presiding over an inauguration. This very unusual request was one way to boost the status of librarians in developing countries like ours. I immediately gave my consent.

On Monday, January 29, 1979, U.S. Ambassador Douglas Heck and I inaugurated the newly renovated facilities. The library was beautiful, featuring improved lighting, a new entrance that facilitated access, and new furnishings and carpeting. The function itself was short but colourful and was attended by almost all local professional librarians and prominent educationalists.

Ms. Stanley gave the welcoming speech. In beautifully chosen words, she emphasized that the renovation of the library reflected the importance that the U.S. International Communication Agency attached to libraries. "Certainly we believe this library, which has served the Kathmandu community for 27 years, is a very important part of our program here", she noted. In his toast to the continued success of the American Library, Ambassador Heck congratulated all those who had worked to make the library a new and handsome facility. I too made a brief speech, admiring Ms. Stanley's praiseworthy interest in the development of libraries and the library profession in Nepal and appreciating this kind of ceremony, which would surely highlight the importance of libraries and the significant service that libraries with an honest and dedicated professional staff provide the community. At the end I too proposed a toast to the continued success of the American Library in providing commendable services, not only to the Kathmandu community but to the whole nation. It was a memorable event for me, and I thought it was an encouraging gesture to all persons involved in the library profession in the Kingdom.

Honour from Without

The Third International Conference of the Friendship Leagues with Israel, June 1979

Ever since I had visited Israel with my husband in 1970, at the invitation of the government and through the good offices of the Israeli ambassador Mordichai Avgar, I had been an admirer of that country's spirit of working for the common good even in an atmosphere of hostility all around. Our country was peaceful compared to theirs, yet our development had always been much slower.

In 1979 there arrived a letter, dated May 25, from the Israeli ambassador, Mr. S. Z. Laor, another great friend of T.U. Central Library and Nepal, inviting me on behalf of the Council of the Israel-Asia Friendship Association to participate in the Third International Conference of the Friendship Leagues with Israel to be held in Israel between the 1st and 8th of June. It was a very impressive conference, which I have already mentioned briefly in a previous chapter.

Here I would simply like to recall some of the remarkable speakers and participants I met and shared thoughts with during the conference: Benzamine Jaffe (moderator), A. L. Dulzin (chairman of the World Zionist Organization), Prof. Daniel Elazar, Yitzhak Shamir (speaker of the Knesset) Mr. Moshe Dayan (minister for foreign affairs), Netanel Lorch (secretary-general of the Knesset), Prof. Yigal Yadin (deputy prime minister), Teddy Koller (mayor of Jerusalem), and Yitzhak Griffel (deputy mayor of Tel Aviv). Some of the memorable places I visited were Yad Vashem, the Holocaust Memorial, the Knesset, Bet Hatefutsoth, the Museum of the Jewish Diaspora, Ben Gurion University, Rafih Salient, Capernaum and the Mount of Beatitudes, and the Golan Heights.

Honour from Without

I will always cherish memories of the fruitful conference and will remain grateful to Ambassador Laor and his wife Nura for their trust.

A Visit to the Soviet Union, 1979

Invitations to visit the Soviet Union were never directly made to the person concerned, as in other countries, but sent first through government channels. When I was the recipient of one such invitation in 1979, I did not know how to proceed, and at the time I was too busy with my work to follow up on it. I got no response from our government. Nothing moves in Nepal unless you make it move yourself, and I had always hated to go around on such business. Still, it was not only an honour for me but also to the government and the University.

I waited to hear from our government. Days passed and months went by with no news, though the embassy kept in touch with me. I always relished breaking our custom of having to go after things, even if I had to miss out on opportunities. To my great happy surprise, though, I received another letter from the head of the Cultural Department, Artour G. Novikov, renewing the invitation to visit the USSR in April, 1980 and informing me of the permission confirmed to the embassy by our Ministry of Foreign Affairs. I was grateful to all concerned staff of the ministry for enabling me to break with the above-mentioned deplorable custom. I left with a happy heart for the USSR, a visit described in a previous chapter. I am ever grateful to the ambassadors Boris Kirnasovsky, Dr. Kamo B. Udumyan, and Abdul Rakhman Khalil Ogly Vezirov, and to Mr. Artour G. Novikov, who made my visit possible and very interesting and fruitful.

Honour from Without

The Inauguration of the British Council Course on Librarianship, 1982

Mr. A. J. Pattison, the representative of the British Council took a great and admirable interest in reversing the deteriorating library situation in the academic life of Nepal, having joined the British Council in the hope of doing just such a thing. I used to share with him freely and frankly my thoughts on the existing educational and cultural problems, sensing an extraordinary urge in him to help the librarians and libraries in Nepal at a time when everything was going very badly. It was always a joy and inspiration for me to host him regularly in my office for consultations regarding library matters. He knew quite well how unhappy I had been for years, no adequate budget having been allotted to T.U.C.L. to perform its various functions. Due to this lack of support, T.U.C.L had had to stop even its training programmes, which were very essential to ensure sufficient manpower. I was happy, then, to learn of a plan he had to arrange a short course in basic librarianship to be conducted by Ms. R. M. Nicholas and Ms. P. Batley from Great Britain. During our discussion he made the request to me to officially inaugurate the course. I accepted the invitation with great pleasure, taking it as an honour not only for me but for the library profession.

The date was set for February 1, 1982. The ceremony was elegantly simple and short. Mr. Pattison, a man of many deeds but few words, was very brief in his welcoming speech. I took a bit more time, speaking on the importance of training and on the role that the British Council had played in the development of library services in Nepal. I highly praised it for its interest in helping libraries to improve their information services by providing such training.

Honour from Without

The course was attended by 25 participants. Preference was given to library staff of those institutions and campuses of Tribhuvan University which had received book presentations from the British Council.

A Visit to the Democratic People's Republic of Korea, 1983

Since its very inception T.U. Central Library had been always successful in establishing close ties with almost all embassies of countries with which Nepal had diplomatic relations. I had always strongly believed that libraries could play a key role in cementing cultural and educational links between countries through information exchange; knowledge, I felt, should never have any boundaries. Thus I never hesitated to accept book presentations from such Communist countries as the USSR, China, North Korea, Poland, and East Germany, if the books were useful for teaching and research purposes. Mr. Kim Won Gil, second secretary of the embassy of the Democratic People's Republic of Korea, used to bring personally such book presentations to T.U. Central Library. I was extremely impressed by his unusual skill of speaking fluent Nepali; he was better than any non-native speaker I had ever met. I always admired any foreign friend who took such interest in our language and culture.

The ambassador, Mr. Hwang Hu Ho, was also a good friend of Nepal, and he too believed that books could strengthen relations between countries. During his tenure of office quite a number of delegations from the DPRK came to visit Nepal, during which he always arranged for them to visit T.U. Central Library.

Mr. Kim agreed with my philosophy that academic institutions like T.U. Central Library should be above politics and free from any party influence within and without. Whenever he or the ambassador came to the library, they expressed their desire to have me visit their country. By my nature I never went after such invitations; they just seemed to come. Maybe my hard work spoke for me.

In April 1983 I received an invitation to visit the DPRK during the ambassadorship of Mr. Chang Gwang Son, who took equally praiseworthy interest in the library and books. I was excited to do so, but it was not easy, I was told, to get permission to go to Communist countries. As advised, I went myself to the Foreign Ministry. Some people there, including high officials, told me that I might not enjoy the trip, as there was nothing much to see in the DPRK. My sixth sense told me to go to the foreign minister, Padma Bahadur Khatri, to inform him about the invitation. I was glad to find him supportive. Nor did the University raise any objections.

I left Kathmandu on May 13, 1983 for Bangkok and then Beijing, somewhat surprised not to find any direct air link to Pyongyang. I was received at the airport in Beijing by Mr. Bake, the second secretary of the DPRK embassy, and he took me to the Capital Hotel for an overnight stay. It was my first visit to China, a neighbouring country about which I had read and heard a lot, yet it seemed like a world away. I was very curious to see more of it, but time did not allow.

A small plane with few people on board took me to Pyongyang, the capital of the DPRK. The flight was very enjoyable, and the scenic mountains appealed to my heart. Members of the Korean Socialist Scientist Association along with a pretty Korean girl dressed in the beautiful national costume and holding an attractive bouquet of flowers were at the airport to welcome me. The brightly smiling girl came to greet me first and saluted me so cutely in the Korean manner that I immediately felt attracted to her and hugged her tightly.

Honour from Without

Some reporters were also present to interview me. Afterwards I was taken to a guest house situated in a serenely scenic setting. That same evening a grand dinner was hosted in my honour. Following local custom, formal toasts were exchanged between my host and me, and brief speeches were delivered before dinner. It was the first dinner speech I ever made. Everyone present seemed to like it.

The Korean dishes came one after another — all very tasty. I enjoyed the occasion thoroughly. The only thing that grieved me was the barrier of language. Without the help of an interpreter, no conversation was possible. How I wished I had known Korean, and they English.

The next day I got up early and tried to tune in BBC news but could only get a local station. I was rather disappointed, being so used to different media for up-to-date information. At first I thought I did not know how to tune the Korean-made radio, so as soon as the guide came I told him about the problem. With a big smile he told me that the radio had only the local band.

Having got myself ready to visit Pyongyang city, I went downstairs, leaving my well-furnished room with its bed (covered with oriental silk), small refrigerator full of different soft drinks, a basket of big, fresh red apples, Korean sweets, a thermos of hot water, and tea bags. I was led to the dining hall for breakfast, but it was still quite deserted. I was the first to arrive, as I was anxious to get out and around as soon as possible. There was nothing to do but to wait for the other visitors who would also be going to the city. Within half an hour the hall was full of people from different countries, including India, Norway, Denmark, Sweden, Peru, Ethiopia, Mexico, Zimbabwe, and Gambia. Most of them were educationalists (vice-chancellors and professors), with a sprinkling of politicians. During the breakfast I noticed that

Honour from Without

some of the elderly professors from India who were vegetarians did not seem at ease with the food offered them, as most of the dishes contained meat. I myself got along, though.

After breakfast all the visitors were taken sightseeing in separate black Mercedes, each with its own guide. The scenes seen from the windows of my speeding car were my first significant impressions of Korea. I was struck immediately by the wide pavements fringed by willows, poplars, plantains, and shade trees, and by little red-cheeked boys and girls greeting me by waving their hands, and, as the car approached the heart of the capital, by the modern buildings, trolley buses and ordinary buses carrying passengers past pedestrians walking without fear of crowded traffic. The streets were beautiful and clean, and the whole of Pyongyang seemed to be a well-planned city with extraordinarily decorative gardens containing a variety of flowering plants, all of which impressed me deeply.

While in North Korea I visited many interesting places: the 150-metre-high stone Tower of Juche, built to honour their great leader President Kim Il Sung for his contribution to the ultimate victory of the revolutionary cause of Juche; Mangyongdae, the site of the birthplace of Kim Il Sung, now a well-preserved museum containing memorabilia of his childhood; the Grand People's Study House, with more than 600 rooms which can be used by 1,200 readers, built in 1982 under the guidance of the president. I wished that every head of state took that kind of interest in the spread of information.

The Secondary Girls' High School was a model school, containing all the facilities needed to boost student creativity. There I was given a warm welcome and treated to a beautiful cultural show organized in my honour. Many kinds of musical instruments were played with great proficiency by the girls.

Honour from Without

Watching the show, I couldn't help but wish that our schools also offered such educational opportunities.

Then there was beautiful Mt. Myohyang with its numerous waterfalls, fragrant flowers, and spellbinding scenery; the unique Pyongyang Grand Theater, built in Korean-style architecture; Kim Il Sung University, the International Friendship Exhibition, an attractive monumental edifice full of native decorative art and more than 25,000 valuable gifts sent to President Kim Il Sung by different nations; and Panmunjom, the military demarcation line and demilitarized zone set up after the unfortunate division of Korea. At this last site, I prayed for a peaceful reunification.

Korean friends gave me a friendly welcome wherever I went and often either interviewed me or asked me to write my comments in visitors books after every tour. I had never met such fastidious ways in any country I visited before.

Besides touring interesting places, I enjoyed regular talks on the Juche philosophy given by Prof. Kim through an interpreter. We often discussed the history of Korea, especially as the Juche idea pertained to it — the base of their development, as emphasized by Prof. Kim. He seemed to be fully knowledgeable on this particular philosophy, which was first propounded by President Kim Il Sung. I liked some of its ideas, as expressed by their leader:

> In order to establish Juche thoroughly, we must completely eliminate dogmatist attitudes to the universal principles of Marxism-Leninism, blind worship of big powers and reliance on them and national nihilism. At the same time we must oppose national chauvinism and national isolation and strictly guard against restorationism which attempts to revive the ancient uncritically on the plea of valuing own things. This is

317

precisely the revolutionary essence of the Juche we advocate.

One of the highlights of my visit was a memorable meeting with Mr. Hwang Chang Yob, the president of the Association of Socialist Scientists. I was deeply impressed by his profound knowledge of international issues, particularly as they related to my country. He spent much time with me in what was a very fruitful discussion.

Though at the end of my visit I felt a bit like a bird in a golden cage, I enjoyed my visit thoroughly. To put my impressions of Korea in proper perspective: It is a model socialist country, a land where children are treasured and the land kept clean. What I saw there was an entire people striving with great confidence to implement the Juche teaching of President Kim Il Sung — living proof to small nations that if they have an honest and selfless leader, whether a democrat or not, and the support of the masses, they can develop and prosper. It was really very amazing to see the country so well developed and adorned with indigenous architecture and gardens thirty-four years after its founding. I prayed that my country would also develop with such speed; given the right policies it would.

After I returned from my trip to Korea, I loved to tell both my Nepalese and foreign friends about my visit to the small agricultural country, which was competing hard to develop. I felt that the country was a showcase of the Communist system. Some American diplomats thought I had become a full-fledged Communist. Sometimes I wondered at how people hastened to evaluate others without giving thought to their past history. When I praised the development work of Korea, I was called a Communist, and when I refused to have a display on the Soviet Union in the library because it had nothing to do with academic concerns, I was regarded by Russian diplomats as an anti-Communist.

I never wished to be involved in world politics, only to be true to my own philosophy of stressing human rights and human well-being and praising any nation's development work as long as it was geared to the public good. I fully subscribed to the saying of Plato: "True happiness consists in making others happy."

The International Seminar on the Juche Idea, Lisbon, 1984

Due to the cold, the month of January had never been a pleasant one either for the library staff or for the readers; there were no heating facilities of any kind. From the very inception of the Research Centre for Applied Science and Technology (RECAST), I had been making regular requests to its directors to apply their knowledge of solar energy to the problem of heating reading rooms heavily used both by teachers and students. Alas, nothing ever materialized. The year 1984 was no different. I was sad not to be able to carry out such development work in the library due to the lack of support from within.

One afternoon, while I was having a meeting with some outside scholars and writers, a letter was brought to me. From the envelope I could see it was from Lisbon, Portugal. I was very curious to open it but waited till the visitors left. To my great surprise it was an invitation letter, dated January 1, 1984, from the well-known ex-president of the Republic of Portugal, Marshal Francisco da Costa Gomes, to participate in an international seminar on the Juche idea to be held in Lisbon from April 6 to 8, 1984.

Honour from Without

Not unnaturally, I was overwhelmed to get such an invitation. God, it seemed, did not like to see me freezing in the library without work to do and anything to look forward to.

I discussed with my husband how to go about attending the seminar. We decided that I should go on my own, taking a few days leave because I was not sure I would be given the green signal from the University. Without any problem I got permission from the government of Nepal and, with the help of the embassy of the Democratic People's Republic of Korea in Nepal, a visa from Delhi for Portugal, a country I had longed to visit ever since I had been in sunny Spain, the land of picturesque cathedrals, palaces, and the remnants of a world empire.

I landed at the Lisbon airport on April 5, 1984. The Portuguese Organization Committee members had arranged everything nicely for delegates from all over the world. We were all given a warm welcome by the members of the Reception Committee and escorted to the cosy Hotel Penta.

I had read about the country when I was a student of history long back: Though a small, largely mountainous land, Portugal was a great European power in the fifteenth and sixteenth centuries. Lisbon, its capital, is a great international air centre and offers excellent port facilities. Travelling from the airport to the hotel, I enjoyed the beauty of the city but wondered at not seeing the coast. I always loved to see large bodies of water. As soon as I reached the hotel, I expressed my surprise but was assured that the delegates would be taken for sightseeing.

It was already late, so I went to my room, taking some information on the seminar given to me. While going through it, I started to wonder who might have so kindly recommended my name for the seminar. Some Korean friends seemed to have

Honour from Without

remembered me and my dedication to my work since my visit to their country.

The next day I woke up early and looked out the window of my room. The view was stunning. I was utterly taken by the small, traditional red-brick houses with tiled roofs. The total effect was one of soothing beauty — the very antithesis of modern concrete jungles. Taking in the scene, I thought of my country and wished that it would also remain true to its architectural traditions.

The seminar started in a grand hall of the Hotel Penta. All the delegates very cheerfully exchanged greetings with each other. I too took the opportunity to introduce myself, eager to let other delegates know more about my country and happy to be representing it in an international seminar. I believe strongly in global friendship — a true key to world peace.

The seminar hall was full of distinguished guests. Marshal Francisco da Costa Gomes looked very dignified, and I did not wonder that General Spinola had resigned, in the face of increasing leftist pressure, for him to become the president of Portugal in 1974. Blasco Hugo Fernandes and other members of the Organization Committee kept themselves occupied with ensuring that everything went smoothly. The committee was composed of persons from different political parties and social and scientific circles.

The seminar had both a formal and informal air to it. All the delegates delivered their speeches in either English, French, Spanish, Arabic, or Portuguese, and simultaneous translation facilities in these languages were available to the delegates. As the title of the seminar itself indicated, the delegates were called upon to give their view of the Juche idea propounded by President Kim Il Sung of the Democratic People's Republic of Korea. Every delegate sang beautifully and earnestly the song of Juche. I too made a brief speech, in which I touched

321

especially upon the development work being carried out inside Korea in accordance with the Juche idea. It was well applauded.

During the three-day seminar, I was happy to meet some of the same top personalities of Korea whom I had previously met when I visited their country. It was a memorable experience for me.

A Visit to Great Britain under the British Council Visitorship Scheme, 1984

I had never realized that it had been so long (fourteen years) since I had last visited Great Britain, at the invitation of the British government, until I was offered another invitation in 1984 to visit the country to keep abreast of recent developments in the library field. This time it was under the British Council Visitorship Scheme and at the initiative of British Council Representative A. J. Pattison, a wonderful friend of libraries and the library profession and also a great supporter of Tribhuvan University Central Library in its period of stagnation. He did much for the betterment of the British Council Library, adding different sections, including a children's section to help young students in their pursuit of knowledge. I was happy that he attached so much importance to the needs of children, the future of Nepal. One way to improve children's reading habits was to make good reading materials available in libraries.

Mr. Pattison became a regular visitor to our library; sometimes he came by himself and sometimes with distinguished visitors. I always enjoyed seeing him and sharing with him my thoughts about existing library and academic problems, as I found him to be deeply interested in helping our country through cultural, educational, and technical cooperation.

Mr. Pattison sent the letter inviting me to visit Great Britain to the rector of Tribhuvan University, Dr. Chandra Prasad Gorkhali. I was extremely happy to get the invitation, though I was not sure whether I would get the okay from the University, as the situation was momentarily not that encouraging for me; though the rector was very supportive verbally, he did not always follow suit in his actions. I let things take their own course, however, and waited for the reply from the rector to Mr. Pattison's invitation letter without even asking him about it. My joy was all the greater, then, to get a copy of the reply sent to Mr. Pattison informing him of the decision by the University to accept the invitation. I was particularly surprised at the quickness of the reply — just twelve days.

The British Council staff, especially Mr. A. Bothwell, the education officer, took great interest in my visit and my participation in two important upcoming conferences: the Library Association in Brighton and the Aslib Conference in Norwich. Mr. Bothwell, a true educationalist and supporter of library development in Nepal, had wanted me to go to Britain in 1983 to participate in a seminar on "Library Resources in Higher Education" organized by the British Council and run by the well-known British librarians D. J. Foskett and D. T. Lewis. Unfortunately circumstances did not allow me to. Thus M. Bothwell seemed genuinely pleased that I was going this time around.

I left Kathmandu on September 8, 1984 and reached London safely the next day. I was driven from the airport by a courier from the British Council to the cosy Savoy Court Hotel. The courier gave me a letter of welcome from the programme organizer of the Visitors Department of the British Council,

Honour from Without

Mr. Steve Kenna, informing me of my programme during my stay in Britain. It was good to be back in London after fourteen years. After a good dinner, I returned to my room to do some reading and TV watching.

The next morning I left London for Brighton after a brief discussion of my programme with Mr. Kenna at the British Council office. I was escorted to the station by my assigned guide, who made moving around London quite easy. It took about one hour to reach the seaside resort of Brighton by rail — a comfortable and enjoyable trip. A shuttle coach service was already in operation to take delegates to the Metropole Hotel, situated in a very scenic spot close to the sea.

Quite a number of delegates had already reached the hotel. I hurriedly went to my room to deposit my luggage and came down to mingle with the crowd. I was extremely excited: it was the first library conference I had ever attended since I began my career as the chief librarian of Tribhuvan University almost 25 years before. It was the annual conference of the Library Association in conjunction with the British Council; the purpose of the conference was spelled out in a detailed handbook provided to the delegates. There was a grand exhibition organized for the occasion featuring more than a hundred booths representing many well-known publishers, leading suppliers and manufacturers of library equipment, micromedia, and the like. I was very much impressed and wished Nepal could have held such an exhibition; it would be a wonderful opportunity to show our educationalists and librarians how much we still needed to do.

I was invited to a reception and dinner held to mark the British Council's 50th anniversary. Mr. H. R. F. Keating, the chairman of the Society of Authors, was there to toast the Library Association in honour of the Society's centenary year. It was indeed a wonderful coincidence that important

Honour from Without

anniversaries of two of the institutions — the British Council (50) and the Society of Authors (100) — fell in same year. The dinner was followed by a Cabaret Evening of Magic performed by Roy Field, a member of the International Brotherhood of Magicians (and the deputy country librarian of Shropshire). I enjoyed the show thoroughly and went up to congratulate the artist, at which time I jokingly said, "I never knew a good magician also could be a good librarian." He gave me his visiting card, which I kept in my file, hoping to invite him to Nepal so that he could do some propaganda work for the library profession through magic shows, thereby helping to create interest, mainly in children, in using libraries.

The next day the conference started in a large hall amidst a very impressive gathering of distinguished delegates from different parts of Britain. All of them looked very dignified and cheerful. Very few non-Britons were present. I was sitting very close to the podium. Since it was my first such meeting, I wanted to observe everything closely and to show, moreover, that Nepal was also represented.

The first session was chaired by Sir Harry Hookway, a former chief executive of the British Council and the president-elect of the Library Association. Mr. R. G. Surridge, the president, gave a sparkling welcoming speech, and Sir John Burg, the director-general of the British Council, delivered an equally delightful keynote address. Prof. Randolf Quirk, the vice-chancellor of the University of London, presented an interesting paper on the role of the printed word in global English. Just after his paper the chairman gave the foreign delegates an opportunity to say a word or two. I was never one to let such chances pass, so I went to the podium to convey my greetings from Nepal and Nepalese librarians to one and all, express my gratitude to the British Council for bringing me to the conference, and paint a brief picture of the library situation in Nepal and the challenges I had been facing since the very beginning of my career. I was highly applauded and naturally felt very honoured. Many delegates were prompted to convey their moral support to me to continue to face the never-ending task of boosting the development of libraries and the library profession in my country. Afterwards I handed over notes (Appendix IX) to the president of the Association to submit to their committee in future and requested him to think over the existing unaddressed problems and try to come up with solutions to them.

On the same day, interspersed with morning coffee and a lunch break, five other topical papers were given: "The British Book Overseas" by Tim Rix, the chief executive of Longman Publishers, who praised the British Council's first fifty years of supporting a "natural flow of British books overseas through to meeting intense competition"; "Librarianship Worldwide: the British Council's Contribution" by Prof. Wilf Saunders, the head of the Library and Information Services Council, who considered the very wide-ranging contributions and influence of the British Council's libraries and librarians in more than 80 different countries; "Africa" by Stan Made, the librarian of the University of Zimbabwe, focusing on the need of aid to library development in the Third World and the British Council's contribution to the creation of national public library services in sub-Saharan Africa; "South-East Asia" by Dr. D. E. K. Wijasuriya, the director-general of the National Library of Malaysia, discussing the major problems and issues regarding library services in Malaysia as well as the prospects for the future, particularly in relation to the British Council; and European Librarianship: "The British Influence" by Dr. Hans-Peter Geh, the librarian of the Wurtemberg State Library and vice-president of the International Federation of Library Associations (IFLA), giving a short review of past activities and describing problems of collection development, the transborder flow of bibliographical data, and the universal availability of information.

After the session a civic reception was held in grand British fashion by The Worshipful The Mayor of Brighton Councillor John Blackman on behalf of the borough in honour of the delegates. I had a brief but memorable chat with the mayor and his wife, who showed genuine interest in Nepal.

The first session of the second day of the conference was chaired by Jean Steward, the president of the Association of Assistant Librarians. I felt happy and proud to see a lady doing the chairing. There were two thought-provoking papers: one on "The Boundless Librarian" by Raymond Astbury, the principal lecturer of the School of Librarianship and Information Studies at Liverpool Polytechnic, and the other titled "Advice versus Information: A Barrier in our Minds" by Mr. W. Gwyn Williams, the county librarian of Clwyd. I again took the floor to make some comments on the poor image of librarians in the Third World and on the challenges I had to face to raise their status in Nepal. The delegates showed me their encouragement by their applause. Some ladies came to tell me that some of them had shed tears while listening to my story. I was indeed touched and thanked God for giving me the power to move an audience of fellow professionals.

After a coffee break the second session started, with Mr. H. Faulkner-Brown chairing. There were two interesting papers on library buildings: "The State of the Art" by Alan Longworth, formerly the county librarian of Lancashire, and "Librarianship without Buildings" by Dr. William Martin, the head of the Department of Library and Information Studies at Queen's University, Belfast.

Afterwards there was an enjoyable tour to Sheffield Park, and in the evening I went to attend a short interdenominational service. This service was arranged by the Librarians' Christian Fellowship Association. I was greatly moved by the powerful talk by Rev. Alec Gilmore, the secretary of the Association for Christian Communication. After the service I went back to my hotel to rest and do some paper reading.

September 13 was the last day of the conference. It was chaired by Doris Palmer of the Conference Subcommittee. Kenneth R. Cooper, the chief executive of the British Library, and George Cunningham, the chief executive of the Library Association, delivered inspiring speeches. Afterwards fellowship presentations were introduced by Peter R. Lewis, the chairman of the Board of Fellowship. Then, with great dignity, Mr. Surridge, the president of the Library Association, stepped up to deliver the presidential address on the theme of the conference, "Librarianship without Frontiers," which dealt, among other things, with the profession and its role in the academic world. The Library Association was lucky to have him as its president, I thought. Later he invited me to have a quiet lunch with him and his wonderful wife — a highlight of the trip for me.

I was sad as the conference came to an end. I really wished it had been a longer one. I was full of admiration for the management of the conference sub-committee which had made my stay so happy. It was indeed a very enriching experience for me to finally attend such a professional conference. I left Brighton for London on September 13 with pleasing memories of the past days and the scenic beauty of the conference site.

Before I left London to attend the 57th annual Aslib conference at the University of East Anglia in Norwich, the British Council arranged a meeting with Mr. Cooper, the chief executive, and Mr. B. C. Bloomfield, the director of Collection Development of the British Library, a visit to David Waterhouse, a former representative of the British Council in

Honour from Without

Nepal, and his family, and a happy reunion with Mr. and Mrs. Winifred Coulson, who had spent a few years in Nepal working in different projects to help Nepalese women in the early 1970's.

I left London by train for Norwich on the afternoon of September 18. The weather was rainy, and I was also not feeling so well. It took about one and a half hours to reach Norwich Thorpe Station. Buses had been arranged to convey delegates from there to the university. In spite of the weather I enjoyed the bus ride. On my arrival I was given some brief printed information prepared by Sherry Jesperson, the manager of the Professional Development Group. With it in hand, I got ready for the opening of the conference and exhibition, which was to start the same evening. Though the whole conference was totally different from the one in Brighton, it was also an enriching experience for me. On the morning of September 21 I left Norwich to return to London.

The next day was Saturday, a day for sightseeing and also a little shopping. Linda Morris of the Libraries Department of the British Council was to accompany me. She had been so kind to me during my stay in the capital. Shopping had never been an interest of mine, yet I did some for my daughter and husband. Everything seemed costly to me, as I always calculated in Nepalese rupees before purchasing anything. It was a very relaxing day, and Linda's companionship made it even more so.

On September 23 I left London for Hull. It took five hours to reach my destination. I was accommodated at the fine Pearson Park Hotel. There I was happy to receive a nice letter from Mrs. A. Hornsby, the programme officer of the British Council, containing a busy programme and extending a warm welcome to the city. The weather was not good at all, though. It was pouring heavily. Unfortunately I had to remain confined to the hotel that evening, feeling too cold to move anywhere. I went to bed early, hoping to see sunshine the next day.

The sun was out as wished to welcome me. Oh, was I happy! The sky was so blue and clear, so I went to the park for a morning walk. I was somewhat sorry to have to cut the walk short to get ready for my visiting programmes. British Council Representative Ms. N. Branton came on the dot to take me to the University of Hull, where two meetings had been arranged: one with Helen Stephens, the South-East Asia librarian of Brynmore Jones Library at the University of Hull, and the other with the director of the Centre for South-East Asian Studies. I enjoyed talking with Ms. Stephens. Unfortunately the director of the centre, Mr. D. K. Basset, was not available.

After visiting different libraries of the University of Hull and a nice lunch with Ms. Branton, I was taken back to the station to catch a train to London to finish out my few remaining programmes: a meeting with Mr. Palmer of VSO to make a special request for British volunteer help for T.U. Central Library and a visit to the School of Oriental and African Studies to check their collection on Nepal and to establish ties. There I met some fond British and Nepalese friends, including Dr. David Matthews, author of *A Course in Nepal* (London, School of Oriental and African Studies, 1984) and Mr. Padma Prakash Shrestha, the editor of *Nepal Rediscovered: The Rana Court 1846-1951* (New Delhi, Time Books International, 1986) and other members of the Nepal Kingdom Foundation. I also made a tour of the House of Commons and House of Lords and each of their libraries. How I wished that the National Panchayat had such library facilities and services so that all the members could have access to the knowledge they needed to contribute to the nation's development.

Honour from Without

I was sad my visit had come to an end. It was really a very fruitful experience for me. With all the happy memories and new ideas I left London on September 29 for Nepal, expressing silently my gratitude to all, especially Mr. Pattison, for making my visit to Britain a great success.

The Library Mission to Bhutan, 1985

From the beginning of my career as a librarian, I was involved in the activities of the National Commission of Nepal for UNESCO as one of the commission members. All the members were seriously intent on achieving the goals of the commission to support UNESCO's activities in Nepal. I was wholly in agreement with the preamble of the UNESCO charter (Since wars begin in the minds of men, it is in the minds of men that the defence of peace must be constructed), which was largely inspired by British Prime Minister Clement Attlee and the American poet Archibald MacLeish, and with its commitment to "collaborate in the work of advancing the mutual knowledge and understanding of people through all means of mass communication..., give fresh impulse to popular education and to the spread of culture..., [and] maintain, increase and diffuse knowledge." Thus I was extremely happy to receive a letter from UNESCO inviting me to undertake a mission to Bhutan, about which I have written in a separate chapter. I still love to remember the few words from Mr. J. Murdock of the Division of Higher Education and Training of Educational Personnel at UNESCO headquarters in Paris after I completed my mission: "The creative improvisation you displayed in getting yourself to Bhutan was much appreciated.... Should the need ever be expressed by one of the projects for which I am responsible for the services of a consultant in the library field, I would like to think I could

Honour from Without

count on your willingness to be considered as candidate." I remain always grateful to UNESCO for the honour.

The International Library Movement Award (medal and citation) 1985 with the Title "Surya"

About the International Library Movement Award I knew nothing till I received a letter from Mr. N. K. Bhagi, the founder of the award, on November 6, 1984 informing me that my name was included in the list of persons to be submitted to the judges for it. I was quite surprised and of course happy. I read and reread his letter and the circular describing the ILM Award. The circular stated that

... the International Library Movement has achieved a distinction in the field of Library and Information Science all over the world. An award entitled International Library Movement Award was instituted from the year 1974. From 1984 onwards seven persons each hailing from continents of Asia, Africa, Australia, Europe, North America, South America and the sub-continent of India who have made distinct contribution in the field of Library Movement in any part of the world every year, will be honoured with this award. Nominations from all over the world are invited and details of the contributions of a nominee should be sent to the Editor International Library Movement, Ambala, India.

I wondered who could have recommended my name; it was surely not someone from Nepal, I thought, because unless you're in a group here you rarely get prizes or awards, no matter how much you contribute honestly and sincerely to the development of your institution and country. In any event, I

Honour from Without

felt quite honoured to have been recommended. Renowned or otherwise, an award is an award, an appreciation of someone's contribution to a particular field of endeavour and a most necessary means of encouragement and inspiration. I immediately replied to Mr. Bhagi, thanking him for the decision to honour me and the six other persons, the effect of which would surely be to bring librarians together to act more effectively in the field of library science in all parts of the world.

Days passed and months went by. I heard nothing further about the award, though I was sure I would end up getting it if the judges evaluated my contribution to the library movement in Nepal honestly. After thirteen months a registered and insured parcel came from Mr. Bhagi. With great excitement I opened it and was extremely happy to find the award (medal and citation) along with his letter informing me that my name had been approved for the ILM Award, 1985 with the title "Surya" (sun) by the International Award Committee. The awards were to be presented at the Indian Library Association Conference at Baroda on November 1, 1985. I was thankful for this recognition of my service to my people, which I regarded as service to God. I have continued to treasure the medal and citation.

The news of the award was carried prominently by important newspapers, which reproduced the beautiful wording of the citation:

Mrs. Shanti Mishra, Chief Librarian of Tribhuvan University, has been awarded the International Library Movement Award (medal and citation) for the year 1985 for distinct contribution toward World Library Movement, for work on World Peace, Universal Brotherhood, National Integration, Social Work, Scientific Research and Education. The awards were presented at the Indian Library Association (ILA) Conference at Baroda, India. The recipients for previous years are Dr. Patrick R. Penland, University of Pittsburgh, U.S.A., and Prof. A. I. Mikhailov, director, VINITT, USSR.

The International Conference on Ranganathan's Philosophy, Delhi, 1985

Although I had had a long-cherished desire to meet Dr. S. R. Ranganathan, ever since to my student life in the Peabody Library School in the U.S.A., I never did. I was so sad when he passed away on September 27, 1972 at the of age of 80. He was not only the pride of Indian librarians but of librarians the world over. Despite all the challenges he had had to face from the beginning of his career as a librarian, he succeeded beyond all expectation in contributing to the development of libraries and the library profession in India. He is called the "father of the library movement" in India. I was told that he was a close friend of India's former president the late Sarvepalli Radhakrishnan, the renowned philosopher, who invited Ranganathan to Banaras Hindu University to develop a library system when he was vice-chancellor from 1945 to 1947. If Ranganathan had not embraced the neglected profession of library science, he would have easily made his way to some high position.

Since my student life I had been a great admirer of Ranganathan. His writings and thoughts always greatly appealed to me — so thoughtful, wise, and practical, and tailored to the situation in this part of the world. After returning from the United States, I took the opportunity to write to him whenever I had problems, especially regarding library-related legislation and library training. His prompt replies became a source of inspiration and encouragement to me from the very beginning of my career. I also collected all the issues of *Herald of Library Science* which carried his articles, under the heading "A Librarian Looks Back." They were very enlightening and full of the experiences he faced during his career, whether sweet or sour.

What could be more exciting than to receive a message, dated August 20, 1985, from Mr. Girja Kumar, the president of the Indian Library Association (founded in 1933), inviting me to attend the International Conference on Ranganathan's Philosophy. I immediately sent my acceptance with a few words of appreciation of their praiseworthy idea to hold such a conference, which would surely be a great event in the history of the library profession in this part of the world.

I left Kathmandu on November 10 for Delhi. It was late evening. I never felt easy travelling alone in India and so was happy to find Mr. S. K. Kochhar, the regional manager from UBS Publishers with his wife to receive me at the airport. Unexpectedly everything had been arranged for me — a token of their high regards, as they put it. Whenever somebody like Mr. Kochhar or the general manager, Mr. R. K. Sahni, came to Kathmandu, they always extended me an invitation to visit Delhi so that I could select books on site. I was glad to be back in the beautiful capital city of India after fourteen years, in the pleasant month of November, the best time to visit. The weather was excellent; flowers were blooming everywhere. I made a special request to Mr. Kochhar to take me to Raj Ghat, Shanti Vana, and the Indira Gandhi Museum, where I could feel and be in touch with the presence of India's great leaders and pay my homage to them.

The conference began on November 11. It was inaugurated by the dynamic ex-librarian of the National Library of India, Mr. B. S. Kesavan, for whom I had had high regards ever

Honour from Without

since I met him in 1967 at INSDOC (Indian National Scientific Documentation Centre) in Delhi when he was its director. He had a pleasing and forceful personality, the qualities needed to advance the cause of the library profession. He delivered a very impressive speech in which he outlined the unique contribution made by Ranganathan. While listening to him, I suddenly remembered the following greeting sent to Ranganathan by the American Library Association on his 71st birthday in 1962, about which I had read and noted down long back:

> To S. R. Ranganthan — Librarian to the World: On behalf of the cataloguers and classifiers of America we greet you. Your words are the words of an Anglo-American but your language is the language of the East, and your ideas are universal. You answer the challenge of the future with a challenge. Most of us are not your disciples: all of us are your students. For a generation you have forced librarians to think. We are proud to be in your debt.

More than sixteen countries were represented at the conference and sixty papers were presented. Many well-known foreign personalities of the library profession were present, including Jean Atchison and Mr. D. J. Foskett. Almost all the active librarians from the different parts of India were also present. Top Indian librarians, such as Mr. P. N. Kaula, Mr. Girja Kumar, Mr. Krishna Kumar, and Mr. P. P. Mangla, gave impressive speeches. I too took the opportunity to speak and pay my tribute to Ranganathan, while at the same time expressing my deep concern about the deteriorating situation of Indian librarianship, especially in the areas of teaching, training, and research in the library schools, and pleading with all to take immediate corrective action, which in itself would be a great tribute to Ranganathan; without such action the conference would have little meaning. I also humbly made a request to do away with groupism in the Indian library world so that Indian librarians like Girja Kumar would not have to express in future, as he did in his foreword to the proceedings of the conference titled *Ranganathan's Philosophy: Assessment, Impact and Relevance*:

> Gandhian philosophy is in danger of being forgotten in the country of its origin. Mahatma Gandhi has been deified in India simultaneously. This dialectical process is typical of Indian culture and civilizations throughout the centuries. It shall indeed be surprising, if the case of Dr. S. R. Ranganathan were to be an exception to the general rule. Dr. Ranganathan has been mummified by his self-proclaimed followers. They seem to be insistent on having inherited his legacy unilaterally. His thoughts are treated like incantations chanted ritually like mantras without comprehending their true meaning or significance.

Before I ended my brief speech, I thanked the president of the Indian Library Association, Mr. Girja Kumar, and the association for honouring me with their invitation to attend the conference. Most of the top librarians — Mr. D. R. Kalia, Mr. P. N. Kaula, Mr. T. Viswanathan, and others — made a point to express appreciation of my truthful comments. I was happy; it was indeed a very interesting experience for me.

Recommendation to the Post of Director of the United Nations Dag Hammarskjöld Library

Among the greatest honours I have been accorded have been offers to apply for a post abroad. One of the most memorable of these was contained in a letter dated July 19, 1989 from Angela E. V. King, the director of the UN Recruitment and

Honour from Without

Placement Division, informing me that I had been recommended as a candidate for the post of director of the Dag Hammarskjöld Library. It was an honour I shall ever remain grateful for.

I have never, however, felt the urge to serve outside of Nepal. One might consider this unwise in a country that is supposedly under a curse (see page 43). The fact that Nepal suffers from such a brain drain would suggest that indeed it is. The attraction that affluent countries exercise is understandable. Still, I am convinced that many expatriates would opt to remain in their homeland if a few set of basic working conditions could be met. The government, by failing to reward merit and tolerating those who pull strings, is driving away some of its most creative talent. It is time to get out from under the curse.

Chapter 13

Librarianship on the Global Scene

Until 1970 I was largely confined to my own small world — Tribhuvan University Central Library. I aspired to nothing other than to devote the whole of my energy to its progress and prosperity. Nothing came into my head if not plans and programmes on how to support the academic goals of the University — the only one in the whole of Nepal. I strongly believed that God helps those who help themselves. My philosophy was not to go after greater things before achieving some plan of limited scope. Expansion would come by itself. Thus I never sought any opportunity to focus my ambitions outside my country.

I received much information on seminars, conferences, and the like organized by IFLA. The International Federation of Library Associations and Institutions, founded in 1927, is a worldwide, independent, non-governmental organization with headquarters in the Hague, Netherlands. It is the voice of librarianship on the global scene. Its constantly growing membership now numbers over 1,250 in more than 122 countries, 82 of them in the Third World. It functions through 32 sections and 10 round tables grouped together in 8 divisions. The sections deal partly with types of libraries, partly with library activities, and range from university libraries to libraries for the blind, and from information technology to services for multicultural populations. Included are three sections for regional activities: Asia and Oceania, Africa, and Latin America and the Caribbean.

Librarianship on the Global Scene

IFLA activities, especially its core programmes in the Advancement of Librarianship in the Third World (ALP), which was officially launched at the general conference in Nairobi in 1984, immediately appealed to me, as I was very much interested in founding a model library association of purely professional membership for Nepal. As I envisaged it, it would maintain close contact with IFLA and target its activities to change the old image of librarians in a society which was not yet quite ready to accept them as being as important as professors, doctors, or engineers. Further, it would be free from the petty group politics endemic to associations in this part of the world, especially South Asia. My husband and I had drafted a prospective constitution in 1970, but there things stood.

I had noticed that quite a number of developing countries were included in the directory of IFLA and had become intent on getting Nepal included also. Early in 1970 I sent an enquiry to IFLA on how to apply for membership. IFLA responded in a very encouraging way, and by 1974 T.U. Central Library's application had been accepted, thanks to the Dutch Library Centre, which came up with the $50 membership fee for us.

Now I had more access to IFLA publications, which I kept separately in the library after displaying them for some time publicly. My interest grew, and correspondence with dedicated professionals from different countries cemented my links abroad. As a result, I was nominated and then elected to be one of the members of the standing committee for Asia and Oceania, for a two-year term, at the 53rd IFLA General Conference held in Brighton, England in August 1987. I took this as a great personal honour. I will always remain grateful to ex-Secretary-General Margreet Wijnstroom of IFLA and ex-Chairman J. S. Soosai of the IFLA Regional Section for Asia

Librarianship on the Global Scene

and Oceania for their admirable support — a source of inspiration to me.

The main government and private newspapers featured the news of my election. I was filled with joy and vowed silently to God to carry on my professional activities in Nepal, with the help of IFLA, as a model for the region.

Shortly after my election I was sad to hear that Margreet Wijnstroom had retired from IFLA. She had been a highly competent and active secretary-general with a deep interest in helping developing nations to boost library activities. In just recognition, the Executive Board of IFLA decided to establish the Margreet Wijnstroom Fund for Regional Library Development and to present her with a scroll containing the following words: "Margreet Wijnstroom has represented the voice of librarianship, particularly for developing countries, which she has wholeheartedly assisted to help reach their goals of self-determination and self-development through a broader access to information."

The first meeting of the Regional Standing Committee for Asia and Oceania was held at the Lodhi Hotel in New Delhi on April 21 and 22, 1988. I was very happy to be attending the meeting — the first such in my professional career. Prof. P. B. Mangla, the local organizer and a member of the IFLA Executive Board, managed everything scrupulously.

The meeting commenced under the chairmanship of the outgoing president, Mr. J. S. Soosai. He gave an impressive welcoming speech, pledging his continued help and support to IFLA. I was touched and sad, because it was he who had supported my nomination to the committee. I was now in, he was now out.

Prof. Mangla also extended a warm welcome in his dignified voice. I took pride in him for being on the IFLA Executive Board from our part of the world. Mr. Guust van

Librarianship on the Global Scene

Wesemael, the IFLA deputy secretary-general and professional coordinator, then briefed the meeting on the role of the standing committees in IFLA.

After the election the meeting was chaired by the new chairman, Dr. D. E. K. Wijasuriya, the director-general of the National Library of Malaysia. He gave an impressive speech in which he vowed to work for the development of the library profession in the region through the standing committee.

During the meeting the Nordic proposal on the implementation of ALP and other proposals of merit were discussed; these had been put forward by Mariam Abdul Kadir (assistant director of the National Library of Malaysia), Dr. Showky Salem (director of the Information Department of Safat Kuwait), and Mr. Anthony Ketley (acting director for National Coordination Services of the National Library of Australia). Since it was my first appearance I had no concrete proposal of my own to submit, yet my participation in the meetings was appreciated. I admired the spirit of the new chairman shown in proposing Ms. A. K. Anand, the librarian of Punjab University Library in India, for the post of secretary of the committee, as I always supported increased participation from South Asia.

Afterwards I discussed the library situation in Nepal with Mrs. Abdul Kadir, Mr. Ketley, and Dr. Salem. The charming and dynamic Mrs. Kadir assured me of her help in arranging one-month training courses for my staff as well as access to attachment programmes under the Malaysian Technical Cooperation Programme (MTCP). It was truly a joy for me to be interacting with people of the same profession from different nations.

I came back with happy memories from Delhi. From the airport I went directly to the library to share the experiences of my first IFLA standing committee meeting. The staff showed great interest. A package from Australia was waiting for me.

Librarianship on the Global Scene

Opening it, I found information on the IFLA Conference to be held in Sydney in September. My desire to attend was strong, but how could I, given the lack of funds? Still, I knew that when I wished from the bottom of my heart, by the grace of God, the wish usually came true.

Visit to Australia: The IFLA and LAA Conferences

After some weeks my husband and I were invited to a reception. If memory doesn't betray me, it was held in the Israel embassy. It was a very impressive gathering of dignitaries and diplomats. The American ambassador, Milton Frank, saw me, and a few moments later he was making his way towards me in the company of a tall and dignified lady. He introduced me to her as the new Australian ambassador, Diane Johnstone, who said she had been looking forward to meeting me, having been told by one of her diplomatic colleagues at one the first official functions she attended that one of the people she really must meet was "the dynamic and capable librarian of T.U. Central Library, Mrs. Shanti Mishra."

These were similar to the words with which Ambassador Frank praised me and my library work in a letter, dated July 18, 1988, after his visit to T.U.C.L. on July 6: "Your warm welcome to 'your' library was deeply appreciated. It is clearly evident that the University is indebted to you for all that you have accomplished in building what is surely the most important repository of knowledge in Nepal." I was overwhelmed to be so close to two ambassadors of great nations who were so interested in T.U. Central Library and the library profession. I will always cherish the memory of Ambassador Frank's keen interest in quality education and library development in Nepal along with his involvement in other equally important fields. During his tenure a number of academicians from the United States visited Nepal, including Mary S. Metz, the president of Mills College — an outstanding women's college in California.

Ambassador Frank gave my husband and me numerous opportunities to meet such guests in his residence. One incident I still remember was a grand reception he hosted in honour of Prof. Leo E. Rose, the American expert on Nepal, Sikkim, Bhutan and other countries and author of the book *Nepal — A Strategy for Survival* (Berkeley, University of California Press, 1972), for whom I always have had highest regards, his skilfully wielded pen having kept outsiders aware of the true state of affairs in Nepal. With his help I was able to complete the Asian Survey file in T.U. Central Library, a tool which allows our teachers, students, and scholars to consult the writings of foreigners concerned with Asia.

While talking to Prof. Rose on this occasion along with other friends, I noticed a peculiar change in his face. Suddenly he fell to the thickly carpeted floor and lost consciousness. Everyone was enjoying the reception so well that few at first took notice. Luckily he soon recovered, though his broken glasses had cut his face. He was taken to a room to rest.

I had requested Ambassador Johnstone to visit the library, and .she had expressed her desire to do so. She wished to discuss a gift programme initiated by the National Library of Australia to donate books published in Australia, which were sent according to receivers' needs, and to establish contacts with libraries of the Asia/Pacific region.

Whenever I meet lady ambassadors I am excited and filled with pride. In our male-dominated society I strongly believe that capable, dynamic, and well-respected women, no matter to which country they belong, should be accounted the equals of their male colleagues — this on the basis of their achievements.

Librarianship on the Global Scene

Jealousy and envy have no place among women, who are still lagging behind socially. I like to remember what Nannerl O. Keohane, the president of Wellesley College in the U.S.A., said:

... the problem lies with men; men control the gateways to success, and they are reluctant to let women in. Men fear successful women, are uncomfortable with women leaders, resist threats to male bonding and changes in the familiar scenery. So when it comes time for the big promotion, they look for reasons to promote a man instead. ...perhaps we lack ambition: perhaps women do not really want other women to succeed.

Perhaps, yet so true to the Nepalese context. I was very grateful to Ambassador Frank for introducing me to Ambassador Johnstone.

The next day I told my senior staff about my meeting with the new ambassador, who immediately struck me as a great friend of the library world. I always loved to share experiences with my staff so as to boost their urge to be true to the profession.

Sometime later a call came from the Australian embassy to confirm the visit of the ambassador for August 12, 1986. We waited expectantly. Our guest came at the exactly appointed time, and we extended her a simple but warm welcome. She showed appreciable interest in inspecting the collections in the different sections of the library during the tour I conducted and stayed longer than I expected.

During our meeting I showed her the information I received from Australia about the upcoming IFLA conference. She immediately took interest. She sounded astonished to learn that I not gone to any IFLA conferences in my 25-year career and promised to look for ways to sponsor my trip to Sydney.

Before leaving, Ambassador Johnstone wrote a few comments in the visitors book: "A most impressive collection. I look forward to returning to the library many times over the next three years." Very friendly and encouraging indeed. I too promised my sincere cooperation in making the Australian National Library's programme a success.

As Ambassador Johnstone had promised, she later came back to the library with books donated by the National Library. The day was November 23, 1987. I organized a simple function, inviting all the heads of the departments and teachers who had helped me to select the books from the catalogue sent from Australia. The ambassador gave a thought-provoking speech with laudatory comments about my staff, me, T.U. Central Library, and the contributions made by the Australian National Library to the development of libraries and the library profession in the Asia/Pacific region:

It is clear that Mrs. Mishra and her dedicated staff have worked very hard — with limited resources — in building T.U. Central Library into the institution it is today. It is an institution which services the growing thirst for knowledge and information in Nepal — both inside and outside the University — and which is providing assistance to other budding libraries in remote areas. It is clear that it is an institution represented by other institutions in the field, and with which they have established links. It is also clear that Mrs. Mishra and her staff have no intention of resting on any laurels — that they are determined that the library will continue to grow and to improve its services. We at the embassy look forward to a continuing relationship with T.U. Central Library, as does the National Library of Australia — a relationship which can only further the links both between our two countries and between the peoples of our countries.

I too promised my wholehearted cooperation in cementing the cultural ties between our countries through the dissemination of information, adding that exemplary activities would be promoted in T.U. Central Library to contribute to the success of the National Library of Australia's mission to help libraries of the Asia/Pacific region. All the departmental heads seemed quite impressed by the ambassador. I expressed my gratitude for their presence.

What a joy it was for me to receive a copy of the letter, dated July 8, 1988, from Ambassador Johnstone to Vice-Chancellor Mahesh Kumar Upadhyaya informing him of the decision of the Australian government to provide financial assistance to enable me to visit Australia for the IFLA/LAA (Library Association of Australia) conference. I was extremely excited at the prospect, the first such conference I would be attending.

Ever since I had started my fight to raise the status of librarians in Nepal, I had been citing the example of Australia's high recognition of librarianship for the benefit of our own authorities. Even before T.U. Central Library had any links with the National Library of Australia, I was able to make T.U.C.L. a depository of the Commonwealth Scientific and Industrial Research Organisation (CSIRO), Australia's main scientific research body, and thus to receive for some years its useful publications on rural industries, management of the natural environment, mineral energy, and water resources, along with publications from the Development Study Centre of the Australian National University. These I kept separately housed for easy accessibility to researchers. The Australian National Bibliography also came free of cost to the library.

Librarianship on the Global Scene

This trust and support shown to T.U. Central Library was a great encouragement, and whenever I got such publications I always took the time to go through them.

I always thought that Australia was the right country to be taking a leading role in helping the developing countries of Asia and Oceania in all possible fields, including librarianship. I had cherished a longstanding desire to visit the country to see with my own eyes what I had read about it. The invitation from the government of Australia to pay a visit and to attend the IFLA/LAA conference thus meant much to me.

There was no problem in obtaining a passport and visa. All the staff of the Australian Embassy were helpful, especially Mrs. Raewyn Henelius, an attaché, who put together an interesting touring programme and arranged everything for me. Vice-Chancellor Upadhyaya, who always introduced me to foreign friends as a legendary lady, Rector Chandra Prasad Gorkhali, and Registrar Dr. Parthibeswar Timilsina also did their part to move the papers quickly.

On August 24, 1988 I left Kathmandu. My husband came to see me off. I was sad to leave him behind and wished he could have accompanied me.

The overnight stop in Hongkong seemed, in my yearning to reach my destination, much too long. The next day at 9.30 a.m. I reached Melbourne, one of the world's great cities and the fashion capital of Victoria. Barry Martin of the University of Melbourne Library was at Tullamarine Airport to meet me and take me to the university to visit the library. While driving from the airport to the university, I enjoyed viewing the garden-like landscape more than talking. Seeing is believing, and now I understood why Melbourne is called the Garden City.

After a tour of the library, senior library staff and Mrs. Cheryl Shauder of the Royal Melbourne Institute of

Librarianship on the Global Scene

Technology's School of Library and Information Science joined me for an enjoyable lunch. They all took admirable interest in Nepal and the library situation there.

My schedule for the visit to Melbourne was tight. Immediately following lunch Mrs. Shauder took me to the School of Library and Information Science for a tour, during which we discussed my future plan to establish a library school in T.U. Central Library as a teaching and serving institution. It was a highly interesting meeting but far too short, as I had to return to Melbourne Airport for my flight to Sydney. My desire to visit the plant cell research centre at the University of Melbourne under the directorship of Prof. Adrienne Clarke, a world leader in the study of plant fertilization, to see the magical and mysterious arcades of Melbourne, and to walk through and explore some of its magnificent gardens and parks did not materialize. The beautiful surroundings, containing gardens with sweeping lawns, bright flowerbeds and century-old trees, enraptured me so much that even now I yearn to go back. With lasting memories of the Garden City, I left for Sydney at 7 p.m.

It took less than two hours to reach the capital of New South Wales, one of the great seaports of the world, where 200 years ago the first European settlement in Australia was founded. It was already late evening. I was a bit nervous because I saw no one waiting for me. It was no problem, though, taking a bus to my destination, the YWCA. I was too tired to go out to explore the sites of Sydney at night and so went to bed in anticipation of waking up to the morning beauty of the city.

It was indeed a fine morning, better than I expected. With an American lady, Eileen Rost, who had helped me to open my room on my arrival, I went down to the reception hall, where I was given a message from Elizabeth Watt of the National

Librarianship on the Global Scene

Library of Australia that she would come to meet me at 1 p.m. I looked forward to discussing my programme in Sydney with her. Before she came I quickly phoned Mrs. Sheela Johnstone, the mother of Ambassador Diane Johnstone, to inform her of my arrival. She sounded very happy to be welcoming me to Sydney and expressed a desire to come to see me and take me to her home.

I don't remember how many times I checked my watch while waiting for Elizabeth Wait, such was my anticipation. She showed up with a gentle smile at one o'clock sharp. After a brief discussion about my programme, she took me to the New South Wales University campus, where all other delegates, from all over Australia, were to gather for the conference meetings.

Later I went to the entrance of the university to wait for Sheela to make it easier for her to find me. We had never met before but had no problem at all recognizing one another. When a tall, graceful lady with a beautiful smile walked towards me, drawn by my sari, I was quite sure that she must be Diane Johnstone's mother. We fell into an affectionate embrace.

Our first meeting was a portent of lasting friendship. She showed me around the beautiful harbour area for about two hours, pointing out where her daughter had gone to school on Darling Point, near where the well-known Blanche d'Alpuget lived, author of three novels and two biographies, including a widely acclaimed profile of Australian Prime Minister Bob Hawke. Darling Point seemed to produce persons of distinction. Then she took me to her residence to meet Mr. Johnstone, who was unfortunately not in good health at the time. In spite of his sickness, he put every effort into welcoming me with all due cheer.

Librarianship on the Global Scene

I was really very much touched by the Johnstones' admirable hospitality. Whenever I had free time from meetings, Sheela was always ready to show me around, taking great pride in her country's charms. To be with her was to learn much about the role of women in Australia and other aspects of its culture.

The most enjoyable and memorable of the outings which Sheela arranged for me was the Captain Cook Cruise of Sydney harbour. She got me the *Captain Cook Guide*, which provided me with a knowledge of Australian history and an insight into the spectacularly colourful character of Sydney and its harbour, now forever engraved deeply in my memory with its beautiful surroundings.

Never was I so charmed in all my life. Having been born in a landlocked country, I love water, and my first spellbound experience with Sheela in the harbour, which was extraordinarily decked out to celebrate the Bicentennial, was that of a masterpiece of art. Oh, how I wish I were a poet and could write of the scenic beauty of Sydney harbour as I saw it! I will always remain grateful to Sheela for making my visit to Sydney so delightful and making me feel so at home. It was thus sad to have to bid farewell to the Johnstones. I no longer wondered why Diane had made such a strong impact on Nepalese: like mother, like daughter.

I eagerly awaited the opening of the LAA (Library Association of Australia) conference, which was to be followed by IFLA's. It started on August 27 at 5:30 p.m. amidst a very impressive gathering of more than 1,000 Australian librarians. They all looked so dignified and knowledgeable; no wonder the image of librarians was so high in Australia. How I wished our librarians enjoyed the same esteem. I silently paid homage to the LAA for its remarkable role as the successor of the Australian Institute of Librarians, which had been founded in

1937 to raise the status of the profession by convincing educational institutions to develop graduate schools to provide quality training to future librarians.

Since I was not yet quite used to big library conferences and big receptions, I felt somewhat lost at times. I did not know whom to talk to or where to go. Later on I pushed myself hard to adapt to the situation. I then enjoyed every bit of it. The whole library world was uniquely different. Whenever I went back to my hotel after attending such gatherings, I returned to thinking how much Nepal's library profession lagged behind and how we could accelerate its progress.

At 9:30 on the 29th, before the opening of the IFLA conference, I went to attend the meeting of the IFLA Regional Standing Committee as its member from Nepal. More observers than regular members took part in the meeting. The new chairman, Dr. Wijasuriya, welcomed the members, and the ex-chairman, Mr. Soosai, also spoke. During the meeting I was happy to meet Lalita Brond, the director of IASL (International Association of School Librarianship) for Australia, with whom I had several times corresponded. We discussed how I could get support to open a library for children in Nepal.

Then came the big event for all the librarians from all over the world gathered in Sydney: the opening day of the IFLA conference, August 30, 1988. It was a lovely afternoon. No more beautiful place could have been the venue than the world-famous Sydney Opera House, designed by Danish architect Jorn Utzon. I reached the destination earlier to attend the closing ceremony of the LAA conference, whose tightly planned and beautifully focused programme was "Living Together: People, Power, Persuasion." This was followed by the impressive opening ceremony of the IFLA conference, which followed the same main theme, "Living Together," with the subtheme, "People, Libraries, Information."

The function started with some lovely music played by City of Sydney Organist David Rumsey. Enjoying its strains, I observed everything carefully. When all present in the hall stood, I too stood as the Vice Regal Salute was played. What a disciplined crowd, I thought. Then everyone gracefully sat back down to hear a fine welcoming speech by the chairman of the IFLA 1988 conference and master of ceremonies, Barrie Mitcheson. Next the president of the LAA, Alan Bundy, addressed the conference, expressing his joy at the IFLA's decision to hold its 54th general conference in the 200th year of Australia and in the 51st year of the LAA.

I, like everyone else, was eager to hear the governor-general of Australia, Sir Ninian Stephen. I silently admired Sir Ninian and Lady Stephen for their interest in the library world. Their presence meant a lot to all the librarians. His opening address was very appealing. He praised very eloquently the librarians as leaders in their profession, and also the wealth of experts in many other fields who were brought together by the conference. I was happy to hear him say, "There is of course no profession which is more familiar with the concept of cultural exchange than librarians." This was very close to my philosophy that libraries can play an important role in strengthening cultural ties between nations to bring peace and prosperity to the world. Another thing I liked was his account of Australian librarianship then and now: how within 45 years librarianship had been revolutionized. Listening to him, I thought that if I got to talk to him I would certainly tell him that librarianship in Nepal had not changed much and greatly stood in need of a similar revolution.

Then the president of IFLA, Hans-Peter Geh, delivered a long but interesting presidential address. His remarks ranged

Librarianship on the Global Scene

from the history of Australia to the importance of books, which are "the most valuable ambassadors of human esteem... [They] serve to promote understanding and cooperation within and between countries and are, therefore, especially important for peaceful coexistence of peoples." This was the same tune I often sang to my countrymen.

The UNESCO representative, Thomas Keller, came forward to convey the good wishes of the director-general of UNESCO, Frederick Mayor, for the success of the IFLA conference. My high hopes to meet Mr. Mayor, about whom I had heard and whose speeches I had read and enjoyed, thus came to naught. Still, Mr. Keller spoke very well about how UNESCO, from its inception in 1946, had considered that libraries, information, books, and reading had an important part to play in fostering international understanding, and about the ongoing general information programmes, including the revival of the old Library of Alexandria, the foundation stone of which had been laid by Hosni Mubarak, the president of the Arab Republic of Egypt, and the director-general of UNESCO on June 26, 1988 at the meeting point of the three continents of Asia, Africa, and Europe. Mr. Keller hoped that this great library of Alexandria, which burnt down nearly 2,000 years ago, would serve as a modern instrument of communication and one of the nodes of a network linking up all the great libraries of the world — a link with the past and a window on the future.

It was good for me to be getting all this information about UNESCO's assistance and concern for the development of libraries and information. I made up my mind to meet Mr. Keller, and also Hans Booms and Peter Judge, who represented the ICA (International Council on Archives) and FID (International Federation for Information and Documentation) respectively and were on hand to give a brief description of their activities.

The opening ceremony was followed by a plenary session chaired by Dr. Geh. Warren Horton, the director-general of the National Library of Australia, delivered a fine plenary address entitled "IFLA in the Antipodes: A Regional Perspective." He touched upon many areas in which Australia was willing to cooperate. Given my background, I was happy when he mentioned his deep interest in further developing IFLA's programme for the Advancement of Third World Librarianship.

Since this was my first IFLA general conference, I was confused about IFLA procedures. There were so many meetings in so many rooms, and all this amid 150 exhibitors. The participants were busy in a multitude of different ways. I enjoyed being caught up in it all and peeping into different meetings to find out what was going on and to try to find an opportunity to contribute something, even if in a small way, so that the presence of Nepal in an IFLA conference for the first time could be felt. Later on I came to know that I could do this more emphatically in the Professional Board's Open Forum and in the Round Table for the Management of Library Associations. I waited very eagerly for that opportunity.

Another opportunity I was seeking was to meet the current IFLA president, Dr. Geh, the former secretary-general, Margreet Wijnstroom, and the current secretary-general, Paul Nauta, along with Mr. Hurton, the director-general of the National Library of Australia. It was on August 31, during a grand reception given in honour of the IFLA participants, that I finally met all of them except Mrs. Wijnstroom. It was very memorable. I requested them to visit Nepal to see firsthand the situation of libraries in my country. I was gratified that they responded positively.

Librarianship on the Global Scene

At the same reception I met William J. Welsh, deputy librarian of the Library of Congress, and Mr. B. C. Bloomfield, the director of Collection Development in the British Library, who also took admirable interest in Nepal. How I wished I had had more time. The social gathering was thoroughly interesting, as the people in it were.

On September 1 I went first to the Professional Board's Open Forum, chaired by Joseph Price. There I listened very carefully to Sarah J. Tyack, vice-chairwoman of the PB and chairwoman of the Division of Special Libraries, and Mr. Guust van Wesemael, the deputy secretary-general of IFLA. As soon as the floor was open for discussion, I took the opportunity to convey greetings from Nepal and to describe in brief the library situation in Nepal. I was well received and thus felt very much encouraged.

Then I went to attend the Round Table for the Management of Library Associations, which had already started. The floor discussion was going on. After listening to some speakers, I took the floor to solicit help in my mission to give new life to the Nepal Library Association in order to make it a model in South Asia. This was met with applause. My brief participation in the discussion stimulated interested participants to approach me afterwards. I was really happy.

Before the closing ceremony of the IFLA conference I met Averill M. B. Edwards, the principal librarian of the National Library of Australia, a very dynamic lady with whom I had corresponded several times before my visit. Within a short period of time we became good friends. In spite of her busy schedule, she took me to the zoo in Sydney, hearing that I loved animals and natural surroundings. It was so relaxing to be out in the fresh air. I will always cherish the memory of my visit and sharing with her the story of my struggles and challenges.

Librarianship on the Global Scene

We came back on time for the closing session in the Chaney Auditorium on the beautiful campus of the University of New South Wales. The meeting was brief yet impressive. Dr. Geh presented the IFLA Medal with thanks to Mr. Mitcheson of the Australian Organisation Committee. At the end of the meeting Dr. Geh, on behalf of IFLA's Executive Board, also conferred the IFLA Medal upon William J. Welsh for his outstanding contributions as one of the founding members of IFLA's Programme Management Committee. I prayed for more librarians like Mr. Welsh who would be able to play a major role in improving international relations through librarianship. I was sad that the 54th IFLA general conference came to a close so soon. It was indeed a fruitful experience for me.

The next day I was to leave beautiful Sydney by bus early in the morning for Canberra to attend the Conference of Directors of National Libraries as Nepal's representative. I enjoyed my trip. It took about four hours but was still too short for my tastes. The advantage of going by bus was that I could see more of the countryside. The bus service was superb.

I found Canberra, the capital of Australia, exemplary in many ways — well planned, quiet, spacious, clean, rich in the scenic beauty of green forests, unspoiled mountains, and natural landscapes. But the weather was cold. I spent a very quiet and relaxing night in the Kythera Motel.

The Conference of the Directors of National Libraries was to start the next day. My schedule was very tight. I was given the opportunity to visit in one day a host of fine libraries and museums, including the library of the College of Advanced Studies and the Australian National Gallery. I got ready quite early to start my tours. By the time I was back at the conference hall, the meeting had already been called to order.

I enjoyed seeing slides of the new building of the Chinese National Library and the national libraries of Japan and

Librarianship on the Global Scene

Indonesia and hearing them described by their directors. It was really one of the highlights of my visit to Australia to represent Nepal in the conference, but I was sorry not to be able to paint a bright picture of our so-called National Library.

Once in Canberra, I longed to visit the National Library of Australia and was happy when it was finally arranged for September 6 at 9:30 a.m. I wanted to find out more about the Regional Cooperation Programme, through which our library had been getting book donations. During the visit I spent some time with John Thompson, the director of Australian Collections and Services, catching up with their modern methods of acquiring materials to enrich the Australian Collection, so that I too could put them to use to enrich the Nepal Collection and improve its services; and then with Chief Librarian Bryony Wilcox of the User Support ABN Office (Australian Bibliographic Network), as I was planning to begin such a network in Nepal, using modern technology.

There were many departments and sections which I wanted to observe, but time was too short. I read somewhere a description of the National Library of Australia in one impressive sentence: "the National Library of Australia is the custodian of Australian written and published heritage — there isn't a book you won't find there." I wished I could make T.U. Central Library the same for Nepal. It was a very enriching experience.

From the library I walked three minutes to reach the Australian National Gallery, where Raewyn Henelius's friend Helen Ulrich, the membership manager at the gallery, was waiting to give me a tour. I was extremely happy to meet Helen and visit the gallery, an exciting place where one can view Australian history through art, fashion, and decoration. The building itself was beautiful and worthy to house the spectacular exhibits of Australian painting, sculpture, drawing,

Librarianship on the Global Scene

photography and decorative art. During my brief visit Helen and I discussed how I could acquire materials which would interest artists in Nepal, who need all the encouragement they can get to bring out their hidden talents and skills. How I wished Nepal would establish a national gallery on Australia's model.

Afterwards I joined in a lunch party with all the directors of the national libraries at a nature reserve that provided me with a real wilderness experience — kangaroos and all. I could have stayed indefinitely, but I had to get ready to leave Canberra by plane to go to Sydney to connect with another flight to Brisbane. My short stay in the youthful capital had been very memorable. I could see why the American architect Walter Burley Griffin had been awarded first prize in a global competition for designing the capital. I was told that from its inception in 1913 it had been developed as a garden city, with thousands of trees being planted to create its unique mix of nature and urbanization. God has given Nepal unmatched snow-capped mountains, but what were we doing to preserve this beauty?

With happy memories I flew to Brisbane, grateful to the government of Australia for giving me the opportunity to visit World Expo 88. It was like a vacation trip — no official appointments, no meetings. The only thing I knew I would do without fail was to stop in to see some of my own compatriots who were there to organize a stall. Mr. Gaurinath Rimal, the chief of the Expo Organizing Committee Nepal, was so kind as to inform his staff in Brisbane of my coming. I was thrilled to see Mr. Binayak Shah at the airport to take me to the place where I was to spend one night before going on to Expo. Without his company I doubt that it would have been easy for me to find my destination so late in the evening. I thanked him profusely for his patience in waiting for the hour the plane was delayed.

Early the next morning I woke up to the beauty of Australia's Sunshine City, Brisbane, the capital of Queensland, and was eager to visit World Expo 88, the largest single event in Australian history, to celebrate the Australia's Bicentenary. I reached the exposition grounds at 9:30 a.m. The crowd was already substantial, and the queues long. The whole setting was so grand and dazzling that I felt I was on some imaginary plane. I was told that more than 30 nations and 20 corporations were participating in Expo, under the theme "Leisure in the Age of Technology," to provide a taste of the world of tomorrow. Some eight million people were expected to attend it.

My first interest was to see Nepal's exhibit and to find how it was represented. To make my moving around easier I went to find Greda, the daughter of my close friends Robert and Lotti Weise; she had settled in Brisbane and was working at Expo. Unfortunately she was off that day. I was thus on my own. It took awhile but at last I came within range of the flute of Prem Rana Autari, a well-known artist of Nepal. How happy I was to find a piece of Nepal away from home! The exhibit was very well decorated and quite presentable. I heartily praised Prem for playing so melodiously and attracting visitors to learn about our country.

I made up my mind to visit as many other country exhibits as possible that day, as I was to leave on the morrow. Luckily I had been given some passes to get into different shows. I found that World Expo really had, as the brochure said, "an international flavour with everything from the religious cultures of Nepal to the timeless traditions of Europe, the tropical paradise of the Pacific to the grand style of the United States of America and the intrigue of the Union of Soviet Socialist

Republics to present an unforgettable technological and cultural showcase." It was really great fun and a once-in-a-lifetime experience for me.

I did eventually met Greda before leaving Brisbane. She took some photos of me in the Expo fairgrounds before taking me to the airport. I still treasure those pictures.

Thus ended my trip to Australia. Every moment I spent there was exquisite — both enriching and enjoyable. I was deeply grateful to the government of Australia for this unique opportunity.

It took hours to reach Singapore, where I was to catch a Royal Nepal Airlines flight back to Nepal. I was anxious to share my memorable experiences with others, especially my husband and my staff in the library. But then I was informed at the Singapore airport that I would be staying four additional days in town due to the cancellation of the flight. No wonder RNAC ran at a loss, I thought.

Now the problem was how to make best use of my stay. I had never enjoyed just sightseeing and window-shopping. Luckily I met some Singapore friends, Peter Campbell and his wife. Peter drew up an interesting programme to visit his 3M office to see their modern equipment and services and then take in the National University of Singapore Library, where I was to meet the chief librarian, Peggy Wai Chee Hochstadt. I found her very dynamic and dedicated and enjoyed the hours together with her, spent as if we were old friends. The university was nicely laid out and attractively landscaped.

Though my four days' stay was relaxing and fruitful, I still longed to be back home. At last, on Tuesday, September 13, 1986, I touched down on native soil. My husband, displaying his usual big smile, was right there to receive me.

Since my first participation in the IFLA conference in Australia, I was very much determined to help IFLA through active membership in the Regional Standing Committee for Asia and Oceania, wanting to prove worthy of IFLA's trust in me. I called a meeting of my professional colleagues to share my experiences with them and to discuss the future. Whenever I remembered my request to Dr. Geh, the president of IFLA, and Mr. Nauta, its secretary-general, to visit Nepal, I hoped and prayed that they really would come. I didn't quite believe it, though when I received a letter from Mr. Nauta dated November 28, 1988, informing me, "As promised in Sydney, Dr. Geh and I will include in our so-called Asia trip a visit to your library for four days, January 29 - February 1, 1988. As you requested, our main objectives are to see your library and to discuss librarianship in Nepal."

How kind of them to remember a request hastily tendered amid such a crowd of delegates. I immediately sent a Telex acknowledging their message and happily broke the news to colleagues, university authorities, and high officials in the Ministry of Education and fixed appointments with some of them.

Dr. Geh and Mr. Nauta reached Kathmandu on January 29. They seemed glad to see me waiting to welcome them, and I myself was glad to be able to. I gave them copies of the programme I had planned for them, which they looked forward to very much. It included visits to some important libraries, appointments with high officials, luncheons, receptions, and sightseeing. In the end they would have some idea about the situation of libraries in Nepal.

I was so grateful to Australian Ambassador Diane Johnstone for hosting a memorable reception in their honour and inviting some local dignitaries and diplomats to meet them at her residence. I was equally grateful to our university authorities, professors, and librarians, who made the reception I hosted in their honour at T.U. Central Library a great success. Although

Librarianship on the Global Scene

their visit was short, I did my best to make it fruitful and enjoyable. I felt it was a great opportunity to be able to share with them my views on the challenges and problems of the library profession in Nepal in the hope of getting support from international organizations like IFLA.

Later I received a letter of thanks from Dr. Geh with the following kind words: "We have very much enjoyed your company, all our talks and of course the library visits. And we were deeply impressed by seeing the places of your great ancient culture. As far as the development of librarianship in your country is concerned, we will try to be of assistance to you in your great endeavours; please let us know in which way we can help..."

Similarly I was sent a copy of the report prepared by Mr. Nauta on their mission to different Asian nations, including Nepal, that was circulated to IFLA's members. It was very encouraging and inspiring to read about the objective of their mission to Nepal: "promotion of librarianship in Nepal, visit at the request of the 'First Lady' of librarianship in Nepal, Mrs. Shanti Mishra, for the discussion on the situation of Nepalese librarianship.... A worthwhile, very well-organized visit.... IFLA committed itself to try to find the necessary funds for workable projects in Nepal." How happy I was to receive such assurances to boost librarianship in Nepal from no less important an international body than IFLA. It had always been my dream to make the library profession both the pacesetter of other professions in Nepal, through exemplary library services, and the backbone of development.

I again express my deep gratitude to the government of Australia for sponsoring my visit to Sydney to attend the IFLA conference, where I met Dr. Geh, Mr. Nauta and so many leaders of the library world, and for its moral support to continue my struggle for the library profession in Nepal.

Librarianship on the Global Scene

Forgetting all the challenges and struggles I was still up against, I began to concentrate on making three proposals to submit to the IFLA Standing Committee for Asia and Oceania:

(1) The extension of bibliographical activities to help implement one of IFLA's core programmes, the Universal Bibliographic Control and Universal Availability of Publications Programme, which promotes the exchange and use of compatible bibliographic records among libraries in general, and national bibliographic agencies in particular. With the admirable support of the Nepal Research Centre under the directorship of Dr. Axel Michaels, I brought out the first *Nepalese National Bibliography* in 1981 in a joint venture between T.U. Central Library and the research centre. The latter was established in Nepal under an agreement between Tribhuvan University and the German Oriental Society with the objective of furthering research work in the humanities and the natural and applied sciences.

I will never forget the help I received from Dr. Michaels to fulfil my long-cherished desire to bring out this bibliography — a must in any country to help scholars to gain easy access to available resources. It had always been very difficult for both local and foreign scholars to find such resources in Nepal. Realizing this fact, I tried my utmost for years to convince the government and our university authorities to provide some more funds to bring out the national bibliography and other specialized bibliographies on subjects like education, foreign policy, environment, and family planning, but unfortunately I never succeeded.

I happened one day to share my plight with Dr. Michaels. He praised my endeavour and immediately extended his support. On November 12, 1982 an agreement was signed by him on behalf of the Nepal Research Centre and by me on behalf of the University. Arrangements were made to provide nominal financial support (Rs. 1,000 a month) for those of my staff engaged in the compilation. They were glad to have a little extra money for their extra work. I made it a rule, though, not to have the money paid out in cases of long leave but to have such sums deposited instead in the bank as a separate fund for the welfare of the library staff in times of emergency. This account was handled by one of my senior staff, and whenever someone was in need, permission was sought from me to draw a loan. The amount in the fund later came to total nearly Rs. 50,000 — a happy surprise for me.

Thus the *Nepalese National Bibliography* had been coming out since 1981. After its publication, I started to notice a new attitude among people in power and position: they gradually changed their tune on bibliographies. I thought it was now the right time to approach some research institutions to solicit their cooperation and financial support to bring out research tools in support of their activities.

The first positive response I got was from Dr. Kedar Lall Shrestha, the director of RECAST (Research Centre for Applied Science and Technology) and member secretary of the National Council for Science and Technology (NCST). I was so happy. I immediately called a meeting of senior professors and the heads of all science departments to discuss the proposal I had made to RECAST, as I sincerely wanted to involve them in it. Everyone was supportive and expressed their willingness to help me to make the project a success even without an abundance of money. Accordingly I was able to bring out some important publications: *Ph.D. and M.Sc. Dissertation Abstracts* (1985) in botany, chemistry, physics, and zoology, five volumes of *Research Papers* in botany, chemistry, physics, and zoology (1987), and the *Catalogue of Nepalese Scientific Publications* (1988). I would always cherish the indispensable help I got from all science teachers, especially Prof. Dayananda

Librarianship on the Global Scene

Bajracharya, Dr. Kamal Krishna Joshi, Dr. Jeevan Shrestha, Dr. Devendra Mishra, Dr. Devi Dutta Poudyal, Dr. Mohan Bikram Gyawali, Dr. Chhabi Lall Gajurel, Dr. Krishna Manandhar, Dr. Mangala Manandhar and Mr. Rhidaya Shrestha. I admired their spirit in joining with me in this endeavour. Special gratitude is owed to Dr. Kedar Lall Shrestha for his financial support.

(2) The establishment of a training facility in T.U. Central Library as a model teaching and servicing institution in Nepal, in line with another IFLA core programme, the Advancement of Librarianship in the Third World. Ever since I started my career, I had had a strong conviction that without honest, sincere, and well-trained personnel, no library could play an important role in the development of any country. Thus I wanted to establish a training facility, but this would not be possible unless a well-organized library was already in place as a laboratory in which to carry out practical work. T.U. Central Library had been running training courses from time to time since 1965 to demonstrate the importance of such training, though the budget was very small. Gradually I began to get some funds to run formal courses, which were much in demand, not only from colleges but also from different ministries, departments, banks, corporations, organizations, missions, and associations — a very good assemblage of interested parties to support my contention that there was a need for this kind of training. Some authorities agreed but some didn't.

Besides these short courses, I was able in May 1975, after more than one decade, to start the first long-term in-service training programme in librarianship. It was one of the happiest moments in my professional career, and the training was itself historic. We had more applicants than we could possibly accommodate. Only 27 candidates were selected. I wrote a note

Librarianship on the Global Scene

of thanks to the rest for their interest in training and assured them that another course would be offered in future.

Whenever I got support I held the training; if not I temporarily suppressed my urge to do so. When the urge again became strong, however, friends from different foreign missions and organizations, such as VSO (the British Voluntary Service Overseas) and IDRC (International Development Research Centre, Canada), always seemed to turn up to help, as if they had been sent by God to keep my spirits high. After a long interval I received some limited financial aid from the British and again started a training course in 1986 during the time of the first VSO training coordinator, Christopher Cunninghame, a very capable and hard-working man, who joined T.U. Central Library in December 1985, at my request, to help me to plan library and information science training courses, starting first with a certificate course and then a degree course, both to be held in the library. We invited Mr. F. Black, a VSO field officer, to speak on the occasion of the distribution of certificates to trainees. He spoke very well, on the importance of library and information training, quoting Edward de Bono, the British writer and thinker: "Information is so great a part of effectiveness that without information a really clever person can never get started. With information a much less clever person can get very far."

To continue our training programme we submitted a proposal, through Mr. Cunninghame, to British Council Representative Peter Moss for a British Council sponsored visit to T.U. Central Library by Mr. Christopher Needham in 1987. The latter was a curriculum development specialist in librarianship. During his two-week visit he worked so vigorously that he hardly had much time to do sightseeing. The period was too short to cover such a wide subject as library science and education. The purpose of his visit was to examine the state of education and training for librarianship and information work in Nepal; to make proposals for future developments; and to help in planning appropriate curricula by evaluating our existing curricula in librarianship and advising on ways to improve short-term training, with a view to developing a permanent certificate course within four to five years, particularly for non-professional library staff. He also spent a good amount of time in assisting VSO volunteer Mrs. Savitri Brandi (Mr. Cunninghame's successor) and my deputies who were responsible for future training programmes at the library in designing a two-month curriculum.

I was extremely happy to have had Mr. Needham with us. He understood me and my challenges and struggles so well that I wished he could have stayed on longer, until I had established a model teaching facility. He provided me a happy surprise by writing a very detailed report. I was thrilled to read the following inspiring words:

Apart from my curriculum planning meetings I normally spent a part of each day talking with Mrs. Mishra, the Librarian of the Central University Library. I found those meetings extremely valuable. Mrs. Mishra has created almost single-handed a university library that can bear comparison with university libraries elsewhere. She has accomplished this by sheer force of personality and political acumen. In a country where "professionalism" is rudimentary she has been, at one and the same time, institution and association, and I learned a great deal from her by simple listening. She also arranged for me a number of meetings with past and present rectors, registrars, vice-chancellors and professors — from which I gathered much information and invaluable help in assessing the broad climate of opinion in Nepal.

Librarianship on the Global Scene

I shall always be grateful to Mr. Moss and his charming wife Norma for making Mr. Needham's visit fruitful and enjoyable, and I shall never forget Mr. Moss's interest in helping me to establish a training facility in T.U. Central Library.

I was sad that Mr. Cunninghame was no longer in the library during Mr. Needham's visit. He had helped me in many ways. One important bridge he constructed on my behalf was with the Asia Regional Office of IDRC. Its programme officer was a professional librarian, Clive Wing, who had once been a VSO volunteer in Nepal and since then had remained a good friend of Nepalese librarianship. I had already had many friendly contacts with Maria Ng Lee Hoon, the regional programme officer of IDRC's Information Science Division in Singapore, even before approaching IDRC in Delhi. I still remember her visit to T.U. Central Library and am grateful to her for assisting me in whatever way she could. She faithfully corresponded and arranged for my staff to participate in seminars and workshops sponsored by IDRC. Later on Mr. Wing also took equal interest in the library. For instance, he arranged for Shahid Akhatar, the associate director of the International Science Division in Ottawa, to visit it. During this visit we discussed our needs. I submitted two proposals to IDRC for financial help, one to continue my training programmes, and another to automate the Nepal Collection. Mr. Wing represented T.U. Central Library so well that both the proposals were approved by IDRC. The training programme started receiving support in April 1988. We had several courses up to 1990, not only in the library but also in other parts of the kingdom, to meet local needs for such training and to create interest in career development in librarianship.

Librarianship on the Global Scene

Under a second project, some of my library staff were trained abroad in automation techniques. The total amount spent on the two projects already exceeds $46,275. I shall remain always grateful to IDRC for the financial support at a crucial time when support from our own authorities was almost on hold. Thus my plans could be kept going. My dream was to start a certificate and diploma course in the library in 1995 with the help of IFLA under its Advancement of Librarianship in the Third World programme.

(3) Another project was to activate the Library Association of Nepal to run according to IFLA guidelines by establishing a close relation between it and IFLA's Round Table for the Management of Library Associations.

IFLA Conference, Paris, 1989

While I was working on the above-mentioned projects, I received a letter dated May 22, 1989 from Mr. van Wesemael, the coordinator of professional activities at IFLA, informing me of the decision of the Preparatory Committee, chaired by Mr. Henry Sene, the director of the University Library in Dakar, Senegal, to invite me as a paid participant to the Seminar on Interlending and Document Supply, August 14-19, 1989, and to the IFLA General Conference, August 19-26, 1989, both in Paris. What happier news could there be for me than this? I immediately informed my husband and my senior staff.

On August 13, 1989 I was back in the City of Lights after nineteen years to attend my second IFLA conference. I reached there with pleasant memories of my last visit together with my husband just after our marriage, at the invitation of the French government.

Librarianship on the Global Scene

The pre-session Seminar on Interlending and Document Supply was well attended, mostly by librarians from the Third World, and provided a good opportunity for those present to air their problems freely and to seek solutions to them. A background document for the seminar was prepared by Hope Clement, the chairwoman of the IFLA Section on Interlending and Document Supply. I was also requested to prepare a short paper offering a survey of the situation in Nepal as it pertained to the section's agenda. I was glad I could attend this, my first pre-session. I appreciated the forum it offered to address Third World concerns in the presence of more experienced library leaders from developed nations.

It was nice to renew ties with colleagues from different parts of the world whom I had previously met in Sydney. I felt much more at ease this time, knowing how to move around and how to participate.

On August 20 I attended the orientation to IFLA's Core Programme. It was worthwhile for a relatively new person like me. On the same day, I took the opportunity to speak out about UNESCO's activities, especially with reference to Nepal, and to plead that more attention be paid to Third World needs in the UNESCO Open Forum. I was loudly applauded. After the meeting many came to express appreciation to me personally for speaking out.

The main speaker on the programme was Mr. J. Tocatlian, the director of UNESCO's Office of Information Programmes and Services in Paris, who was kind enough to have a brief meeting with me afterwards. I also took the opportunity, during UNESCO's open house, to have a short talk with Gianfranco Romerio, who had visited me when he was in Nepal, to discuss my future plans for the automation of T.U. Central Library. Another person I well remember was Alastair McLurg of the Division of Promotion and Rights at the UNESCO Press; he assured me that he would send UNESCO publications regularly.

As on the previous occasion, I attended two Regional Standing Committee meetings, this time chaired by Dr. Wijasuriya and held at the Palais de Congrès, to discuss the ALP Programme, the report of the new regional manager, Mrs. Pongpan Rattanabusit, and the upcoming Regional Standing Committee meeting in Bangkok. I was happy to find some very deeply interested observers of Third World librarianship, such as Dr. Suzine Har Nicolescu (U.S.A.), Mrs. Natsuko Furuya (Canada), and Dr. Faroug Mansor (Jordan).

The opening of the 55th IFLA General Conference took place with great fanfare in the Palais de Congrès, which was furnished with large, well-equipped meeting rooms. Marie-Louise Bossual had planned chamber music amidst beautiful floral arrangements and a beautiful silk tapestry, upon which all member countries of IFLA were listed in a panoply of colours. I silently took great pride to see Nepal included. I was told that the conference was one of the largest on record. There were 2,069 participants from 104 countries, 245 from the United States alone, making it the largest delegation.

The theme of the conference was "Libraries and Information in Yesterday's, Today's and Tomorrow's Economy." The opening ceremony included a performance by the Trio Wanderer of the Trio in A minor by Maurice Ravel. Marc Chauveinc, the vice-president of the IFLA 1989 Steering Committee, welcomed the participants. Then the president of IFLA, Hans-Peter Geh spoke, reflecting upon the ideals of the French Revolution and on how IFLA has tried to achieve liberty, equality, and fraternity for its members. He emphasized that IFLA was working to reduce the growing gap and disparity among nations through many of its programmes. Thomas Keller, UNESCO's assistant director-general, Jean

Librarianship on the Global Scene

Favie, the president of ICA (International Council on Archives), and Ben Goedegebuure, the executive director of FID (International Federation for Information and Documentation) also spoke. Jack Lang, minister of culture, communication, large-scale projects, and the bicentenary, described plans for the Bibliothèque de France. Initiated by President François Mitterrand, it is slated to be equipped with computer terminals that will link readers throughout France and even the world to its published and electronic resources. Its book collection will contain items published after 1945.

At the end of the opening ceremony a grand reception was hosted by Minister Lang and Lionel Jospin, the minister of national education, youth, and sports. As usual, I took the opportunity to introduce myself to them to let my hosts know that Nepal was also taking part in the conference and to thank them for the reception. Their interest in my country was genuinely gratifying.

The number of meetings scheduled was 232, and the papers totalled 162. It took awhile to make up my mind which meetings would be useful for me to attend; I ended up going to ones on mobile libraries, children's libraries, regional activities, rare and precious books and documents, university libraries, and national libraries. One of the highlights of the conference for me was my participation in the meeting of the librarians and directors of national libraries. Some pertinent questions I addressed to the top librarians of the developed world regarding the deteriorating status of librarians, even in the United States, stirred everyone gathered in the room; I could hear a long applause echo after I concluded. My words seemed to have focused some attention on my country and me. Wherever I went I was appreciated for speaking the truth. It made me feel good, and I thanked God for encouraging me to stand up and speak out.

Librarianship on the Global Scene

Another thing I remember well was my participation in the workshop on the Dewey decimal classification. Due to my own negligence I had not been included in the workshop, yet upon request I was allowed to participate and speak about the problem faced by developing countries like Nepal, to which Dewey had assigned just one number each, and about how to make the system more suitable to our local needs. I requested that these matters be given attention when the next edition was brought out and offered my own services if needed.

The conference was very rewarding. I wanted to congratulate Catherine Cannot, the coordinator, for her excellent management, but I failed to find her in lavish receptions organized for all participants in the Pyramid of the Louvre, where the food and drinks were selected to reflect the themes of "The Earth," "The Air," "The Sea," "The Forest," and "The Light," and at the Bibliothèque Nationale, where our French friends dressed in 18th-century clothing. I requested some French colleagues to convey my greetings and congratulations to all the organizers who worked so hard to make the conference a great success. As one experienced IFLA participant described the conference, it was "luxurious, a largesse, a labour of love, elegant, effervescent, edifying, fabulous, faultless and formidable."

With such enriching experiences I left Paris, grateful to IFLA, and especially to Paul Nauta, the secretary-general, and Guust van Wesemael, the coordinator of professional activities, for providing me this rare opportunity to participate in the 55th IFLA General Conference and to be part of the bicentennial of the French Revolution.

Chapter 14

Nepalese Writers and the P.E.N. Club

Since my college life I have been a great lover of literature. I always enjoyed reading such authors as Shakespeare, Wordsworth, Coleridge, Milton, Keats, Shelley, Browning, and Tennyson to my friends in the hostel in Calcutta. My Bengalese friends inspired me to take reading seriously. Too late I realized that I should have majored in literature. With history as my choice, I had little time for literature for some years. As soon as I started my career as a pioneer librarian, I began to revive my interest not only in literary works but also in literary figures, especially the writers of Nepal whose roles were most clear-cut in furthering their indigenous literature, both inside and outside the country.

My library profession acted as a strong bridge between Nepalese writers and me. I always felt happy to be with them and have always had profound regards for their walk of life. It was my constant wish that they have abundant opportunities to develop as writers and at the same time to maintain the peace of mind necessary for bringing beautiful works into being for the public. Their work should be accorded the recognition and respect it deserves, as they are the jewels of the nation. No nation can be called developed unless it has a storehouse of good literature written by writers of its own soil. And these writers should be supported by the nation, for "ability is of little account without opportunity."

I quite often heard the cry of writers who faced the problem of marketing and distribution their works after having published them with great difficulty. In the beginning I was successful in securing special funds to buy multiple copies of

Nepalese Writers and the P.E.N. Club

imaginative literature not only for T.U. Central Library but for all the college libraries. Unfortunately the funds were cut after some years. I was extremely sorry but had no power to change things.

Well-known writers of Nepal were regular visitors to the library. I always took the opportunity to welcome them if I happened to see them, knowing that I owed my livelihood to them: without writers, no books; without books, no libraries. Every nation needs a plentiful supply of writers for its own well-being.

I kept 0returning to the thought of how I could help our writers to take a leading role in bringing about social change, towards the end of fulfilling development goals. A few lines from poems of Nepal's literary genius and great poet of the twentieth century Laxmi Prasad Devkota — "I have suffered both at the hands of man and God" and "I am the most unfortunate of writers of Nepal" — often made my mind reel. I wondered whether we still had suffering writers and why we voiced protest against such suffering only after their deaths. I always felt that had he lived longer Laxmi Prasad Devkota would have received the Nobel Prize and thus acquired the greater recognition he deserved. He was the first and only Nepalese poet widely known to foreigners.

I reacted with joy when David Rubin told me of his deep interest in writing a book on Devkota. Such an effort would serve to focus outside attention on the great genius, I thought. I still cherish the memory of David's visits to the library while he was engaged in writing his wonderful *Nepali Visions, Nepali Dreams: the Poetry of Laxmi Prasad Devkota* (New York, Columbia University Pres, 1980). What could be a more praiseworthy tribute to Devokta from a foreign friend than such a book? The great poet and genius of West Bengal, Rabindranath Tagore, became famous in India only after he

Nepalese Writers and the P.E.N. Club

received the Nobel Prize. Thereafter praise of him could be heard on everyone's lips. That is the way things go in this part of the world. My hope is that each nation in this part of the world will praise writers of merit regardless of caste, creed, or sex, even before they receive prizes from the outside.

Thus I, for one, realized that the writers of my country needed recognition both from within and from without. I was still hunting. Suddenly an idea flashed through my mind, and I began to concentrate on reading materials I got from time to time from International P.E.N., a world association of writers. After some research I came to know more about the organization. I kept up contacts with other countries in order to find ways to draw outside attention to our writers and also perhaps to interest some foundation in financing the publishing of good books on Nepalese literature and in helping to market already written books.

I once discussed my ideas with Nick Langton and Jill Tucker of the Asia Foundation, thinking that they might buy books written by our well-known writers and distribute them to all the campuses and other, unaffiliated libraries in Nepal. They were very supportive and I was very persistent, but for some reason the project never materialized, perhaps because in the meantime Mr. Langton had been transferred to the Asia Foundation office in Sri Lanka. I was sad to see him go.

I was just a librarian without any power and position, and without the money I would have liked to have to establish prizes and awards to honour our writers. As a librarian, though, I began to organize functions in the library to salute prize-winning authors.

One such memorable function was in honour of the well-known dramatist Mohan Raj Sharma, held when he received the prestigious Madan Puraskar (Madan Award), which had been established by Rani Jagadamba in 1955 to pay recognition

Nepalese Writers and the P.E.N. Club

to the best Nepali litterateurs. This function was well attended by writers and university teachers, who appreciated my modest efforts to further the cause. I was so happy.

As for our great deceased writers, such as Bhanubhakta Acharya, the first poet in the history of Nepali literature and an opponent of the existing social system based on foolish religious norms two centuries ago, Motiram Bhatta (1866-96), who has been described as Nepal's first biographer, first critic, first publisher, first composer of *gazals*, and first romantic poet, the poets Lekhnath Poudyal (1884-1965) and Laxmi Prasad Devkota (1909-1959), and others, I used to organize various displays and exhibitions in the library in order to draw public attention to their unforgotten contribution to our literature and language. One, for example, helped to celebrate Lekhnath Poudyal's centenary in 1984. As soon as I read of the plans regarding the centenary programme published in newspapers by the Lekhnath Centenary Committee, I called a meeting of my own staff to put to them my idea of arranging a grand library exhibition incorporating all kinds of materials on and by the poet laureate and bringing out a bibliography on him as our salute to his achievements. I loved his poems from my early days of student life and learned by heart his poem *"Pinjarako Suga"* (The Parrot in the Cage), which I liked very much. He wrote in a very simple blank verse that appeals to both common man and scholar and had a gift of entering into the minds and hearts of everyone. I loved his poems because they boosted me morally and spiritually. He was a great humanist poet, a torchbearer of Hindu culture, and a great lover of nature — the William Wordsworth of Nepal. Here is one extract from "The Parrot in the Cage" in translation:

The bird to whom the open boundless blue
Was filled for flights of pleasure to renew

Nepalese Writers and the P.E.N. Club

> Has now, alas! for his life's single stay
> A narrow cage of iron here today.
> So long as on this wild terrestrial plain
> A single human being shall remain,
> O Lord! Let not a parrot's life be given —
> Suddenly comes a sense to me, o Heaven!

My staff wholeheartedly supported my idea. It took several months to collect all the materials needed for the exhibition. I thoroughly enjoyed my literary hunt to procure them. It was a worthy bit of research, I thought. Wanting to display a large photo of the poet, manuscripts, unpublished materials, letters to friends and family members, such cherished personal effects as pen, ink pot, a traditional trunk used as a writing table, spectacles, *daura suruwal* (the national dress with cap) and *chakati* (cushion), I approached his daughter Mrs. Punya Prava Dhungana, his son Mr. Ananta Poudyal, and his poet nephew Damaru Ballabh Poudyal. Their response was very encouraging. I was happy that they agreed to loan me everything I requested. My main aim in including such items in the exhibition was to make people conscious of the need to establish a Lekhnath museum along the lines of the one at Stratford-on-Avon, the birthplace of Shakespeare, which attracts visitors from all over the world.

During my visit with my husband to Great Britain in 1970 at the invitation of the British government, we made a special request to the programme organizer, Mrs. Paynton, to include a visit to Stratford so that we could pay tribute to my favourite English author, the greatest of playwrights and chief symbol of British culture. Mrs. Paynton was so kind as to arrange not only the visit but also to get us in to see *Richard III* performed by famous actors and actresses. We were extremely impressed by the performance — so real to life and moving; we felt as if

Nepalese Writers and the P.E.N. Club

we were really watching historical events unfurl before our eyes. Watching the play, I became convinced that what the Pulitzer Prize winner (1945) Prof. Russell B. Nye had written was true: "Though they speak in English, Shakespeare's characters act out universal human problems. Shakespeare's art is English, but it is also international."

Since my visit to Stratford I had often wished that Nepal too might respect its dead and living writers in the way the British people have Shakespeare: Devkota; Bala Krishna Sama, the greatest playwright of Nepal; the poets Dharanidhar Koirala, Siddhicharan Shrestha, and Hari Bhakta Katuwal; along with such great living writers as the poet Kedar Man Byathit, the poet Madhab Prasad Ghimire; the novelist Daulat Bikram Bista; the first Nepali woman novelist of note, Parijat; the dramatist Bijaya Bahadur Malla; and the short story writer Govinda Bahadur Gothale, to name a few.

Oh, how happy I felt when I got every item I needed for the display! I conveyed information about the coming event to the professors of the Nepali Department, knowing that they too would be happy. Everyone asked me to approach some high-ranking person like the prime minister or a cabinet minister to inaugurate the exhibition so that Nepal Television and the other media would cover it and provide the publicity to attract more visitors. My idea was quite different: I wanted not a politician but a renowned poet. I did some research to find out who might be suitable and narrowed my choice down to Siddhicharan Shrestha "Yuga Kavi" (the epithet means "poet of the age," given to honour him for his contributions to Nepali literature and language). He was Nepal's eldest living poet.

It was no problem for me to approach him, because he always showed a fatherly affection towards me. He used to address me as *chhori* (daughter) and my husband as *jwai* (son-in-law) whenever he met us; it was a great cause of joy for us

380

Nepalese Writers and the P.E.N. Club

to feel such warmth from such a luminary. I respected him immensely for daring, during the Rana regime, to publish his poem entitled *"Krantibina Yaha Shanti Hudaina"* (There Will Be No Peace Here without a Revolution), which I used to often recite whenever my husband and I visited him in the hermitage-like quarters at Tribhuvan Park given to him to stay in so long as he was working as the chairman of the Tribhuvan Memorial Committee. I used to sing this poem, and he brightened up so much that I could see joyous tears in his sparkling eyes under his thick glasses. He would then narrate stories of his suffering during his early life and how he was called the poet of agony and romantic ecstasy. Of all the stories of his early life, I loved to hear most of his imprisonment for five years for writing the above poem. I felt so happy when he was honoured by the Royal Nepal Academy with its prestigious Tribhuvan and Prithvi awards in recognition of his contribution to Nepali literature and language during his lifetime.

One afternoon I called him for an appointment. He sounded so happy over the phone that I wished I could fly straightway to his home, but due to my busy library work I had to wait for the next day. I reached his traditional-style residence at Ombahal in Kathmandu at the exact set time. I was pleased to hear him say, "*Chhori*, I have been waiting for you, as I always long for your visit. How is *jwai saheb*?" Oh, those few affectionate words from him meant a lot to me! When I conveyed my desire to have his consent to inaugurate the exhibition on Lekhnath Poudyal, he at once accepted and was full of admiration for my plan to hold such an exhibition on the poet laureate. I conveyed the happy news of his acceptance to my library staff.

The exhibition was ready to be inaugurated. The whole show seemed so grand that I couldn't help feeling a great sense of satisfaction. It looked like a well-managed museum for

Nepalese Writers and the P.E.N. Club

Lekhnath, as I had wished. The inauguration by the seniormost living poet Siddhicharan took place amidst an impressive gathering of respected writers, professors, students, and lovers of literature and language. All of them were full of praise, some of it preserved in writing in the visitors book. Viewing the exhibition, many people asked me how I had managed to collect so many items in such a short time, all of which made them feel the presence of Lekhnath. My reply to them was simple: through the support, cooperation, inspiration, and encouragement of everyone I approached.

As predicted by people in the know, Nepal Television and representatives from other major media did not come because the exhibition was not attended by people in power. I was sad not for myself but for the writers. I hardly cared for publicity because I have always preferred subtler ways of getting messages across. Most of the visitors urged me to request Nepal Television to film the exhibition, thinking that the public would be delighted to see it. Somewhat hesitantly I did approach a number of people, including some in the palace, but nothing came of it.

We had more visitors than expected. By popular request, we extended the exhibition an additional week. During this period I got a call from the palace to inform me of the possible visit of the king and the queen to grace the exhibition. How happy I was to hear this, knowing that their visit would surely inspire all the writers of Nepal, but to my great dismay, the visit for some reason never occurred. In any case, the exhibition was a great success. Later, with the help of my staff, I brought out a bibliography on Lekhnath, entitled *Kavi Siromani Lekhnath Bangmaya Suchi*, which is now highly appreciated by writers and scholars as a useful research tool. I still remember being flattered by the remark made by the respected writer Kamal Mani Dixit: "Shanti's bibliography on the poet Lekhnath even

Nepalese Writers and the P.E.N. Club

surpasses the bibliography compiled by Prof. Basudev Tripathi in his Ph.D. thesis on Lekhnath [which was published as a book]."

I kept up contact with other countries to find ways to bring wider attention to bear upon our writers from the outside. After doing some research, I came to know more about International P.E.N. It was established in 1921 in London by C. A. Dawson Scott under the presidency of John Galsworthy; its main aim was to promote friendship and close understanding between writers and to defend the freedom of expression within and between all nations of the world. The initials P.E.N. stand for Poets, Playwrights, Editors, Essayists, Novelists, but membership is open to all writers of standing (including translators), whether men or women, and without distinction of creed or race, who subscribe to the above fundamental principles. I was impressed by its stand not to be involved in state or party affairs, strongly believing that writers, as writers, should be above politics. P.E.N. has made very praiseworthy efforts to raise money for refugee writers and writers imprisoned for exercising their right to freedom of expression. Another couple of things I liked about P.E.N. were its scheme in collaboration with UNESCO to promote the translation of works by writers in lesser-known languages and its international congresses to bring together writers from different nations of the world.

I became more interested in P.E.N. activities and came to know that if we could start a P.E.N. centre in Nepal, we could apply for membership of International P.E.N. I learned that more than 84 autonomous centres exist throughout the world. This drove me to search out interested writers in Nepal who might share my dream to open a local P.E.N. centre.

Months passed and years went by. I could never decide whom to involve in the establishment of a P.E.N. centre in

Nepalese Writers and the P.E.N. Club

Nepal, where groupism is so strongly entrenched. It was really a hard decision to make because I wanted the initiators to be selfless writers who practised what they preached in their writings and who were willing to do something to improve society and to nurture talented writers within and without and to abjure groupism, favouritism, partiality, and racial and religious discrimination. Knowledgeable persons told me that I would never be able to achieve my goal. For years I kept quiet, but my divine drive and urge to serve our writers was never still; it pulsed through my mind and thoughts.

Greta Rana had long been one of my favourite poetesses and writers. Having read her articles in *The Rising Nepal* and her poems, I wanted to meet her, but I had never had the opportunity to. In 1975, though, when I was working as the member secretary of International Women's Year Committee Nepal, I found the opportunity I had been waiting for and requested her to write an article on the role of women in social work to be published in a book, *Women in Nepal*, one in a series in English on Nepalese women brought out by the IWY Committee. She kindly came in person to my office to accept my request. That was the first time I met her. I was quite impressed by her deep concern for women and the country's problems. I always loved to hear her free and frank comments and remarks on Nepalese society, which has been slow to accept domiciled foreigners' contributions to its development.

Her own story struck sympathetic chords in me. She was born and brought up in England and became a lover of books and reading. At her request I gave her membership of T.U. Central Library under the policy of the library to serve writers, historians, and scholars of Nepal. She came to borrow and return books, and whenever I was free I used to invite her into my office. Since then we have been close friends, sharing our joys and woes. Whenever I went to literary functions I used to

Nepalese Writers and the P.E.N. Club

mention her name but always discovered that she was still little known and appreciated. Many people had no idea that she was a poetess, a writer, and a good translator. Her poem entitle "The Tomb Around" conveys her own sense of isolation:

> Who reads my words,
> In my alien tongue,
> and understands the secret of my exile?
> Who reads my words,
> in my alien tongue
> and understands the cipher of my soul,
> that hides a thousand truths against the light?
> Who reads my words
> does not read me,
> but the tomb around
> that's built for all to see!

She told me that she had been writing poetry since she was seven years old, so that poetry was naturally her preferred medium. I loved to hear her reciting her poems; she is a truly gifted poetess. Her work includes three volumes of poetry (*Mara*, *The Stone God Thunders*, and *Middle Lode*), and three novels. Apart from these she has written numerous short stories and articles along with unpublished fiction manuscripts. Recently her short story "The Hill" won first prize in the Internationale Arnsberger Kurzprosa 1991 competition. It was first published in German by the Stadt Direktor-Kulturrat of Arnsberg, West Germany.

I used to wonder whether, if she had not become a Nepalese *buhari* (daughter-in-law), she might have more easily fulfilled her childhood ambition to make a special mark on the literature of the English-speaking world. To have her as a *buhari* can only be a source of pride for the Rana community. She

Nepalese Writers and the P.E.N. Club

translated the well-known Nepali writer Diamond Shumshere Rana's book *Seto Bagh* (Wake of the White Tiger) which has since been also translated into Japanese and French.

I usually kept some literary works of such Nepalese women writers as Parijat, Banira Giri, Toya Gurung, Prema Shah, Maya Thakuri, Bhagi Rathi Shrestha, Benju and Manju Sharma, Shusila Koirala, and Padmavati Singh on my table. Greta's books also occupied a prominent place in my office. In fact, I was planning to bring out a bibliography on and by Nepalese women writers and was working hard to open a separate section in the library on women's issues so that those interested in doing research on the subject could have easy access to information.

Our great woman writer Parijat, who was honoured with the Madan Award for her novel *Shirishko Phool* (the first Nepali novel to be translated into English, by Tankavilas Acharya and my American friend Sondra Zeidenstein, under the title "The Blue Mimosa" (1972)), organized a grand display of books on and by Nepalese women at the Nepal-Bharat Cultural Center in March 1986. I was given the honour of inaugurating this unique exhibition, which was well attended and highly praised. It was a great joy for me to see so many literary works on display together in such a way as to bring all Nepalese women writers into the limelight. I have a strong conviction that all writers should be respected without discrimination under any system on the basis of their merits. They should be above politics and groupism and should use their pen not just to boost their own interests but those of all writers and their country as a whole, so that its people can go forward, breaking with foolish traditions while sustaining its own true values.

One fine afternoon in October 1987 the well-known novelist Dhruba Chandra Gautam came to visit me to get some information on his research. He saw the many literary works

Nepalese Writers and the P.E.N. Club

of Nepalese women writers, including Greta's. I told him about her talent and requested him to meet her once in my office in the library. He agreed. I arranged for them to meet on October 18. He was contributing articles and interviews to different weeklies, having already won the Madan Award for his novel *Alikhit* (translated into English ("Unwritten") by my American friend Philip Pierce).

When his interview with Greta was finally published, it was a thrill to read. I was touched that felt led to quote "If you prick us, do we not bleed? If you tickle us, do we not laugh" from *The Merchant of Venice*, as this is so true of all of us. Now, I felt sure, Greta would be read by more Nepalese writers.

Greta, Gautam, and I began to meet quite often. One of the topics of discussion was the deteriorating situation in Nepal and the plight of its writers, who besides writing have to work hard on the side for their livelihood. The more we met, the more confidence I gained that we could band together to improve the condition of writers. My long-cherished desire to introduce International P.E.N. into Nepal drove me one day to broach the subject to Greta. She immediately offered her support to make my dream a reality. I knew that when Greta said yes she meant it. She sat down and wrote to International P.E.N. to apply for membership.

According to P.E.N. International procedures, we needed to prepare a document along with the P.E.N. Charter signed by twenty prospective founding members of P.E.N. Nepal. On March 30, 1988 Greta and I had a serious discussion about who would sign the P.E.N. Charter at that time, before the pro-democracy movement, though I never found any clauses in it that might be objectionable to government authorities. The P.E.N. Charter is reproduced in Appendix IX. To be on the safe side, and also to deny troublemakers the chance to twist matters, I informed palace secretaries about the plan before we formally submitted the P.E.N.N. (P.E.N. Nepal) constitution to the Bagmati Zonal Commissioner for registration.

When Greta and I decided that it was time to commit ourselves, we broke the news to Dr. Gautam and requested him to get writers who would willingly sign the P.E.N. Charter without fear and reservation. Once we were established we could draw other notable writers into it, I always thought. I urged Greta to use her own judgement in planning the first executive body with the help of Dr. Gautam in getting at least twenty prospective founding members to sign the charter. Dr. Gautam's efforts resulted in the following list of signatories, without whose support P.E.N. Nepal would never have come into existence: Mr. Nagendra Sharma, Mr. Dhruba Sapkota, Mr. Diamond Shumshere Rana, Ms. Benju Sharma, Mr. Sailendra Sakar, Mr. Asesh Malla, Manjul (Mr. Megh Raj Sharma), Mr. Pushkar Lohani, Ms. Sharada Sharma, Mr. Rochak Ghimire, Mr. Ramesh Toofan, Mrs. Shanti Kunwar, Mr. Nayan Raj Pandey, Mr. Janardhan Joshi, Dr. Kumar Bahadur Joshi, Mr. Binod Mani Dixit, and Mrs. Prabha Thacker.

Greta called me one afternoon to get my reaction to an executive body of P.E.N. Nepal that would be formed under my presidency, with Dr. Gautam as vice-president and herself as secretary-general. That sounded fine, yet I wanted to give some thought to whether I should accept the offer to become the first and founding president, when there were so many well-known writers available. I did not want to disappoint Greta and Dr. Gautam by rejecting their idea, as their trust in me was an honour I could not take lightly. Moreover, I had always wanted to be in a position to serve writers by attracting outside interest to them. Thus I decided to accept the call. The attraction for me was not the attending of literary congresses

Nepalese Writers and the P.E.N. Club

and conferences but the serving of writers in a kind of sacred trust: to be with them in their needs and to arrange for them opportunities within and without so that they could write freely and joyfully works of literature worthy of national and international recognition. "O God, give me strength and make me worthy to serve writers in the way they wish and deserve" — that was my prayer.

During the last part of 1988 several meetings among the three of us and also with other interested writers who had signed the P.E.N. Charter were held in T.U. Central Library to discuss the drafting of the constitution of P.E.N. Nepal Centre and its logo. According to national law, it was necessary to submit the constitution to the zonal commissioner for registration.

Greta kept herself engaged writing to International P.E.N. and other international organizations for help and cooperation in getting our new-born centre on its feet and able to achieve its set goals. Dr. Gautam agreed to work on the constitution with the help of other members. When the draft was ready we needed legal advice, but we had no money yet. Greta came up with the idea to get help from the well-known lawyer Kusum Shrestha, who was much admired by foreign friends for taking on political cases and also working as a consultant for them. He acceded to our request, and I expressed my deep gratitude to him personally for waving the cost. The constitution was filed for registration.

In the meantime, even before we got the green light, many encouraging letters in reply to the secretary-general's enquiries poured in. It was a great joy for all of us to receive a letter dated September 29, 1988 from Alexandre Blokh, the International P.E.N. secretary, congratulating P.E.N. Nepal Centre officially for being unanimously accorded membership in International P.E.N. at the 52nd International P.E.N.

Nepalese Writers and the P.E.N. Club

Congress held in Seoul from August 28 to September 3, 1988. His letter not only praised our efforts to create the centre but also assured P.E.N.'s help and support to writers of Nepal in making their literature, their culture, and their present situation better known to the world and in establishing contacts with writers of other countries where P.E.N. International is active. I don't remember how many times I read and reread his letter. As the founding president, I shall remain ever grateful to Mr. Blokh, International P.E.N. President Francis King, and others for their support in getting P.E.N. Nepal Centre inducted into International P.E.N. much sooner than I thought possible.

Although Mr. Blokh wrote not to worry about the membership fee, our problem was not only foreign exchange but funding itself. I dared not request contributions from Nepalese writers even before anything concrete appeared on the horizon to boost their opportunities. Writers of the Third World are not as well off as those of developed countries. They need both moral and financial support from within and without to keep their creative spirit alive. Thus I was deeply concerned how to tide the centre over for a few years until it developed some momentum. Then, out of the blue, Greta's sister Ruth Jones of Yorkshire, came forward to offer a handsome contribution. Though I wanted to write a letter of appreciation to her personally, she left this world before I could fulfil my desire. I silently prayed for her eternal peace when Greta broke the sad news to me, and I remembered a quote I loved so much:

They who give have all things;
They who withhold have nothing.

Now P.E.N. Nepal was in a position to keep its promises — (1) to act and speak with a collective voice for writers; (2) to improve relations among writers; (3) to

Nepalese Writers and the P.E.N. Club

encourage, stimulate, and foster the production of translations of Nepalese works into main European languages; (4) to honour Nepalese writers and give them international exposure; (5) to help eminent Nepalese writers to publish their unpublished works; and (6) to support International P.E.N.'s goal of promoting the ideal of universality both in the field of international intellectual cooperation and the defence of freedom of expression.

The news of the formation of P.E.N. Nepal under my presidency, with Dr. Dhruba Chandra Gautam as vice-president and Greta Rana as the secretary-general, and Mrs. Benju Sharma and Messrs. Diamond Shumshere Rana, Shailendra Sakar, Dhruba Sapkota, Nagendra Raj Sharma, and Ashesh Malla as executive members was flashed out through R.S.S. (the state news agency) to the major newspapers on December 10, 1988. Our founding member Ramesh Toofan, who is experienced in such things, was responsible for drafting news releases.

The first P.E.N.N. executive meeting was held at the British Council at the latter's kind invitation on February 9, 1989. The British Council representative, Peter Moss, his wife Norma, and the assistant representative, John Mackenzie, were very supportive, and P.E.N.N. remains grateful to them. With great joy I chaired the meeting with a silent prayer within me for a show of team spirit. The vice-president and other members listened cheerfully while the secretary-general informed us about contacts she had made with International P.E.N. and other P.E.N. centres and organizations, and about invitations sent to P.E.N. Nepal, after it was inducted into International P.E.N., to attend international congresses and meetings, among them the Maastricht P.E.N. meeting in the Netherlands, in May 1989, and the 54th International World

Nepalese Writers and the P.E.N. Club

Congress in Toronto and Montreal from September 23 to October 1, 1989.

I was invited to attend the Canadian meeting by P.E.N. Toronto at their cost but I had already decided not to go, as I wanted to offer such an opportunity to our eminent writers and thus help fulfil my long-cherished desire to give them an international platform. Greta's written and my informal request to William Dawson, director of the USIS, and staff of the Asia Foundation succeeded in getting their financial support to send a delegation of two, our vice-president and the secretary-general, for which P.E.N. Nepal will always remember their encouraging help.

As planned, Dr. Gautam and Greta took English translations of some Nepali poems, short stories, and excerpts from novels along with curricula vitae and photographs to display in the congress. I was proud of their contribution and of the fact that Nepal was represented in such an important gathering of writers from all over the world.

After their return I received a brief report along with a copy of an interview of Dr. Gautam held by Mark Abley and published in *The Montreal Gazette* on September 30, 1989. I was glad of this exposure but a little astounded to find the story of the establishment of P.E.N. Nepal incomplete: the interview guest was either too shy to mention me as the founding president or simply forgot to.

Since we had no steady source of money on our own as yet, we could not send our writers to every P.E.N. conference and meeting. Still, until my presidency ended on December 13, 1991, P.E.N. Nepal managed to send delegations of writers to such different conferences as those that took place in Canada, Madeira (Portugal), and Vienna (Austria).

P.E.N. Nepal was officially registered in 1990 during the interim government following the pro-democracy movement.

Nepalese Writers and the P.E.N. Club

The first P.E.N. general meeting was held on July 5, 1990 at the British Council Hall. I made a brief welcoming speech in which I reiterated my commitment to the welfare of writers of Nepal and vowed to give them international exposure. The vice-president and secretary-general also spoke about P.E.N. At the end of our meeting six committees were formed — (1) the Fund Committee under the convenorship of Diamond Shumshere Rana, with Dr. Kumar Bahadur Joshi, Ramesh Toofan, Janardhan Joshi, and Nagendra Sharma as members, (2) the Publication Committee, of which Pushkar Lohani was the convenor, with Megh Raj Sharma "Manjul," Ashesh Malla, and Nayaraj Pandey as members; (3) Rochak Ghimire agreed to be the convenor of the Translation Committee, with Mrs. Prabha Thacker, Dhruba Sapkota and Binod Dixit as members; and (4) the Women's Committee, consisting of Mrs. Sharada Sharma as convenor and Mrs. Benju Sharma, Mrs. Shanti Kunwar, and Mrs. Archana Karki.

Our business over, British Council Assistant Representative John Mekenzie held a reception in honour of the writers at the British Council and expressed his happiness to be with them on that auspicious occasion.

P.E.N. Nepal has been under a very propitious star since its inception. News of its establishment spread quickly. One of the happiest moments in my life was the day when Greta informed me, very confidentially, about a letter P.E.N. Nepal had received, signed by members of the Nobel Committee of the Swedish Academy, inviting us to nominate a candidate for the Nobel Prize for literature for the year 1991. I always dreamt of and prayed for such a mark of distinction for our writers. Greta and I gave serious thought to the task and decided to seek the opinions of as wide a variety of writers, readers, intellectuals, and public figures as we possibly could before P.E.N. Nepal nominated its candidate. Everyone we wrote to

Nepalese Writers and the P.E.N. Club

sent a response. The writer whose name was put forward most (75% of the total) was nominated for the Nobel Prize. We both took great pride in forwarding the name of the first ever Nepalese candidate to the committee and offered strong reasons for the nomination. As instructed by the committee, we kept the nomination strictly confidential.

From August 1990 to April 1991 we had opportunities to welcome such eminent writers as the German critic Dr. Joseph Peter Strelka (settled in the U.S.A.), Lynne Reid Banks from Great Britain (a friend of our good friends Sidonie and Brian Garton, great lovers of Nepal, whose contribution to the development of Budhanilkantha School and whose keen interest to further quality education will always be remembered), and Jan Szcpanski from Poland. At our request they kindly gave talks to our writers. All the talk programmes were highly appreciated. In each I took an opportunity to make a very brief speech to welcome the speaker, the writers, and other lovers of literature. Greta then introduced the guests to the audience, offering a concise sketch and appreciation of their past life and works.

The representative of the British Council, Richard Hale, always generously provided the hall and refreshments. Refreshments, be it said, are regarded as an important component of any gathering that seeks to attract an audience in developing countries. One of the local writers made the remark that if in future we held our programmes in big hotels, the number of writers would automatically go up. Though I didn't entirely agree with what he said, I couldn't gainsay it either. I was happy with our guests for talking to whoever showed up, believing strongly that such talks were knowledge in the making. I still cherish the memory of their visits and thought-provoking lectures.

Nepalese Writers and the P.E.N. Club

One of the highlights in the history of P.E.N. Nepal was its first annual literature festival and short story shield awards at Hotel Annapurna. It was generously sponsored by Nepal Grindlays Bank Ltd. and inaugurated by the prime minster, Krishna Prasad Bhattarai, who unfortunately came to the function almost two hours late, by which point we were almost ready to start without him, not wanting to make all the eminent writers and diplomats, such as the British ambassador Timothy George and his wife, who were faithfully present for most of our programmes, wait indefinitely. Luckily we happened to have an impressive display of books by Nepalese and foreign writers organized by Pilgrim's Bookstore at our request.

The minister for home and communications, Yoga Prasad Upadhyaya, who came on time, seemed very restless and kindly went to call the prime minister. After a while the guest of honour strode in with a broad smile and made the waiting audience laugh by apologetically confessing that he had completely forgotten about the programme. I appreciated his confession, as people in power usually do not react so honestly in our culture, which encourages those at fault to make up some story or other to cover up the truth.

The prime minister proceeded with the inauguration and gave a speech expressing his confidence that P.E.N. Nepal, the only international literary association in the country, would play a due role in heightening literary awareness. I made a brief welcoming speech in which I complimented the prime minister for singing always from the Song Celestial, the *Bhagavadgita*, to remind people to go about their honest duty without attachment and to worship their work by committing themselves to do what they preach. I ended my speech with a prayer:

O God, give our writers courage to write the right as they see it, not seeking the favour of men, women, or the applause of people, but believing simply that a piece of good literature can make a million souls think and move. And give them such courage that they can scale the hardest peaks themselves and transform every stumbling block into a stepping stone.

Greta spoke beautifully about the objectives of P.E.N.N. Dr. Gautam thanked all, apologizing humorously for his weakness in English — a malady since boyhood.

Chairing the function was the outstanding novelist Daulat Bikram Bista. The prime minister gave away the P.E.N. Nepal shield to Bibas Pokharel, the winner of the award for the best short story. Then the chairman presented the first prize to the same recipient, Bibas Pokharel, the second prize to Govind Bhandari, and third prizes to Kishore Pahari and Jyoti Koirala. The function came to an end with the recitation of poems by the poets. Mrs. Archana Karki, a P.E.N.N. executive member, performed with flair the job of announcer. The news was well covered by the different media, including Nepal T.V. The festival turned out to be a grand success.

P.E.N. Nepal was generating some momentum, so my next mission, I felt, would be to begin a campaign to request outstanding old and promising new writers to join P.E.N. Nepal and help the centre to achieve its goal of uplifting writers without any discrimination on the basis of sex, caste, or creed, and to give the lie to the Nepali proverb, "As dogs bark at one another, so too do intellectuals envy one another" (*kukurle kukurlai bhukchha; bidwanle bidwanlai irsya garchha*). I had noticed the queer and unfortunate relationships existing between literary organizations in developing countries and wanted to break that tradition by an exemplary effort on the part of P.E.N. Nepal to unite all writers. But one quiet night I suddenly heard the divine whisper, "Daughter, stay

Nepalese Writers and the P.E.N. Club

still." Thus I decided not to stand for reelection, though Greta requested me to do so, if I felt so inclined. As its founding president, I will always be closely tied to P.E.N. Nepal. I am very grateful to all founding members, especially to Greta, for her key role as an energetic and dedicated secretary-general. I thank God for giving me such
an opportunity to be associated with writers, the jewels of Nepal.

Chapter 15

The People's Movement and the Library Episode

After my first ten happy years (1963-1972) as chief of T.U. Central Library things changed. Every moment turned into a challenge and struggle because I had always needed to stand for truth in order to get things done for the library, the library staff, and the library profession. I had become used to raising my voice against wrong, no matter from which quarter, and to pointing out faults with the sincere intention of instigating improvement. I worried not only for the library but also for the University as a whole. I had a strong conviction that, while aloof from politics, the University should play a crucial role, through the honest exercise of its academic mission, in pointing out the right direction if the government took a wrong path. I quite often argued with university authorities and professors for not raising their voice openly against dishonest deeds during the Panchayat period, as I strongly believe that with hard and honest work and determination we can achieve something, if not everything, under any system.

If all the elite and enlightened souls of Nepal had engaged in constructive criticism without fear of speaking and writing, the corrupt people in power and position under the Panchayat system would not have been able to prolong their dishonest activities for thirty years. These people became so blind that they failed to see the deteriorating situation in the country. King Mahendra certainly did not introduce the Panchayat system in

The People's Movement and the Library Episode

order to have a people's movement do away with it within such a short time.

In the beginning, I was told, the king's men were not that crooked and selfish. King Mahendra himself took a leading role, feeling out the pulse of his subjects, and was eager to prove that his brainchild, a Panchayat system suitable to Nepal's needs, was more democratic than the multiparty democracy introduced by his father, King Tribhuvan in 1951 following 105 years of autocratic Rana rule. He was a shrewd, farsighted, and patriotic king who worked hard to cement Nepal's self-identity. His death was untimely and sudden.

The young Eaton- and Harvard-educated Crown Prince Birendra succeeded his father as the eleventh Shah King of Nepal. His first photo as king was published in *The Rising Nepal* against a very impressive background picture of his grandfather, King Tribhuvan, the leader of the democratic movement of Nepal in 1950. People were full of hopes that King Birendra would become the leader of a reformation movement of Panchayat democracy. However, there were more Sakunis than Bidurs (respectively villainous and ideal characters in the *Mahabharata*) in and around the palace. As a believer in the fundamental truths of Hinduism, I still strongly look upon the king as a symbol of unity, love, and kindness — an ideal human above petty concerns who has nothing of his own; the whole nation belongs to him and he belongs to the nation.

It was a great shame that people had to take to the streets to defy the Panchayat system. The irresponsible persons in power were too slow to recognize the aspirations of honest and sincere citizens, including leaders of banned political parties, who wanted rational democratic reform in the Panchayat system so that not only a few privileged groups of people but all the people would have a say in running the country. The powerbrokers were too busy escaping realities to be tolerant of healthy criticism.

My husband and I went through many painful experiences which inhibited us from exercising our will to contribute to the development process, not only of the University but also of the nation. We were saddened, as we could feel that something momentous was in the offing — the torch of liberty set to be lit. To have peace of mind and keep his conscience clear, my husband wrote many pseudonymous articles and poems (such as the one entitled "Panchayati Gita," published October 18, 1984 in *Nepal Post*), hoping to open the eyes of people in power to the deteriorating situation in the country. Whenever I got a chance to speak out against wrong, I never feared to do so. My mind, too, was revolting.

King Birendra had earlier called for a referendum to choose between multiparty democracy or a reformed Panchayat system, and I, like many, had seen this as a great opportunity. The referendum took place peacefully on May 2, 1980. The result was in favour of a reformed Panchayat system; the people had spoken. Unfortunately the word "reform" remained only on paper and was not put into practice. People's high hopes gradually faded, but plans were hatched to induce reform by public outcry.

On April 6, 1990 the whole Kathmandu Valley rose in revolt against the system, and on April 8, 1990 King Birendra showed where his true instincts lay by declaring his assent to multiparty democracy for Nepal, thus forestalling the shedding of further blood.

The struggle at the last moment had turned into a popular uprising. The Revolution of 1990 drew people, especially young people, onto the streets, to the great surprise of all party leaders. It was said that these leaders were not quite sure whether the revolution would really come off. It came like a

The People's Movement and the Library Episode

miracle, at a time when the leaders themselves were in a compromising mood, hoping that the king's men would simply implement what the king had said in his historical proclamation on December 16, 1979, a few months after the announcement of the national referendum on May 2: that "whatever the outcome of the National Referendum, the election to the Legislature henceforward is to be through adult franchise, the prime minister elected by it, and the cabinet responsible to it." Up until the Movement, as it came to be called, this proclamation had not been translated into reality, and this was what had sparked the torch of liberty and freedom in the whole of Nepal. It took the Movement just a few days to gain its ends. A detailed account of the Revolution of 1990 is very well presented in the book *Spring Awakening: An Account of the 1990 Revolution in Nepal* by William Raeper and Martin Hoftun (New Delhi, Viking, 1992).

Thus multiparty democracy was back after thirty years of Panchayat rule. Processions and illuminations throughout the Kathmandu Valley and all over Nepal were held to celebrate. I myself was very curious to view the scene in the streets, as neither my husband nor I had experienced any revolutions or wars or conflicts in our lives. I always take pride in saying that Nepal is a land of peace — the birth place of Gautam Buddha and a small Shangri-la that had never been under any foreign domination. It was a land of patriots like Bhimsen Thapa, Bala Bhadra Kunwar, Bhakti Thapa, and Amar Singh Thapa, who fought against the British. There had been no major wars — civil, religious, or otherwise — and no communal conflicts for centuries. The country had existed without even a revolution until, in 1950, the Glorious Revolution occurred; it had always managed to preserve its own identity.

In the company of my husband I went to witness the jubilation of the people on the main streets of Kathmandu. It

The People's Movement and the Library Episode

was an utterly unique occasion, incomparable even to any of the big festivals. Never had I seen in my life such a cheerful crowd singing songs of victory. Watching the scene, I thought that the king had made a very wise and gracious decision in giving freedom to the people. He had averted a serious crisis, realizing the truth that suppression is no remedy and more expensive than liberty. We shared much personal pride with the people of Nepal in celebrating the day that marks the coming of age of Nepal as a democratic society.

To our great surprise, we happened to see some of the ardent *pancha* elites throwing red powder to celebrate the occasion publicly. This was unbelievable hypocrisy! How could they change their tune so quickly after having sung only praises for the old system for so long? Making a list of them was a must, I thought, because they could never be loyal either to any system or to the nation. Theirs was the mercurial behaviour described by the Nepali proverb, "Where the water goes, so goes the fish" (*jata pani uta machha*).

Such behaviour went back many years. When the king announced the national referendum, one of the Panchayat elites called up multiparty leaders to tell them that he was behind the idea and totally sure that victory would go to the multiparty system. In anticipation, he even bought a *khasi* (goat) to sacrifice in celebration, thinking to throw a grand party and to invite a host of freedom fighters. At the time, the outcry of the masses supporting the different parties was quite high.

When the people's verdict turned out to be for the reformed Panchayat system (a total of 2,433,452 votes as against 2,067,965 for the multiparty system out of a voting population of 7,155,438), the same man still threw a big party and sacrificed the same goat, but he was careful to invite not the freedom fighters, only ardent *panchas*. In the same way, I heard, some *panchas* called various multiparty leaders late at

The People's Movement and the Library Episode

night on April 8, 1990, when King Birendra had just lifted the 29-year ban on political parties, to inform them that they had been hard at work for decades to clear the path for the multiparty system. When I heard such incredible stories, I could not help laughing for a while, but I was also saddened to think that these were the kinds of people attracted to public service.

The close of the long struggle for democracy initiated decades ago by the most respected Congress leader within and without, Mr. B. P. Koirala, and the most popular Communist leader, Mr. Pushpa Lall Shrestha, marked the beginning of a new chapter in Nepalese history — an era of transition towards a revitalized democracy.

I was extremely anxious to reopen the library after the Movement. It had been closed for seven days, April 5-11, 1990. On April 12 I reached the library, as usual, on time. My disciplined staff, as close to my heart as ever, were also punctual. I was standing in the entrance hall close to my office to greet everyone, hoping to hear of their experiences. I remained somewhat nervous until everyone was accounted for; lives had been claimed, but not among my staff, and for this I was grateful.

I made a brief speech, urging one and all to renew their efforts to be disciplined, sincere, honest, and hard-working, so that T.U. Central Library would be able to meet the new challenges that the new era would demand of it. I prayed for the peace of the departed souls lost in the Movement.

The staff was abuzz with many exciting stories. They and people from the outside seemed happy. Democracy was in the air. The situation seemed to be returning to normal very quickly. But events soon proved this to be far from the case. The interim government soon got involved not only in its declared task of drafting a new constitution and arranging for elections but also had in dealing with unforeseen challenges,

The People's Movement and the Library Episode

including demands put forward by different groups, such as journalists, ethnic communities and, most crucially, the civil servants, whose agitations were initiated by the Communists. Hunger strikes, token hunger strikes, demonstrations, public speeches, and the like took place almost daily as a means of registering protest. The word "democracy" came to be used by different people in different ways — not at all a healthy sign. If democracy was to survive, it could not afford to be misused to justify lax behaviour. On the contrary, it required even more honesty, sincerity, and discipline. Without these it would have no meaning.

Ironically, in spite of having made people conscious of the real meaning of democracy, the two main political parties, the Congress Party and the Communists, began to compete with each other to exploit the unstable situation for their own ends, with discontented groups being used as levers. The need for self-restraint was lost sight of within a short period. At the same time, the university employees also started to show their strength by establishing associations throughout the country. I closely watched these developments, while also remaining deeply involved in planning a strategy to upgrade library and information services to enable the new university authorities and political decision-makers to benefit from the tested methods expounded in various library material for bringing about social change.

I had always loved to thrash things out with my senior staff and the more knowledgeable members of my junior staff, having established decades before the democratic tradition of holding monthly meetings with them for a free discussion of library work and services. To my dismay, however, I seldom got even the senior members to open their mouths during such meetings. I found myself doing all the talking. Quite often I hinted that I would stop holding monthly meetings if the staff

The People's Movement and the Library Episode

disliked the idea. I frequently read out Swami Vivekananda's saying, "You should work like a master not as a slave; work incessantly, but do not do a slave's work."

Some occasions were still fresh in my memory. Way back in 1966 and in the 1970's my staff were already telling me that they had nothing to report in the meetings. I requested them to read some newly acquired books, periodicals, and newspapers and then prepare précis of them for the next meeting; by increasing their knowledge, they could better guide readers. After some months of this, I came to know that certain staff members were grumbling that they were employed to do library work, not to make précis. I this took in stride. I had always wanted my staff to exercise their freedom of speech by learning to conceptualize problems and to think for themselves, in monthly meetings or otherwise, so I kept at it. I looked for great things from my staff, who cooperated with me for decades to achieve my goal to make T.U. Central Library a model under my much talked-about administration of strict discipline — a must for development, though it goes against the grain of our culture: *rajako kam kahile jala gham* ("It's government work. When will the day end?" — the attitude of someone whose thoughts are more on the clock than on the job).

I had never had reason to complain about my staff. Most of them were nurtured in the library, having joined it fresh out of school and having grown into adult men and women while pursuing a higher education on the side. I took great pride in them.

A few weeks after the success of the Movement, though, I began to scent change. My trust in my staff was so high that I didn't pay any heed at first. Then, on April 20, I returned to the library in the afternoon after a fixed meeting with the vice-chancellor to find that the library had, for the first time ever, been closed without my knowledge and without prior notice

The People's Movement and the Library Episode

being given to the readers and visitors. I was shocked to see visitors turn back disappointed. It had been a longstanding policy of the library not to close during the posted hours, as people depended upon it for its services. Moreover, Kirtipur is quite far from Kathmandu, and people had to take the trouble to squeeze into crowded buses to reach the University.

Earlier that day Mr. Chandra Kanta Jha had come to me with some of my other staff to inform me of a big meeting that was being organized by the university employees on the open ground of the Kirtipur campus. I told them to participate actively and to petition for better bus service and cafeteria service so that the library would have greater opportunities to serve more readers — this my own years-old request with so many vice-chancellors. Perhaps, I thought, this meeting would finally get the ball rolling.

Thus the meeting was attended, but the library was closed. Even the senior staff were lured away. For a while I almost lost my senses in front of the locked entrance. I could feel the crisis of discipline that had spread all over Nepal finally coming to haunt T.U. Central Library, which had been so well known for its good administration and efficient services.

With heavy heart I returned home. I spent a sleepless night thinking how to proceed; I was not used to such undisciplinary acts on the part of my staff. I prayed and prayed for the power to remain cool.

Luckily the next day was Saturday. Usually I avoided worrying about work over the weekend. I went out with my husband to a nearby village to enjoy the natural beauty of the country surroundings and to put all disturbing thoughts out of my mind. But no peace came to me. We returned earlier from the village than we had planned.

Arriving at the office the next day, I was told the shocking news that Mr. Jha, whom I had taken on at T.U. Central Library from the Janakpur campus (swayed by his wish to give

The People's Movement and the Library Episode

a good education to his children in Kathmandu), and whom I had asked to participate in the meeting, had spoken nothing but lies. He had insinuated through the mike to the crowd that I had forbidden the participation of the library staff in the meeting, whereupon the staff had taken the bold step to come anyhow. This he did to rouse antipathy against me and to sow the seeds of discord in the library — a gross misuse of the spirit of democracy and freedom of speech.

I was terribly mad at Mr. Jha. I called a staff meeting and spoke very fiercely in it against his knavery and naked lies. He put on a display of ingenuousness, confessing that since he was not used to speaking through microphones in front of large audiences he didn't know what he was saying that afternoon and should therefore be treated leniently. Oh, what a cruel hypocrite! Listening to his cunning words, I remembered a warning I had received from some of my staff when I made the decision to take him on: "*Some* people from the Terai lowlands can act like mice so long as they need your help but can easily turn into cobras later to poison you." I never believed this, being against any kind of discrimination towards Terai people. I strongly believed that every citizen of Nepal, whether from the Terai or the hills, should enjoy equal opportunities on the basis of ability, sincerity, and honesty. Knowing that to err is human, I warned Mr. Jha not to bluster forth such blatant, shameless lies ever again.

At the end of the staff meeting I read out a news item on Eastern Europe after the collapse of Communism there. This I did to make my fellow librarians conscious of their responsibility to sustain freedom. The situation in Eastern Europe could be compared with the demolition of an orphanage. Suddenly no one was around to play the guardian. Citizens used to being cogs in a machine, having information filtered down from above, and being kept in line by the state had now to be told to assume responsibility for their own lives.

The People's Movement and the Library Episode

Coming to terms with new-found independence would be hard for many. Some would feel that there were no longer constraints of any kind and therefore no obligations towards society as a whole. Many people would behave as if they could do what they wanted. They would live in a dream world.

After the meeting Mr. Jha came up to me in private to tell me that he had been misled and promised to consult me in the future before acting. In spite of his assurances, I remained very suspicious of his every move, both inside the library and out, especially when he got himself elected president of the association of library employees without my knowledge, having promised promotions, confirmations, and new posts to innocent-minded lower staff.

Later, to my great surprise, I came to know through different sources that Mr. Jha had been used by external forces to create problems in the library, as part of a more general plot against me personally. These conspirators were exploiting the newly aroused democratic spirit of innocent persons in and outside the library.

After these few incidents, suspicions at times arose in my mind towards some other members of my staff, including senior ones, yet I could hardly distrust persons who had spoken nothing against me and my working methods all through the years and had always showed admirable team spirit. I did not think that they would ever renounce that spirit, and thinking that, I kept free from worry.

On the afternoon of May 11, 1990 I was happily leafing through the Nepali translation of *Alice's Adventures in Wonderland* by Lewis Carroll. Prof. Chudamani Bandhu had done the translation at my request to represent the Nepali language at exhibitions to be held in different parts of the world at the initiative of the Carroll Foundation in Australia. My absorption was broken when all the members of the newly founded association of library staff entered and handed over a

The People's Movement and the Library Episode

list of fifteen demands, requesting me to answer in writing whether they could be met. I scanned through the list and found it very extravagant. The demands included: (1) removal of two register books, kept to record the exact arrival time of the staff as well as their comings and goings during office hours so that they could learn to appreciate the value of time — to come exactly at 10 and not to waste office hours, (2) free use of the office vehicle, in contravention of the strict precedent to make use of it only for official work, (3) free use of the office telephone, against the library practice of using it only for official business except in cases of emergency.

I thought it best not to discuss further what made no sense. I told them that the demands could easily be met if they took responsibility to run the library in the way I had run it with their cooperation for decades. I realized now what malign presence had entered the library. I told my husband about all these disturbing developments, hoping that he would be able to find out who was behind it all. Before he even got down to work, though, I learned from members of the T.U. Teachers' Association that Mr. S. B. Thakur, who for decades had been conducting a personal vendetta against me, was behind the conspiracy: he had been going around to various associations, including student associations, with a letter, written on stationery of the Nepal Library Association, demanding my resignation — and this even before any serious agitation had broken out. Now my staff, once so disciplined, had caught the contagion. Their looks and tone had changed completely. Later on I also found out that Krishna Gopal Shrestha, the president of the T.U. Employees' Association and currently an M.P. (Communist Party of Nepal / United Marxist-Leninists) had also been wooed over to strengthen the hands of my adversaries.

Though now on my guard, I still basically trusted my senior staff, whom over the years I had been gradually trying to

The People's Movement and the Library Episode

charge with greater responsibility. They had been given many opportunities to go abroad, as far as Australia, to broaden their knowledge and to prepare themselves to take charge one day of T.U. Central Library and to assume a leading role in the development of the campus libraries.

I realized, however, that I was growing tired of my unending struggle for the profession as day by day the academic atmosphere in the country deteriorated. The people in power had become merchants who peddled not knowledge but influence and money. And now, if the authorities did not show any interest in stemming undemocratic developments in the library with the very advent of democracy, I made up my mind that I would take this opportunity to leave the library.

All these many years my friends in power, in particular palace secretaries, never showed interest in seeing me promoted out of the library. Whenever I expressed my desire to them to serve my country in a different capacity by taking on some larger responsibility than T.U. Central Library, as other university colleagues of mine had done, having been given such posts as minister, ambassador, or member of the Planning Commission or Development Council, they played coy with me: "Oh Shanti, how can we see you leave the library. You have become an institution yourself..." In this way they managed to sidestep the issue.

Whenever I thought about my colleagues whose careers were advanced in spite of their having made no evident contributions in any field to the development of the nation, I felt chafed. Our culture's practice of filling vacant posts with *aphno manchhe* (one's own people who can be used as pawns), regardless of their qualifications, was a great stumbling block to steady development. Since my path was the path of truth, I belonged to none but to God. Moreover, as a woman, I was eager to show male-dominated Nepalese society that capable and competent women could participate in the development

The People's Movement and the Library Episode

process of the nation if only equal opportunities were given to them. Perhaps these two aspirations went too much against the grain of our culture. Thus I had to confine myself to the library for decades even after making it "the pride of the nation" and "almost unique in South Asia," as stated by the British Book Development Mission as far back as 1969.

Before I could resign on my own terms, another deplorable incident occurred that forced my hand. It seemed to have been in the making since April 8, Democracy Day. On May 16, I took down a notice about a reception to be given to the T.U. Employees' Association Ad Hoc Committee, thinking that it no longer was needed because a different understanding had been reached as to its contents. Immediately the misleading rumour was spread that the chief librarian had torn up the minutes of a very important meeting. This resulted in a decision to start a campaign to gather signatures from my library staff to demand my resignation.

I was stunned. I sat alone in my office for some time trying to decide the best course of action. It was already late evening. My husband, as usual, came from his office to pick me up. I told him of the situation and about how improper efforts were being made by the instigators to prevent any kind of compromise from being reached between the library staff and me. The staff had been roused to a pitch of fury, to the point where I had completely lost trust in them. Responsibility was being sacrificed in the name of democracy, which had come to mean the freedom to do anything anyone wanted.

I told my husband that I would not return to the library and would relinquish my duty as chief of T.U. Central Library. It was a burden I had taken on with great pride and pleasure decades ago, but it now had become greater than I was willing to bear.

Before leaving the library, I uttered a prayer for courage to face the challenge gracefully and took a final look around. My

The People's Movement and the Library Episode

eyes ran over the book stacks and the pictures of kings and other distinguished visitors taken during their tours of the library while I was enthusiastically showing them around. I walked out with my husband, closing the door behind us. I knew that I would not be coming back again.

I was unable to sleep that night; I lay awake and prayed. It had not been an easy decision to make — perhaps one of the hardest decisions I had ever made in my life, as I had always looked forward to leaving the library with grace and dignity.

Early the next morning I told my husband that, the vice-chancellor, rector, and registrar having already resigned, I should like to report the details of the current situation to the acting rector, Dr. Bhisma Raj Prasai, hoping that he would find a means to bring down the curtain on what I felt was a "hideous tragedy." I did meet him, but no concrete steps were taken to remedy the situation in the library. My foes were now calling me a "dictator" and the library rules and practices were termed "despotic, dictatorial, and authoritarian."

On May 18 I notified the acting rector in writing that I would not remain in the library under such anarchic, undemocratic, unmanageable, and undisciplined conditions. Thoroughgoing changes had to be made in the deplorable conduct of the library staff, and the group leading the campaign against me penalized. Dr. Prasai backed off from taking any action immediately, however, and politely requested me to take a month's leave. Thus I voluntarily relinquished my library duties and also gave notice in writing on May 20 to the library staff of my decision not to return to the library, including a plea to them to look after the library properly.

The agitators drew on the support of discontented ex-library staff who had either been transferred or fired for misconduct or negligence, some of those who had been found guilty in court of misappropriation of library money, and others who always showed dissatisfaction at the administration. The T.U.

The People's Movement and the Library Episode

authorities for their part made no decision on how to deal with the situation. The agitators took advantage of the power vacuum and called for a token hunger strike to demand my resignation, oblivious of my written notice. Five days after I had voluntarily left the library, a relay hunger strike was staged in front of the library to demand what was already a *fait accompli*. The mastermind behind this deplorable farce was S. B. Thakur, and he was backed by others, including Krishna Gopal Shrestha.

For a few days I sat and pondered. I looked for reasons why my devoted staff, who had supported me so strongly so long, had let themselves be wooed by the cry of devils. They were innocently being caught up in the countrywide revolt of employees against authority — condoned by both the Congress and Communist parties. I cried out to God against human treachery and naive selfishness — against the wrong people deaf to their own conscience (the whisper of God) do.

At last, on May 25, 1990, a new set of university authorities was announced: a strange combination of Congress and Communist followers to officiate at the temple of higher learning. Honest academicians and administrators, among whom I counted myself, felt ill at ease with such politicalization of the educational process in the newly emerging democratic period. Still, I kept up hopes that the team, consisting of Prof. B. C. Malla (Congress) as vice-chancellor, Prof. Ram Man Shrestha (Communist) as rector, and Mr. Bishweshwar Man Shrestha (Communist) as registrar, might somehow take advantage of the new democratic conditions to bring about radical change by applying, for instance, a just policy of rewards and punishments. But days passed and months went by with little headway being made. The new officials were too busy just placating various mob-like factions to be effective aca-demicians. When they came, I thought that they would surely get at the truth of the library episode so that the agitators would be punished, but to my great dismay they did nothing of the sort. They didn't even bother to make enquiries with me. Their timid, do-nothing attitude was mystifying.

During this whole time my sole duty was to show up daily at the rector's office; otherwise I was as free as a bird. No responsibilities were assigned to me. I often thought and also expressed openly that it was not right to be drawing a salary under such circumstances. But what could I do? I was in limbo, having been neither transferred from my old post as the chief librarian nor assigned to a new one with new responsibilities. The only thing left to cherish was the unfailing outward respect shown to me whenever I turned up here and there.

While I was still hoping that the vice-chancellor, rector, and registrar would come to some concrete decision, they unexpectedly resigned from their posts. They had served about fourteen months, during which they had accomplished one thing: the mass promotion of more than 3,000 personnel (teaching and administrative staff), a mistake they should have done everything possible to avoid if they had wanted to be remembered as good educationalists. When under mass pressure to turn temporary posts into permanent ones without honest scrutiny, they had ironically had no trouble in making decisions to please the mob to the detriment of the University.

To console myself I silently recalled my own efforts and achievements during the 27 years as a chief librarian fighting a one-woman crusade for what I believed in. During that crusade I loved to quote the verses I had penned, trying to remember something similar I had seen and then forgotten:

What is the Library Profession?

The Library Profession is a Challenge - Meet IT.
The Library Profession is a Struggle - Accept IT.

The People's Movement and the Library Episode

The Library Profession is a Devotion - Devote Yourself to IT.
The Library Profession is an Opportunity - Grasp IT.
The Library Profession is God's Gift - Cherish IT.

This was copied by visiting librarians whenever they saw it hanging on the wall of T.U. Central Library. Its wide circulation made me proud.

I had done my utmost to be true to that pledge. As a result of my endeavours, I was confident that not only Tribhuvan University but also Nepal as a whole now had a model library both for Nepalese and Nepal-loving scholars of all nations, and that teachers and students who thirsted after knowledge and wisdom now had a better opportunity of quenching their thirst than before.

Thus my mission to make T.U. Central Library a model in the country had come to a tragic end only in a personal sense. The challenges and unending struggles I went through came back one by one to stir my soul to make me want to become more mature and a stronger God-loving woman so that I could serve my country in better ways ahead. I took great pride in having accepted those challenges, whether pleasing or unpleasing, for the development of quality education — the backbone of development so needed to change the deep-rooted attitudes of a people stricken with outdated traditions.

God's message that "A prophet is honoured everywhere except in his own country and among his own people," long enshrined deep in my heart, now flashed out again into my memory. That message was so true. My divinely guided decision to leave my profession shocked my foreign friends all over the world more than my countrymen. My phone brought calls from such friends at home and abroad, and many others wrote to me to express their deep concern not only for me but also for the newly reestablished democracy in Nepal. They

The People's Movement and the Library Episode

praised my contribution to the nation-building process through library services. I treasured their letters and calls as a source of inspiration that encouraged me to take the vow that I would not shrink back and would not shed tears, a woman's weakest weapon, but would shine out the stronger with an iron will to serve the men and women of my country and to show male-dominated societies like ours that women of competence, honesty, sincerity, and devotion can serve humankind equally well, having accepted challenges as the road to glory. "Stones have been known to move and trees to speak against bad deeds." O God, you know that I have never repented having been born as a woman. May I be born as a woman again in my next life and help swell the ranks of those who bring peace and prosperity to the world.

Appendix I

Debt to Mt. Everest

In Honor of our Friend,
Shanti Shrestha
From Kathmandu, Nepal

'Tis not alone to thy majestic heights
Or rock-ribbed shoulders and ice-crusted crown,
To awesome crevasses and blinding lights
Which guard thy crest, or snowfields sweeping down
To which we are indebted; nor the power
Which isolates thee like an unclaimed throne
Above the earth, once usurped for an hour
When two men struggled to thy top alone.
But also this: That from the range below
Once came a child to view a foreign land;
A daughter nurtured by thy melting snow,
More than a child - who took us by the hand
And told us of green pastures far below
Thy heights, where hills of untold beauty stand.
                    - Charlie Coggin

Appendix I

For Shanti

    She came among us when our lives were full,
Replete with many blessings, in a way
Most singular - a sari-ed eastern way,
Wearing her laughter like a tinkling bell,
Bidding us welcome to share her lovely thoughts,
Her bright surmise, her expectation of
Fair new worlds of hope and gentle peace.
    Like morning in the springtime did she come,
Like a flower unfolding she brought into our home
And showered on our occidental minds
A new respect for ancient, honorable lands
Staked out among the stars, beneath the snows
Of Everest, and their customs and their ways,
And taught us many things, though still a child.
    Later, in absence, when maturity
Had wrought its wonders in her inner life -
First, love, and then the joy of motherhood,
Reunion with her family and her land,
And worthwhile tasks, the sharing of a home,
The privilege of duty and of toil.
We found her memory mirrored in our minds.
    Now, half a generation afterwards,
Grief and age having claimed their ancient rites,
Having hung their ancient wreaths upon our door,
She has returned. Upon our lives once more
Shines beauty, pride, and welcome, faith restored.
The East has smiled upon the West again,
And we rejoice to greet and call her daughter.
    With love/1-5-78

Appendix I

How We Felt on Receiving Your Letter, Shanti

Halfway around the world tonight
Within another world,
Past oceans and the highest height
Our planet has unfurled,
Within a home there shines a light
Bidding us share a friendship bright
With promise, and unto that home we answer from afar:
Dear Friends, there is no way to tell
How much your welcome means
To us! it was like a temple bell
And all the distant scenes
We envisioned now cast a magic spell
And chime in unison, "All is well,
Here and where you are!"
If home is where the heart is, we
Already share your home,
And five already dwell when three
Extend such true welcome!
We shall indeed your own guests be,
We do accept most gratefully,
So set your door ajar.
And tell your little Daughter, whose
Bright eyes we'll see so soon,
To stay with her indeed we choose!
Together we'll watch the moon
Climbing the sky in silver shoes,
And every golden moment use,
And bless the day that made you like you are!

Appendix II

IWYCN 1975 Programme

Preface

Nepalese society has its own typical identity in the context of the country's religion, culture and historical tradition, and the society has indeed left a deep imprint on the Nepalese women. Kindness, love, service, mercy, modesty, magnanimity, tenderness, obedience, faith and confidence form the basis of our cultural values and religion. The character of the Nepalese women should be inspired and guided by these very values. Nepalese women should be capable of playing an arduous role — that of a good housewife who discharges social responsibilities befittingly. Individualistic selfish attitudes do not find rapport with the character of the Nepalese women. Social service and welfare, and the Nepalese women are synonymous. The Nepalese women should be of the firm resolve that their personality can be built up only through social service. If modern education and training tend to alienate the Nepalese women from their responsibility towards home and society and drive them towards the brink of harsh and selfish individualism, it should be understood as the approach of a great degeneration in the character of the Nepalese women. The knowledge and talent attained through modern education should be regarded not only as a medium for developing self-reliance but also as a supplement based on religious and cultural values for conscientiousness and preparedness so essential for the development of the significant character of the Nepalese women. In short, Nepalese women's ideal character depends on the grand blend of positive

Appendix II

traditional values and modern education coupled with a broad attitude acquired through advanced technology.

Hence, in response to the United Nations' call to its member states to observe the International Women's Year, 1975, His Majesty King Birendra Bir Bikram Shah Dev constituted the International Women's Year Committee Nepal under the patronage of Her Majesty Queen Aishwarya Rajya Laxmi Devi Shah. Keeping in view the aforementioned ideals of the Nepalese women, the International Women's Year Committee Nepal (IWYCN) has worked out a comprehensive programme based on the International Women's Year's three main objectives: 1) to bring about harmonious co-ordination between men and women, the basis of equality; 2) to fully associate women in the task of development; 3) and to give due recognition to the ever growing importance of women so as to contribute to world peace and to maintain cooperation and friendship among various countries. The following programme has been drawn up to fulfill these objectives.

Programme

Agriculture:
1) Afforestation, cotton growing, fruit cultivation and vegetable cultivation programmes will be carried out in the kingdom's four regional development centres — Dhankuta, Surkhet, Kathmandu and Pokhara.
2) With the help of J.T.A.s [junior technical assistants], short-term training programmes will be launched for the effective service of rural women in the production of fruits and vegetables.

Education:
3) Whereas the practice so far of the women's literacy campaign was to include only one district from each zone

Appendix II

under its programme to increase the number of literate women, henceforth two districts from each zone will be included in the competition and the winning districts will be awarded the "Ratna Literacy Award" and certificates.

4) In connection with the International Women's Year, a women's handicrafts competition is to be held on the basis of development regions, and the districts declared as the winners will be given the "International Women's Year" prizes, certificates, etc.

5) Women's multi-purpose work centres are also to be established in the four development regions with the assistance to be provided by the Ministry of Panchayat.

6) At the request of the IWYCN, St. Mary's High School is to award free scholarships to fifteen deserving girl students. Under the scheme, five girls representing the four development regions, with the exception of Kathmandu Valley, will be awarded free boarding scholarships while the other ten scholarship — five for class I and five for class 2 — will be granted to day scholars of Kathmandu Valley.

7) The primary schools that help the most in increasing the number of literates among the girls of 18 remote districts will also be awarded.

8) A book for imparting practical education to literate adult women will be prepared with the help of the Ministry of Education.

9) Quiz contests will be held at the high school level in the four development regions.

10) An essay competition on equality and co-ordination between man and woman will also be organised.

11) Debates at campus level will also take place.

12) Efforts will be made under the auspices of the Ministry of Education to institute Her Majesty Queen Aishwarya

Appendix II

Women's Scholarships under which, for the present, provision will be made for one revolving fund to each of the four development regions of the Kingdom.

13) An evaluation committee will be formed with the co-operation of the Education Ministry to prescribe school textbooks that will highlight the importance of women in the society.

Seminars:

14) International doll exhibition will be held.
15) Seminars on the main objectives of the International Women's Year, 1975, and family planning and other related subjects will be organised in three different development regions.
16) Teams will be sent to various districts so as to acquaint the rural women with the non-aligned foreign policy of Nepal, the provision of women's rights under the law and other related matters.
17) A literary conference will also be held.

Health:

18) People of various districts will be enlightened on the importance and necessity of family planning, and family planning programmes will be carried out with the co-operation of the Ministry of Health.
19) Women will be acquainted with the importance of nurses and midwives, and a training programme will be conducted under the auspices of the Ministry of Health and the Family Planning Association.
20) With the help of the Ministry of Health provision will be made for health facilities so as to maintain sound health among the women and children.

Social Service:

21) A national campaign will be launched in order to remove child marriage, polygamy and other similar social evils.

Appendix II

22) Maximum efforts will be made to provide drinking water, water mills and other benefits to the women of a number of villages under the four development regions.
23) The Women Training Centre will organise campaigns for encouraging women to take to social service, housewife training, kitchen garden, cleanliness, poultry, education and the like.
24) Cultural programmes, talks and film screenings with the theme of the urgency to get rid the country of social evils will be held.

Law:
25) Suggestions will be made for formulating laws and also for introducing timely amendments in the existing law in order to bring about reform and end hindrances and obstacles perpetuated by outmoded practices and traditions.
26) The provision of women's rights under the Constitution, Law and other rules and regulations are to be compiled and written in simple language for distribution and, at the same time, teams will be sent to acquaint the women with their rights.
27) The Ministry of Law is to make provision for disposing of speedily pending cases affecting women.
28) A seminar on Law will be organised.

Publicity:
29) The IWYCN has been conducting programmes based on the objectives of the International Women's Year over Radio Nepal from 1:45 to 2:00 in the afternoon every Monday.
30) With a view to providing opportunities to women to show and develop their artistic talents, painting, handicraft and other exhibitions will be held.
31) Women's sports will also be organised.

Appendix II

32) Pamphlets and posters concerning the International Women's Year will be released for distribution.
33) Special stamps and coins are to be issued to commemorate the International Women's Year.
34) A documentary film reflecting various aspects of the Nepalese women society will be produced and screened.
35) To mark the International Women's Year, 1975, a calendar will be issued.

Miscellaneous:

36) A research committee will be formed to carry out research studies on subjects relating to the role and status of the Nepalese women and also to analyse women's problems and find their solutions.
37) A women's welfare home will be opened with the help of the Ministry of Panchayat.
38) A mothers' club will be opened in Kathmandu with the help of the Nepal Red Cross Society.
39) Efforts will be made to open centres for women's training in three development regions with the help of the Ministry of Panchayat.
40) In compliance with the recommendation of the ILO, efforts will be made to provide 84 days of maternity leave instead of 45 days to the women employees.
41) The Tribhuvan University Central Library will help the IWYCN to publish a Directory of Working Women.
42) With the help of the Ministry of Education, a women's hostel will be opened in Kathmandu and efforts will also be made to open similar hostels in the other three development regions of the kingdom.

Appendix III

IWYCN 1975 Report

His Majesty the King constituted a seven member committee under the patronage of Her Majesty Queen Aishwarya Rajya Laxmi Devi Shah on November 7, 1974 to observe 1975 as the International Women's Year amidst special, befitting programmes all over the Kingdom in response to the call made by the United Nations, and provision was also made for including eight representatives of the Ministries of Home, Panchayat, Law and Justice, Industry and Commerce, Food and Agriculture, Education, Health and Foreign Affairs of His Majesty's Government in the committee. Accordingly, the International Women's Year Committee Nepal 1975 emerged under the inspiring leadership of and in conformity with the clarion objectives and glorious ideals so graciously provided by Her Majesty the Queen so as to be able to forge ahead in the task of acquainting the general people with the significant importance of services rendered in connection with the Women's Year and also to associate them in the development endeavours by doing away with the hindrances and obstacles that creep in the way of women's progress. The committee's office was opened at Bhrikuti Mandap with the cooperation extended by the Ministry of Home and the Bagmati Zonal Commissioner's Office. The total financial assistance provided by His Majesty's Government to the committee was received through the Ministry of Panchayat, which also made available one acting internal auditor and one peon on a lien basis. The committee has so far received a budget of Rs. 868,394/-, for which it expresses its gratitude to His Majesty's Government.

Appendix III

The committee published its proposed programme-list for realising the objectives of the theme "Equality, Development and Peace" of the International Women's Year within 1975. The committee formulated the programme after due consideration and on the basis of the time factor, financial assistance, resources and co-operation expected from various sources. Coming as it did to fulfill its responsibilities with the co-operation and goodwill of all, the committee worked out programmes mainly divided in two groups: programmes to be carried on the committee's own efforts on the one hand and those to be implemented with the help of various offices on the other. Of the two programmes grouped in two, if some clearly indicated permanent help for the upliftment of women, others included programmes related to seminars and publicity designed to make direct or indirect, but significant, impact on the general people's attitudes that could contribute to the fulfillment of the objectives enlisted for the Women's Year. Both the programmes were of equal importance. The programmes were further divided in eight groups under the headings of Agriculture, Education, International Affairs and Seminars, Health, Social Service, Law, Publicity and Miscellaneous, brief reports of which are mentioned herewith.

With a view to ensuring greater co-operation and services from the womenfolk to the country's agriculture sector, trainings were imparted through J.T.A's. to a total of 119 women, of whom 26 were from the Central Development Region, Kathmandu, 26 from the Western Development Region, Pokhara , 28 from the Eastern Development Region, Dhankuta, and 39 from the Far Western Development Region, Surkhet, under the agriculture programme. Similarly, 214 packets of seeds and 7500 saplings worth Rs. 12,692 (twelve thousand six hundred and ninety two) were distributed in all the four development regions for cotton cultivation, orchard

Appendix III

development and vegetable growing. In keeping with the popular saying "Green forests: Nepal's wealth", afforestation programmes were initiated in all the four development regions with the co-operation of womenfolk for the encouragement of womenfolk. These programmes were conducted with co-operation extended by the Agriculture and Forest ministries.

It may also be mentioned that eleven programmes were drawn up under the heading "Education". Under it, two districts from each zone, unlike in the past when only one district was included from each zone, were associated in the literacy campaign schemed to make more women literates. The districts were Jumla, Surkhet, Ilam, Dhankuta, Bhojpur, Saptari, Parsa, Bhaktapur, Kaski, Dolpa, Gorkha, Salyan, Doti, Kanchanpur, Jhapa, Morang, Ramechhap, Palpa, Chitwan, Kathmandu, Tanahu, Myagdi, Rupandehi, Kalikot, Dailekh, Dang, Kailali, Darchula, making a total of 28 districts. A total of 540 works of craft like mats made of maize leaves, bamboo and thread fans were displayed at competitive handicraft exhibitions held on a regional basis in Pokhara, Dhankuta and Surkhet in order to draw out the artistic talents of womenfolk and present it to the general public. In line with the objective of encouraging people towards this sort of effort and industry, "Shree Panch Aishwarya Shilpa Shield" International Women's Year 1975 were awarded to three districts coming first in the handicraft competitions, and three districts from each of the three development regions were given a total of nine cash awards. One of the visible achievements of the International Women's Year is the establishment of women's multipurpose work centres in Pokhara, Dhankuta and Surkhet which aim at national development and additionally enhancing women's income. Two such centres in Pokhara and Surkhet have already started to function. Responsibilities for running these centres have been entrusted to the concerned

Appendix III

district unit of the Women's Oraganisation. As the St. Mary's High School had expressed its willingness to make available ten scholarships for day scholars of Kathmandu Valley and five for boarders coming from the four development regions, accordingly, fifteen poor, but talented and deserving girl students as required by the provision have been selected and recommendations to this effect sent to the said school. It is hoped that, if properly utilised, the school's willingness to provide free scholarships which will be given to the selected girls till the final year of the school will help the girl students to attain success and, hence, make considerable contribution to women's education. Likewise, with the financial assistance of the Ministry of Education five additional scholarships for girl students of remote areas have also been provided in Mahendra Bhawan High School.

Rs. 200,000/- (two hundred thousand rupees) has been handed over to the Tribhuvan University to set up revolving funds for making provision for four Aishwarya Women's Scholarships for medicine, four for science and two for humanities, making a total of ten scholarships and each of them involving Rs. 2,752 (two thousand, seven hundred and fifty-two rupees), are to be provided from the fund. Under the remaining education programmes, thirteen districts of remote areas that enrolled the highest number of girl students were awarded Rs. 500/- each; medals and certificates were given to schools and concerned teams standing first, second and third in quiz contests held in the four development regions; those coming out first, second and third in essay contests organised in Dhankuta, Surkhet and Kathmandu received medals and certificates; while nine persons standing first, second and third in debate contests held in Pokhara, Surkhet and Kathmandu were awarded with medals and certificates. A book designed for imparting practical knowledge to adult women literates was

Appendix III

also published with the help of the Ministry of Education. An evaluation committee was also constituted with the help of the Ministry of Education to formulate a school level syllabus that would highlight the importance of women's society. Further, I would also like to mention that the donation of Rs. 10,005 made available by Hon'ble Mrs. Angur Baba Joshi in connection with the Women's Year has been handed over to the Tribhuvan University. The donation will be appropriated for making a provision for one scholarship to one woman every year. To be instituted as "Laxmi Scholarship", it will be awarded to financially poor women hailing from remote areas so that they may be able to continue their study with Nepali as their major subject, be it at the diploma level (graduate) or degree (post-graduate) level. Similarly, Rs. 10,598 received from the Women Artists Committee under its cultural programme has been handed over to the Tribhuvan University in aid of poor but talented girl students of music and dance.

As regards our programmes under the third group — Seminars — a doll exhibition was held. Organised with the objective of acquainting people with fascinating ways of life and cultures of others living in various nooks and corners of the world, the exhibition was participated by altogether twenty-three countries — Bangladesh, Belgium, Burma, Czechoslovakia, People's Republic of China, France, Democratic Republic of Germany, Federal Republic of Germany, Greece, Hungary, India, Israel, Japan, Republic of Korea, Nepal, Pakistan, Poland, Rumania, Sri Lanka, Switzerland, Thailand, the U.S.A. and the U.S.S.R. About 10,000 persons are estimated to have viewed the exhibition. Under the same heading, seminars on "Women's Participation in National Development", the "Promotion of Equality between Men and Women" and the "Significance of Literacy in the Development of Women" were held in Pokhara, Dhankuta and

Appendix III

Surkhet respectively in consonance with the programme of holding seminars on the main objectives of the International Women's Year, 1975. Opinions and suggestions of the participants were also compiled, as a result of which it is hoped that it will contribute to the task of launching necessary measures in this respect in future. In accordance with the decision to send vigilance teams to acquaint rural women with various subjects, touring teams were dispatched to sixteen districts — Dhankuta, Rajbiraj, Biratnagar, Ilam in the Eastern Development Region, Surkhet, Nepalgunj, Dhangadi, Mahendranagar, Jumla, Dang in the Far Western Development Region; Baglung, Kaski, Rupandehi in the Western Development Region; and Sindhupalchok, Parsa, Mahotari in Central Development Region. In addition, a literacy conference was organised in Kathmandu with a view to contributing to the accomplishment of the International Women's Year's objectives in the field of literature as well. Altogether 84 literati participated in the conference. There were sufficient indications that a good response would be received from the field of literature also in women's development. Together with these, fourteen representatives of the International Women's Year Committee participated in international conferences held in countries like Mexico, the United States, Israel, Czechoslovakia, the U.S.S.R., German Democratic Republic at the invitations received from the United Nations and other friendly countries.

The fourth group of programmes is Health. Firstly, mobile health teams comprising gynecologists were sent to eleven districts — Nepalgunj, Mahendranagar, Siraha, Baglung, Gulmi, Taplejung, Jumla, Salyan, Namchebazar, Okhaldhunga and Dhading. Secondly, 119 persons were given mid-wife trainings; and thirdly, laparoscopy operations were performed on 637 women, while vasectomies were performed on 3,424

Appendix III

men, and family planning devices distributed to 657,000 persons. I would like to point out that full co-operation was received from the Ministry of Health as well as Family Planning and Maternity Child Health Centre in carrying out these programmes. I would also like to mention that a sum of Rs. 276,293/- collected under the leadership of the Minister of State for Health, Mrs. Sushila Thapa, who presented it to Her Majesty the Queen, has contributed considerably to the women's health programmes. A "Shree Panch Aishwarya Medical Fund" will be instituted with the amount collected. I would also like to express gratitude to the Minister of State for Health for taking keen and special interest in providing necessary help to carry out the programmes. In this respect, I would also like to inform that Kathmandu district Women's Organisation had provided Rs. 7,505/- (seven thousand five hundred and five rupees) to open a fund in aid of poor, new mothers and it has been handed over to the executive committee of "Shree Panch Indra Rajya Laxmi Devi Prashuti Griha".

As fixed in the programme already published, programmes under the heading "Social Service" were also carried out as per schedule. In this regard, two interesting cultural programmes, "Karmachhetra" and "Ek Seema Yahin Tunginchha," were staged. Films on International Women's Year and various aspects of women were also screened in Kathmandu, Pokhara and Dhankuta. Further, necessary arrangements for opening a day-care centre at Indrayani village panchayat are being made.

As protection of laws for women's development and upliftment are of considerable importance and as laws play a role of special significance in removing obstacles and hindrances that impede women's progress, the bulk of the people are interested in and expect protection of laws. His Majesty the King has promulgated Civil Code (6th

Appendix III

Amendment) Ordinance with a view to ensuring to all the Nepalese women their essential rights and benefits. A gracious gift from His Majesty the King, the Ordinance is concerned with the changes in the law of procedure, and other legal provisions concerning husband and wife relations, women's property rights, adoption, partition of property, marriage, paramour, inheritance and the like. Besides this, a seminar on law was held, and a booklet entitled "Legal Status of Women" written in simple language on the rights of the Nepalese women was published.

Another group of programmes was Publicity, under which was included a radio programme every Monday. A total of 175 articles were broadcast over the radio. The first painting exhibition brought to the limelight many hidden women artists, inspiring and encouraging others. Altogether 64 artists participated in the painting exhibition. Similarly 60 girl athletes joined in the women's sports events organised with the co-operation of the National Sports Council. Pamphlets and posters relating to Women's Year were published and distributed. Postal stamps of one rupee denomination featuring the portrait of the patron of the International Women's Year Committee Nepal, Her Majesty the Queen, together with the symbol of the Women's Year and three coins of the denominations of Rs. 20, Re. 1 and 10 paisa featuring Their Majesties the King and Queen were also brought out in commemoration of all the events of the International Women's Year observed in a grand manner in the nation. A documentary film reflecting various aspects of the Nepalese women's society is also being produced. The calendar brought out by the International Women's Year Committee Nepal, provides us not only the days and dates of 1975 but also reminds us of the 1975 Women's Year.

Appendix III

Likewise, I would also like to remind that seven programmes were included under the Miscellaneous programmes.

I would also like to present you with the facts that in the bid to raise maternity leave from 45 days to 84 days, His Majesty's Government has made a provision for 60 days of maternity leave, a report on the Nepalese women's status and problems encountering them and some solutions has been prepared by the "Panch Boojh Kendra"; a mothers' club was established with the help of the Nepal Red Cross Society; foundation stones of women's training centres in Dhankuta and Surkhet were also laid; a directory of working women has been published; and under the programme to open a girls' hostel in Kathmandu, the foundation stone has already been laid down at Padma Kanya Campus, while construction work of a girls' hostel in Pokhara is nearing completion. I would like to take the opportunity of informing the distinguished persons present here that under this group of programmes necessary arrangements have been made for opening a centre for helpless women destitutes, though the foundation stone of the centre has yet to be laid down, while works for opening the women's training centre in Pokhara remain to be completed.

Besides these, though not included earlier in the programmes, Ratna Recording Corporation has already made arrangements for recording some of the lofty ideals and guidelines extracted from the "Geeta" written in Nepali for men and women having faith in religion to commemorate the Women's Year. And Sharada Thapa's collection of lyrics exhorting women and Manju Tiwari "Kaanchuli's" *Kiranka Chhalharu* were published in connection with the aim of encouraging women writers in need of financial help.

That we were able to implement almost all the programmes within the allotted period of one year was precisely because of

Appendix III

the patronage, leadership, directives, inspiration, guidelines and infinite affection granted by Her Majesty the Queen to the committee. Her Majesty not only provided leadership and directives to the committee in carrying out its programmes but participated in its programmes held in different nooks and corners of the country. It was due to Her Majesty's immense love and affection towards the women community that Her Majesty visited Bhrikuti Mandap in connection with the opening of the committee's office and graciously granted four inaugural speeches in the Women's Year 1975, including those on January 1, 1975, October 3, 1975, October 31, 1975, and November 28, 1975 which by themselves, indeed, constitute a historical event. That these invaluable speeches strewn with pertinent and thought-provoking words of wisdom will always act as a guiding force to all of us is indisputable. Her Majesty the Queen graced 16 functions in Kathmandu, 5 in Pokhara, 6 in Dhankuta and 6 in Surkhet besides laying foundation stones and declaring open 8 centres, hostels for the welfare and benefit of women community, and the like. Her Majesty also presided over the committee's meetings five times during the year. These will be written in golden letters and Her Majesty the Queen will be known as women's leader first and foremost.

I hope that the aforementioned report will suffice to make it clear as to what were the programmes and activities of the committee during the International Women's Year, 1975 and which of them were implemented. The objectives of the Women's Year and our needs cannot be met in one year. Therefore, it is beyond the shadow of any doubt that stress should be on channelising activities initiated by the committee in the process of development and these types of campaigns should be conducted on a regular basis. I feel that Book Year, Population Year, Women's Year or Agriculture Year were observed not merely with a fanatical spirit of completing the

Appendix III

related activities within the fixed period of one year but largely due to the express need felt for inculcating a spirit that would enable the majority of the people to set telling examples by initiating new activities in order to bring about rapid development in every field. In this way, I think, the bulk of people can grasp the meaningful significance of the activities of the International Women's Year Committee Nepal in promoting the welfare of the country and the society, and the interests and harmony of women as well as in publicising the need for associating women in all spheres of national development and developing a positive attitude towards women so that the latter can be associated side by side with men in the task of effectively carrying out activities in all spheres of development endeavours, including fields like agriculture, industry and commerce on the one hand and subjects like duties, rights and benefits on the other. It may also be mentioned that the committee has initiated a number of significant activities within the period with the co-operation of all, which is well evident if compared with others.

These achievements belong to us all. I would like to express my profound happiness at the fact that many associations, individuals and various ministries of His Majesty's Government have been associated with the activities of the committee. My thanks to all of them. To conclude, we pray for the continued love, affection, directives and leadership of our mentor and the patron of the committee Her Majesty the Queen.

Chronological list of the Programmes graced by the patron of the committee, Her Majesty the Queen:

1. Inauguration of the International Women's Year Committee Nepal 1975, City Hall, January 1, 1975.

Appendix III

2. Initiation of afforestation programme, Chovar, January 1, 1975.
3. Laying of foundation stone of the central office building of Nepal Women's Organisation, Pulchowk, January 1, 1975.
4. Inauguration of first Women's Painting Exhibition, NAFA Hall, February 19, 1975.
5. Inauguration of International Doll Exhibition, Rotary Club, August 19, 1975.
6. Women's First Seminar on Law, City Hall, August 24, 1975.
7. Gracing of the talks and cultural programmes organised on the occasion of "Teej" festival, Ved Vidyashram, September 8, 1975.
8. Inauguration of the first literary conference on women, City Hall, September 19, 1975.
9. Inauguration of mid-wife training programme, Narayan Bhawan, October 3, 1975.
10. Inaugural speech of the seminar on "Women's Participation in National Development", Pokhara, October 3, 1975.
11. Initiation of afforestation programme, Pokhara, October 3, 1975.
12. Inauguration of the women's multipurpose work centre, Pokhara, October 3, 1975.
13. Inspection of women's handicraft exhibition, Pokhara, October 3, 1975.
14. Prize distribution, Pokhara, October 3, 1975.
15. Inauguration of mothers' club, Kalimati, October 20, 1975.
16. Witnessing of women's sports competitions, Dasharath Stadium, October 24, 1975.
17. Inaugural speech of the seminar of the "Promotion of Equality between Men and Women", Dhankuta, October 31, 1975.

Appendix III

18. Initiation of afforestation programme, Chuli Ban, Dhankuta, October 31, 1975.
19. Laying of foundation stone of women's multipurpose work centre, Dhankuta, October 31, 1975.
20. Laying of foundation stone of women's training centre, Dhankuta, October 31, 1975.
21. Inspection of women's handicraft exhibition, Dhankuta, October 31, 1975.
22. Prize distribution, Dhankuta, October 31, 1975.
23. Laying of foundation stone of girl's hostel, Dhankuta, November 7, 1975.
24. Witnessing of cultural programme, Padma Kanya Campus, Royal Nepal Academy, November 7, 1975.
25. Affixation of concellation mark on stamps issued on the occasion of the International Women's Year, Royal Palace, November 8, 1975.
26. Acceptance of coins minted to mark the International Women's Year, Royal Palace, November 8, 1975.
27. Inaugural speech of the seminar on the "Significance of Literacy in the Development of Women", Surkhet, November 28, 1975.
28. Initiation of afforestation programme, Kakre Bihar, Surkhet, November 28, 1975.
29. Inauguration of women's multipurpose work centre, Surkhet, November 28, 1975.
30. Laying of foundation stone of women's training centre, Surkhet, Nomvember 28, 1975.
31. Inspection of women's handicraft exhibition, Surkhet, November 28, 1975.
32. Prize distribution, Surkhet, November 28, 1975.
33. Prize distribution, Narayan Bhawan, Jawalkhel, December 22, 1975.

Appendix III

34. Gracing of felicitation function, City Hall, December 24, 1975.

Publications of the International Women's Year Committee Nepal 1975

1) *Programme-list of the International Women's Year Committee Nepal 1975* (Nepali/English)
2) International Women's Year 1975 — Calendar
3) *Women's Legal Status* (Nepali)
4) *Short Biography of Members of Women Artists Committee* (Nepali)
5) *Shorts Biography of the Artists* (English)
6) *Directory of Working Women* (Nepali)
7) Sharada Thapa's *Collection of Lyrics* exhorting women (Nepali)
8) Manju Tiwari "Kanchuli's" *Kiranka Chhalharu* (Nepali)
9) *Report on the seminar on the "Significance of Literacy in the Development of Women"* (Nepali)
10) *Report on the seminar on "Women's Participation in National Development"* (Nepali)
11) *Report on the seminar on the "Promotion of Equality Between Men and Women"* (Nepali)
12) *Work-oriented Adult "Home Science" Teachers' Manual* (Nepali)
13) *Women in Nepal* (English)

Appendix IV

Elimination of All Forms of Racial Discrimination

Madam Chairman,

May I begin by congratulating you on your election as the Chairman of this important committee. Your elevation is really a tribute to your wide-ranging knowledge of world affairs as well as to the important role played by you in this committee. It is indeed an inspiration to all the distinguished delegates gathered here.

Madam Chairman, I would also like to express sincere appreciation of my delegation to Madam Sipila for her thought-provoking introductory statement which, I am sure, will provide us with a framework within which this committee can take up items entrusted to it.

Madam Chairman, it is a great joy for my delegation to be able at last to welcome the representatives of the Socialist Republic of Vietnam. My country has consistently supported the admission of Vietnam and my delegation hopes that the Socialist Republic of Vietnam will contribute positively to the work of this committee. We also feel happy to welcome the Republic of Djibouti, whose independence marks another step in the process of decolonization.

Madam Chairman, it has been four years now since the General Assembly declared the Decade for Action to Combat Racism and Racial Discrimination. This very praiseworthy declaration is itself a historic chapter in the annals of the struggle begun by the UN in 1946 against all forms of racial discrimination. The United Nations should be congratulated for this.

Appendix IV

My delegation has noted with satisfaction that this committee always gives top priority to the item under discussion and to focusing the debate on racial discrimination and the inhuman policy of apartheid enforced by the racist regime in South Africa. Yet racial discrimination has not stopped at the borders of Zimbabwe, Namibia or South Africa. My delegation's stand on the problem is well known. My delegation can again assure this committee that our government will do all that is necessary to make these inhuman racist regimes renounce their policies of apartheid and to mobilize world public opinion in support of the cause of the oppressed people of South Africa in their freedom struggle to gain their just and legitimate right to live in freedom, dignity and a majority-ruled, non-racial society. It is known to all that my country is presently a member of the Special Committee against Apartheid. My delegation finds it very difficult to understand how some countries continue to support the racist regimes against the opinion of the international community.

Madam Chairman, the report of the secretary-general (A/32/187) on the Status of the International Convention on the Suppression and Punishment of the Crime of Apartheid shows that up to September 1, 1977, the total number of countries to ratify and accede to the convention had reached 35. My delegation is happy to inform the committee that His Majesty's Government of Nepal acceded to this convention on July 12 of this year. As a party to the convention we would like to assure the committee that Nepal will comply fully with the obligations under the International Convention. At the same time my delegation would urge earnestly other countries to become a party to this convention and help to eliminate apartheid, the abominable system of racial discrimination.

As a state party to the International Convention on the Elimination of all Forms of Racial Discrimination, Nepal has

Appendix IV

been submitting its periodic reports to the Committee on the Elimination of Racial Discrimination. The third periodic report submitted by Nepal to the committee on July 6, 1977, enumerates the non-discriminatory provisions laid down in our constitution and other legislative measures adopted on the basis of that. My delegation proudly informs this committee that my country has never followed any policy of discrimination. Our constitution and legal code prohibit discrimination based on caste, creed, sex or race. We live in great harmony under the able leadership of our beloved King Birendra, who, in his message to the World Conference for Action against Apartheid, held in Lagos, Nigeria, has forcefully observed that "apartheid is not only an anachronism in the modern world but a grave crime against humanity". My delegation believes that there cannot be peace in South Africa unless the policies and practices of apartheid are totally terminated.

Let us support the views expressed by Secretary-General Mr. Kurt Waldheim, that the human issues at stake in the South African situation are too great and too grave for the world to remain indifferent to them. We look forward to the forthcoming World Conference to Combat Racism and Racial Discrimination and hope that this conference will come up with concrete proposals and a programme of action to eliminate all forms of racism and racial discrimination.

Madam Chairman, racism, racial discrimination and apartheid in Southern Africa and elsewhere cannot be eliminated unless all the members of the United Nations make sincere efforts to implement the programme of action for the decade to combat racism and racial discrimination. It is encouraging to note the analysis on the replies, contained in document A/32/196, submitted by some countries on various measures they have taken to combat racism and racial discrimination. But the strongest measures on the part of the

Appendix IV

international community, such as the sanctions including an arms embargo against the racist regimes of Southern Africa, can help to achieve the objectives of the decade.

My delegation thinks that the stage of discussion and debate is over. The time has come to face three questions honestly and with a sense of urgency: Firstly, why, in spite of all efforts and repeated appeals made by the United Nations and its agencies, has it not been possible to solve the problem of racial discrimination? What measures can we take that are appropriate to a solution of these problems? Secondly, how can we deal with those countries who continue to support the racist regimes in opposition to the repeated requests and demands of the General Assembly and the Security Council to break off diplomatic relations, to boycott South African goods, to refrain from all exports to South Africa, to impose a strict arms embargo, etc? Thirdly, what pressures can we bring to bear on those countries who continue to encourage these racist regimes?

Madam Chairman, when we study the problems raised by discrimination of all kinds, we find that discrimination finds its root in sentiment, prejudice, ignorance, poverty, superstition and social evils. It seems, therefore, that the demands and appeals made by the United Nations alone are inadequate to improve the situation caused by racial discrimination. In the light of this, it would seem that we are obliged to educate and enlighten the masses in order to help them realise that the practice and policies of apartheid are a crime against humanity. In view of this, my delegation would like to request that this committee consider the ways and means by which UNESCO can help, through its educational activities, to eradicate all forms of racial discrimination rooted in the minds of the uneducated masses.

Appendix V

United Nations Decade for Women: Equality, Development and Peace

Madam Chairman,

At the very outset, my delegation would like to express our deep appreciation and thanks to the United Nations Organization and to the concerned officials for the various resolutions, recommendations and decisions that have been made regarding the recognition of women's rights.

Madam Chairman, we would also like to thank those distinguished personalities from different countries throughout the world for their efforts in successfully implementing these resolutions that were adopted to raise the status of women in conformity with the main UNO objective of promoting the welfare of mankind. This has been a significant step towards peace and happiness. My delegation would like to assure you that we fully welcome most of these resolutions and decisions and that we look forward to their successful implementation.

Madam Chairman, in response to the call made by the UNO, Nepal, like many other countries, observed International Women's Year with great enthusiasm. Her Majesty the Queen of Nepal herself provided leadership to ensure the attainment of the Year's lofty objectives of bringing about equality of women and fostering development and peace. As a result, important measures designed for the improvement of the status of women were initiated. Considerable advances have been made in awakening women to a realization of their rights. One of the outstanding achievements of International Women's Year

Appendix V

has been the promulgation of legislation designed to promote and secure the status of women in Nepal. Under Nepalese law, no legal discrimination can be made today between men and women. Legally, we are all equal.

Madam Chairman, it is obvious that years of tradition and outmoded customs that have been the root cause of the deprivation of women's rights cannot be changed overnight. The efforts and labour of a particular year or a limited period of time, no matter how concentrated and effective, are not going to change centuries of custom. While we were celebrating International Women's Year, 1975, in Nepal, we realized that we should stress the institutionalization of the activities initiated by the International Women's Year Committee by incorporating these into the very process of development. We also decided that campaigns such as those introduced during International Women's Year should be conducted on a regular basis in Nepal. We observed International Women's Year not merely with a single-minded devotion to completing the programme of activities within the fixed period of one year but we also felt that we should take advantage of this opportunity to inculcate a spirit that would prompt a majority of the people to help set significant precedents in using the talents and energies of women in all phases of Nepal's development efforts. In this way, we thought that the people of Nepal could actually see the importance of International Women's Year in its effects; that we would not merely be highlighting the need to recognise women's rights and awaken women to their opportunities and responsibilities, but we would also be incorporating these new attitudes into the development effort. Thus we hoped that men would realize that women had a real role to play and that women themselves would actually begin to fulfil that role. The results of this effort have been very gratifying. We have not arrived at our final

Appendix V

goal, but we are very definitely on the way towards that goal. Naturally, Nepal is very happy to welcome the United Nations' decision to make 1976-85 a decade for women.

Madam Chairman, in view of this fact, a women's services co-ordination sub-committee, which aims at paving the way for the continuous progress of women, was formed on February 13, 1977, as a part of the Social Services Coordination Committee, which functions under the chairmanship of Her Majesty Queen Aishwarya. It is a matter of pride to us, and it is of great significance in its own right, that this has been made possible by the able and active leadership of His Majesty King Birendra. Her Majesty the Queen has taken particular interest in this work, and her affectionate interest has been a major source of encouragement and inspiration for us.

Madam Chairman, similarly, our Constitution provides for a Women's Organization, whose duty it is to integrate and utilize the united strength of the women of the community for the development of our nation and to assist the local Panchayats (local political units) to mobilize the general public. The Women's Organization has been included in the central advisory committee of class organizations for the "Back-to-the-Village" National Campaign Central Committee, which has been instituted to provide leadership in the political sphere. The four nominated representatives of the Women's Organization are required to offer advice, suggestions, and cooperation to the Back-to-the Village National Campaign Central Committee in respect of women's organization. The Advisory Committee is also expected to maintain contact with similar organizations in foreign countries as well as with international organizations and associations. The National Planning Commission has also started to give due attention to the improvement of women's status in Nepal.

Appendix V

Madam Chairman, all of these offices have been conducting various activities on a regular basis in order to contribute to women's progress and the greater participation of women in development activities in accordance with the World Plan of Action. They are also preparing a long-range programme to ensure the continuance in a systematic and effective manner of the activities that they have initiated. His Majesty's Government, with the help of US/AID (Nepal) is currently conducting an in-depth research study on the status of women in the social-economic development of Nepal. The purpose of this project is to collect and generate information on the status and roles of a representative range of Nepalese women in order to support planning to facilitate the increased integration of women into the national development progress. A survey will be conducted of the legal, social and economic position of women in traditional and modernizing Nepalese society. More specifically, this project aims at a preliminary assessment of the contribution of women to the household and national economy, not only in their crucial roles as mothers and home-makers, but also as an important component of Nepal's active labour force, a role often underestimated in macro-economic thinking. The general objectives of this survey may be stated as follows:

a. To prepare a national statistical profile of women in Nepal.
b. To prepare a summary of women's legal rights as set forth in the national civil code.
c. To prepare an inventory of Nepalese institutions concerned with women.
d. To compile a list of information resources on women in Nepal.
e. To gather information on the extent to which women's participation in agriculture, industry, trade and science and

Appendix V

technology is reflected in Nepal's national plans and programmes.

f. To develop methodologies and implement pilot socio-economic case studies of women in important sub-groups in both traditional rural and urban communities.

g. To evaluate the extent to which AID (Nepal)'s on-going and proposed programmes reflect women's participation in the development process and make recommendations about how these programmes could further encourage the involvement of Nepalese women.

This survey plans to complete its summary report within two years.

A seminar was also held in Nepal this year to discuss an integrated programme for women, in connection with the Women's Decade. In order to formulate a national plan of action, the seminar presented suggestions to Her Majesty the Queen, who is the Chairman of the Social Services Coordination Committee.

Madam Chairman, a national plan of action will definitely be formulated in connection with the Women's Decade that will be effective, and therefore significant. We anticipate full cooperation from the UNO and its various agencies and services in this regard. My delegation is happy to inform this Committee that we have already submitted some projects on women's development to the UN for necessary financial assistance. In the same context, it may be noted that the Regional (Asia-Pacific) Seminar on the Participation of Women in Political, Economic, and Social Development, with special emphasis on the machinery to accelerate the integration of women in development, was held from February 15 to 22, 1977, in Kathmandu, Nepal. We hope that all concerned nationals will give due attention to the successful implementation of the recommendations th' seminar has

Appendix V

adopted. We would also like to take this opportunity to express our deep gratitude to Madam Helvi Sipila for her participation in the seminar. Madam Sipila, who has worked for so long and so arduously for the causes of women, contributed a great deal to the success of the seminar.

Madam Chairman, legal provisions and other opportunities alone are inadequate to achieve the objectives of the International Women's Year and the UN Decade for Women: equality, development, and peace. Legal provisions and programmes of action are important, but, even among men competing with men, the decisive criterion is often knowledge, experience, and other qualifications. If women are to have equal opportunity, they will have to be given adequate education so that they can acquire both the necessary knowledge and experience to prepare them to contribute equally for development and peace. In view of this, my delegation feels that we must face and answer four questions if we are to make the decade a success: Firstly, what is required of women to permit them to compete on a basis of equality with men? Secondly, what are the essential requisites for associating women at par with men in bringing about development and peace? Thirdly, how can these essential requisites be fulfilled and what kind of plan and programme do we need to achieve the goals of the UN Decade for Women: equality, development, and peace? And fourthly, how can we implement these plans and programmes in such a way that menfolk willingly and with full hearts associate themselves effectively in the promotion of women's status, without disturbance to the peace and harmony of family life and the social fabric?

Madam Chairman, in order to concentrate more on these facts, Her Majesty Queen Aishwarya, who is the leader of Nepalese women, noted in a message given on the occasion of

Appendix V

International Women's Year, 1975. "It seems to me that education is the most vital fact for the realisation of the goals of the International Women's Year, which seeks equality, development, and peace. Without the consciousness which education helps to develop, it will not be possible to move towards equality. Likewise, in the absence of knowledge and skill, one cannot effectively contribute to development." In line with the stress laid by Her Majesty the Queen, due priority has been given to the promotion of the cause of women and to the increase of the number of educated women. Nepal is encouraging the community of women to improve their education by providing scholarships, opening girls' hostels, and the like. Since the majority of women cannot afford to abandon their work, which is an important source of domestic income, it is very difficult to expect them to attend classes. To meet the challenges posed by this situation, women's multi-purpose work centres, women's training centres, and mothers' clubs have been established for making available a source of income and development in needed skills. These will be gradually expanded. We also have some noteworthy educational projects sponsored jointly by UNICEF/UNESCO for training young girls from remote villages to become primary school teachers. UNICEF has helped in the funding of the project by building hostels for students, giving supplies to the training campuses and the hostels, providing scholarships to the students, and helping in recruitment of candidates with a publicity campaign including publicity booklets, posters, and radio programmes. As a result of this, the recruitment has now increased. So far over 300 women teachers have been trained under this programme. UNICEF is giving considerable assistance to the strengthening of a community development-oriented training launched by His Majesty's Government of Nepal for rural women. Emphasis in this programme is placed on nutrition and

Appendix V

child care. Increasingly, the training of workers is being conducted in rural areas.

Madam Chairman, distinguished delegates of this Committee are fully aware that many women living in the villages or districts of the developing countries want to become more active and ideal members of society in accordance with the stress laid by the Women's Decade. But if they wish to join schools or attend literacy classes, they will have to face the consequence of reduced family income. Persistent problems such as the inadequate supply of drinking water conveniently located near the village, the absence of electricity, the lack of marketing facilities and many other problems prevent them from attaining the additional knowledge and skills they need, the acquisition of which requires considerable time. I, therefore, feel that the development projects sponsored by UNDP, UNICEF and other UN special agencies like UNESCO, WHO, ILO, and FAO should be coordinated and operated in specific areas that will mitigate some of the most persisting problems of daily life, thereby contributing considerably to the task of meeting the objectives of Women's Decade. Furthermore, I would also like to draw your attention towards the fact that more concrete and effective results can be achieved if national development programmes are formulated and implemented in this spirit. In view of the fact that it is only through comprehensive research work and intensive studies that easy and suitable methods can be drawn up for bringing about women's development or development in any other field, we welcome the establishment of the Asia & Pacific Centre for Women and Development on February 27, 1977. We also express our appreciation of the keen and active interest shown by Iran to establish the centre, whose effective service is expected to contribute a lot to women's development.

Appendix V

In conclusion, Madam Chairman, we are confident that with the cooperation, goodwill and mutual understanding of all, women will be able to contribute more towards a brighter world future.
Thank you, Madam Chairman.

Appendix VI

Question of the Elderly and Aged

Madam Chairman,
　At the outset my delegation would like to thank the acting assistant director, Mr. Evner Ergun, for his introductory statement on the question under consideration. It is gratifying to note that more and more attention is now being paid to the question of the elderly and the aged. We have noted with appreciation Malta's initiative in including this item for the first time in the agenda of the twenty-fourth session of the General Assembly in 1969. We hope that the efforts made by the United Nations to study the changing socio-economic and cultural role and status of the aged in countries of different levels of development will achieve positive results.
　Madam Chairman, the report of the Secretary-General (A/32/130) on the Question of the Elderly and the Aged is indeed informative and encouraging. My delegation is, however, of the opinion that the problem of the elderly and the aged concerns more the developed countries than the developing ones. The urban societies of the developed world have a large number and a high proportion of aging adults; yet, often the majority of these adults are forced to be non-productive and are then penalised for their non-productiveness with reduced income and relatively low status. This decrease in status has a severe negative effect on the psychological, social, and economic well-being of the aging individuals. Whereas in developing countries like Nepal, we believe in the active participation of the aged in the life of the family and the community. Their active participation in the family or in the

Appendix VI

society can have a positive effect on their psychological and social well-being. In our country it is not yet common to live independently as it is in the more developed societies. The family is still the major social support system for all the elderly and the aged. The aged and the elderly have a strong relationship with their children that involves mutual affection and assistance, and depend on them for support. The aged always command great respect and affection in our society. We encourage children to look for alternatives to institutional care such as home-help services in order to enhance the independence and dignity of the aged. Homes for the aged and shelter-care services are discouraged in our country as we want to maintain the family tie. So we feel if the developed countries could give some thought to family attachment, the older section of the population may have feelings of security in society.

Madam Chairman, the distinguished delegates in this committee are aware of the fact that during the early stages of modernization, changes do take place that create some discrepancies between the aged and the non-aged; and with increased industrialization, urbanization, and other related social and economic changes, the developing countries, like ours, increasingly face these problems. My delegation welcomes the United Nations' plan to consider an international seminar to discuss this phenomenon of the aging population and its social and economic implications. My delegation hopes that the seminar will adopt some concrete decisions which will help the lot of the aged without disturbing the cultural and traditional values of the societies of the developing countries.

In conclusion, Madam Chairman, my delegation strongly urges the United Nations to give due consideration to the question of the aged within the framework of its social development programme and in cooperation with the agencies concerned. Consideration should also be given to the more

Appendix VI

effective method of information exchange system on the aged in order to give required information to policy makers, planners, and decision makers concerned with the conditions of the aged so that they can make improvements in planning and in developing new and better programmes to meet these human and environmental needs. My delegation would also like to request the United Nations to provide governments of the developing countries with the information and results of the experience, which would enable them to take timely action to meet difficulties which are likely to arise especially as a result of rural-urban migration among young people.

Appendix VII

Policies and Programmes Relating to Youth

Madam Chairman,

The Committee is considering one of the important items of its agenda: policies and programmes relating to youth. May I, on behalf of my delegation, pay tribute to Acting Assistant Director Mr. Evner Ergun for his statement in introducing the item in the Committee. My delegation would like to express our appreciation of the United Nations' constant interest in the activities of youth, because it is clear that the energies of youth can be used as a vital instrument for mobilizing the development process.

In a rapidly changing world, the younger generation should be given an opportunity to play an important role and participate actively in the development of their countries and in the creation of a better world. It is common knowledge that Nepal joined the sponsors of Draft Resolution A/C.3.31.L.35. Just as my country has always supported the decision of the United Nations regarding youth activities, so also do we give equal importance to youth's participation in nation-building. In Nepal there are both governmental and non-governmental organizations for the mobilization of youth. Under the partyless political system of Nepal, politics are directed towards development. Young people, too, are encouraged to participate in development politics. A number of young people, members of youth organizations, are participating actively in political units in our country in order to mobilize the people's participation in national advancement. Nepal is of the opinion that youth should be involved in social welfare activities too.

Appendix VII

Recently His Majesty King Birendra has constituted a Social Services Coordination Committee under the chairmanship of Her Majesty Queen Aishwarya to look after all social welfare programmes of the country. A sub-committee of this committee, the Youth Activities Coordination Sub-Committee, has been entrusted with the duty of looking after the welfare of the youth of the country. This committee plans to bring out its detailed programme of youth activities very soon.

In addition to these activities, we have the National Development Service under university education to mobilize the energies of young people for the development of the country and to acquaint youth with the real problems and needs of Nepal. This programme was introduced in 1974 as part of the New Education System. It aims primarily at enabling young men and women to dedicate a certain period of their student life to the cause of national development. These students teach in schools to meet the very great shortage of teachers in rural areas; they undertake development projects in such fields as soil conservation and reforestation, family welfare work (including health education and the promotion of family planning), literacy programmes, agriculture extension work, the improvement of village water supplies, and simple construction work (e.g. latrine building, simple local roads, bridges, water supply systems, and school buildings). At the present time there are 543 students serving under the National Development Service Programme. This programme will certainly contribute greatly towards a solution of the manpower needs required for the development task in rural areas. It will also have a tremendous impact on the education of thousands of university graduates, our future leaders in many fields.

It is worth mentioning that Nepal has initiated a number of programmes which aim at ensuring the participation of youth in different fields in order to prepare them for future leadership

Appendix VII

and give them opportunities to serve as representatives in different organizations, committees, etc. For instance, two student representatives serve on the University Council, the highest governing body of the university. The National Sports Council of Nepal has encouraged youth participation in the fields of sports. Also, the Boy Scouts, the Girl Scouts, the Junior Red Cross, Youth Clubs, and UNESCO Youth Clubs are all active for the cause of youth. Since our government gives great importance to meetings, seminars, and conferences for the exchange of views for mutual benefit, many seminars on youth have been held in the country, and youth are encouraged to participate in both national and international seminars.

My delegation, which believes in the mobilization of the energies of youth, expresses the hope that the international community will succeed in creating an atmosphere favourable to the full participation of youth in the quest for world peace.

My delegation thinks more attention should be paid to the implementation of the United Nations Volunteers Programme, through which youth participation could be increased. The United Nations University must also be encouraged to focus research on the problems of youth which have become universal in character.

Madam Chairman and distinguished delegates, while the United Nations publications in the field of youth have been informative, they have miserably failed in providing answers to questions regarding:
- the specific mechanism to involve youth in development processes in general and decision-making processes in particular,
- mechanisms and methodologies we should use in creating interest among youth to contribute their share to the development process,

Appendix VII

- the possible methods and means to establish and strengthen the channels of communication between youth and development planners, between youth and the rest of the community members, and among youth themselves,
- and finally integration of youth policies and programmes with the national development strategy.

Madam Chairman, we in the least developed countries cannot afford to continue experimenting with the lives of our people and the lives of those who shall soon bear the burden of development, namely, youth. Therefore, we look to this august body with hopes for transmitting to us the results of successful experiments already carried out by other nations. We also expect the United Nations and its specialised agencies and offices to provide us with guidance not on the general philosophies, for philosophies are sometimes difficult to translate into practical terms, but with concrete plans and proposals, measures and methodologies already experimented elsewhere. We are ready to study them, modify them according to our needs and requirements and implement them wherever and whenever it is possible to do so. In our opinion, ideas that the United Nations is equipped with are not enough. What is important is the actual delivery of these ideas.

Thank you, Madam Chairman.

Appendix VIII

Elimination of all Forms of Religious Intolerance

Madam Chairman,
The item before us is an important one. Mr. Muller's thought-provoking introductory statement provided us with a framework within which to deal with so sensitive a subject as religion. We all know that the issue under discussion was on the General Assembly's agenda at its seventeenth session which adopted resolution 1781 (XVII) to stress the need to put into effect the principles of equality as stated in the Charter of the United Nations and to take all possible steps conducive to the final elimination of all manifestations of discrimination based on differences of race, colour or religion. We also know that since 1961 the General Assembly has been making continuous efforts to take necessary action to speed up the work on the elaboration of a single draft declaration on the elimination of all forms of intolerance and of discrimination based on religion or belief. These efforts of the General Assembly must be appreciated by all of us. Since the question on religious intolerance has been on the agenda, many ideas have been put forward and the committee has heard many similar statements by the distinguished representatives of many countries, but we sadly note that we have not been able to adopt even a draft declaration. The question arises as to why, in spite of all efforts made by the General Assembly and other concerned agencies, we have failed to adopt such a draft declaration.

Madam Chairman, my delegation is strongly in favour of the principle of the elimination of religious intolerance in all its forms. We firmly believe that freedom of religion and belief

Appendix VIII

could contribute to the attainment of the goals of world peace, social justice and international understanding and also to the elimination of policies and practices of racial discrimination. We feel the final elimination of all forms of religious intolerance demands strong United Nations decisions followed by effective implementation. We look forward to such decisions and their implementation.

Madam Chairman, my country has the distinction of being the only Hindu kingdom of the world. The bulk of the population professes that faith. However, Hinduism has been influenced by and has a great influence on a large Buddhist minority. A unique variation of the two religions has been created. Due to the intermingling of Hindu and Buddhist customs and beliefs, Hindu temples and Buddhist shrines are mutually respected. Buddhist and Hindu festivals are occasions for common worship and rejoicing. These two faiths are so inextricably interwoven that any attempt to draw a line of difference between them would be somewhat difficult. Thus we think this religious homogeneity existing between Hindu and Buddhist communities who have cherished mutual regard and respect for one another is indeed a unique example of religious tolerance. Besides Hindus and Buddhists, we have some Moslems and Christians. Since the constitution of Nepal ensures the right to religious freedom, the Moslems and Christians are free to profess their religion and practise it according to their beliefs. Madam Chairman, my delegation proudly informs that we have never had any religious conflict of any kind in our country and our people with all religious denominations always live in complete harmony and peace. Naturally, my delegation is very much concerned by manifestations of intolerance and by the existence of discrimination in matters of religion or beliefs still in evidence in some areas of the world.

Appendix VIII

Madam Chairman, when we study the problem of the existence of discrimination in matters of religion or belief, we find that such discrimination finds its root in sentiment, prejudice, ignorance, poverty and social evils. It seems, therefore, that demands and appeals made by the General Assembly are inadequate to improve the situation caused by such discrimination. Those enlightened are obliged to enlighten the people in order to make them realize that the policies and practices of religious intolerance are against the norms of civilization. My delegation strongly believes that the various religious institutions can be used more effectively as appropriate instruments than any other agencies to eliminate all forms of religious intolerance. In view of this my delegation would like to request the United Nations Organization to consider the ways and means by which all the existing religious institutions can help, through their different activities, to solve the existing problem of religious intolerance. But, Madam Chairman, my delegation is also convinced of the fact that unless the United Nations obtains cooperation from all the members of the United Nations, even the adoption of a draft declaration, resolutions, or conventions, will not help solve the problem since it requires first the political will on the part of all governments, social consciousness among people, and legal provisions to ensure religious freedom. Therefore, we appeal to all to cooperate in this noble endeavour to eradicate all forms of religious intolerance.

Thank you.

Appendix IX

Notes on Some Unspoken Problems of the Librarians of the Developing World

The library has a vital role to play in the development of a nation. It should be an intellectual workshop instead of a mere collection of reading materials. This is known to all. But most of the developing countries have not yet fully recognized this modern concept of librarianship. So librarians of developing countries have to face many problems and challenges due to the lack of this realization.

Poverty in developing countries is another factor which creates some problems in the library field. Some of the problems created due to the lack of a modern concept of librarianship and poverty are discussed below:

Documentation

The library should be an intellectual workshop to support study, teaching and research. It may have different names, such as documentation centre, information centre, reference centre, or learning resources centre, but the services of the library cannot be separated to such names. A library can't be called a library if it cannot provide services needed for readers and research scholars. A library and its services — reference service, documentation service, etc. — are as inseparable as a body and its shadow or the moon and moonlight. But, fortunately or unfortunately, some librarians of developed countries who are ashamed of calling themselves librarians are trying hard to separate libraries from library services by creating new names like documentation centre, learning

Appendix IX

resources centre etc. As a result, high officials in developing countries are attracted to these new names and support the establishment of such centres even when their services are provided by already existing libraries. These officials overlook the fact that libraries are established for the task of identifying, procuring, processing, documenting, and preserving reading materials for the use of present and future scholars. As a result library services are duplicated. The economy of developing countries can't afford such duplication, which serve the development neither of the different centres nor of libraries. So this peculiar concept of new names for library services is creating increasing problems for the development of libraries. Therefore librarians from developed countries should be discouraged from propagating new names for libraries.

Stock-taking

Stock-taking is important in making library services effective. Even with the best safeguards, books are lost in the library. The percentage of missing books considered tolerable is different in different countries. If the loss is higher than the allowed percentage, the authorities make the library staff responsible for the loss. Books are stolen by clever thieves and honest library staff are punished. This is one of the main reasons even dedicated people are not attracted to the library profession. It makes the library staff a jealous guardian of books instead of an enthusiastic promoter of the use of books. An allowable percentage of loss has no meaning. Instead of allowing a certain percentage as tolerable loss, we should make a standard rule by which we can punish dishonest library staff even for the loss of a low percentage and spare honest library staff even when the loss is high. Honest library staff should not be punished when there is no reason to suspect them of misconduct, no matter whether the percentage of missing books

Appendix IX

is low or high. This procedure, once widespread, will support the development of libraries.

Book prices

One of the reasons of dishonesty is poverty. In developing countries cheating is very common. If the price is not printed on the back of the title page of a book there is always a possibility for dishonest booksellers to cheat by charging inflated prices. The price of books cannot be checked easily due to the lack of up-to-date bibliographical tools. Thus the price should be printed on the back of all books published throughout the world.

Discounts

Bribery may be more common in developing countries than in developed countries. Businessmen often try to bribe the concerned parties to promote their business. This is the case in the buying and selling of books. Booksellers often offer commission to the buying party. This practice is indeed regrettable, as under the influence of the commission the buying parties may not pay attention to the needs of the library. A further consequence is that even honest buyers come under suspicion. To solve this acute problem, the publishers of the world should reduce the price of the books by reducing the percentage given to the booksellers as commission so that they are no longer able to offer commission to the buying party. It will also help to make reading materials cheaper for all. In short the discount system should be abolished.

Library seminars and non-professionals

The library profession has not been fully recognized in developing countries. Non-professionals are thus often selected by officials to participate in library seminars and conferences hosted by foreign countries. This is a discriminatory attitude towards the library profession that should be discouraged — that is, such candidates should not be accepted.

Appendix IX

The sponsoring agencies should take full note of the problem and act accordingly.

Appendix X

P.E.N. Charter

P.E.N. affirms that:
1. Literature, national though it be in origin, knows no frontiers, and should remain common currency between nations in spite of political or international upheavals.
2. In all circumstances, and particularly in time of war, works of art, the patrimony of humanity at large, should be left untouched by national or political passion.
3. Members of P.E.N. should at all times use what influence they have in favour of good understanding and mutual respect between nations; they pledge themselves to do their utmost to dispel race, class and national hatreds, and to champion the ideal of one humanity living in peace in one world.
4. P.E.N. stands for the principle of unhampered transmission of thought within each nation and between all nations, and members pledge themselves to oppose any form of suppression of freedom of expression in the country and community to which they belong, as well as throughout the world, wherever this is possible. P.E.N. declares for a free press and opposes arbitrary censorship in time of peace. It believes that the necessary advance of the world towards a more highly organized political and economic order renders a free criticism of governments, administrations, and institutions imperative. And since freedom implies voluntary restraint, members pledge themselves to

Appendix IX

oppose such evils of a free press as mendacious publication, deliberate falsehood and distortion of facts for political and personal ends.

INDEX

A

Academic Council member -
  Librarian, 50-51, 118-119,
  158-164
Acharya, Bhanubhakta, 378
Adhikari, Jagat Mohan, 122-
  124, 129, 131, 138, 154,
  174-177
Akihito, *Emperor*, 70, 169
Allen, Vincent W., 282
d'Alpuget, Blanche, 350
Amatya, Dhruba Man, 62
Amatya, Purna Prasad, 21,
  38-40, 41-45, 202-203
Amerasinghe, H.S., *Rep.*, 272
American Chemical Society,
  71
American Library -
  Inauguration, 308-309
American spirit, 53
Americans, 23, 25, 34, 37
Anusooya, 224
Arbuthnott, Robert, 64-65,
  125-126, 298
Arbuthnott, Robina, 64
Architecture, Traditional,
  286, 289-291, 295, 320
Aryal, Krishna Raj, 71, 262,
  265-266
Ashim, Gopal Pandey, 9
Asia Foundation, 68-69, 165-
  166, 304-307, 377, 392
Astrologer, 227-228
Attlee, Clement, *P.M.*, 331

Auditor general's office,
  248-255
Australia, 348-361, 363
Australian National Gallery,
  358
Autari, Prem Rana, 360
Authors, Nepalese, 375-397
Automation - T.U.C.L., 370-
  371
Avgar, Mordechai, *Amb.*, 63,
  96, 309
Avgar, Shoshana, 63

B

Bandhu, Chudamani, 408
Bangdel, Manu, 102
Bangladesh, 304-307
Banks, Lynne Reid, 394
Baroody, Jamil M., *Rep.*, 272
Basnet, Netra Bahadur, 153-
  158, 250, 253
Beck, Terence R., 71, 276
Bhagavadgita, 138, 140, 297,
  395
Bhagi, N.K., 331-333
Bhaju Bir, 243-245
Bhatta, Motiram, 378
Bhattarai, Gopal Prasad, 52
Bhattarai, Guna Dev, 19
Bhattarai, Krishna Prasad,
  P.M., 395-396
Bhutan, 283-295, 330-331
Bidur, *P.M. of Mahabharata*,
  140, 161, 399

Bista, Dor Bahadur, 51, 161-164
Bista, Gopal, 210-215, 232, 243, 246-247
Bista, Keshar Bahadur, 159, 161-163
Bista, Kirti Nidhi, *P.M.*, 238, 266
Black, F., 367
Blokh, Alexandre, 389-390
Bloomfield, B.C., 328,356
Bonn, George S., 111-112
Book price, 465
Book selection and purchase, 204-206, 208
Books for Nepal Project, 168-169
Bothwell, A., 323
Brain drain, 338
Branch Library - T.U.C.L., 125-126
Brisbane, Australia, 359-361
British Book Development Council, 296-299, 411
British Council course on librarianship - Inauguration, 312-313
British Council, Kathmandu, 64, 71, 96, 125, 204, 297-299, 312-313, 322-331, 367-368, 391, 394
Brond, Lalita, 352
Budhathoki, J.B., 38-42
Burleigh, Peter, 63

C

CEDA, 105-107

CSIRO depository, 347
Cafeteria, 58-59
Calcutta University, 9-15, 17, 21-22
Campbell, J. Gabriel, 71, 276
Campbell, Peter, 361
Campus libraries, 125-126, 165, 169, 410
Canberra, Australia, 357-359
Carroll Foundation (Australia), 408
Carter, Jimmy, *Pres.*, 269
Caste system, 77
Central Bureau of Investigation (CBI), 256
Central Library, 45-46
Chakadi, 51, 163-164, 214
Chang Gwang Son, *Amb.*, 314
Charut, Henri, 63
Cheney, Frances Neel, 26-27, 30, 32, 34
Clarke, Catherine, 31-32
Clough, W.L., 38
Coggin, Charles U., 24-25, 417-419
Coggin, Edith, 24-25
Coggin, Randy, 24
Collings, Dorothy, 32-33
Colombo Plan, 11, 19
Colon Classification, 44
Commission for the Prevention of Misuse of Authority, 236
Cooper, Kenneth, 327-328
Corruption, 202-257
Costa Gomes, Francisco da, *Pres.*, 319-321

Coulson, Winifred, 329
Council, Senate member - Librarian, 49-51, 118-120, 129, 158-164
Cunninghame, Christopher, 366-368

D

Dag Hammarskjöld Library, 33, 267, 337-338
Dalai Lama, 283
Dar, Raj Kumar, *Rep.*, 293-294
Dawadi, Gopi Nath, 264, 268
Dawson, William, 392
Dayan, Moshe, 273, 310
Delhi University, 78
Democracy, 1990 - Jubilation, 402-403
Desai, Morarji, *P.M.*, 59-60
Dettmann, John, 106
Deutsch, Andre, 297
Devkota, Laxmi Prasad, 76, 376, 378, 380
Dewey Decimal Classification, 44
Dhar, D.P., 67
Dhungana, Punya Prabha Devi, 187, 192-193, 379
Dhungel, Bipin Dev, 124
Dillard, James M., 304, 307
Discounts, 205, 465
Displays, exhibitions, 45, 51-52, 184-185, 378
Dixit, Jayanti, 183
Dixit, Kamal Mani, 123-124, 168, 382-383
Dixit, Kumar Mani Acharya, 183
Dixit, Narendra Mani Acharya, 182-183
Documentation, 463-464
Dove, Thomas C., 64
Dowry. *See* Wedding gifts
Dunant, Henri, 52
Durga Kawach, 225

E

Economic assistance. *See* Foreign aid
Education - Nepal, 5, 8, 10, 113-115
Education - U.S., 28
Edwards, Averill M.B., 356
Environment, 349, 351, 357, 359
Erickson, E.W., 30-31, 55
Extortion, 204-245

F

Family, Joint, 1, 9, 75
Female education, 4-5, 8-10
Fessler, M. Doris, 24, 26, 30
Field, Roy, 325
Flemming, Bethel, 97, 103-104, 264
Flemming, Robert, 97, 110
Folo, Keith de, 164
Ford Foundation, 106
Foreign aid, 296
Forgery, 207-208, 210, 215-221, 229, 234-236, 240-241, 255-257

Français, Jean, *Amb.*, 63, 96
Frank, Milton, *Amb.*, 343-344
Fulbright Programme, 71, 245, 276
Furniture - Library, 34, 41, 63

G

Gaige, Austra, 278
Gaige, Frederick H., 278
Gandhi, Indira, *P.M.*, 152, 302-303
Garden - T.U.C.L., 65-66
Gardner, Sentress, 64
Garton, Brian, 394
Garton, Sidonie, 394
Gautam Buddha, 401
Gautam, Dhruba Chandra, 386-396
Gayatri mantra, 224
Geh, Hans-Peter, 326, 353-357, 362-363, 372
George Allen Unwin Ltd., 98
George, James, *Amb.*, 63
George Peabody College for Teachers, 24
George, Timothy, *Amb.*, 395
Ghose, Subrata, 14-15
Ghose, Sujata, 14
Gifts, donations, 61-72, 140-141, 165-183
Giri, Kanti, 102-103, 187
Giri, Tulsi, *P.M.*, 215, 238, 266
Giri, V.V., *Pres.*, 300-301
Girja Kumar, 335-337
Gita. *See* Bhagavadgita

Glass, Patty, 264
Gorkhali, Chandra Prasad, 154-158, 323, 348
Goyal, J.C., 287-290
Grantham, Herbert H., *Rep.*, 33, 260
Great Britain, 96-99, 298-299, 303-304, 312, 321-331
Gurung, C.K., 285-290
Gurung, Harkha, 117, 167
Guttmacher, Alan F., 103
Gyawali, Shambhu Prasad, 50-51, 209

H

Hafenrichter, John L., 23, 28-29, 46
Haffner, Willibald, 70
Hale, Richard, 394
Handwriting expert, 219, 242
Harrison, G.E., 98
Harsha Nath Khanal Collection, 171
Hatch, Allison Maya, 277
Hatch, Douglas, 90, 94, 101, 277
Hatch, Kamala, 277
Hatch, Nancy, 90, 94-95, 101-102, 104, 110, 262, 264, 276-278
Hatch, Shanti Ruth, 277
Hawke, Bob., *P.M.*, 350
Heating - T.U.C.L., 319
Heck, Douglas, *Amb.*, 143, 306, 308
Henelius, Raewyn, 359

Herzog, Chaim, *Pres.*, 273
Hidaka, Shinrokuro, *Amb.*, 70
Hochstadt, Peggy Wai Chee, 361
Höfer, András, 70
Hoftun, Martin, 401
Homa, 222-225
Hookway, Sir Harry, 325
Hopwood, Richard, 64
Horton, Warren, 355
Humphreys, K.W., 98
Husain, Zakir, *Pres.*, 66
Hwang Chang Yob, 318
Hwang Hu Ho, *Amb.*, 313
Hypocrisy and hypocrites, 402, 406-407

I

IDRC (Canada), 367, 369-370
IFLA, 229, 339-356, 362-364
IFLA Conference, Australia 1988, 347, 353-356
IFLA Conference, Paris, 1989, 370-374
IFLA membership - T.U.C.L., 340
Ibrahim, Neelima, 306
Inayatullah, *Amb.*, 63
Indian Aid Mission, 61, 78
Indian Library Association, 332, 335
Interim government, 1990, 403-404
International Conference of the Friendship Leagues with Israel, Jerusalem, 1979, 310
International Conference on Ranganathan's Philosophy, Delhi, 1985, 334-337
International Federation of Library Associations and Institutions. *See* IFLA
International Library Movement Award, 332-334
International P.E.N., 383, 387-397
International Red Cross, 52
International Seminar on the Juche Idea, Lisbon, 1984, 319-321
International Summer School, Sheffield, England, 1975, 303-304
International Visitors Programme (IVP), U.S.A., 1977, 96, 281-282, 307
International Women's Delegation to Iran, 1978, 307
International Women's Year, 1975, 184-195, 303
International Women's Year Committee Nepal, 1975, 186-195, 303, 384, 420-439
Israel, 125, 144, 310

J

Jaanch Boojh Kendra, 128-129, 197-198
Jacobs, John Hale, 32
Japan-Nepal Friendship Association, 70, 170
Jewish National and University Library, 167
Jha, Bishnu Raj, 143
Jha, C.L., 300
Jha, Chandra Kanta, 406-407
Johnstone, Diane K., *Amb.*, 343-348, 350-351, 362
Johnstone, Sheela, 350-351
Jones, Ruth, 390
Joseph, Andrew, *Rep.*, 260
Joshi, Angur Baba, 187, 192, 235, 239
Joshi, Bhuwan Lall, 9
Joshi, Mangal Raj, 222-223, 227-229, 239
Joshi, Nanda Lall, 5, 8
Joshi, Ram Prasad, 253-254
Joury, Jacoub J. *Rep.*, 260
Juche philosophy, 317-321
Junior librarians - Misunderstanding, 147-148

K

Kadir, Mariam Abdul, 342
Kafle, P.L., 219
Kaiser Library, 171, 173
Kalia, D.R., 337
Kambara, Tatsu, 70
Karki, Gyanendra Bahadur, 115
Karmacharya, Narayan Dass, 95
Kaula, P.N., 336-337
Keating, H.R.F., 324
Kellas, A.R.H., *Amb.*, 63
Keller, Thomas, 354
Kennedy, John F., *Pres.*, 269
Keohane, Nannerl O., 345
Kesavan, B.S., 335-336
Khanal, Guna Raj. *See* Ramdas
Khanal, Ranjan Raj, 191, 221-222, 227, 243
Khatri, Padma Bahadur, 314
Kim Il Sung, *Pres.* 316-318, 321
Kim Won Gil, 313
King, Angela E.V., 337
King, Coretta Scott, 281
King, Francis, 390
King, Martin Luther, 269, 281
Kira, Hidemichi, *Amb.*, 63, 70
Kirnasovsky, Boris E., *Amb.*, 68, 144
Kobayashi, Haruhisa, *Amb.*, 70
Kochhar, S.K., 335
Koirala, B.P., *P.M.*, 20, 275, 403
Koirala, Dirgha Raj, 49
Koirala, Matrika Prasad, *P.M.*, 237-238
Kölver, Bernhard, 70
Korea (DPRK), 313-318
Krishna Bahadur, 243-245
Kulkarni, S., 268

Kumari. *See* Virgin girls

L

Lady teacher, 17, 19

Lang, Jack, 373
Langton, Nick, 164-165, 377
Laor, S.J., *Amb.*, 144, 311
Lawrence, M.H., 98
Lekhnath Centenary Committee, 378
Lekhnath exhibition, 378-382
Leuchtag, Erika, 10
Libraries - Australia, 339-361
Libraries - Bhutan, 283-295
Libraries - Great Britain, 97-99, 322-330
Libraries - Nepal, 21, 23, 38, 44-45
Libraries - U.S., 30-34, 39
Libraries - U.S.S.R., 144-147
Library Association of Australia, 347, 351
Library Association of Australia Conference, Sydney, 1988, 351-352
Library Association of Bangladesh, 305-307
Library Association, Great Britain, 323-330
Library building - Inauguration, 59
Library Committee, 1968 (Convenor - Shanti Mishra), 168
Library Committee - T.U.C.L., 120-126

Library schools and training, 131-132, 312, 366-369
Library schools - U.S., 23-34
Library science, 23, 27, 29
Library science - Book, 137-138
Library science education, 23
Library seminars and non-professionals, 461-462
Lindel, Jonathan, 97
Lindsey, Marjorie, 63
Lindsey, Quint, 63
Lodge, Eileen, 140
Lohani, Mohan Prasad, 263, 267-268
Loss of books, 39, 154-155, 250-251
Lufthansa, 262
Lyle, Guy R., 251

M

Mackenzie, John, 391
MacLeish, Archibald, 331
Madan Puraskar, 182, 377, 386-387
Madan Puraskar Pustakalaya, 124
Magar, Maya, 107-108, 111
Mahabharata, 161, 199, 399
Mahendra Prasad, 139-143, 145, 147-149, 153, 207-208, 235, 251
Mainali, Chhatra Prasad, 43-44
Mair, Lucille, 268
Malla, Kamal Prakash, 117, 128-139

Manandhar, Krishna Bahadur, 237
Manandhar, Krishna Man, 137
Manandhar, N.B., 46
Mangla, P.B., 336, 341
Maria, Ng Lee Hoon, 369
Marriage, Arranged, 77, 82
Marriage customs and rites, 84, 90
Marriage, Intercaste, 77, 92
Martin, James H., 60
Martin, Jane E., 60
Mathema, Nanda Ram Bhakta, 143
Matthews, David, 330
Mayor, Frederick, 354
Medal and award, 332-333
Meir, Golda, *P.M.*, 153, 302
Melbourne, Australia, 348-349
Meyer Lyndemann, Hans-Ulrich, *Amb.*, 70
Michaels, Axel, 364
Michiko, *Empress*, 70, 169
Miller, Father Casper J., 63
Miller, Dorothy, 60, 90
Mirow, Eduard, *Amb.*, 70
Mishra, Narayan Prasad, 49, 52-57, 74-117
Mishra, Pragya, 103-105, 107-108, 111, 179, 225, 256
Misuse of democracy, 404-416
Mitterand, François, *Pres.*, 373

Mohsin, Mohammad, 117, 167
Monarchy - Hinduism, 399
Moran, Father Marshall, 110
Morris, Linda, 329
Moss, Norma, 369, 391
Moss, Peter, 367-369, 391
Mubarak, Hosni, *Pres.*, 354
Multinational Librarian Project, 96
Multiparty system, 399-400
Murdoch, J., 285, 331
Myrdal, Alva, 301
Myrdal, Gunnar, 301

N

NESP. *See* National Education System Plan
Namgyal, Chogyal Palden Thondup, *King*, 281
Nance, Mildred, 147-148
Nashville, U.S., 24-25
National Education System Plan, 1971, 113-138
  Mid-term evaluation, 128-136
National Library of Australia, 344, 346-347, 349-350, 357-358
Nauta, Paul, 355, 362-364, 374
Navon, Yitzchak, *Pres.*, 144
Needham, Christopher, 367-369
Nehru, Jawaharlal, *P.M.*, 11, 269
Nemoto, Hiroshi, *Amb.*, 70

Nepal Collection, 99, 147, 166-169, 358, 369
Nepal Library Association, 340, 356, 370, 409
Nepal Research Centre, 364-365
Nepal Women's Organization, 185
Nepalese National Bibliography, 364-365
Nepali, Chitta Ranjan, 5, 8
Nepali literature, 375-397
Nepalology, 58
Netherlands Literature Programme, 170
Neupane, Ram Chandra, 52
Nijananda Yogi, Hermit, 222-227, 239
Nitschke, Liane, 207
Niwa, Jean, 285
Niwa, Toshiyuki, *Rep.*, 285
Nobel Prize, 15, 376, 393
Novikov, Artour G., 311

O

Office management, 57, 87, 163, 405
Old age, 278, 453-455
The One Asia Assembly, New Delhi, 1973, 299-303
Oppenheimer, Tamar, 281

P

P.E.N. Charter, 387
P.E.N.N., 383, 387-397

Palmer, Robert, 245, 275-277
Panchayat system, 398-402
Panchayati Gita - Poem, 400
Pandey, B.D., 62
Pandey, Devendra Raj, 23
Pandey, K.R., 284-285
Pandey, Kul Raj, 208-209, 215-216, 232-233, 246-247, 255-256
Pandey, Lekh B., 218-219, 232
Pandey, Rudra Raj, 47-48, 57-60, 96, 106, 115-116, 121, 127, 130, 300
Pandey, Shamba Dev, 62
Pant, Krishna Prasad, 238-239
Papineau, Sarah J., 293-295
Parijat, 380, 386
Pattison, A.J., 312, 322-323, 330
Peabody Library School, 24
Peace Corps Volunteers, 59-60, 91, 101, 260, 277
Pearson, J.D., 98
People's movement, 1990. *See* Revolution, 1990
Philip, J.B., 140
Physical verification. *See* Stock-taking
Pierce, Philip, 387
Pilferage of gasoline, 189-190
Poets, Nepalese, 376-397
Politicalization of University, 412-414
Portugal, 319-321
Poudyal, Lekhnath, 378-382

477

Poudyal, Ram Prasad, 202-203, 209, 211, 213, 236, 241, 248-249, 256
Poudyal, Ram Raj, 52, 300
Power worship, 194-195
Pradhan, Lava Bahadur, 9
Pradhan, Panna Lall, 234-235
Pradhan, Parasmani, 182
Pradhan, Ram, 143
Pradhan, Shankar Prasad, 126
Pradhan, Yubaraj Singh, 139, 147-149, 152-153, 207-209
Prasai, Bhisma Raj, 412
Pregnancy, 95-96
Priests, 228-229
Professors' quarter, 101, 104
Pundit Chhetri, Sundar Keshar, 89
Puri, Aditya Prasad, 143

Q

Qualtrough, R., 61-62

R

Race problem, 25, 268, 440-443
Radhakrishnan, S., *Pres.*, 334
Raeper, William, 401
Rahman, Sheikh Mujiber, *Pres.*, 306-307
Rai, C.B., 219, 242, 244
Raj Bahadur, *Amb.*, 300
Rajbhandari, Pradhumna Lall, 33, 49

Ramakrishna Paramhansa, 15, 138
Ramayana, 171, 199
Ramdas, 171-172
Ramunny, M., 61, 65
Rana, Akhanda Shumshere J.B., 90
Rana, Chandra Shumshere J.B., 176
Rana, Damodar Shumshere J.B., 230-231
Rana, Greta, 384-397
Rana, Jagdish Shumshere, 142
Rana, Juddha Shumshere J.B., 4
Rana, Kaiser Shumshere J.B., 171
Rana, Kamal, 187, 192-193
Rana, Kendra Shumshere J.B., 233-234
Rana, Pashupati Shumshere J.B., 105-106, 177-178
Rana, Prabhakar Shumshere J.B., 91
Rana, Rabi Shumshere J.B., 4
Rana, Rajya Laxmi, 233-234
Rana, Rama Rajya Laxmi Devi, *Princess,* 173-174, 177, 180
Rana, Shingha Shumshere J.B., 171-181
Rana, Samrajya Shumshere J.B., 172, 235, 243
Rana, Saraswoti Kumari, 172, 236

Rana, Subarna Shumshere
  J.B., 19
Rana, Surendra Shumshere
  J.B., 4
Ranas, 4, 6-7, 10-11, 231,
  399
Ranganathan, S.R., 28, 44,
  130, 249-250, 334-337
Rao, V.K.R.V., 67-68
Raoof, A., 287, 289
Rayamajhi, Dan Gamvir
  Singh, 231-232, 243
Redco, I.B., 147
Referendum, 1980, 400-401
Religious intolerance, 278,
  460-462
Revolution, 1950, 10, 399
Revolution, 1990, 400-401
Rice-feeding ceremony, 104
Rimal, Gauri Nath, 359
Rimal, S., 130
Rinchen, Dasho Nado, 290,
  292
Roach, John, 23
Romerio, Gianfranco, 371
Rongong, Rajendra Kumar,
  137
Rose, Leo E., 344
Rubin, David, 376
Ruegg, Irma, 58

S

Sahni, R.K., 335
Saiju, Mohan Man, 123, 125
St. Mary's High School, 108,
  110
Samchi, Bhutan, 286-290

Saturn, 228
Semester system, 114-115
Seminar on Libraries in
  National Development,
  Bangladesh, 1976, 304-
  307
Senate. See Council
Serenity Prayer, 164
Shah, Aishwarya Rajya
  Laxmi Devi, *Queen*, 177-
  179, 185-188, 191-196,
  198-201, 234, 258-259,
  382
Shah, Basundhara Bir
  Bikram, *Prince*, 10
Shah, Bhogya Prasad, 189-
  190
Shah, Binayak, 359
Shah, Gyanendra Bir Bikram,
  Prince, 230
Shah, Helen, *Princess*, 52
Shah, Himalaya Bir Bikram,
  Prince, 10-11, 93
Shah, Ishwari Rajya Laxmi
  Devi, *Queen*, 19-20
Shah, Kanti Rajya Laxmi
  Devi, *Queen*, 19-20
Shah, Khadga Bikram, 93-94
Shah, Netra Rajya Laxmi,
  172-173
Shah, Princep, *Princess*, 11,
  13, 52, 82, 87-91, 93,
  100, 200, 229
Shah, Ratna Rajya Laxmi
  Devi, *Queen*, 163
Shah, Sharada, *Princess*, 93
Shah Dev, Birendra Bir
  Bikram, *King*, 115, 118-

119, 129, 160, 170, 172, 176-180, 185-187, 195, 201, 267, 382, 399-403
Shah Dev, Mahendra Bir Bikram, *King,* 19, 32, 114, 119, 163, 180, 185, 231, 398-399
Shah Dev, Tribhuvan Bir Bikram, *King,* 6, 7, 10, 13, 19, 180, 399
Shahi, K. B., 262, 268
Shanti Nikunja Secondary School, 5
Shakespeare, William, 379-380
Shakya, Surya Bahadur, 120, 123-125, 174, 177-178, 191
Shakya, Thakur Man, 117, 128
Sharif, M., 274-275
Sharma, Madhab Prasad, 135-136
Sharma, Mohan Raj, 377
Sharma, P.R., 121-122
Sharma, Rabindra Nath, 161
Sharma, Suresh Raj, 204, 249
Shauder, Cheryl, 348-349
Shaw, Patrick, *Amb.,* 63
Shingha Collection, 171-180
Shrestha, Amala Devi, 1
Shrestha, Bhawani Devi, 1
Shrestha, Bishweshwar Man, 413
Shrestha, Gopal Das, 213, 300

Shrestha, Gopal Dhoj, 129-130, 139, 154-155
Shrestha, Jayanti, 3, 16-18 34-36, 81-86, 90
Shrestha, Jyanki Lall, 1, 4, 7, 10-18, 34-37, 81-91, 94, 100, 104, 216
Shrestha, Kedar, 94
Shreshta, Kedar Lall, 365
Shrestha, Krishna Devi, 2-3, 5, 9, 13-18, 34-37, 81, 83, 86
Shrestha, Krishna Gopal, 409, 413
Shrestha, Kushav Lall, 1
Shrestha, Kusum, 389
Shrestha, N.P., 143
Shrestha, Narayan Prasad, 115, 160, 220-221, 258, 266
Shrestha, Nirmal, 274
Shrestha, Padma Prakash, 330
Shrestha, Pushpa Lall, 82, 86
Shrestha, Pushpa Lall, Communist leader, 403
Shrestha, Raj Bahadur, 206
Shrestha, Rajendra Lall, 3, 16-18, 34-36, 81-86, 90, 216
Shrestha, Ram Man, 413
Shrestha, Renu, 82-83, 90
Shrestha, Siddhicharan, 380-381
Shrestha, Subarna Lall, 1, 94
Shriman Narayan, *Amb.,* 60-61, 63
Sikkim, India, 283

Singapore, 361
Singh, Anirudra Prasad, 236
Singh, Bhagawati Prasad, 49-50, 123
Singh, Gehendra Man, 186, 198-199, 258-259
Singh, Ishwar Man, 52
Singh, Ram Chandra Bahadur, 139, 150-156
Singh, Ramananda Prasad, 49, 218
Singh, Shailendra Prasad, 208, 211, 213, 215-216, 220, 232-233, 240, 247-248
Singh, Shiva Shankar, 62
Sipadole Mahadev Temple, Bhaktapur, 75
Sipila, Helvi, 275, 279-281
Social service, 196-201
Soosai, J.S., 340-341
Special Police Department, 207-219, 229, 232, 235-237, 239-240, 243, 246-247, 255-257
Spock, Benjamin, 104
Staff - T.U.C.L., 52-57, 403-413
Stanley, Diane, 143, 307-309
Status of librarians, 49-50, 127, 130-134, 139-140, 153, 261, 308, 351
Status of university employees, 261
Stebbins, Barbara, 63
Stebbins, Henry, *Amb.*, 63
Steinem, Gloria, 308

Stephen, Sir Niniam, *Governor-General,* 353
Stock-taking, 248-255, 464-465
Strelka, Joseph Peter, 394
Subba, Ranadhir, 16-17, 22-23, 38-41, 47
Summers, Jon L., 166
Superstition, 222-229
Surridge, R.G., 325
Surya (Medal and Citation), 331-333
Surya Prasad Upadhyaya Collection, 140-141
Sutton, S.C., 58, 98
Suwal, P.N., 16-17, 23, 38, 40
Sydney, Australia, 349-353
Szcepanski, Jan, 394

T

T.U.C.L. *See* Tribhuvan University Central Library
Tagore, Rabindra Nath, 376
Tantric healer, 2
Teaching, 21-22
Thakur, S.B., 121-123, 134-135, 212, 248-249, 409, 413
Thapa, Bhekh Bahadur, 49
Thapa, Bhimsen, 43-44, 401
Thapa, Chiran Shumshere, 160-161, 266
Thapa, Durlav Kumar, 217-218

Thapa, Ram Bahadur, 217-218, 235
Thapa, Ramesh Jung, 168
Thapa, Surya Bahadur, *P.M.*, 60, 214-216, 243
Thimpu, Bhutan, 290-295
Thinley, Pema, 287-291
Tibet, 283
Timilsina, Parthibeshwar Prasad, 158, 348
Tobgyal, Dasho T., 292
Tocatlian, J., 368
Tribhuvan University, 12, 16-17, 19-22, 38, 50-51, 57, 61, 115-118, 120, 156-157
Tribhuvan University Central Library, 21, 23, 30-31, 38-72, 113-183, 200-257, 296-374, 398-417
Tripathy, Basudev, 124
Truthfulness and falsehood, 398
Tshering, Dago, 283
Tshering, Lhamu Dorjee, 283
Tucker, Jill, 377
Tuker, P.E., 98
Tyulina, Natalya, 267

U

UNESCO, 284-287, 330-331, 354, 371-373
USAID, USOM, 23, 29-30, 45, 51, 71, 149
USIS, 64, 71, 143, 204, 305, 308- 309
U Maung Maung Gyee, 63

U Thant, *Secretary-General*, 300
Udumyan, Kamo B., *Amb.*, 144, 147, 311
Ulrich, Helen, 358-382
USSR, 144-147, 311, 318-319
United Nations, 258-282
United Nations Depository Library, 33, 142-143, 184, 259-260
United Nations General Assembly, 32nd, New York, 1977, 258-281
United States, 23-34, 39, 281-282
U.S. Educational Foundation (Kathmandu), 71, 276
U.S. Library of Congress, 167
Unsold, Jolene, 60
Unsold, Willi, 59-60
Unwin, Rayner, 98
Upadhyaya, Kali Prasad, 181
Upadhyaya, Mahesh Kumar, 157-159, 163, 347-348
Upadhyaya, Shail, 275
Upadhyaya, Shailendra Kumar, 238, 263, 266-267, 274-275
Upadhyaya, Sharada Prasad, 42-43
Upadhyaya, Surya Prasad, 140-141, 181
Uprety, P.N., 49
Uprety, Trailokya Nath, 47-48, 53, 58-59, 96, 101,

106, 115, 120-121, 127, 130, 168-169

V

VSO, 330, 367, 369
Vajapayee, Atal Behari, 268
Vehicle conspiracy, 149-152
Vezirov, A.K., *Amb.*, 144
Vice-chancellor's appointment, 156
Violin, 4, 7, 10-11, 36
Virgin girls, 225-226
Vivekananda, 15, 138, 405

W

Waldheim, Kurt, *Secretary-General*, 142-143, 300-301
Wanchuck, Jigme Singhe, *King.*, 291
Waterhouse, David, 303-304, 328-329
Watt, Elizabeth, 350
Weaver, Henry D., 71
Wedding gifts, 85, 92, 100
Weise, Lotti, 110
Weise, Robert, 61, 108-111
Welfare fund, 365
Wells, A.J., 98
Welsh, William J., 356-357
Wesemael, Guust van, 342, 355, 362-364, 374
Wezler, Albrecht, 70
White, Carl M., 67
Wijnstroom, Margreet, 340-341, 355

Williamson, Messi, 270, 272
Wing, Clive, 369-370
Winter, Lois, 262, 276
Winter, Robert, 262, 276
Winton, Harry N., 33
Woman boss, 46, 54-57
Women in Nepal, 184-195, 410-411, 416, 444-451
Women writers in Nepal, 386
Wood, Hugh B., 168-169
Woodcock, James L., 304-305
World Expo, 1988, Australia, 360

Y

Yogi, 222-224, 226-227
Youth, 278, 456-459

Z

Zeidenstein George, 59-60
Zeidenstein, Sondra, 60, 386

BFI
ALSO AVAILABLE FROM BOOK FAITH INDIA

A selection of titles already published or in preparation

- **Secret Tibet** Fosco Maraini
- **Through Asia, 2 Volumes** Sven Hedin
- **Himalayan Dialogue** Stan Royal Mumford
- **Building Bridges to the Third World** Toni Hagen
- **Oracles and Demons of Tibet** Rene De Nebesky Wojkowitz
- **Confession** Kavita Ram Shrestha
- **Lost in the Himalayas** James Scott and Joanne Robertson
- **Secret Oral Teachings in Tibetan Buddhist Sects** Alexandra David Neel and Lama Yongden
- **The Throne of the Gods** Arnold Heim and August Gansser
- **Thakalis Bon Dkar and Lamaistic Monasteries Along the Kali Gandaki** Ratan Kumar Rai
- **Tribal Ethnography of Nepal** Rajesh Gautam and Asoke K. Thapa-Magar
- **Silk Road** Sven Hedin
- **Peaks and Lamas** Marco Pallis
- **Mustang: A Lost Tibetan Kingdom** Michel Peissel
- **A Conquest of Tibet** Sven Hedin

These books can be ordered by post. For ordering information and catalogues, please write to the following address:

Book Faith India
Mail Order Department
PO Box 3872
Kathmandu, Nepal
Fax: 977-1-229983